THE FATHERS
OF THE CHURCH

MEDIAEVAL CONTINUATION

VOLUME 12

THE FATHERS
OF THE CHURCH

MEDIAEVAL CONTINUATION

PETER ABELARD

COMMENTARY ON *THE EPISTLE TO THE ROMANS*

Translated by

STEVEN R. CARTWRIGHT

THE CATHOLIC UNIVERSITY OF AMERICA PRESS
Washington, D.C.

The paper used in this publication meets the minimum requirements
of the American National Standards for Information Science—
Permanence of Paper for Printed Library Materials,
ANSI z39.48-1984.
∞

LIBRARY OF CONGRESS CATALOGING-IN-PUBLICATION DATA
Abelard, Peter, 1079–1142.
[Expositio in Epistolam ad Romanos. English]
Commentary on the Epistle to the Romans / Peter Abelard ; translated
by Steven R. Cartwright.
p. cm. — (The fathers of the church mediaeval continuation ; v. 12)
Includes bibliographical references (p.   ) and index.
ISBN 978-0-8132-1860-1 (cloth : alk. paper)
1. Bible. N.T. Romans—Commentaries.
I. Cartwright, Steven R.   II. Title.   III. Series.
BS2665.53.A2313 2011
227'.10709021—dc22
2010042542

CONTENTS

ACKNOWLEDGMENTS

I began translating Abelard's Romans commentary as part of my dissertation work in 1995. Consequently I owe my dissertation committee a debt of thanks for their encouragement, particularly Dr. Rozanne Elder, Dr. David N. Bell, and the late Dr. Otto Gründler. Additionally, thanks are due to Dr. Rand Johnson of Western Michigan University, Dr. Martin Tweedale, Emeritus of the University of Alberta, and Dr. John Cavadini of the University of Notre Dame for their help and suggestions. Thanks also to my editors at Catholic University of America Press for their confidence and patience.

I would be remiss if I did not also thank my colleagues at the Western Michigan University Libraries for their support in producing this work. I translated this commentary using print and electronic resources purchased or borrowed by the University Libraries, which has an exceptionally fine medieval studies collection. Without the work of the Acquisitions, Serials, Cataloging, Resource Sharing, Reference, and Special Collections personnel, I could never have even started, let alone finished, this project.

Finally, my thanks to the most important people of all, my wife Barbara and daughter Katie, for their loving support, and to my parents for their confidence and encouragement.

Steven R. Cartwright

ABBREVIATIONS

Primary Sources
Many single-word titles are not abbreviated.

Common titles

Ep.	*Epistulae*
Rom.	*In epistulam ad Romanos* (exact title varies from author to author)
S.	*Sermones*

Peter Abelard

Dial.	*Dialectica*
Hex.	*Expositio in Hexameron*
Rom.	*Expositio in epistolam Pauli ad Romanos*
S.	*Sermones*
TChr.	*Theologia Christiana*
TSch	*Theologia Scholarium*
tsch	*Theologia Scholarium, recensiones breviores*

Ambrose

Isaac	*De Isaac vel anima*

Ambrosiaster

quaest. test.	*Quaestiones veteris et novi testamenti*

Anonymous

cap. haer.	*Anonymi Capitulum Haeresum Petri Abaelardi*

Augustine[1]

b. conjug.	*De bono conjugali*
c. ep. Pel.	*Contra duas epistulas Pelagianorum*

---

1. From *Augustine Through the Ages: An Encyclopedia*, ed. Allan Fitzgerald, xxxv–xlii.

c. Jul imp.	*contra Julianum opus imperfectum*
cat. rud.	*De catechizandis rudibus*
civ. Dei	*De civitate Dei*
conf.	*Confessiones*
cons. Ev.	*De consensu Evangelistarum*
div. qu.	*De diversis quaestionibus octoginta tribus*
doc. Chr.	*De doctrina Christiana*
en. Ps.	*Enarrationes in Psalmos*
ench.	*Enchiridion ad Laurentium de fide spe et caritate*
ep. Io.	*In epistulam Ioannis ad Parthos tractatus*
ep. Rm. inch.	*Epistulae ad Romanos inchoata expositio*
ex. Gal.	*Expositio epistulae ad Galatas*
ex. prop. Rm.	*Expositio quarundam propositionum ex epistula Apostoli ad Romanos*
f. et symb.	*De fide et symbolo*
gest. Pel.	*De gestis Pelagii*
Gn. litt.	*De Genesi ad litteram*
Gn. litt. imp.	*De Genesi ad litteram imperfectus liber*
Jo. ev. tr.	*In Johannis evangelium tractatus*
lib. arb.	*De libero arbitrio*
mend.	*De mendacio*
mor.	*De moribus ecclesiae catholicae et de moribus Manichaeorum*
nat. et gr.	*De natura et gratia*
nupt. et conc.	*De nuptiis et concupiscentia*
pecc. mer.	*De peccatorum meritis et remissione et de baptismo parvulorum*
praed. sanct.	*De praedestinatione sanctorum*
qu. Exod.	*Quaestiones in Hepateuchum, Exodus*
qu. Lev.	*Quaestiones in Hepateuchum, Leviticus*
retr.	*Retractationes*
spir. et litt.	*De spiritu et littera*
Trin.	*De Trinitate*

Ps.-Augustine

symb.	*De symbolo*

Boethius

c. Eut.	*Contra Eutychen et Nestorium*
diff. top.	*De differentiis topicis*
in Per.	*In Periermenias*
syll. hyp.	*De syllogismo hypothetico libri duo*

Burchardus of Worms

decret.	*Decretorum libri viginti*

Cassiodorus

compl.	*Complexiones in epistolis apostolorum*

Cicero

inv.	*De inventione*

Ps.-Cicero

Heren.	*Ad C. Herennium*

Cyprian

eccl. cath.	*De ecclesiae catholicae unitate*

Eusebius of Caesarea

hist. eccl.	*Historia ecclesiastica*

Fulgentius of Ruspe

fid.	*De fide ad Petrum*

Gratian

Decret.	*Decretorum magistri Gratiani*

Gregory of Tours

Franc.	*Historia Francorum*

Gregory the Great

homil.	*Homiliae XL in Evangelia libri duo*
moral.	*Moralia in Iob*

Hilary of Poitiers

Trin.	*De Trinitate*

Hugh of St. Victor

sac. chr.	*De sacramentis christianae fidei*
didasc.	*Didascalicon*
sum. sent.	*Summa sententiarum*

Isidore of Seville

fid. Cath.	*De fide Catholica ex Veteri et Novo Testamento contra Judaeos*
etym.	*Etymologiarum sive originum libri XX*
sent.	*Sententiarum libri tres*

ABBREVIATIONS

Ivo of Chartres

decret.	*Decretum*

Jerome

Phil.	*Commentariorum in epistolam ad Philemonem*
Exod.	*De Exodo, in vigilia Paschae Sermo*
Ezech.	*Commentariorum in Ezechielem prophetam*
Is.	*Commentariorum in Isaiam prophetam*
Math.	*Commentariorum in Matheum libri IV*
Osee	*Commentariorum in Osee prophetam libri III*
vir. ill.	*De viris inlustribus*
hebr. quaest.	*Hebraicae quaestiones in libro Geneseos*
hebr. nom.	*Liber interpretationis Hebraicorum nominum*

Ps.-Jerome

Tyras.	*Ad Tyrasium super morte filiae suae consolatoria*

John Chrysostom

Hebr.	*Enarratio in epistolam ad Hebraeos*
Mutiani	*Mutiani Scholastici interpretatio homiliarum S. Joannis Chrysostomi in epistolam ad Hebraeos*

Macrobius

somn.	*Commentarii in somnium Scipionis*

Marius Victorinus

rhet.	*Explanationes in rhetoricam Ciceronis*

Origen

princip.	*De principiis*

Pelagius

Claud.	*Epistula S. Severi ad Claudiam sororem de virginitate*

Plato

Tim.	*Timaeus*

Ps.-Quintilian

Decl.	*Declamationes XIX maiores Quintilian falso ascripto*

Richard of St. Victor

stat.	*De statu interioris hominis*

trib.	*De tribus appropriatis personis in trinitate, ad divum Bernardem abbatem Claraevallensem*
Trin.	*De Trinitate libri sex*

Seneca

ep. mor.	*Ad Lucilium epistulae morales*

Ps.-Seneca

epist. Paul.	*Epistulae Senecae ad Paulum et Pauli ad Senecam*

Sextus

sent.	*Sexti philosophi sententiae a Rufino translatae*

William of St. Thierry

Aenig.	*Aenigma fidei*
cont.	*De contemplando Deo*
disp.	*Disputatio adversus Petrum Abaelardum*
nat.	*De natura et dignitate amoris*

Abbreviations of Series and Editions

AGLB	Aus der geschichte der Lateinischen Bibel. Freiburg: Herder.
ATTA	*Augustine through the Ages.* Grand Rapids: Eerdmans.
BSGRT	Bibliotheca scriptorum Graecorum et Romanorum Teubneriana.
CCCM	Corpus Christianorum, Continuatio Mediaevalis. Turnholt: Brepols.
CCSL	Corpus Christianorum, Series Latina. Turnholt: Brepols.
CSEL	Corpus scriptorum ecclesiasticorum Latinorum. Vienna: Hoelder-Pichler-Tempsky.
DS	*Dictionnaire de spiritualité ascétique et mystique.* Paris: G. Beauchesne.
DTC	*Dictionnaire de théologie catholique.* Paris: Letouzy et Ané.
FC	Fontes Christiani. Freiburg: Herder.
LCL	Loeb Classical Library. Cambridge: Harvard University Press.
LXX	Septuagint.
PG	Patrologia cursus completus, Series Graeca. Ed. J.-P. Migne. Paris.
PL	Patrologia cursus completus, Series Latina. Ed. J.-P. Migne.
PLS	Patrologiae Latinae supplementum. Paris.
SCBO	Scriptorum classicorum bibliotheca Oxoniensis. Oxford: Oxford University Press.
Vg.	Vulgate.

SELECT BIBLIOGRAPHY

WORKS WRITTEN BEFORE 1500
Peter Abelard

Romans commentary:

Commentaria in epistolam Pauli ad Romanos. Edited by E. Buytaert. CCCM 11. Turnholt: Brepols, 1969.

Commentariorum super S. Pauli epistolam ad Romanos libri quinque. PL 178:783–978.

Expositio in epistolam ad Romanos/Römerbriefkommentar. Edited by Rolf Peppermüller. Fontes Christiani. Band 26/1–3. Freiburg: Herder, 2000.

Other relevant or cited works:

Dialectica. 2d ed. Edited by L. M. De Rijk. Assen: Van Gorcum, 1970.

Ethics. Edited by David Luscombe. Oxford Medieval Texts. Oxford: Oxford University Press, 1971.

Expositio in Hexaemeron. PL 178:729–784.

Sermones. PL 178:379–610.

Theologia Christiana. Edited by E. Buytaert. CCCM 12. Turnholt: Brepols, 1969.

Theologia Scholarium. Edited by E. Buytaert and C. Mews. CCCM 13. Turnholt: Brepols, 1987.

Theologia Scholarium, recensiones breviores. Edited by E. Buytaert. CCCM 12. Turnholt: Brepols, 1969.

Theologia Summi Boni. Edited by E. Buytaert and C. Mews. CCCM 13. Turnholt: Brepols, 1987.

Other Cited Authors and Works

Adam the Scot. *Sermones.* PL 198:91–440.

Ambrose. *De Isaac.* Edited by K. Schenkl. CSEL 32. Vienna: Tempsky, 1896–97.

———. *Epistulae.* Edited by Otto Faller and Michaela Zelzer. CSEL 82. Vienna: Hoelder-Pichler-Tempsky, 1968–1990.

———. *Hexameron.* Edited by K.. Schenkl. CSEL 32. Vienna: Tempsky, 1896–97.

Ambrosiaster. *Ambrosiastri qui dicitur commentarius in epistulas Paulinas.* Edited by J. Vogels. CSEL 81. Vienna: Tempsky, 1966–69.

———. *Quaestiones veteris et novi testamenti CXXVII.* Edited by Alexander Souter. CSEL 50. Vienna: Tempsky, 1963.

Anonymi Capitulum Haeresum Patri Abaelardi. Edited by E. Buytaert. CCCM 12. Turnholt: Brepols, 1969.

Aristotle. *Categoriae vel praedicamenta.* Translated by Boethius, ed. Lorenzo Minio-Paluello. Aristoteles Latinus. I.1–5. Bruges-Paris: Desclée de Brouwer, 1961.

Atto of Vercelli. *Expositio epistoli sancti Pauli ad Romanos.* PL 134:125–288.

Augustine. *Confessiones.* Edited by Luc Verheijen. CCSL 27. Turnholt: Brepols, 1981.

———. *Contra duas epistulas Pelagianorum.* Edited by Karl Franz Urba and Joseph Zycha. CSEL 60. Vienna: Tempsky, 1913.

———. *Contra Julianum opus imperfectum.* Edited by Michael Zelzer. CSEL 85. Vienna: Hoelder-Pichler-Tempsky, 1974–2004.

———. *De bono coniugali.* Edited by Joseph Zycha. CSEL 41. Vienna: Tempsky, 1900.

———. *De catechizandis rudibus.* CCSL 46. Turnholt: Brepols, 1969.

———. *De civitate Dei.* Edited by B. Dombart and A. Kalb. CCSL 47 and 48. Turnholt: Brepols, 1955.

———. *De consensu Evangelistarum libri quatuor.* Edited by F. Weihrich. CSEL 43. Vienna: Tempsky, 1904.

———. *De diversis quaestionibus LXXXIII.* Edited by A. Mutzenbecher. CCSL 44A. Turnholt: Brepols, 1975.

———. *De doctrina Christiana.* Edited by J. Martin. CCSL 32. Turnholt: Brepols, 1962.

———. *De fide et symbolo.* Edited by Joseph Zycha. CSEL 41. Vienna: Tempsky, 1900.

———. *De Genesi ad litteram libri XII.* Edited by Joseph Zycha. CSEL 28. Vienna: Tempsky, 1894.

———. *De gestis Pelagii.* Edited by Karl Franz Urba and Joseph Zycha. CSEL 42. Vienna: Tempsky, 1902.

———. *De libero arbitrio.* Edited by William M. Green. CCSL 29. Turnholt: Brepols, 1970.

———. *De mendacio.* Edited by Joseph Zycha. CSEL 41. Vienna: Tempsky, 1900.

———. *De nuptiis et concupiscentia.* Edited by Karl Franz Urba and Joseph Zycha. CSEL 42. Vienna: Tempsky, 1902.

———. *De peccatorum meritis et remissione et de baptismo parvulorum.* Edited by Karl Franz Urba and Joseph Zycha. CSEL 60. Vienna: Tempsky, 1913.

———. *De praedestinatione sanctorum.* PL 44:959–92.

———. *De spiritu et littera.* Edited by Karl Franz Urba and Joseph Zycha. CSEL 60. Vienna: Tempsky, 1913.

———. *De Trinitate.* Edited by W. J. Mountain. CCSL 50, 50A. Turnholt: Brepols, 1968.

———. *Enarrationes in Psalmos.* Edited by D. Dekkers and J. Fraipont. CCSL 38–40. Turnholt: Brepols, 1956.

———. *Enchiridion ad Laurentium de fide spe et caritate.* Edited by E. Evans. CCSL 46. Turnholt: Brepols, 1969.

———. *Epistulae.* Edited by Alois Goldbacher. CSEL 34, 44, 57–58. Vienna: Tempsky, 1895–1923.

———. *Epistulae ad Romanos inchoata expositio.* Edited by Paula Fredriksen Landes. In *Augustine on Romans: Propositions from the Epistle to the Romans, Unfinished Commentary on the Epistle to the Romans.* Early Christian Literature Series. Chico, California: Scholars Press, 1982.

———. *Expositio Epistulae ad Galatas.* Edited by Johannes Divjak. CSEL 84. Vienna: Hoelder-Pichler-Tempsky, 1971.

———. *Expositio quarundam propositionum ex epistula Apostoli ad Romanos.* Edited by Paula Fredriksen Landes. In *Augustine on Romans.*

———. *In epistulam Ioannis ad Parthos tractatus.* PL 35:1977–2062.

———. *In Iohannis evangelium tractatus CXXIV.* Edited by R. Willems. 2d ed. CCSL 36. Turnholt: Brepols, 1990.

———. *Quaestionum in Heptateuchum libri VII.* Edited by J. Fraipont. CCSL 33. Turnholt: Brepols, 1958.

———. *Retractationes.* Edited by Almut Mutzenbecher. CCSL 57. Turnholt: Brepols, 1984.

———. *Sermones.* PL 38–39.

Ps.-Augustine. *De symbolo.* PL 40:1189–1202.

Bede. *Expositio Actuum Apostolorum.* Edited by L. W. Laistner. CCSL 121. Turnholt: Brepols, 1983.

Bernard of Clairvaux. *Epistulae.* Edited by J. Lecercq, C. H. Talbot, and H. M. Rochais. *Opera*, 7–8. Rome: Editiones Cistercienses, 1957.

Boethius. *Commentaries on Aristotle's De interpretatione: Anicii Manlii Severini Boetii commentarii in librum Peri hermeneias.* Edited by Karl Meiser, 1877. Reprint. Greek & Roman Philosophy. New York : Garland, 1987.

———. *Contra Eutychen et Nestorium.* In *The Theological Tractates.* Edited by H. F. Stewart. LCL. Cambridge: Harvard University Press, 1973.

———. *De syllogismo hypothetico libri duo.* PL 64:831–76.

———. *De topicis differentiis.* PL 64:1173–1216.

Burchardus of Worms. *Decretorum libri viginti.* PL 140:537–1058.

Cassiodorus. *Commentarius in epistulas Paulinas* (under name of Ps.-Primasius). PL 68:413–794.

———. *Complexiones in epistolis apostolorum.* PL 70:1321–80.

Cicero. *De inuentione.* Edited and translated by H. M. Hubbell. LCL. Cambridge: Harvard University Press, 1960.

Ps.-Cicero. *Ad C. Herennium.* Edited by Harry Caplan. LCL. Cambridge: Harvard University Press, 1954.

Claude of Turin. *Commentarius in epistulam ad Romanos.* Unedited. Paris BN Lat. Ms. 12,289.

Cyprian. *De ecclesiae catholicae unitate.* Edited by M. Bévenot. CCSL 3. Turnholt: Brepols, 1972.

———. *Epistulae.* Edited by W. Hartel. CSEL 3. Vienna: F. Tempsky, 1871.

Eusebius. *Die Kirchengeschichte. Die lateinische Übersetzung des Rufinus.* Edited by Eduard Schwartz. Die Griechischen christlichen Schriftsteller der ersten drei Jahrhunderte. Leipzig: J. C. Hinrichs, 1908.

Fulgentius of Ruspe. *De fide ad Petrum.* Edited by Johannes Fraipont. CCSL 91A. Turnholt: Brepols, 1968.

Gratian. *Decretum Magistri Gratiani. Corpus iuris canonici 1.* Edited by Emil Friedberg. Reprint. Graz: Akademische Druck- u. Verlagsanstalt, 1955.

Gregory of Tours. *Historia Francorum = Libri historiarum X*. Edited by Bruno Krusch and Wilhelm Levison. Monumenta Germaniae historica.; Scriptorum rerum Merovingicarum. Hannover: Impensis Bibliopolii Hahniani, 1951–1965.

Gregory the Great. *Homiliae XL in Evangelia libri duo.* PL 76:1077–1312.

———. *Moralia in Iob.* Edited by M. Adriaen. CCSL 143, 143A, 143B. Turnholt: Brepols, 1979–85.

Haymo of Auxerre. *In epistolam ad Romanos.* PL 117:361–508.

Herveus of Bourg-Dieu. *Expositio in epistolam ad Romanos.* PL 181:595–814.

Hilary of Poitiers. *De Trinitate.* Edited by P. Smulders. CCSL 62, 62A. Turnholt: Brepols, 1979–80.

Horace. *Odes and Epodes.* Edited and translated by Niall Rudd. LCL. Cambridge: Harvard University Press, 2004.

———. *Satires. Epistles. The Art of Poetry.* Edited and translated by H. Rushton Fairclough. LCL. Cambridge: Harvard University Press, 1961.

Hugh of St. Victor. *De sacramentis christianae fidei.* PL 176:173–618.

———. *Didascalicon.* PL 176:739–838.

———. *Summa sententiarum.* PL 176:41–174.

Isidore of Seville. *De fide Catholica ex Veteri et Novo Testamento contra Judaeos.* PL 83:449–538.

———. *Etymologiarum sive originum libri XX.* Edited by W. M. Lindsay. SCBO. Oxford: Clarendon Press, 1911, 1987.

———. *Sententiarum libri tres.* PL 83:537–738.

Ivo of Chartres. *Decretum.* PL 161:47–1022.

Jerome. *Commentariorum in epistolam ad Philemonem.* PL 26:599–618.

———. *Commentariorum in Ezechielem prophetam.* Edited by F. Glorie. CCSL 75. Turnholt: Brepols, 1963.

———. *Commentariorum in Isaiam prophetam.* Edited by M. Adriaen. CCSL 73, 73A. Turnholt: Brepols, 1963.

———. *Commentariorum in Matheum libri IV.* Edited by D. Hurst and M. Adriaen. CCSL 77. Turnholt: Brepols, 1969.

———. *Commentariorum in Osee prophetam libri III.* Edited by M. Adriaen. CSEL 76. Turnholt: Brepols, 1969.

———. *De Exodo, in vigilia Paschae Sermo,* CCSL 78.538.

———. *De viris inlustribus.* Edited by Wilhelm Herding. Leipzig: Teubner, 1879.

———. *Epistulae.* Edited by I. Hilberg. CSEL 54–56. Vienna: Tempsky, 1910–18.

———. *Hebraicae quaestiones in libro Geneseos.* Edited by P. de Lagarde. CCSL 72. Turnholt: Brepols, 1959.

———. *Liber interpretationis Hebraicorum nominum.* Edited by P. de Lagarde. CCSL 72. Turnholt: Brepols, 1959.

Ps.-Jerome. *Ad Tyrasium super morte filiae suae consolatoria.* PL 30:278–82.

Joannou, P. P. *Discipline générale antique.* Grottaferrati, 1962.

John Cassian. *Collationes XXIII.* 2d ed. Edited by Michael Petschenig and Gottfried Kreuz. CSEL 13. Vienna: Verlag der Österreichischen Akademie der Wissenschaften, 2004.

John Chrysostom. *Enarratio in epistolam ad Hebraeos.* PG 63:9–236.

———. *Mutiani Scholastici interpretatio homiliarum S. Joannis Chrysostomi in epistolam ad Hebraeos.* PG 63:237–456.

John of Salisbury. *Metalogicon.* Edited by J. B. Hall. CCCM 90. Turnholt: Brepols, 1991.

Juvenal. *Satires.* Edited and translated by G. G. Ramsay. LCL. Cambridge; Harvard University Press, 1965.

Lucanus. *Pharsalus.* Edited and translated by J. D. Duff. LCL. Cambridge: Harvard University Press, 1957.

Macrobius. *Commentarii in somnium Scipionis.* Edited by James Willis. BSGRT. 2d ed. Leipzig: Teubner, 1994.

Mansi, Giovan Domenico, ed. *Sacrorum conciliorum nova, et amplissima collectio.* Paris: H. Welter, 1901–27.

Marius Victorinus. *Explanationes in Ciceronis rhetoricam.* Edited by Antonella Ippolito. CCSL 132. Turnholt: Brepols, 2006.

Ps.-Maximus of Turin. *Homiliae.* PL 57:221–530.

Origen. *Commentarii in epistulam ad Romanos/Römberbriefkommentar.* Edited by Theresa Heither. FC 2. Freiburg: Herder, 1990–99.

———. *Der Römerbriefkommentar des Origenes: Kritische Ausgabe der Übersetzung Rufinus.* Edited by C. P. Hammond Bammel. AGLB 16. Freiburg: Herder, 1990–98.

———. *Origenis commentariorum in epistolam S. Pauli ad Romanos.* PG 14:837–1292.

———. *De principiis.* In *Vier bücher von den Prinzipien.* Edited by Herwig Görgemanns and Heinrich Karpp. 2d ed. Texte und Forschung. Darmstadt: Wissenschäftliche Buchgesellschaft, 1985.

Ovid. *Amores.* Edited and translated by Grant Showerman. LCL. Cambridge: Harvard University Press, 1977

Pelagius. *Epistula S. Severi ad Claudiam sororem de virginitate.* Edited by C. Halm. CSEL 1. Vienna: F. Tempsky, 1866.

———. *Expositio in epistulam Pauli ad Romanos.* Edited by Alexander Souter. In *Pelagius' Expositions of Thirteen Epistles of St. Paul.* Texts and Studies, 9. Reprint ed. Nendeln/Liechtenstein: Kraus Reprint, 1967.

Peter Lombard. *In epistolam ad Romanos.* PL 191:1301–1534.

Plato. *Timaeus.* Translated by Calcidius. Edited by J. H. Waszink, *Plato latinus, Corpus Platonicum Medii Aeui.* London: Warburg Institute, 1962.

Ps.-Quintilian. *Declamationes XIX maiores Quintilian falso ascripto.* Edited by Lennart Håkansson. BSGRT. Stuttgart: Teubner, 1982.

Richard of St. Victor. *De statu interioris hominis.* PL 196:1115–60.

———. *De tribus appropriatis personis in trinitate, ad divum Bernardem abbatem Claraevallensem.* PL 196:991–994.

———. *De Trinitate libri sex.* PL 196:887–992.

Seneca. *Ad Lucilium epistulae morales.* Edited by Richard M. Gummere. LCL. Cambridge: Harvard University Press, 1925–53.

Ps.-Seneca. *Epistulae Senecae ad Paulum et Pauli ad Senecam.* Edited by C. Barlow. PLS 1, 673–78.

Sextus. *The Sentences of Sextus.* Edited by H. Chadwick. Texts and Studies. Cambridge: Cambridge University Press, 1959.

Sulpicius Severus. *Epistulae.* Edited by C. Halm. CSEL 1. Vienna: Tempsky, 1866.

Terence. *Andria.* Edited by G. P. Shipp. London: Bristol Classical, 2002.

Theodore of Canterbury. *Capitula.* PL 99:935–952.

Virgil. *Aeneid.* In *Virgil.* Edited by H. Rushton Fairclough. LCL. Cambridge: Harvard University Press, 1916–18.

William of St. Thierry. *De contemplando Deo.* Edited by P. Verdeyen and S. Ceglar. CCCM 88. Turnholt: Brepols, 2003.

———. *De natura et dignitate amoris.* Edited by P. Verdeyen and S. Ceglar. CCCM 88. Turnholt: Brepols, 2003.

———. *Disputatio adversus Petrum Abaelardum.* Edited by Paul Verdeyen. CCCM 89A. Turnholt: Brepols, 2007.

———. *Enigma fidei.* Edited by Paul Verdeyen. CCCM 89A. Turnholt: Brepols, 2007.

———. *Expositio super epistolam ad Romanos.* Edited by Paul Verdeyen. CCCM 86. Turnholt: Brepols, 1989.

MODERN WORKS

Bardy, G. "Trinité," *DTC* 15.2, 1681–92.

Bell, David N. *Many Mansions: An Introduction to the Development and Diversity of Medieval Theology West and East.* Cistercian Studies Series, no. 146. Kalamazoo: Cistercian Publications, 1996.

Blomme, Robert. *La doctrine du péché dans les écoles théologiques de la première moitié du XIIe siècle.* Louvain: Publications Universitaires de Louvain, 1958.

Bond, H. Lawrence. "Another Look at Abelard's Commentary on Romans 3:26." In Campbell, *Medieval Readings of Romans,* 11–32.

Buytaert, Eligius M. "Abelard's Trinitarian Doctrine." In *Peter Abelard. Proceedings of the International Conference. Louvain, May 10–12, 1971,* 127–52. Leuven: Leuven University Press, 1974.

Campbell, William S., Peter S. Hawkins, and Brenda Deen Shildgen, eds. *Medieval Readings of Romans.* Romans Through History and Cultures Series. New York: T & T Clark, 2007.

Carruthers, Mary. *The Book of Memory: A Study of Memory in Medieval Culture.* Cambridge Studies in Medieval Literature. Cambridge: Cambridge University Press, 1990.

Cartwright, Steven R. "The Romans Commentaries of William of St. Thierry and Peter Abelard: A Theological and Methodological Comparison." Ph.D. diss. Kalamazoo: Western Michigan University, 2001.

Châtillon, François. "Sur la place de l'expérience dans la théologie d'Abélard." *Revue du Moyen Age Latin* 45, no. 3–4 (1989): 88–91.

Clanchy, M. T. *Abelard: A Medieval Life.* Oxford: Blackwell, 1997.

Cottiaux, Jean. "La Conception de la Théologie Chez Abélard." *Revue d'histoire ecclésiastique* 28 (1932): 247–95, 533–51, 788–828.

de Rémusat, C. *Abélard.* Paris, 1845.

Djuth, Marianne. "Will." In *ATTA,* 881–85.

BIBLIOGRAPHY xxi

Doutre, Jean. "Romans as Read in School and Cloister in the Twelfth Century: The Commentaries of Peter Abelard and William of St. Thierry." In Campbell, *Medieval Readings of Romans*, 33–57.

Evans, G. R. *The Language and Logic of the Bible: The Earlier Middle Ages.* Cambridge: Cambridge University Press, 1984

Fairweather, E. R., ed. and trans. *A Scholastic Miscellany: Anselm to Ockham.* The Library of Christian Classics. Philadelphia: Westminster, 1956.

Fischer, H. J. "Intention." In *DS*, 7.2, 1838–58.

Fitzgerald, Allan D., ed. *Augustine through the Ages: An Encyclopedia.* Grand Rapids: Eerdmans, 1999.

Gilson, Étienne. *The Mystical Theology of St. Bernard.* Translated by A. H. C. Downes. Cistercian Studies Series. Kalamazoo: Cistercian Publications, 1940; reprint, 1990.

Gross, Julius. "Abälards Umdeutung des Erbsündendogmas." *Zeitschrift Für Religions- und Geistegeschichte* 15, no. 1 (1963): 14–33.

Hill, William J. *The Three-Personed God: The Trinity as a Mystery of Salvation.* Washington, DC: The Catholic University of America Press, 1982.

Jolivet, Jean. *Arts du langage et théologie chez Abelard.* Études de Philosophie Médiévale, Vol. 57. Paris: Librarie Philosophique J. Vrin, 1969.

———. "Sur quelques critiques de la théologie d'Abélard." *Archives d'histoire doctrinale et littéraire du Moyen Age* 38 (1963): 7–51.

Kelly, J. N. D. *Early Christian Doctrines.* 2d ed. New York: Harper and Row, 1960.

Kemeny, Paul C. "Peter Abelard: An Examination of His Doctrine of Original Sin." *Journal of Religious History* 16, no. 4 (1991): 374–86.

Kors, J.-B. *La justice primitive et le péché originel d'après S. Thomas.* Bibliothèque Thomiste, Vol. 2. Paris: Librairie Philosophique J. Vrin, 1930.

Landgraf, Artur. *Dogmengeschichte der Frühscholastik.* Regensburg: Verlag Friedrich Pustet, 1952–56.

Leclercq, Jean. *The Love of Learning and the Desire for God: A Study of Monastic Culture.* Translated by Catherine Misrahi. New York: Fordham University Press, 1961.

Lottin, Odo. "Les théories du péché originel au XIIe siècle." *Recherches de théologie ancienne et médiévale* 11–12 (1939–40): 17–32, 78–103, 236–74.

———. *Psychologie et morale aux XIIe et XIIIe siècles.* Gembloux, Belgium: Éditions J. Duculot, 1948–60.

Lubac, Henri de. *Medieval Exegesis.* Translated by Mark Sebanc. Grand Rapids: Eerdmans, 1998–.

Luscombe, D. E. *Peter Abelard.* London: The Historical Association, 1979.

———. *The School of Peter Abelard: The Influence of Abelard's Thought in the Early Scholastic Period.* Cambridge: Cambridge University Press, 1969.

Marenbon, John. *The Philosophy of Peter Abelard.* Cambridge: Cambridge University Press, 1997.

Martin, Raymond-M. "Pro Petro Abaelardo: Un plaidoyer de Robert de Melun contre S. Bernard," *Revue des sciences philosophiques et théologiques,* 12 (1923): 308–33.

McGrath, Alister E. *Iustitia Dei: A History of the Christian Doctrine of Justification.*

The Beginnings to the Reformation. Cambridge: Cambridge University Press, 1986.

Mews, Constant J. *Abelard and Heloise.* Great Medieval Thinkers. Oxford: Oxford University Press, 2005.

———. "On Dating the Works of Peter Abelard." *Archives d'histoire doctrinale et littéraire du Moyen Age* 52 (1985): 73–134.

———. "Un lecteur de Jérôme au XIIe siècle: Pierre Abélard." In *Jérôme Entre l'Occident et l'Orient: XVIe Centenaire du Départ de Saint Jérôme de Rome et de Son Installation à Bethléem. Acts Du Colloque de Chantilly (Septembre 1986).* Edited by Yves-Marie Duval. Paris: Études Augustiniennes, 1988. Pp. 429–44.

Minnis, A. J. *Medieval Theory of Authorship.* Edition no. 2. Aldershot, England: Wildwood House, 1988.

Minnis, A. J., and A. B. Scott, eds. *Medieval Literary Theory and Criticism, c. 1100– c. 1375: The Commentary-Tradition.* Oxford: Clarendon Press, 1988.

Murray, A. Victor. *Abelard and St. Bernard: A Study in Twelfth Century 'Modernism.'* Manchester: Manchester University Press, 1967.

Niermeyer, J. F. *Mediae latinitatis lexicon minus.* Leiden: E. J. Brill, 1993.

Ostlender, Heinrich. "Die Theologia 'Scholarium' des Peter Abaelard." In *Aus der Geisteswelt des Mittelalters, Beiträge zur Geschichte der Philosophie und Theologie des Mittelalters,* vol. Supplementband III.1, 263–81. Münster i. W., 1935.

Pelikan, Jaroslav. *The Growth of Medieval Theology (600–1300). The Christian Tradition: A History of the Development of Doctrine,* vol. 3. Chicago: University of Chicago Press, 1978.

Peppermüller, Rolf. *Abaelards Auslegung des Römerbriefes.* Münster: Verlag Aschendorff, 1972.

———. "Exegetische Traditionen und theologische Neuansätze in Abaelards Kommentar zum Römerbrief." In *Peter Abelard. Proceedings of the International Conference, Louvain, May 10–12, 1971.* Edited by Eligius M. Buytaert. Leuven: Leuven University Press, 1974. Pp. 116–26.

———. "Zum Fortwirken von Abaelards Römerbriefkommentar in der mittelalterlichen Exegese." In *Pierre Abélard, Pierre le Vénérable. Les Courants Philosophiques, Littéraires et Artistiques en Occident au Milieu du XIIe Siècle. Abbaye de Cluny, 2 au 9 Juillet 1972.* Paris: Éditions du Centre National de la Recherche Scientifique, 1975. Pp. 557–68.

———. "Zur kritischen Ausgabe des Römerbrief-Kommentars des Petrus Abaelard." *Scriptorium* 26, no. 1 (1972): 82–97.

Quinn, Philip L. "Abelard on Atonement: 'Nothing Unintelligible, Arbitrary, Illogical, or Immoral About It.'" In *Reasoned Faith: Essays in Philosophical Theology in Honor of Norman Kretzmann.* Edited by Eleonore Stump. Ithaca: Cornell University Press, 1993. Pp. 282–300.

Rashdall, Hastings. *The Idea of the Atonement in Christian Theology.* Bampton Lectures for 1915. London: MacMillan and Co., 1925.

Reasoner, Mark. *Romans in Full Circle: A History of Interpretation.* Louisville: Westminster John Knox Press, 2005.

Rivière, Jean. *Le dogme de la rédemption au début du moyen age.* Bibliothèque Thomiste, Vol. 19. Paris: Librairie Philosophique J. Vrin, 1934.

Rydstrøm-Poulsen, Aage. *The Gracious God:* Gratia *in Augustine and the Twelfth Century.* Copenhagen: Akademisk Forlag, 2002.

Saarinen, Risto. *Weakness of the Will in Medieval Thought: From Augustine to Buridan.* Studien und Texte zur Geistesgeschichte des Mittelalters, Vol. 44. Leiden: Brill, 1994.

Schmidt, Martin Anton. "Zur Trinitätslehre der Frühscholastik: Versuch einer problemgeschichtlichen Orientierung." *Theologische Zeitschrift* 40:2 (1984): 180–92.

Sikes, J. G. *Peter Abailard.* New York: Cambridge University Press, 1932. Reprint. New York: Russell & Russell, 1965.

Smalley, Beryl. *The Study of the Bible in the Middle Ages.* 2d ed. Oxford: Basil Blackwell, 1952. Reprint. Notre Dame, IN: University of Notre Dame Press, 1964.

Taylor, R. O. P. "Was Abelard an Exemplarist?" *Theology* 31 (1935): 207–13.

TeSelle, Eugene. "Faith," *ATTA,* 347–50.

Thouvenin, A. "Intention." In *DTC,* 7.2, 2267–80.

Weingart, Richard E. *The Logic of Divine Love: A Critical Analysis of the Soteriology of Peter Abailard.* Oxford: Clarendon Press, 1970.

Wetzel, James. "Sin." In *ATTA,* 2000, 800–802.

Williams, Rowan. "De Trinitate." *Augustine through the Ages.* Pp. 845–51.

Williams, Thomas. "Sin, Grace, and Redemption." In *The Cambridge Companion to Abelard.* Edited by Jeffrey E. Brower and Kevin Guilfoy. Cambridge: Cambridge University Press, 2004. Pp. 258–78.

INTRODUCTION

INTRODUCTION

Significance

Peter Abelard's commentary on the Epistle of St. Paul to the Romans is one of the more notorious works of medieval biblical exegesis and theology, on account of both its content and its methodology. Both of these made it different from other commentaries on Romans, both those written long before and those contemporary with it; and both these factors were significant in making it a controversial work, one that led to Abelard's second condemnation at the Council of Sens in 1140. Its heavy use of dialectics, especially in the numerous *quaestiones* to be found in it, and its pronouncements on redemption, original sin, intention, and the Trinity, added fuel to the fire already set by Abelard's other theological works. But it is also significant for its spirituality and theology of love, which were not controversial, but which rather show great insight and depth of religious experience.

This significance was recognized by both medieval and modern scholars. The commentary was read throughout the Middle Ages, as evidenced by its being copied as late as the fourteenth century,[1] and modern analyses of Abelard and his thought routinely refer to it.[2] In spite of this acknowledged importance on a variety of topics, the commentary has never been translated

---

1. See the discussion below on manuscripts and editions.

2. These analyses are, of course, numerous; and some of them deal very heavily or even exclusively with the Romans commentary. Most importantly, these include the studies of Rolf Peppermüller: *Abaelards Auslegung des Römerbriefes* (Münster: Verlag Aschendorff, 1972); "Exegetische Traditionen und theologische Neuansätze in Abaelards Kommentar zum Römerbrief," in *Peter Abelard. Proceedings of the International Conference, Louvain, May 10–12, 1971*, edited by Eligius M. Buytaert (Leuven: Leuven University Press, 1974), 116–26; "Zum Fortwirken von Abaelards Römerbriefkommentar in der mittelälterlichen

Exegese," in *Pierre Abélard, Pierre le Vénérable. Les courants philosophiques, littéraires et artistiques en occident au milieu du XIIe siècle. Abbaye de Cluny, 2 au 9 Juillet 1972* (Paris: Éditions du Centre National de la Recherche Scientifique, 1975), 557–68; and "Zur kritischen Ausgabe des Römerbrief-Kommentars des Petrus Abaelard," *Scriptorium* 26, no. 1 (1972): 82–97; and the introduction to his critical edition and German translation of the commentary, *Expositio in Epistolam Pauli Ad Romanos: Römerbriefkommentar,* Fontes Christiani (Freiburg: Herder, 2000), v. 1, 7–59. Others that must be mentioned include: Constant J. Mews, *Abelard and Heloise,* Great Medieval Thinkers (Oxford: Oxford University Press, 2005); A. J. Minnis and A. B. Scott, eds., *Medieval Literary Theory and Criticism, c. 1100–c. 1375: The Commentary-Tradition* (Oxford: Clarendon Press, 1988); M. T. Clanchy, *Abelard: A Medieval Life* (Oxford: Blackwell, 1997); Richard E. Weingart, *The Logic of Divine Love: A Critical Analysis of the Soteriology of Peter Abailard* (Oxford: Clarendon Press, 1970); J. G. Sikes, *Peter Abailard* (New York: Cambridge University Press, 1932; repr., 1965); A. Victor Murray, *Abelard and St. Bernard: A Study in Twelfth Century 'Modernism'* (Manchester: Manchester University Press, 1967); D. E. Luscombe, *The School of Peter Abelard: The Influence of Abelard's Thought in the Early Scholastic Period* (Cambridge: Cambridge University Press, 1969); John Marenbon, *The Philosophy of Peter Abelard* (Cambridge: Cambridge University Press, 1997); Jean Cottiaux, "La conception de la théologie chez Abélard," *Revue d'Histoire Ecclésiastique* 28 (1932): 247–95, 533–51, 788–828; R. O. P. Taylor, "Was Abelard an Exemplarist?" *Theology* 31 (1935): 207–13; Jean Jolivet, "Sur quelques critiques de la théologie d'Abélard," *Archives d'Histoire Doctrinale et Littéraire du Moyen Age* 38 (1963): 7–51; idem, *Arts du langage et théologie chez Abelard,* Études de Philosophie Médiévale, Vol. 57 (Paris: Librarie Philosophique J. Vrin, 1969); Julius Gross, "Abälards Umdeutung des Erbsündendogmas," *Zeitschrift für Religions- und Geistegeschichte* 15, no. 1 (1963): 14–33; Paul C. Kemeny, "Peter Abelard: An Examination of His Doctrine of Original Sin," *Journal of Religious History* 16, no. 4 (1991): 374–86; Constant J. Mews, "On Dating the Works of Peter Abelard," *Archives d'Histoire Doctrinale et Littéraire du Moyen Age* 52 (1985): 73–134; Hastings Rashdall, *The Idea of the Atonement in Christian Theology,* Bampton Lectures for 1915 (London: MacMillan and Co., 1925); H. Lawrence Bond, "Another Look at Abelard's Commentary on Romans 3:26," in *Medieval Readings of Romans,* ed. William S. Campbell, Peter S. Hawkins, and Brenda Deen Shildgen, Romans Through History and Cultures Series (New York: T & T Clark, 2007), 11–32; Jean Doutre, "Romans as Read in School and Cloister in the Twelfth Century: The Commentaries of Peter Abelard and William of St. Thierry," in *Medieval Readings of Romans,* 33–57; Aage Rydstrøm-Poulsen, *The Gracious God: Gratia in Augustine and the Twelfth Century* (Copenhagen: Akademisk Forlag, 2002); and Philip L. Quinn, "Abelard on Atonement: 'Nothing Unintelligible, Arbitrary, Illogical, or Immoral About It,'" in *Reasoned Faith: Essays in Philosophical Theology in Honor of Norman Kretzmann,* edited by Eleonore Stump (Ithaca: Cornell University Press, 1993), 282–300. See also Steven R. Cartwright, "The Romans Commentaries of William of St. Thierry and Peter Abelard: A Theological and Methodological Comparison" (Ph.D. diss., Western Michigan University, 2001).

into English in its entirety; only small portions have appeared.[3]
This translation makes the whole work available to the general
public for the first time, and allows further discussion of Abelard's thought.

Authorship

There has never been any doubt that this commentary was
written by Abelard. Though he does not mention the work in
his *Historia calamitatum,* and therefore in all likelihood wrote it
after his autobiography, there are ample indications within the
commentary itself that it comes from Abelard's pen, and significant references to it from other sources.

All three surviving manuscripts of the commentary, as well
as the earliest printed edition of it, based on a now-lost manuscript, list Peter Abelard as the work's author. The oldest of the
manuscripts, dating from the fourteenth century, includes several other works of Abelard's.

The text of the commentary itself contains strong indications
of Abelardian authorship. It refers to several others of his works,
including his *Ethics* and *Theologia Scholarium,* citing specific passages in those works dealing with the identical subject being
discussed in the commentary. Additionally, numerous parallels
with others of Abelard's works have been identified.

Abelard's contemporaries also mention this commentary.
Most famous of these is Bernard of Clairvaux, who refers to it
in his treatise against Abelard, in which he describes, accurately,
the theology of redemption contained in it.[4]

---

3. A translation of the complete Prologue appears in Minnis and Scott,
Commentary-Tradition, 100–105; the question on redemption appears in E. R.
Fairweather, ed., *A Scholastic Miscellany: Anselm to Ockham,* The Library of Christian Classics (Philadelphia: Westminster, 1956), 276–87 (trans. Gerald E. Mof-
fat); translations of other parts of the commentary appear in Marenbon, *Philosophy;* Weingart, *Logic;* Bond, "Romans 3:26"; Doutre, "School and Cloister"; and
Thomas Williams, "Sin, Grace, and Redemption," in *The Cambridge Companion to
Abelard,* ed. Jeffrey E. Brower and Kevin Guilfoy (Cambridge: Cambridge University Press, 2004), 258–78.

4. *Ep.* 190.5.11. An English translation of this epistle may be found in *The
Works of St. Bernard,* trans. S. J. Eales (London: Burns & Oates, n.d.), II.565–91.

Date and Place of Composition

The date of Abelard's composition of his commentary must be discerned through careful scholarship, because, as noted above, Abelard does not mention this work in any of his other writings, and because no original manuscripts survive which might also provide decisive codicological evidence. Abelard's autobiographical *Historia calamitatum* takes the reader only up to 1132, while he was still abbot of St. Gildas, and there is no indication in that work of any interest in St. Paul's Epistle to the Romans. The commentary itself provides no direct clues or references to place or time. It does provide other information, however: its schoolbook style of question, debate, and answer, and numerous references to other, datable works: his *Theologia,* namely, the *Theologia Scholarium,* the last of his large systematic treatises on Christian doctrine; and his *Ethica,* or *Scito te ipsum.* Additionally, there are numerous parallels with other works, such as Abelard's sermons and letters. Finally, there are the events of Abelard's own life, such as the accusations by William of St. Thierry[5] and Bernard of Clairvaux,[6] which were based on works they had read which they believed to be Abelard's, and which made use of his Romans commentary.

All these factors have led scholars to place the composition of Abelard's Romans commentary in the timeframe 1134–1138, while Abelard was back in Paris teaching in his old school of Mont-Ste.-Geneviève.[7] This is a shadowy time of Abelard's life with little evidence for it from Abelard himself. The evidence is largely external, based on references such as those by John of Salisbury, who reported learning from Abelard at Mont-Ste.-Geneviève in 1136.[8]

5. *Disputatio adversus Petrum Abaelardum.*

6. *Ep.* 190, cited above.

7. For example, Eligius Buytaert, ed., *Commentaria in epistolam Pauli ad Romanos,* CCCM 11 (Turnholt: Brepols, 1969), 37 (hereafter simply referred to as "Buytaert"); Cottiaux, "Conception," 268; D. E. Luscombe, *Peter Abelard* (London: The Historical Association, 1979), 29; Betty Radice, ed. and trans., *The Letters of Abelard and Heloise* (London: Penguin, 1974), 38; *John Marenbon,* Philosophy, 65; Mews, "Dating," 132; and Peppermüller, ed., *Römerbrief Kommentar,* I, 23.

8. *Metalogicon* 2:10, cited by numerous modern scholars, e.g., Clanchy, *Abelard,* 25; Luscombe, *Abelard,* 29; and Radice, *Letters,* 25–26.

Eligius Buytaert, editor of the modern Corpus Christiano-rum edition of the commentary, sifts through the textual evidence at length.[9] He notes that some of Abelard's references to his *Theologia* cite specific books, and others do not, indicating in the latter case parts that had not yet been written, specifically the third book. The *Ethica* refers to some of these passages as already written, thus placing the commentary before these parts of the *Theologia* and the *Ethica*. Additionally, Buytaert considers the relationship between certain passages of the commentary and three sermons and a letter containing similar material, which can all be dated. Based on the development of ideas, Buytaert concludes that *m*, a later edition of the commentary, came after the sermons in question. Overall, Buytaert asserts a date for the commentary's redaction of no later than 1137.

Audience and Purpose of Writing

Abelard does not identify his audience, but based on the above discussion of date and place of composition, as well as on the style and content of the commentary, we may safely state that he was writing for the young clerics at Mont-Ste.-Geneviève, who were preparing for careers in the Church and required instruction in Scripture, doctrine, and morals.

Neither does Abelard state his reasons for commenting on Romans. In his Prologue, to be discussed in more detail below, he mentions that St. Paul's purpose in writing the epistle was to amplify the gift of divine grace and to diminish the merits of our own works, thereby abolishing pride. At the same time, the purpose of this epistle, like that of all the Epistles, is to encourage obedience to the Gospels and evangelical doctrine, to enlarge upon them, and to defend salvation. To be sure, the Gospels are adequate for salvation; but the Epistles function to ornament the Church, and also to establish the authority of the apostles.

Like Paul, therefore, Abelard seeks to proclaim to his students the supremacy of divine grace and obedience to the Gospel. He also seeks to enlarge upon the doctrine he has received and to defend salvation by clarifying the teachings of the

9. Buytaert, 27–37.

Church on key points. His commentary on Romans is at once doctrinal and moral, concerned with providing a knowledge of the biblical text, its meaning, and its application in matters of faith and practice. It is the manner and substance of his teaching that would make his commentary controversial.

Manuscripts and Printed Editions

The extant manuscripts and printed editions of Abelard's commentary reveal a number of problems. There are three surviving manuscripts and three early printed editions containing the commentary. Of the printed editions, two reproduce the first, which publishes a now-lost manuscript.

Buytaert has described these manuscripts and editions at some length and offered his conclusions,[10] which we here follow and summarize. The three manuscripts are Angers Bibliothèque Publique Ms. 68, f. 1va–26ra, designated as *A;* Oxford Balliol College Ms. 296, f. 80r–160v, designated as *O;* and Vaticanus Reginensis latinus Ms.242, f. 1r–74v, designated as *R.* The *editio princeps,* edited by Andrew Duchesne in 1616,[11] is based on a manuscript of Mont-Saint-Michel, and so is designated as *m.* Together Buytaert refers to these witnesses as *AmOR.*

A is a twelfth-century manuscript with a slightly shorter text than the other versions, and Buytaert considers it to be a first draft. Like the other manuscripts, it contains numerous errors, homoioteleuta, and omissions. Up to 11.28 it cites only the first few words of the biblical text under consideration, in accordance with Abelard's standard practice, but after that point gives the biblical text in full.[12] *m* contains the longest version of the commentary, with additional brief comments of Abelard's scattered throughout the work, called *Lectiones abaelardi* by Buy-

10. Ibid., 3–38. Peppermüller also describes them very briefly, *Römerbriefkommentar,* I, 51–52.

11. *Petri Abaelardi sancti Gildasi in Britannia abbatis, et Heloisae conjugis ejus, quae postmodum prima coenobii Paracletensis abbatissa fuit Opera* (Paris, 1616), cited by Buytaert, xxix. The two reprints are the Patrologia Latina, 178:783–978, from 1855, and V. Cousin, *Petri Abaelardi opera hactenus seorsim edita,* II.152–356 (Paris, 1859), both cited by Buytaert, 15–16.

12. Buytaert, 3–5.

taert. It likewise contains many errors, whether Duchesne's or the printer's or the manuscript copyist's, and lengthens the biblical text beginning at 15.27. It also divides the commentary into five books, rather than the four of the manuscripts.[13] *O* is a fourteenth-century manuscript. Its text is longer than *A*'s, but shorter than *m*'s, and frequently gives better readings than those two witnesses.[14] *R* is twelfth-century, and contains numerous corrections and many of the additions of *m*. It seems to have been based on two models, and Buytaert regards its text as better than *AmO*. As a result of the two models, Buytaert distinguishes between the not-annotated and the annotated *R* in discussing the history of the text.[15]

The numerous differences between the manuscripts and the printed edition have led Buytaert to consider the question, first raised by Heinrich Ostlender,[16] of separate redactions of the commentary. Buytaert lists numerous passages in the commentary with readings found in some manuscripts (*m, O,* and the annotated version of *R*) but not in the others (*A* and the original version of *R*). There are, he says, five different forms of the commentary, though only three (*A*, with unannotated *R*; *O* with annotated *R*; and *m*) go back to Abelard. Buytaert does not go so far as to call these redactions; rather, he sees one redaction, twice enlarged. Additionally, he argues that there is no evidence to suggest that Abelard did not write the commentary within a single, uninterrupted period.[17]

Buytaert's work leads us to make two other statements: first, that no autograph manuscripts of the commentary exist; and second, following this, that numerous copies must have been made and circulated over the years. Many must have perished as a result of the later accusations against Abelard, but the fact that copies were being made as late as the fourteenth century speaks to the work's enduring popularity.[18]

---

13. Ibid., 6–7.   14. Ibid., 7–12.

15. Ibid., 12–14.

16. "Die Theologia 'Scholarium' des Peter Abaelard," in *Aus der Geisteswelt des Mittelalters, Beiträge zur Geschichte der Philosophie und Theologie des Mittelalters,* Supplementband III.1 (Münster i. W., 1935), 279, n. 79, cited by Buytaert, 20, n. 27.

17. Buytaert, 20–25.

18. Buytaert cites André Wilmart's research on *R* to the effect that this work

Buytaert's own critical edition is a major advance over previous printed editions.[19] It makes use of all the available manuscripts and editions, and sifts through myriad variant readings to produce a text approximating Abelard's final version of the commentary. Nevertheless, it is not without problems. Rolf Peppermüller, working on the commentary and its manuscripts at the same time as Buytaert, produced a long list, nearly twelve pages, of corrections to Buytaert's text, and most of his readings make better sense than Buytaert's. He would incorporate these corrections into his own critical edition.[20] Additionally, many of Buytaert's scriptural and patristic references are inaccurate, and seem to have been taken over from the Patrologia Latina edition uncritically. In these respects, Buytaert's edition must be used with care.

Peppermüller's edition features a much simplified apparatus, listing few variant readings. Scriptural references are cited in the German translation, and patristic and classical references are footnoted. The translation, on facing pages with the Latin text, is mostly literal, and closely follows the Latin. This present work has followed both Buytaert's and Peppermüller's editions, usually preferring the latter when the two editions differ.

Structure and Organization

Abelard structures his commentary with a Prologue and four books, as follows:

---

was written by the Carthusians of Mont-Dieu (*Codices Reginenses latini*, T. 1, Codices 1–250 [Vatican City, 1937], 578–85; Buytaert, 12). If this is true, and if Paul Verdeyen's speculation that William of St. Thierry sent these same Carthusians a copy of his own Romans commentary is also true (Verdeyen, ed., *Guillelmi a Sancto Theodorico Opera Omnia, Pars I: Expositio super epistolam ad Romanos*, CCCM 86 [Turnholt: Brepols, 1989], lv–lvi), then both works existed almost side-by-side in that monastery. Even if Verdeyen is wrong, it is still interesting that Mont-Dieu can be favorably connected with both William and Abelard, especially since William had warned the Carthusians against Abelard in his *Golden Epistle* (trans. Theodore Berkeley, Cistercian Fathers Series, no. 12 [Kalamazoo: Cistercian Publications, 1971], 6).

19. See above, n. 7.
20. "Ausgabe," 86–97.

Abelard's Divisions	Modern Chapters and Verses
General Prologue	
Book I	1.1–3.18
Book II	3.19–6.18
Book III	6.19–9.5
Book IV	9.6–16.27

Prologue

Abelard's commentary is divided into a prologue and four (or five) books; this structure differs from that of most other medieval expositions of Romans, which were undivided.[21] As we shall see, the divisions are not themselves significant for Abelard's argument.

According to A. J. Minnis, of the three kinds of literary prologue used in late antiquity and the Middle Ages, only two were used in prologues to scriptural commentaries, and of these the one used most in the twelfth century, his "Type C," described the title of the work; the name of the author; the author's intention; the subject matter of the work; its *modus agendi* or *scribendi* or *tractandi*, or stylistic and rhetorical qualities; the *ordo libri*, or arrangement of materials; and its utility.[22] Minnis classifies Abelard's prologue as a Type C prologue,[23] but it discusses only three of the topics commonly found in this type: intention or purpose, subject matter, and the *modus tractandi*. It does treat several of the themes commonly found in ancient and medieval Romans prologues:[24] the place of this epistle, and the epistles in

21. Of the major Latin commentaries on Romans written up to Abelard's time, only those written by Origen (translated by Rufinus), Atto of Vercelli, and William of St. Thierry contain book or chapter divisions. Origen's divisions are as follows: I: 1.1–2.1; II: 2.2–3.4; III: 3.5–31; IV: 4.1–5.11; V: 5.12–6.11; VI: 6.12–8.13; VII: 8.14–9.33; VIII: 10.1–11.36; IX: 12.1–14.15; X: 14.16–16.27. The footnotes of the PL text of Atto's commentary list fifty-one chapter divisions taken from the margins of one of the manuscripts of the commentary, which chapters vary greatly in length, from half a column in the PL to fifteen columns. William's divisions are as follows: I: 1.1–2.9; II: 2.11–4.25; III: 5.1–6.23; IV: 7.1–8.4; V: 8.5–9.21; VI: 9.22–11.36; VII: 12.1–16.27.

22. A. J. Minnis, *Medieval Theory of Authorship*, 2d edition (Aldershot, England: Wildwood House, 1988), 18–29.

23. *Commentary-Tradition*, 69.

24. See, for example, the prologues to the Romans commentaries of Origen,

general, in the canon of Scripture, and the situation Paul was addressing in Rome. Abelard treats these themes by using distinctions and questions to put the epistle in its proper historical and canonical context and to resolve apparent difficulties in understanding that context.

In contrast to Minnis, Rolf Peppermüller subdivides the prologue into a general and special prologue.[25] In the general prologue, which Peppermüller believes is patterned after Pelagius's prologue to his Pauline commentaries,[26] Abelard summarizes the threefold teaching of Scripture: the Law and the Gospels teach commandments of righteousness; the Prophets and the Epistles admonish and encourage obedience; and the histories and the Acts of the Apostles provide object lessons. Though the Gospel is the perfect teaching, one should not consider the Epistles superfluous; they teach lessons not found in the Gospels—for example, that the carnal observances of the Law should cease, or teachings concerning ecclesiastical hierarchies. Using an example from Cicero,[27] Abelard compares the Gospels to those things necessary for the safety and health of the state, and the Epistles to those things beyond what is necessary, such as beautiful buildings and abundance of treasure.

In the special prologue,[28] Abelard then turns to the Epistle to the Romans itself. He describes Paul's *modus tractandi:* to diminish works and exalt grace, by rebuking first Gentiles and then Jews, and through this to recall the two Christian factions at Rome to humility and peace. Abelard also takes up the classic exegetical question of who converted the Romans, examining the opinions of Eusebius of Caesarea,[29] Pseudo-Jerome,[30] Greg-

---

Haymo of Auxerre, Atto of Vercelli, and Herveus of Bourg-Dieu, all of which are very similar.

25. *Auslegung,* 16–22; *Römerbriefkommentar,* I, 28–30.

26. *Auslegung,* 16–17; *Römerbriefkommentar,* I, 28. See also his summary of this prologue, *Auslegung,* 16–18.

27. *Inv.* 2.56.

28. See also Peppermüller's summary of this prologue, *Auslegung,* 18–22.

29. Cf. *Hist. eccl.* 2.14–15, ed. T. Mommsen (GCS 9.1), 139–40 (cited by Buytaert in the critical apparatus); see also PG 20:171B, which has the Latin text.

30. Cf. *In Epistolam ad Romanos,* PL 30:648C, which Abelard and many others considered to be the work of Jerome. In fact, it was an interpolation of Pe-

ory of Tours,[31] and Haymo of Auxerre,[32] dialectically analyzing them to show that there is no contradiction among the authorities. He then discusses another question commonly found in medieval Romans commentaries: why Romans was placed first among Paul's epistles. Abelard's answer differs from those commonly found in the other commentaries: it was placed first not because it was written first, but because it addresses the first of the vices, pride. Finally, he notes that Paul is believed to have written the epistle at Corinth and sent it through Phoebe, and cites the opinions of Origen and "Jerome" on this.

Structure and leitmotif

Abelard does not elaborate a theme for each book. His divisions, in fact, seem to be arbitrary. Often he ends a book in the middle of Paul's arguments, and none of his sections entirely encompasses any of the subjects raised in the epistle. The major subjects of each book are as follows:[33]

Prologue: Functions of the Old and New Testament, the purpose of the epistle, *modus tractandi*, question on the conversion of the Romans, the epistle's place in the Pauline corpus.

Book I: Human and divine natures of Christ, the Trinity, circumcision, intention, reason, natural law, philosophy, Jews and Gentiles.

Book II: Righteousness, redemption, necessity of baptism, grace, circumcision, original sin, the death of Christ and his immunity from sin.

Book III: Love and charity, the nature of the law, grace, redemption, consent, concupiscence, the Holy Spirit, predestination, Christ's incarnation and death.

Book IV: Predestination, election, grace, mercy, righteousness, faith, conscience, Jews and Gentiles, prayer, love, scripture, women in the Church.

---

lagius's commentary on Romans. See the discussion of this work below, p. 26, n. 94.

31. Cf. *Franc.* 1.24.   32. Cf. *Rom.*, Argumentum.

33. See also the more extensive summaries of the commentary in Peppermüller, *Römerbrief,* I, 28–50; and Mews, *Abelard,* 186–95.

The early printed edition of the commentary, *m*,[34] also has a Book V, beginning at 13.8. None of the other surviving manuscripts has this division, and Buytaert argues that a scribe must have made it.[35] The rest of the divisions are unquestionably Abelard's. At 7.8, he speaks of a discussion in "the previous book," referring to Book II. Apart from this, though, one could remove the book divisions and read the commentary continuously, and not ever know it had been divided.

The main theme of Abelard's commentary is grace, but in the process of commenting he discusses many other themes as well. Paul himself was not systematic, and Abelard neither discerns a system within the epistle nor imposes one on it. Nor does Abelard discuss an overall *ordo libri*, though he constantly refers back and forth to earlier and later passages, connecting them thematically and showing how Paul develops his argument.[36]

Abelard's structure has no bearing on his argument or the organization of his material. This is unusual, and marks the commentary off from his other works. Most likely the commentary is a compilation of his own lecture notes on Romans.[37] Abelard may well have lectured on Romans over a long period of time, and may never have finished the lectures. The sketchy nature of his comments on Romans 16, which are drawn almost entirely from patristic sources,[38] suggests that he wanted to move on to other writings rather than refine his lectures on Romans into a literary work with distinct themes and a carefully wrought structure.[39]

---

34. See above, pp. 8–9.

35. Buytaert, 6, n. 8.

36. For example, at 5.18–19, Abelard refers back to 5.12–14; at 7.18–21, he refers back to 7.15–17; at 9.13–20, he refers back and forth to 8.30, 9.20, 9.11, 9.16, and 9.14; at 11.11, he refers forward to 11.14; at 11.30 he refers back to 11.25; and at 12.17 he refers back to 12.14.

37. But see Peppermüller, *Römerbriefkommentar*, I, 23, who argues that the commentary is not a lecture manuscript.

38. See the discussion below on Abelard's sources.

39. Buytaert, 25, suggests that "[p]robably this section was only a marginal gloss in Abelard's copy of the Epistle to the Romans."

Exegetical Methods

Abelard's methods of expounding Romans are one of the distinguishing features of this commentary. He uses both traditional exegetical methods and relatively new ones in expounding the text; he is traditional enough that readers of either his time or ours familiar with the patristic and medieval tradition of Romans interpretation could recognize his familiarity with that tradition; and he is progressive enough that these same readers could recognize in what ways he breaks new ground. These methods include everything from his citation of the text of Romans to his use of dialectics and questions as means of resolving difficulties within the text.

Text citation

Unlike contemporary monastic commentators on Romans, who usually cite long passages of the text prior to commenting on it, Abelard normally cites short pieces of it, typically no more than a sentence of Romans at a time. He assumes that his reader is already so familiar with the Apostle's words that he does not need to have the text quoted at length. Occasionally he cites the text phrase by phrase or word by word, commenting on one small part before citing the next. For example, Abelard breaks down Romans 1.1, "Paul, a servant of Christ Jesus, called to be an Apostle, set apart for the Gospel of God," into five component words and phrases, and comments on each of the first two words (*Paulus servus*) at length. The effect of this throughout his commentary is to atomize the text and focus analysis on each word or phrase, potentially distracting an inattentive reader from the larger text by forcing him to look at the individual trees and ignore the forest as a whole.

Abelard recognized the danger of this approach. Though he rarely pauses to summarize what he has commented on, or to point out what is yet to come, he unquestionably has a sense of the message of the whole epistle, and he frequently tries to connect the words and phrases he has separated and show how an earlier passage is linked to a later one. For example, he makes extensive use of the terms *continuare* and *continuatio* to join concepts and terms from one passage to those of another and show how Paul makes a continuous argument.[40]

As Abelard proceeds with his commentary, he shortens his citations to the point of omitting portions of the text and sometimes giving only the first word or two from the passage under consideration, assuming the reader's familiarity with the text. Rather infrequent in Book One, by Book Four this truncation has almost become the rule.[41] Often Abelard comments on omitted text. For example, at 16.9, Abelard simply gives the word *Nostrum* and proceeds to comment on Urbanus's unmentioned relationship to Paul: "[*Greet Urbanus,*] *our* [*helper in Christ*], namely, of myself and the others."[42] A more extensive omission occurs at 15.3, where Abelard gives a theological explanation of the text he leaves out: "And this is what he says: *For* [*Christ did not please himself*]; that is, that human nature assumed by the Word, who is especially called Christ according to his special anointing, strove to fulfill the resolution not so much of the human will as of the divine."[43]

Abelard occasionally paraphrases the text, changing words and word order as he weaves his comments into the text, as at 14.9 (paraphrased passages in bold italics):

40. 1.20, 2.24, 3.19, 3.20, 4.16, 5.12, 6.12, 6.23, 7.1, 7.7, 8.9, 9.14, 9.22, 10.14, 11.1, 11.12, 11.16, 15.9, and 16.25–27. Peppermüller also refers to this and other commonly used terms (*Auslegung*, 9–10), and Buytaert says that it is a grammatical term meaning "construction of a phrase" or "concatenation of the ideas of a paragraph," and that Abelard uses it to say, "the context of Saint Paul is grammatically or ideologically connected as follows" (Buytaert, 24–25).

41. The extant manuscripts of the commentary cite the text of Romans differently in Book Four. Manuscript *A*, Angers ms. 68, supplies the whole biblical text beginning at 11.28. See Buytaert's description of this manuscript, 3–5. Edition *m* begins to supply missing text from 15.27; see Buytaert, 6–7.

42. "[*Salutate Urbanum adiutorem*] *nostrum* [*in Christo*], mei scilicet et aliorum." Buytaert, 330.116, missing text added. Manuscripts *A* and *m* both supply the whole text of 16.8–9, which is missing in mss. *O* and *R.*

43. "Et hoc est, *Etenim* [*Christus non sibi placuit*], id est homo ille assumptus a Verbo, qui secundum specialem eius unctionem specialiter Christus dicitur, non tam humanae quam divinae voluntatis placitum implere studuit." Buytaert, 312.11, missing text added. Manuscript *A* supplies more of the biblical text than I have. Abelard does give the complete citation later in his comment on this verse.

For to this end, as if he should say, *to this end,* because *he died,* namely, for us and on account of our sins, *and rose again,* likewise for us and *on account of our justification* (Rom 4.25), just as the same Apostle said above; he merited to rule over our death as much as our life, so that, just as he did each for us, so by dying as much as by living we may seek only to obey him and to fulfill his will. For otherwise he is not **Lord of the dead,** but, as it were, an enemy because of his punishments, unless we persist to death in his obedience, having prepared our soul not only for its confession, but also to lay it down for the brothers.[44]

If Abelard regards the words of the text as mutable, then so also does he regard the order of these words. For example, compare the order in which he discusses the words of Romans 5.6 and 5.13 with the order of the text found in most Latin versions of Romans:

5.6: *Abelard:* Ut quid enim…Christus mortuus est…secundum tempus…pro impiis mortuus est…cum adhuc infirmi essemus.
    Versions: Ut quid enim Christus, cum adhuc infirmi essemus, secundum tempus pro impiis mortuus est?

5.13: *Abelard:* Usque ad legem enim…peccatum erat in mundo…cum lex [nondum] esset…peccatum…non imputabatur.
    Versions: Usque ad legem enim peccatum erat in mundo: peccatum autem non imputatur, cum lex non est.

Abelard both paraphrases and changes word order frequently. These alterations, combined with his textual omissions, make it virtually impossible to determine Abelard's text of Romans.

The use of Scripture to comment on Scripture

Most medieval exegetes, up to the time when dialectics became the dominant means of expounding Scripture, consid-

---

44. "*In hoc enim,* ac si diceret: *In hoc quod mortuus est,* pro nobis scilicet et propter justificationem nostram, sicut idem supradixit Apostolus, *meruit tam morti nostrae quam vitae dominari,* ut sicut utrumque fecit pro nobis, ita tam moriendo quam vivendo nonnisi ei obedire et eius voluntatem implere quaeramus. Aliter enim *mortuorum Dominus* non est, sed quasi hostis puniendo, nisi etiam usque ad mortem in eius obedientia persistamus, parati animam non solum propter eius confessionem, sed etiam pro fratribus ponere." Buytaert, 300.137–301.146. Compare with the Vulgate text: "In hoc enim Christus et mortuus est, et resurrexit: ut et mortuorum et vivorum dominetur."

ered Scripture its own best commentary. They believed that the
best way to explain obscure passages or to expound clear ones
was by other passages of Scripture that used the same key words
or concepts. Abelard, steeped in Scripture and the expository
tradition, followed this technique, almost continually citing
Scripture to make an exegetical point.

Medieval exegetes were able to cite Scripture as frequently as
they did because they committed vast amounts of it to memory.
In her *Book of Memory*, Mary Carruthers describes the memory
techniques taught and used by many educated people during
the Middle Ages.[45] These techniques would have enabled well
educated men like Abelard to recall at will any passage they
needed, on the basis of either verbal links or topical, conceptual links. Similarly, Jean Leclercq describes the mentality that
produced this effusiveness among exegetes. In his *Love of Learning and the Desire for God,* he speaks of "the extremely important phenomenon of reminiscence, whereby the verbal echoes
so excite the memory that a mere allusion will spontaneously
evoke whole quotations," of a biblical imagination, of a memory fashioned wholly by the Bible leading to spontaneous ex-
pression in a biblical vocabulary, of how the words of Scripture
become those of the person using them, and of "exegesis by
reminiscence," which aptly describes the exegete's ability to cite
scripture by "spontaneously [supplying] a text or word which
corresponds to the situation described in each text, and which
explains each separate word."[46] While Leclercq was primarily
describing monastic exegesis, his words equally apply to the exegesis of secular exegetes such as Abelard, though what Abelard
recalls he uses dialectically, to argue and dispute.

Abelard's commentary contains over 1,000 quotations, references, and allusions to Scripture.[47] He quotes from or alludes to

45. Mary J. Carruthers, *The Book of Memory: A Study of Memory in Medieval Culture*, Cambridge Studies in Medieval Literature, no. 10 (Cambridge: Cambridge
University Press, 1990), 80–155.

46. Jean Leclercq, *The Love of Learning and the Desire for God: A Study of Monastic Culture*, trans. Catherine Misrahi (New York: Fordham University Press,
1961), 73–77.

47. See Buytaert's index, 371–79; Peppermüller's, *Römerbriefkommentar*
III.933–42; and below, 410.

fifty-two books of the Bible, passing over mostly Old Testament histories and minor prophets, as well as the shorter letters of the New. His favorite books are, of course, Romans, which he quotes almost 300 times, usually to tie earlier passages of Romans together with later ones; the Gospels, which together approach the total of Romans; Genesis, ninety-one times; and the Psalms, eighty-six times. The passage Abelard quotes or alludes to most often is Deuteronomy 7.6/14.2/26.18, which refers to the Jews as "the peculiar people" of God. He cites this passage seven times,[48] to denote the special relationship of the Jews to God. Perhaps reflecting his interest in ethics, he quotes Tobit 4.16, "Do not do to others what you would not have them do to you," six times; he quotes the converse passage from Matthew 7.12, "Do to others," only five times, each time in parallel with the passage from Tobit, omitting it the last time he quotes Tobit.[49] Abelard cites Genesis 21.12, "In Isaac shall your seed be named," five times,[50] to distinguish Israel from the Gentiles. He quotes John 15.13, "Greater love has no man," five times,[51] in the context of redemption and the death of Christ. He refers to Matthew 6.10, "Your will be done,"[52] 1 Timothy 2.5, "Christ the mediator between God and men,"[53] and 1 Timothy 2.7, "the teacher of the Gentiles,"[54] four times each.

Abelard also has favorite passages from Romans. They include 5.12 ("in whom all sinned"),[55] 8.28 ("all things work together for good"),[56] and 13.10 ("love is the fulfillment of the law"), each of which he uses four times.[57] Quite often when he quotes from Romans, he does so only briefly, and in the context

48. 3.19, 4.11, 9.3–4, 11.2–3, 11.25 (from Haymo), 15.10, and 15.25.
49. 2.13, 2.15, 2.27, 12.16, 13.10, and 14.17. Abelard regards these commandments as a summary of the natural law of charity.
50. 2.16, 2.17, 4.11, 9.7 (quotation of the Romans text), and 9.10.
51. 3.22, 3.26, 7.6, 7.13 (allusion), and 8.34.
52. 1.1, 1.10, 5.19, 12.15.
53. 3.12, 3.17, 5.1, and 8.34.
54. 1.1, 15.15, 15.25, and 16.4.
55. 4.11 (from Augustine, *nupt. et conc.* 2.11.24), 5.16, 5.19 (allusion), and 5.19.
56. 1.10, 12.15 (twice), and 13.10.
57. 2.27, 3.31, and 7.6 (twice).

of an adjacent passage. His quotations from outside Romans are usually more substantial and more significant.

Abelard often quotes Scriptures with the same or similar keywords to reinforce and expand his exposition.[58] For example, to expound 2.7, "To those who according to patience in good works seek glory and honor and incorruption, eternal life," he quotes Psalm 20.5 and 3,[59] "He asked life from you, and you gave it to him...you gave him the desire of his soul," finding the obvious link of "life" (*vita*), but also the similar terms "seek," "ask," and "desire" (*quaerunt, petiit*, and *desiderium*).[60] At 3.11, "There is no one who understands (*intelligens*) God," he adds 1 Corinthians 2.14, "The natural man does not perceive (*percipit*) the things which are of the Spirit of God," and Psalm 31.9, "just like a horse and mule which have no understanding (*intellectus*)."[61] At 3.17, "And the way of peace they have not known," Abelard cites a chain of passages linked to the terms "way" and "peace":

And the way of peace; that is, they are utterly destroyed by condemnation in their ways because *they have not known* the way of God, that is Christ, through whom, as mediator between God and men, we have received peace and been reconciled to God, who "is our peace," so that, as the same Apostle says, "he made both into one." [Christ] also said about himself: "I am the way"; "I am the door; if anyone enters through me, he shall be saved."[62]

Such multiple references are common; sometimes Abelard even cites the same chains at different passages of Romans to expound the same theme. For example, Abelard takes up the theme of the will twice, first at 7.16 ("I do not what I wish"), adding Matthew 23.37 ("How often have I wished to gather your sons, and you

58. Concordances did not come into use until the thirteenth century. See Mark-Robin Hoogland, Introduction to Thomas Aquinas, *The Academic Sermons*, Fathers of the Church, Mediaeval Continuation 11 (Washington, DC: The Catholic University of America Press, 2010), 11–12 and 12 n. 18.

59. The Vulgate numbering of the Psalms is used in this volume.

60. Buytaert, 79.111–80.127.

61. 3.11, Buytaert, 104.266–70.

62. 3.17, Buytaert, 109.429–35; as references, cf. 1 Tm 2.5, Col 1.20, Rom 5.10, 2 Cor 5.18–19 ("mediator," "made peace," "reconciled to God"), Eph 2.14, Jn 14.6 and 10.9.

did not wish it"), 1 Timothy 2.4 ("who wishes that all should be saved"), Psalm 113.3 ("Whatever he wished, he did"), and Romans 9.19 ("who resists his will?"). He cites the same passages again at Romans 9.19.

Abelard links passages of Scripture by similar concepts more frequently than by these verbal links. A passage of Scripture may bring to mind another, not with an identical word, but a related concept. For example, a reference to grace, charity, or the Holy Spirit may bring up references to passages containing any of the other two concepts. At 1.7, "Grace to you, and peace," causes Abelard to think of the seven gifts of the Spirit in Isaiah 11.2–3, because grace is the Holy Spirit; it is also a gift, and he argues from the passage of Isaiah that there are seven gifts of grace.[63] Paul's words at 3.24 that we are justified by God's grace cause Abelard to think of 1 John 4.10, "who first loved us." At 9.1, "I speak the truth in Christ Jesus, I do not lie, my conscience bears me witness in the Holy Spirit," he alludes to Ephesians 3.17, "rooted and grounded in charity," from which charity a lie cannot come forth; "therefore [the Holy Spirit] is rightly called 'the Spirit of truth' (John 14.17, et alibi)." The Holy Spirit causes Abelard to think of charity, which leads him back to the truth Paul speaks of earlier in 9.1. Obviously Abelard makes not only conceptual links but conceptual leaps in some of his scriptural citations. He is very creative in linking verse to verse, not only verbally, but theologically, and jumping from the verse at hand to another, less obvious passage that arises from his long study and thought.

Finally, Abelard uses Scripture as a tool of dialectics in his *quaestiones*. Abelard cites Scripture sometimes to argue one position and contradict another, as in his famous question on redemption at 3.26, where he skillfully proof-texts his arguments against the devil's rights, in favor of the idea that God can forgive sins as he pleases, without a sacrifice, and that redemption is a demonstration of divine love. Other times he uses Scripture to demonstrate opposing points of view, *pro* and *contra,* in a balanced manner, as in his question on the imperfection of the law at 7.6, where he sets a number of passages from the Gospels

63. 1.7, Buytaert, 60.454–63.

and the Epistles against each other to determine whether one may achieve eternal life by following the law of Moses, specifically the Mosaic commandments to love God and neighbor, and to show how Christ changed the law from love of friend to love of neighbor. Scripture is an authority to be cited, but because it can support contradictory positions, dialectics may still be required to resolve the question under consideration.

Spiritual senses of Scripture

Although the Epistles of St. Paul did not lend themselves to allegorical interpretation as easily as did the Psalms or the Song of Songs, Abelard was nevertheless able to find spiritual meanings in the text of Romans according to the threefold scheme of the senses of Scripture that he and other exegetes of the twelfth century followed (literal, mystical, and moral senses).[64] To be sure, Abelard's exposition of Romans is mostly literal,[65] but there are some twenty to thirty passages in which he offers a figurative interpretation.

Abelard refers to these senses sparingly in this commentary; he refers to the literal sense usually in contrast to the spiritual understandings of Scripture,[66] or as the Jews' insufficient understanding of their own Scriptures.[67] He refers to the moral sense only once.[68] Much more often, he refers to the mystical sense, which sometimes can have an allegorical meaning, that is, a deeper, hidden meaning of the Old Testament;[69] at other times,

---

64. As opposed to the fourfold scheme better known to modern readers: literal, allegorical, moral, and anagogical. The fourfold scheme was outlined in the early fifth century by John Cassian (*Conference* 14.8), whereas the threefold scheme had been proposed two hundred years earlier by Origen (*On First Principles* 4.2.4). On the differences between these schemes and their prominence at different times during the Middle Ages, see Henri de Lubac, *Medieval Exegesis*, trans. Mark Sebanc (Grand Rapids: Eerdmans, 1998–), I.75–159. Abelard does not directly discuss his scheme in the Romans commentary, though he does refer to the various senses; he does discuss it in his commentary on the Hexaemeron (Preface, *De sexta die*) and in his *Sermon* XIV.

65. As noted by G. R. Evans, *The Language and Logic of the Bible: The Earlier Middle Ages* (Cambridge: Cambridge University Press, 1984), 70.

66. 10.9 and 11.9.   67. 4.11, 7.4, 7.6, 7.13, and 15.4.

68. 2.26.   69. 4.11, 10.9, 11.9, and 16.25–26.

it can convey the anagogical sense of future fulfillment, or even a moral sense of expected conduct.[70]

Alongside these references to the different senses of Scripture, Abelard also refers to the "spiritual" meaning of Scripture,[71] to the figurative nature of the Old Testament,[72] to the way in which one person or thing in the text of Scripture can signify another,[73] and to typology, or the prefiguration of a New Testament person in the life of an Old Testament person.[74] All of these were standard terms and methods of medieval exegetes for finding deeper meanings in Scripture, particularly in the Old Testament.[75]

Abelard's figurative interpretations are mostly unique; only three come from other writers.[76] He usually does not label them as mystical or moral, and in some cases it would be hard to apply a label to them; usually it is not difficult to do so. For example, he mystically interprets the stars and sand of 4.18 as the Jews and the Gentiles; and then again, the stars as the orders of continent men shining brightly while engaged in divine service, and the sand as married people fluctuating like the sands of the sea. He mystically applies Luke 13.8 to his interpretation of the root of Jesse at 15.12, regarding the manure applied to the root of the tree as the filth of the sins which Christ bore, resulting in fruits springing from the tree. Morally, he applies Psalm 136.9 to 8.13, interpreting the children dashed against a stone as sins killed while still suggestions, crushed against Christ. At 12.20, the head signifies the mind and soul; the coals of fire are fires of charity or laments of penitence.[77]

---

70. 2.29, 9.32, 10.15, and 16.3. Abelard refers to the mystical understanding of Scripture almost exclusively in his discussions of Rom 2 and 9–11, which deal extensively with the Jews, circumcision, and the law; he uses it primarily to interpret the Old Testament.

71. 2.25, 3.2, 3.30, 4.11, and 7.6.

72. 2.26, 2.27, 3.20, 3.21, 3.31, 4.13, 4.24, 7.4, and 7.6.

73. 2.27, 3.13, 3.15, 4.11, 6.3, 9.8, and 11.17.

74. 1.1, 4.11.

75. On all these terms, see also Peppermüller, *Auslegung*, 25–26.

76. 4.11, from Origen; 15.28, from Jerome; and 16.3, from Bede.

77. For other examples, see 1.4, 3.16, 4.11, 4.17, 6.6, 6.14, 7.1, 9.26, 9.27, 9.29, 9.33, 10.9, 11.18, 12.14, 13.12, and 15.4.

Patristic and classical sources

In addition to interpreting Scripture with Scripture, medieval Bible commentators also interpreted Scripture by citing those who had commented on it long before them, and to whose wisdom they willingly deferred. The Fathers of the Church—Jerome, Augustine, Gregory the Great, and others—had themselves at length pondered Scripture's mysteries and offered their own opinions on its meaning. Their writings formed a continuous tradition with Scripture, and succeeding generations of interpreters looked to them to greater or lesser degrees for guidance and instruction. No medieval expositor could ignore them and be completely original without running the risk of being called an innovator.

Abelard does not ignore the Fathers at all, though they do not dominate his commentary.[78] He makes very explicit use of them, in contrast to many other commentators of his time, who, while using them extensively, almost never identify them. Abelard almost always identifies his source, author, and often the work, though sometimes he errs. This identification is likely due to his desire to proof-text his arguments and deflect criticism.

A careful analysis of Abelard's use of sources leads one to make the following observations: First, Abelard uses a wide variety of sources, including Augustine, Origen, Gregory the Great, Jerome, Ambrosiaster, Haymo of Auxerre, and several classical authors. Second, Abelard does not usually use any one writer for an extended period, but moves from one writer to another, quoting the most appropriate ones, sometimes several writers in a row. Third, Abelard's citations are largely evenly spaced throughout the commentary, and not concentrated in one place. The exception is in his exposition of Romans 16, which is heavily drawn from patristic sources, especially from Ambrosiaster and Origen.

Of these writers, Abelard uses Origen more than any other,

78. I calculate that approximately fifteen percent of Abelard's Romans commentary consists of patristic quotations, a rather low figure in comparison with other commentaries of the time; for example, William of St. Thierry's Romans commentary is approximately twenty-five percent patristic quotations.

with regard to the amount of text quoted; he cites half again as much material from Origen's Romans commentary[79] as he does from all the works of Augustine, though over half of this material is found in two passages, on the single topic of circumcision. In the first passage, 2.16, Abelard quotes him to demonstrate that circumcision was enjoined solely on the Jews, and was not a universal precept that bound the Gentiles as well. He repeats this theme at 4.11, adding also Origen's discussion of circumcision as an allegory of the cutting-away of sin and entrance into the world to come, and as a necessary sacrifice for the many until the one sacrifice of Christ. Apart from this, Abelard largely uses him for information about the context of Romans and the people whom Paul mentions in Chapter 16.[80] He also uses him to discuss newness of life,[81] the tradition of Christ as one's neighbor,[82] and Christ as a sacrifice for sin.[83] Origen's overall influence on Abelard, with regard to his doctrinal teaching, is thus quite limited, and it would hardly be accurate to call Abelard an Origenist.

Although Abelard quotes less of Augustine than he does Origen, Augustine's influence on Abelard is still significant. Abelard cites him on original sin, and even cites a passage in which Augustine speaks of the sins of parents binding children with guilt, a concept which he himself denies in his own definition of original sin.[84] He also cites him on Christ's sonship, to the effect that Christ is not the son of the Holy Spirit, even though the Holy Spirit is God and Christ is the Son of God.[85] He does not use him on other traditional topics, however, such as grace or the Trinity. He does use him on the topics of feeling, the soul, and the body;[86] of thoughts condemning or justifying a person;[87]

---

79. See Origen, *Commentary on the Epistle to the Romans,* trans. Thomas P. Scheck, Fathers of the Church 103 and 104 (Washington, DC: The Catholic University of America Press, 2001 and 2002).

80. Prologue, and 16.2–27 (*Rom.* 10.16–43).

81. 6.5; *Rom.* 5.8   82. 13.8–9; cf. *Rom.* 9.31.

83. 8.3–4; cf. *Rom.* 6.12.

84. Compare 5.19 with *ench.* 46–47, 68, and 93. See below, pp. 51–55, for a discussion of Abelard's views on original sin.

85. 1.4, cf. *ench.* 38.

86. 2.9, cf. *civ. Dei* 21.3.2; *Gn. litt.* 3.5; ibid., 12.24; *Ep.* 118.14.

87. 2.15, cf. *civ. Dei* 20.26.3; *en. Ps.* 118.24.6; and ibid., 5.13.

on God's permission of evil for a good purpose;[88] on circumcision, baptism, and the covenant;[89] on whether angels should be loved along with our other neighbors;[90] and on the selfless love for God.[91] That is, Abelard uses Augustine less for doctrinal purposes than for moral ones, and fairly often in his questions. If one adds passages which Abelard believes to be from Augustine but which modern scholars have determined to be from other writers, this increase only slightly favors doctrinal purposes.[92] Augustine thus holds a certain weight with Abelard.

After Origen and Augustine, Abelard's favorite patristic and medieval sources are Haymo of Auxerre,[93] Jerome/Pelagius,[94] and Ambrose/Ambrosiaster.[95] Rather than using them to make doctrinal or moral points, however, Abelard uses them primar-

88. 3.6 (cf. *ench.* 95–96), and 3.8 (cf. *civ. Dei* 11.17–18, and *ench.* 11).

89. 4.11, cf. *nupt. et conc.* 2.11.24; and *Gn. litt.* 4.13.

90. 7.6, cf. *doc. Chr.* 1.30.31–31.33.

91. 7.13, cf. *div. qu.* q. 35.1 and *en. Ps.* 53.10.

92. Abelard cites Fulgentius of Ruspé as Augustine three times: 5.19 (cf. *fid.* 41), on irrational animals having no eternal life; 5.19 (cf. *fid.* 70), on the punishment of children dying without baptism; and 14.23 (cf. *fid.* 85), on the goodness of all that God has created. He also cites the same passage of Pseudo-Augustine's *symb.* three times on the definition of faith: 8.30, 15.13, and 16.25.

93. Abelard cites his commentary on Romans twenty-four times, for a total of 104 lines.

94. Abelard cites several authentic works of Jerome's, including his commentary on Matthew, his book on the interpretation of Hebrew names, and his epistles. He also cites works which he attributes to Jerome, but which are, in fact, the work of Pelagius or one of his followers. These include a commentary on Romans (PL 30.643–902) and some letters (*Epp.* 13 and 40 in the PL collection of Jerome's letters, vol. 30). Pelagius's commentaries on the epistles of St. Paul can also be found in Alexander Souter, ed., *Pelagius's Expositions of Thirteen Epistles of St Paul* (Cambridge: Cambridge University Press, 1931), which edition will be referred to in the notes to the translation. On the special regard with which Abelard held Jerome, see Constant J. Mews, "Un lecteur de Jérôme au XIIe siècle: Pierre Abélard." In *Jérôme entre l'occident et l'orient: XVIe centenaire du départ de Saint Jérôme de Rome et de son installation à Bethléem. Acts du colloque de Chantilly (Septembre 1986),* ed. Yves-Marie Duval (Paris: Études Augustiniennes, 1988), 429–44.

95. Like all medieval writers, Abelard ascribes the popular but otherwise anonymous commentary on Romans to Ambrose, and cites it with some frequency. He also refers to two of Ambrose's epistles and his commentary on the *Hexaemeron.*

ily to explain obscure names and terms. He cites a number of other patristic writers as well, though only Boethius, whom he cites five times, contributes anything of significance. The most important of these Boethian citations concern free choice, and occur in Abelard's discussion of original sin, where Abelard uses them to buttress his view that original sin refers only to inherited punishment and not to inherited guilt; where there is no free choice, there can be no sin, and therefore children without free choice are not guilty of any sin.[96]

Of the other patristic writers, Abelard cites historians such as Eusebius of Caesarea and Gregory of Tours, lexicographers such as Isidore of Seville, and canonists such as Theodore of Canterbury. He cites several passages from Theodore's *Penitential Book* on the subject of eating dead animals in the context of his exposition of Romans 14.23, concerning the eating of meat sacrificed to idols,[97] as well as the Council of Gangra.[98]

Abelard also cites a number of classical writers, though few more than once or at any length. His favorite is Cicero, whom he cites three times, twice at some length, on political life, the role of providence in the world, and vice.[99] He also cites Calcidius's translation of Plato's *Timaeus*[100] three times, and a passage from Aristotle's *Categories*.[101] In general, Abelard uses his brief quotations from classical authors to express moral opinions.[102]

In addition to using these writers to make occasional moral points and to explain obscure names and terms, Abelard also

---

96. 5.19, cf. *in Per.*, 3:9.

97. Cf. *Capitula* 15–19, and also Burchardus of Worms' *decret.*, lib. XIX.85–92.

98. Canon 2, in P. P. Joannou, Fonti IX, *Discipline générale antique* (Grotaferrata, 1962), 90.

99. Prologue (cf. *inv.* 2.56), 1.20 (cf. *inv.* 1.34), and 2.24, *Heren.* 2.27.

100. 1.20 (cf. *Tim.* 29e, ed. J. H. Waszink, *Plato latinus*, Corpus Platonicum Medii Aeui [London: Warburg Institute, 1962], IV.22), on the creation of the world; 3.8, and 9.21 (cf. *Tim.* 28a, ed. Waszink, IV.20.21–22), on cause and effect.

101. 3.4, cf. *Categoriae* 13a30, from the edition of Boethius, ed. Minio-Paluello, *Aristoteles Latinus* [Bruges-Paris: Desclée de Brouwer, 1961], 1.1–5, 35.

102. For example, at 7.5, when he quotes Horace's *Odes* 3.16.18 and Juvenal's *Satires* 14.139 on wealth; at 7.9, when he quotes Ovid, *Amores* 3.4.17, on desire for forbidden things; at 7.13, when he quotes Horace's *Ep.* I.1.32 on stubbornness and obedience; and at 7.13, when he quotes Lucanus's *Pharsalus* 8.85 on motives for love.

uses them to buttress his arguments on controversial points, and this is why he regularly identifies his sources: to show that his positions have support from traditional, respected authorities. For example, his question on redemption at 3.26 cites Gratian's *Decretum*, in his argument against the devil's rights.[103] Sometimes he seeks to resolve apparent contradictions between sources, as he does in his Prologue, when he cites several authorities on the question of who converted the Romans.[104] At other times he sets sources against each other, even sources from those whom he believes to be the same writer, as in the question on original sin at 5.19, where he cites "Augustine" (actually Ambrosiaster) and "Jerome" (actually Pelagius) against another passage from Augustine, and finishes with a reference to Gregory the Great.[105] Abelard regards his patristic sources as useful, though not absolutely authoritative, a position he had already taken in the prologue to *Sic et Non*.[106] He must therefore analyze and balance them with logic in his attempt to arrive at the fullest meaning of the ultimate and only infallible authority, Scripture.

Abelard treats his sources all very much the same. Occasionally he quotes entire passages nearly verbatim, with only minor changes, as with Boethius.[107] More frequently, though, Abelard edits his texts, especially the longer passages, using no more of the original than he must and eliminating extraneous material. Sometimes the portions omitted are substantial, as at 2.17, where he reduces a passage from Augustine's sermon on Psalm 75 by over three-fourths, keeping only the most essential material on the origin of the word "Jews," and the definition of true Jews.[108]

Abelard's question at 7.6 offers several examples of his editing skill. He edits a passage from Ambrosiaster, leaving out sev-

---

103. 3.26, cf. *Decret.*, cap. 63, causa XI, ed. Friedberg, 660.

104. Cf. Eusebius of Caesarea, *hist. eccl.* 2.14–15; Ps.-Jerome, *Rom.*, PL 30:648C (Souter places this among the later interpolations of Pelagius's text); Gregory of Tours, *Franc.* 1.24; and Haymo, *Rom.*, Argumentum.

105. 5.19, cf. Ambrosiaster, *quaest.test.*, q. 67; Jerome, *Ezech.* 4, on 16.8; Augustine, *div. qu.*, 24; and Gregory, *homil.*, 32.6.

106. PL 178:1339A–1349C.   107. See 5.19; cf. *in Per.*, 3:9.

108. Cf. *en. Ps.* 75.1.

eral sentences dealing with Paul's intention and with love for one's enemy. What he quotes from Ambrosiaster, he quotes verbatim, but he omits what he considers unnecessary and beside his larger point, namely, that in the Law of Moses, the neighbor is not understood as every man.[109] Abelard immediately follows this with a passage from *De doctrina Christiana* which he reduces by about half, citing it piece by piece, as though it were several different passages and not just one.[110] Shortly thereafter, Abelard summarizes a wordy passage from Origen, eliminating phrases and words that are repetitive or not entirely necessary for his point about Christ as the neighbor of the parable of the Good Samaritan.[111]

Sometimes Abelard omits significant concepts in the process of editing his sources. At 6.23, "The wages of sin are death," Abelard omits from a passage of Haymo what might have been a useful distinction about the kinds of sins that receive the reward of eternal death, something he barely touches on in his comment on this verse.[112] At 11.26, Abelard dissects an entire sentence of Haymo, stringing together pieces of widely separated phrases to create a more concise sentence. He eliminates most of Haymo's references to God's efforts to save Gentiles and Jews equally, concentrating on the ultimate salvation of the Jews, the major focus of his own comments on Romans 11.26. Haymo's larger point is omitted, leaving mostly a Scripture reference.[113] Generally, however, Abelard is faithful to the original meaning of his sources. He edits them with no malicious intent, only the desire to make his point more concisely, while still giving his sources credit.

Dialectics

Not only does Abelard look for divine meanings hidden in the text, but he also analyzes the human meanings of the words of Scripture according to dialectics, or the discernment of true reasoning from false. Dialectics serves two purposes in Abelard's

109. Cf. Ambrosiaster, *Rom.*, 13.10.
110. Cf. *doc. Chr.* 1.30.31–30.33.
111. Cf. Origen, *Rom.*, 9.31.
112. Cf. Haymo, *Rom.*, 6.23.
113. Cf. Haymo, *Rom.*, 11.26.

exegesis: it clarifies the meaning of Scripture through the use of distinctions, definitions, analogies, and syllogisms; and it demonstrates the truth or falsity of propositions. Though Abelard was by no means the first exegete to apply logic to Scripture,[114] he was the first to do so as prominently as he did.

His primary tool of dialectical exegesis is the numerous *quaestiones* found throughout the commentary.[115] These questions are, as G. R. Evans has noted, little treatises within and integral to the commentary, and there is little uniformity in their form or treatment of material.[116] They do not all use dialectics to resolve the matter under consideration, but enough of them do, and some of them have become quite famous because of their content.

The best known is undoubtedly the question on redemption at 3.26, where Abelard rejects two well known theories of redemption in favor of his view that not only Christ's death, but his entire life as well, was a demonstration of divine love that provokes the response of human love. We shall discuss the content below in the section on theology; what concerns us here is his dialectical methodology. Abelard begins by questioning the premise that the devil possesses humanity by right as a result of Adam's sin. He attacks this position by arguing from the authority of scripture—that is, by proof-texting—and by asserting an alternate position, that God has an even stronger right to man, and simply hands him to the devil for torment. Ultimate right lies with Christ, who may forgive as he sees fit, in any way; he was not under necessity to suffer and die, but is free to choose whatever method of forgiveness he wills.[117] He attacks the theory of redemption by ransom through moral argument in the form of continuous questions: Which was the greater wrong, Adam's

114. Beryl Smalley discusses several eleventh- and early twelfth-century exegetes who utilized the *Quaestio* before Abelard did; see *The Study of the Bible in the Middle Ages*, 2d ed. (Oxford: Basil Blackwell, 1952; reprint, Notre Dame, IN: University of Notre Dame Press, 1964), 70–73.

115. Peppermüller identifies twenty-nine: Prologue, 1.1, 1.4, 1.7, 1.32, 2.14, 3.4, 3.26, 3.27, 4.8, 4.11, 4.19, 5.19, 6.9, 7.6, 7.13, 8.10, 8.11, 8.30, 9.21, 10.9, 11.36 (two), 12.14, 12.15, 13.10, 14.23 (two), and 15.3 (*Auslegung*, 12–14).

116. Evans, *Language*, 127–28.

117. See also Weingart, *Logic*, 90–91.

eating of the apple, or the murder of Christ? Could God be pleased by Christ's murder so much as to achieve reconciliation? He then asks to whom the ransom was paid. Certainly not to the devil, whom Abelard had already established as a mere torturer; it must go to God. But then, it would be cruel for someone to demand an innocent person's blood, or to be pleased with that person's death.

Richard Weingart argues that necessity is the underlying principle of Abelard's rejection of these two theories; God is under no extrinsic necessity to atone in any particular way. For Abelard, Weingart asserts, there was no prior necessity that God reveal himself in Christ's incarnation or death; God's only necessity was his intrinsic need to fulfill his essence by acting out of love to save humanity.[118] The particular arguments Abelard advances point to what he regards as either logical or ethical inadequacies: forgetting that God has ultimate right over human beings; ignoring God's freedom from necessity; and overlooking the moral dilemmas of the old theories. In these arguments, morality has as much force as logic. Abelard's dialectics is not entirely dispassionate; its function is to demonstrate the truth of the Christian faith, and this faith underlies his dialectical method.

Also well known is his question on original sin at 5.19, where he denies that the guilt of original sin is transmitted from parent to child. While significant for its content, the question's methodology is also important because it takes the form of a disputed question, or a question that was possibly debated in Abelard's class. A question is posed for discussion (whether God is just in punishing innocent children who lack free choice and the ability to consent to sin, but who are condemned for the sin of their first father, Adam, and who die before baptism), arguments pro and con are made from authority (Augustine, Fulgentius of Ruspé, Boethius, Jerome, and pseudo-Jerome), and the master's response is delivered, in which he analyzes the key authority (Augustine) to find the solution in one word and offer additional understanding. More authorities are cited, and

118. Ibid., 92–93.

the underlying doctrinal and dialectical principles expounded: divine standards cannot be judged by human standards, and God works no injury, whatever he does.

In some questions, Abelard uses dialectics to demonstrate the truth of a scriptural proposition. For example, at 3.4,[119] Paul's words, "God is true, and every man a liar," cause Abelard, or one of his students, to wonder whether Christ's humanity was capable of lying or sinning. Do Paul's words exclude the God-man? Was Christ capable of sin? To answer this question, Abelard makes full use of dialectics as linguistic analysis and the construction of arguments. He addresses the following problems in making his response: How could Christ assume Adam's humanity, since the will and inclination to sin always existed in Adam? Did Christ have free choice, by which he was capable of sinning? Was Christ fully human and self-subsistent? In resolving these issues, Abelard first argues from the authority of Boethius[120] and Scripture[121] to establish Christ's sinlessness as well as his possession of the free choice by which he could sin. He also asserts Christ's full humanity and his possession of a soul and flesh by arguing that he had a nature of substance and not of accident. But arguing for Christ's self-subsistent humanity leads back to the question of ability to sin. Abelard finds himself in a dilemma: to affirm Christ's inability to sin appears to deny his humanity; to affirm his humanity is to affirm his ability to sin. He resolves the difficulty by considering the strengths (*vires*) of the propositions, and the qualifications, or conditions, by which they are made.[122] Are these qualifications possible or necessary? Or is the statement made simply, without a proper qualification? In the case of the man united to God, the following qualification describes the point at which he was united to God: He is able to sin, but not after or while he is so united. Christ could not sin because that very name describes the union of God and man; consequently, "every man is a liar" is a true proposition.

119. See also Peppermüller's brief discussion, *Auslegung*, 41.

120. *c. Eut.* 8.

121. Eccli 31.10 and Is 33.16.

122. For Abelard's own discussion of qualifications, see *Dial.* 1.3.2.1, and 5.2.5.

He does not restrict his use of dialectics to the questions, of course, and one can find numerous other *distinctiones* and dialectical terms and explanations throughout the commentary, in both glosses and questions. For example, at 13.9, expounding "You shall love your neighbor as yourself," he distinguishes between "as yourself" and "as much as yourself," regarding the first as demonstrating similarity, and the second as demonstrating equality, and he shows dialectically how anyone should be loved the more, the dearer he is held by God and the better he is. In the question on the love of God and neighbor at 13.10, Abelard distinguishes the love of God according to the subjective and objective genitives, and then distinguishes between the two forms of loving one's neighbor: by avoiding injuries and granting benefits. Finally, he distinguishes between love of God and neighbor, noting that the former is superior, and thus does not inevitably include the latter.[123] All these distinctions are intended to clarify the text, as opposed to demonstrating the truth of a statement.

Similar in use to distinction is "subdivide," a term Abelard uses three times, usually to describe Paul's enumeration of large numbers of items within a category, such as vices or spiritual gifts.[124] He speaks of "inferring" four times, in the sense of deducing or drawing logical consequences.[125] He mentions the rhetorical or dialectical figure of "contraries" four times, once referring to a "topic," or dialectical maxim, drawn from contraries.[126] He finds all these contraries in the words of Paul under consideration, and usually draws a moral lesson from them.

123. See also 1.20, where Abelard makes his famous distinction between the Persons of the Trinity according to power, wisdom, and goodness, and 15.24, where Abelard distinguishes between enjoying God wholly and enjoying our neighbor in part; we love God for his sake, and our neighbor for the sake of his benefit, placing the end of the enjoyment in the final and supreme cause, which is God.

124. 1.29–31, 12.6, and 15.19. Note that Abelard sees Paul always subdividing *statim*.

125. As a means of learning the skill of a thing's maker from the quality of the work, analogous to learning of the Trinity from their works (1.20 [*coniicimus*]); from contraries (2.26); inferring divine purposes from frequent events (5.19 [*coniicere*]); and an incorrect inference from a particular wording of a statement (8.30).

126. 1.17, 2.26, 6.20 ("topic," or *locus*), and 9.17.

Abelard mentions "cause" at least four times in the commentary, demonstrating familiarity with Aristotle's different kinds of causation: divine providence is the necessary cause of all evil things;[127] we must direct the intention of our love toward God, lest we make ourselves, rather than God, the final and supreme cause of our love;[128] we enjoy God wholly, but our neighbor in part, to make God the final and supreme cause of this enjoyment;[129] and peace is the final cause, or intention, of the Epistle to the Romans.[130]

One also finds some of Abelard's linguistic theory in the Romans commentary. At 1.20, he speaks of how different divine attributes could be assigned to the different persons of the Trinity. At 6.4, he returns to this theme, where, discussing Paul's words "Through the glory of God the Father," he explains, "that is, through the power of divinity which is especially expressed in the name 'Father.'" The names and titles of Jesus also express particular attributes: "Christ," "anointed one," expresses his royal power, and "Lord" expresses the right he has over us, to draw us out of the dominion of sin.[131] Since these terms are ordinarily applied to human beings, Abelard regards the divine expressions as being specially imposed through revelation; God has revealed himself as Father, Christ, and Lord, and used these terms to describe his nature and activity to humanity.

Related to the ability of terms to express divine realities is their ability to signify. We have seen that Abelard uses "signification" to refer to the spiritual understanding of scripture. He also uses it in its related dialectical sense, to analyze the meanings of words in their contexts and determine their precise referents. For example, at 2.17–20, noting Paul's words, "guide… light…teacher…master," Abelard interprets these terms as an inculcation of words, and "not a diverse signification." That is, each succeeding term reinforces the previous one by having a similar meaning to it, rather than a different one. At 7.16, argu-

127. 8.30.
128. 13.10. Note the closeness of this discussion to that of love of neighbor as derived from the genus of love.
129. 15.24. 130. 15.33.
131. 7.25.

ing against the idea that the killing of a man through the throwing of a stone is voluntary, he states that terms frequently change their significations from their essential attributes; while every sin is voluntary, not every act of killing is voluntary, if it lacks the will to murder. Killing is not always voluntary; it has different significations according to the will attached to it.[132] None of Abelard's uses of signification is as complex as what one finds in his *Dialectica*.[133] He has largely avoided complex discussions of signification in favor of more basic usage, though one may assume that his students were capable of understanding such a discussion.

Abelard occasionally mentions dialectical terms and techniques, as though he were giving lessons in application to his students. These have included determinations, topics, distinctions, and subdivisions, not to mention the other terms and techniques we have discussed. At 4.18, Abelard, discussing Abraham's "hope against hope," speaks of how Abraham believed God's promise "according to that rule of dialectic: 'If what seems to be contained more completely is not, what seems to be contained less will not.'" This is the converse of a topic from his *Dialectica:* "If what seems to belong to a lesser degree belongs, then also what seems to belong to a greater degree will belong."[134] Since Abelard applies this rule obscurely at best, it is hard to know if he was deliberately citing the converse or if he had forgotten the original form; at any rate, it is evident that he cites it didactically, to teach his students.

Abelard uses the major tool of dialectic, the syllogism, only three times. At 8.15, he offers the following syllogism on the spirit of adoption:

A. You yourselves received the spirit of adoption in which the sons of God are made.[135]

B. The charity of God is poured out in our hearts through the Holy Spirit who has been given to us.[136]

---

132. See also 5.19, 8.15 (cf. Haymo, *Rom.*, 8.15), and 9.24.

133. 1.3.

134. "Si enim quod magis uidetur inesse non inest, nec quod minus uidetur inesse inerit." Compare *Dial.* 3.1: "Si id quod minus inesse uidetur inest, et quod magis inesse uidetur inerit."

135. Rom 8.15.   136. Rom 5.5.

C. Therefore, the spirit of adoption is a gift of charity through which we are adopted by God as sons.

The conclusion is made from linking the two premises and equating the Holy Spirit with the spirit of adoption, a justifiable equation, and the syllogism answers the question of whether God has many sons—yes, Abelard responds, many, but through adoption, at which point he offers the syllogism.

At 8.30, Abelard answers another question with a syllogism: Do divine providence and predestination take away free choice? He responds with the following argument:

A. Since God foresees that a man who will commit adultery may commit adultery, it is necessary that he commit adultery.

B. If it is necessary that he commit adultery, it is inevitable, and he does not have the free choice to avoid this sin.

C. Therefore, he should not be judged guilty of this sin which he could in no way avoid.

Abelard goes on to overturn this argument, distinguishing between "inevitably" and "unavoidably," for the statement does not imply unavoidability simply, with a qualification.

Finally, at 9.21, Abelard speaks of the "horned syllogism" with which a person is wounded (*cornuto uulneratur syllogismo*), when he responds to the question asked by Paul, whether the potter has a right to do as he pleases with his clay. The "horns" represent contrary opinions: deny the potter this power and condemn his duty and the public welfare (by denying the public vessels for waste), or "choose what is evident," admitting that the potter has this power and may exercise it without injury to the "vessels of disgrace"—that is, that God may treat his creation as he chooses, without accusation of mistreatment.

Abelard also uses a number of analogies to explain some difficult points that might otherwise be obscure, though only rarely does he directly apply them to the text. The best known of them is the analogy of the bronze and the image made in the bronze, which he offers to explain the relationship of the Persons of the Trinity: As the bronze and the image in the bronze have the same substance but different characteristics, and just as the image comes from the bronze but not vice versa, so it is with the

Persons of the Trinity: They share the same substance yet different characteristics, and the Son comes from the Father, not vice versa.[137] Also well known is his string of analogies at 9.21, which includes his analogy of the physician who offers medicine to a sick person, who could not receive the medicine if the physician did not help him; and the analogy of the rich man who offers his wealth to the poor if they will work for him.[138]

Abelard's analogies, especially when they are strung together as at 9.21, offset the difficulty of his rhetoric and make his exposition clearer and more vivid. Dialectically, they clarify the meanings of arguments or statements by means of comparison, though they do not prove them; Abelard never intended to demonstrate the Trinity by means of the analogy mentioned above, but to explain and represent it.[139]

Theology

Abelard's Romans commentary is equally famous for its statements on points of Christian doctrine. Abelard was accused by several people, most notably William of St. Thierry and Bernard of Clairvaux, of serious error on a number of these doctrines.[140] Abelard's Romans commentary, like most medieval Romans commentaries, functions as an encyclopedia of Christian doctrine, and discusses most of the doctrines concerning which Abelard was accused of error. William's and Bernard's accusations can be linked directly to several passages from this work. Some of Abelard's doctrinal statements are quite significant, most notably those on redemption, grace, original sin, and intention; others, such as those on the Trinity, are less so,

137. 1.20. Abelard also uses this analogy, of course, in others of his works: the *TSch.* 2.112–16, and the *TChr.* 4.86–87; and it was one of William of St. Thierry's major points of criticism in his *Disp.* III, which cites the passage from the *TSch.* See also Evans' discussion of this analogy in *Language,* 104–5, which is based on the passage from the *TChr.*; and of analogies and similitudes in general; ibid., 101–5.

138. For his other analogies, see 5.19, 6.9, 7.13, 9.32, 12.14, and 12.19.

139. Cottiaux, "Conception," 819.

140. See above, pp. 5–6, nn. 4–5, for citations of William's *disp.* and Bernard's *Ep.* 190.

and more significant statements can be found in others of his works. Here we will focus on the key doctrines of the Romans commentary, and on those relating to the accusations of William and Bernard, specifically, grace, redemption, original sin, intention, faith, and the Trinity. Additionally, we will discuss the spirituality of the work.

Among the various doctrinal discussions one can detect certain concerns or guiding principles, which arise in others of Abelard's works as well. Chief among these is the tension between the grace of God and human freedom. Abelard asserts the primacy of God's grace as the means of human salvation, but is equally concerned to protect human responsibility both for sin and for accepting grace. This latter concern would lead to the charge of Pelagianism as well as to the controversy over original sin. Related to this is Abelard's linking ethics with his doctrine of God: there can be no injustice with God—a seemingly orthodox statement which would cause Abelard trouble when he criticized the ransom theory of atonement because it required God to demand the blood of an innocent man to save the guilty.

Grace

Grace is ostensibly the major topic of Abelard's commentary; Abelard notes in his prologue that Paul's epistle amplifies the gift of grace, and that grace and works are the epistle's subject matter. Grace was also the subject of one of William of St. Thierry's main accusations against Abelard. William accused Abelard of being a Pelagian, of teaching that a person could receive and cling to grace through free choice and reason, and that God gives grace to all people to excite them to will the good.[141]

---

141. *disp.* 6. William quotes two passages that he attributes to Abelard, but they have never been identified as coming from any of Abelard's surviving works. Peppermüller discusses this, citing Landgraf's belief that Abelard's discussion of grace in his comment on 5.19 (to be discussed below) is as close to what William criticizes as can be found in his works (Landgraf, *Dogmengeschichte* I.1.70, cited by Peppermüller, *Auslegung*, 55, n. 327). Bernard makes no accusation concerning grace in his *Ep.* 190.

That is, William believed that Abelard's doctrine of grace was contrary to the received Augustinian tradition that dominated medieval thought on this subject.

A few scholars have summarized Abelard's doctrine of grace or touched on particular aspects of it,[142] and they vary in their assessment of Abelard's Augustinianism,[143] though they regard Abelard's thought on grace as distinct from that of his contemporaries.

For the most part, Abelard follows Augustine's teaching on grace. For example, he teaches that grace precedes merit in election and justification, though he says little about grace enabling humans to achieve merit through works.[144] He defines grace as redemption.[145] He frequently links grace with redemption, salvation, or liberation from punishment or the dominion of sin.[146] He affirms the remission of sins by grace several

142. The most complete is that of Aage Rydstrøm-Poulsen, *The Gracious God*, 157–98; see also Weingart, *Logic*, 176–83; Marenbon, *Philosophy*, 325–30; Luscombe, *School*, 128–30; Peppermüller, *Auslegung*, 53–59; Murray, *Abelard*, 131–34; and Williams, "Sin, Grace, and Redemption," 269–74. All of these deal with the Romans commentary to greater or lesser degrees.

143. Rydstrøm-Poulsen, for example, argues that "[i]n his teaching on grace,...Abelard has been shown to be quite conservative and Augustinian" (*Gracious God*, 197); and Weingart notes how Abelard develops an idea of Augustine, and says that he is faithful to Augustine's position (*Logic*, 180–81). Murray, on the other hand, says that Abelard "believes neither in grace in the Augustinian sense nor in merits in the Pelagian" (*Abelard*, 133).

144. 1.7, 3.24, 5.2, 5.4, 5.11, 5.17, 5.19, 5.20, 6.11, 7.25, 8.18, 8.22–23, 8.28, 11.5, 11.6, and 11.7. He does not deny the existence or even importance of merits, good or bad. See especially 11.6, where Abelard notes that St. Paul does not say "through merits" (*per merita*) but "by merits" (*ex meritis*), and goes on to say that grace does not exclude the merits of Paul and others. At 13.10, Abelard says that "the entire essence of our merits consists in the love of God and neighbor" (*cum vero tota meritorum nostrorum summa in dilectione Dei consistat et proximi*). And, at 8.18, Abelard notes that grace was "superadded" (*superadditam*) to our merits, obtaining for us what we were not adequate to attain by our own merits. He is not clear, however, about the nature of these merits, though they have to do with the reward for works subsequent to salvation. Cf. Augustine, *Io. ev. tr.* 3.8; ibid., 115.46; *ex. prop. Rm.* 20; *en. Ps.* 31.1.1; and ibid., 67.12.

145. 3.24. Cf. Augustine, *S.* 285.3.

146. 3.26, 4.15, 6.3, 7.14, 8.1, 13.10, and 14.23. Cf. Augustine, *en. Ps.* 30.2.2.13.

times,[147] and likewise justification by grace.[148] And, importantly, he notes that we do not seek grace, but rather it seeks us out.[149] As it does for Augustine, grace for Abelard represents the divine initiative that begins the process of salvation, distinct from human efforts.

Additionally, Abelard mentions several kinds of grace also cited by Augustine: He speaks of *gratia praeveniens,* or prevenient grace;[150] of the grace that calls or chooses;[151] of the grace that adopts;[152] of *gratia adjuvans,* the grace that helps;[153] and of *gratia operans,* the grace that works for salvation and sanctification.[154] He also speaks of the time of grace, that is, human history from the time of Christ on.[155]

Abelard sees grace as well in divine purposes hidden from human beings. He follows Augustine on the matter of God granting grace to whom he chooses, without being accused of iniquity or injury; God can both give grace and withdraw it.[156] Abelard also argues, going beyond Augustine, that God's grace works in children who die before baptism, and who are therefore condemned, because their punishment is lenient, and their parents are moved to self-examination and penance; Abelard attributes this punishment to grace and not to righteousness, because God uses such punishment for the benefit of oth-

---

147. 1.5, 5.16, 5.19, 6.1–2, 6.6, 8.10, and 16.24 (from Haymo). Cf. Augustine, *s.* 131, 7.7; *ep. Rm. inch.* 1.23, ed. Landes, 86–89; *Ep.* 194, 3.9.

148. Prologue, 3.22, 3.24, 5.9, and 5.19. Cf. Augustine, *ep. Rm. inch.* 1.1; I.6; *ex. prop. Rm.* 20, 21.

149. 13.12.

150. 1.7, 4.7, 5.19, and 9.21; cf. Augustine, *en. Ps.* 31.2.1; *s.* 174.4; and *c. ep. Pel.* 4.6.15.

151. 1.7, 9.12, 11.7, and 11.28. Cf. Augustine, *Io. ev. tr.* 86.2.

152. 1.7, 8.22–23, and 9.4. Cf. Augustine, *c. Jul. imp.* 4.132; *Jo. ev. tr.* 2.13; and *ex. prop. Rm.* 52.

153. 8.37 and 8.38. Abelard understands by helping grace the grace that enables Christians to overcome and conquer all spiritual opposition that would separate them from the love of God. As we will see, Abelard was accused of denying enabling or helping grace, on the basis of his comments on 9.21. Cf. Augustine, *gest. Pel.* 65; *ep.* 177.1–2; *ep.* 167.4.39.

154. 5.5; cf. Augustine, *pecc. mer.* 2.19.33; *ep.* 187, 9.319.

155. 3.21, 3.26, and 11.6. Cf. Augustine, *s.* 72, 2.3; *s.* 131, 9.9.

156. 9.14–15 and 9.21.

ers.[157] Grace is ultimately beyond our understanding, but it is apparent that to Abelard it is not universal, and it does not save every person from punishment.[158]

Some of Abelard's most distinctive teachings on grace equate it with deity or with theological virtues. For example, he equates grace with the Holy Spirit some thirteen times in the commentary.[159] Also distinctive and only slightly less frequent are Abelard's identifications of grace with charity or love.[160] He links these eight times,[161] again following Augustine.[162] This latter identification would not have been controversial, but in identifying grace with the Holy Spirit, Abelard made two statements that might have drawn William of St. Thierry's fire had he read Abelard's commentary. At 4.23–24, he states that the goodness of divine grace belongs especially to the Holy Spirit; at 5.5, he equates the Holy Spirit not just with grace, but with the operation of grace. These passages both assign either divine characteristics or operations to specific Persons of the Trinity; William would accuse Abelard of the heresy of modalism, or Sabellianism, for similar statements.[163]

Also distinctive and even more controversial was Abelard's statement that no additional grace is necessary to do good works beyond the grace that God already gives to a person. He arrives at this conclusion in the question he poses at 9.21 on

157. 5.19. Augustine, in *ench.* 93, saw this punishment of those who had added no sin of their own to original sin as the gentlest of all, but saw no work of grace here.

158. Cf. Augustine's statement on grace in *Ep.*190.3.9–12, in which he asserts the primacy of God's choice in giving grace to some people while withholding it from others.

159. See, for example, 1.4 (twice), 1.7, 1.20, 3.13, 4.23, 5.5, 8.4, 8.10, 8.13, and 15.19.

160. Abelard does not seem to distinguish clearly between *caritas, amor,* and *dilectio.* In fact, at two places in his Romans commentary he seems to equate the first two terms: 7.6 and 8.2; and at 5.5, he equates *caritas* with *dilectio.*

161. 3.26, 5.7–8, 5.19, 6.14, 8.2, 11.22, 13.10, and 16.24. This latter reference is taken from Haymo's commentary on Romans, 16.24. Abelard also links the Holy Spirit with charity and love; see the discussion of his teaching on the Trinity.

162. *ex. Gal.* 24; *ex. prop. Rm.* 13–18; ibid., 45–46; and *en. Ps.* 70, 1.20.

163. *disp.* 3.

whether a wicked person to whom God has never given the grace necessary in order to accept grace can be held guilty. How can God condemn such a person? Can a sick man incapable of receiving medicine on his own be blamed if the doctor giving him that medicine does not help him? It is on this basis that Abelard argues against the necessity of additional grace for each good work; the general gift of grace that is given each day equally to all people through the gift of faith is sufficient to inflame desire for the Kingdom of God and its rewards, but not all respond equally to it. Grace goes before each of the elect, enabling him to desire well and then to persevere; additional grace is not necessary to do good.[164] Abelard thus seems to deny helping grace, and for this reason William would accuse Abelard of Pelagianism,[165] though, as we have seen, Abelard does have a concept of *gratia adjuvans*.

Others, such as the author of the *Capitula Haeresum,* would criticize his view that the wicked man seems blameless, and that God does no more for the saved before they receive grace than for the wicked;[166] and Bernard would simply charge that Abelard asserted the sufficiency of free choice for good works.[167] Abelard's emphasis on the desire for reward inflamed by the gracious offer of the Kingdom, his analogy of the industrious who labor hard for the reward, and his statement that "the will is enough to obtain [the reward], and it can be reached by all with much less expense or labor or danger than in the acquisition of earthly kingdoms,"[168] could certainly be regarded as Pelagian. On this basis one can understand the various accusations. What his accusers seem not to have realized was Abelard's point: to relieve God of the accusation of arbitrariness by plac-

---

164. On this passage, see Peppermüller, *Auslegung,* 53–55; Marenbon, *Philosophy,* 325–27; Luscombe, *School,* 128–30; and especially Williams, "Sin, Grace, and Redemption," 269–74.

165. *disp.* 6; see n. 3 above, as well as *Ep.* 326 in the collection of Bernard's letters, PL 182:532B, cited by Luscombe, *School,* 129.

166. *cap. haer.,* 6.

167. *Ep.* 190.

168. Buytaert, 241.339–242.342: ". . . praesertim cum ad ipsum obtinendum sola sufficiat uoluntas, multoque minori impensa uel sudore seu discrimine ab omnibus peruenari possit quam ad acquisitionem terrenorum regnorum."

ing responsibility on human beings for responding to the offer of grace made to all.[169] This simplified grace, but also seemed to overlook predestination, vocation, justification, and remission of sins,[170] and to make grace only an inspiration to do good. On this point William of St. Thierry and the other critics certainly seemed to have valid arguments.

This is not the whole picture of Abelard's theology of grace, as we have seen. Abelard here, as he did so often elsewhere, went to an extreme to make a particular point in defense of his ethical view of God, and it was easy for critics to pick on the obvious flaws in this bolder statement without looking at the shorter, plainer, and more orthodox statements on grace found elsewhere in his commentary.[171] Taken together, Abelard's statements on grace are, for the most part, consonant with traditional Augustinian positions. In contrast with the more elaborate twelfth-century thought on grace, which specified different kinds of grace given at different stages of human need,[172] Abelard presents a simpler, more unified view. He does not address many of the questions on grace raised by other scholars of his time, questions he could easily have raised in a Romans commentary, but pursues his own agenda, to present a morally consistent view of grace, in which God saves by grace, but human beings are responsible for receiving it. This simplification, combined with the bold language of 9.21, led to the accusations against him.

Redemption

Redemption likewise forms an important theme in Abelard's commentary, and not only because it is a major theme of St. Paul's epistle. Abelard's views on redemption, or at least William of St. Thierry's and Bernard of Clairvaux's perceptions

169. Cf. Marenbon, *Philosophy*, 325–27.

170. William of St. Thierry pointed out the absence of the first two of these in *disp*. 6.

171. See above; see also Luscombe, *School*, 128–30.

172. See Artur Landgraf, *Dogmengeschichte der Frühscholastik* (Regensburg: Verlag Friedrich Pustet, 1952–56), I.i, and Alister E. McGrath, *Iustitia Dei: A History of the Christian Doctrine of Justification. The Beginnings to the Reformation* (Cambridge: Cambridge University Press, 1986), 101–3.

of these views, were a central issue in their accusations against him. William accused Abelard of teaching that Christ died for nothing, and that his coming into the world was unnecessary; he also argued that Abelard emphasized the death of Christ as a provocation of charity, to the near-exclusion of his death as the sacrament of redemption and an example of humility.[173] Bernard made similar accusations.[174]

Abelard does not present an entirely consistent theology of redemption in his Romans commentary. At some points he presents what seems to be a strictly exemplarist view of redemption;[175] at other points he presents the objective views he had previously rejected;[176] at still others he seems to mix them. This has likely contributed to the modern controversy over Abelard's views. Many scholars, especially those of the early twentieth century, have adopted the view that Abelard was primarily, if not exclusively, an exemplarist. These include Hastings Rashdall,[177] C. de Rémusat,[178] J. G. Sikes,[179] Jean Rivière,[180]

173. *disp.* 7.   174. *Ep.* 190.

175. By "exemplarism" is meant the belief that Christ's death functioned primarily as an example of obedience to the will of God, or of divine love, which inspires a response in the human heart of love for God (the "provocation of charity" mentioned above) that transforms the person. This is also known as "subjective" redemption, because the emphasis is on the subjective response of the person.

176. By "objective" is meant the belief that Christ's death by itself achieved salvation for human beings apart from any human response. Many theories of how Christ did this abounded in the patristic era and the Middle Ages, and have survived into the modern era; they involve some sort of transaction, between either Christ and the devil or Christ and the Father, and include such theories as satisfaction, ransom, and penal substitution.

177. Hastings Rashdall, *The Idea of Atonement in Christian Theology*, Bampton Lectures, 1915 (London: 1919), 357–62. Rashdall asserts that for the first time, in Abelard's theology of redemption, "the doctrine of the atonement was stated in a way which had nothing unintelligible, arbitrary, illogical, or immoral about it."

178. C. de Rémusat, *Abélard*, 2 vols. (Paris, 1845), II.447–48; cited by Murray, *Abelard* (Manchester: Manchester University Press, 1967), 131. De Rémusat likewise argued for the moral, spiritual character of Abelard's view, favoring it over the traditional views set forth by the Church.

179. Sikes, *Abailard*, 207–10. Sikes emphasizes Abelard's view that Christ's death poured charity into men's hearts, providing a new motive for obedience, and he denies any aspect of sacrifice in Abelard's theology.

180. Jean Rivière, *Le dogme de la rédemption au début du moyen age*, Biblio-

INTRODUCTION   45

and A. Victor Murray.[181] Others, mostly of the late twentieth
and early twenty-first centuries, either deny this exemplarism or see a balance between it and Abelard's more objective
statements. These include R. O. P. Taylor,[182] D. E. Luscombe,[183]
Richard Weingart,[184] Rolf Peppermüller,[185] John Marenbon,[186]
M. T. Clanchy,[187] Philip L. Quinn,[188] Thomas Williams,[189] and

théque Thomiste, vol. 19 (Paris: Librairie Philosophique J. Vrin, 1934), 106–
25. He does not regard as convincing Abelard's statements concerning Christ's
death as a sacrifice, and argues that Abelard's exemplarism takes redemption to
the level of simple psychology.

181. Murray, *Abelard*, 126–34. Murray argues that Abelard's references to
the price of Christ's blood and his sacrifice were intended to demonstrate his
orthodoxy, and that Abelard believes neither in grace in the Augustinian sense
nor in merits in the Pelagian sense.

182. Taylor, "Exemplarist," 207–13. Taylor argues against both Rashdall and
Sikes, presenting Abelard's Passion hymn and re-examining the question on redemption from the Romans commentary.

183. Luscombe, *School*, 137–38. Luscombe sees a greater balance in Abelard's thought between the exemplarist and objective positions than previous
scholars did, and attributes the apparent imbalance to Abelard's style of argument, in which he seemingly denies one point to make another.

184. Weingart, *Logic*, 125–46. Weingart does not regard the question on redemption as a fully developed theory of subjective atonement, or even as subjective at all, and shows how in all of his teaching, Abelard uses traditional language and concepts to create a theocentric theology of redemption.

185. Peppermüller, *Auslegung*, 96–104, 119–21. In many ways Peppermüller
concurs with Rivière, regarding Abelard's teaching as very psychological and
subjective. At the same time, he gives full attention to the other passages in the
Romans commentary that speak of Christ's intercessory work, regarding them
as necessary to complete Abelard's teaching on redemption.

186. Marenbon, *Philosophy*, 322–23, 330–31. Marenbon does not regard the
question on redemption as "pure exemplarism," though it is a prime example
of his ethical teaching, and it does overshadow the teachings on Christ's redemptive death, which can be read as inconsistencies or attempts to fend off
charges of heresy.

187. Clanchy, *Abelard*, 278, 283–87. Clanchy does not deal extensively with
questions of exemplarism or objectivism, though he does assert that Abelard's
theology was based on love, and that it was rooted in his concern for Heloise
and her questions.

188. Quinn, "Abelard on Atonement," 282–95. Quinn argues that while the
example of Christ's death is certainly part of Abelard's teaching, Abelard does
not teach that it is merely an example. Rather, Abelard, like Thomas Aquinas,
was a hierarchical pluralist, affirming that Christ's death was a penal substitution and restored humanity to a state of liberty.

189. Williams, "Sin, Grace, and Redemption," 258–76. Williams argues that

H. Lawrence Bond.[190] There is general consensus among this latter group that Abelard made statements supporting the view that Christ died on behalf of humanity, though there is little agreement about Abelard's motives for doing so and about how important they are for understanding his redemption theology as a whole.

The most important passage in the commentary on redemption, and the one to which both medieval and modern scholars have given so much attention, is the *quaestio* at 3.26. One may make five general observations concerning this question. First, Abelard considers Christ's entire life and death to be a demonstration of God's justice. Second, Abelard several times equates that justice with charity. Christ's life and death are thus demonstrations of divine charity. Third, Abelard also considers this demonstration to be a redemptive act of grace, begun and finished by God in Christ. Fourth, this demonstration actually achieves the remission of sin through the human response of love. Redemption is thus a divinely initiated act that kindles human love. Fifth, Abelard criticizes only two objective theories of redemption, not all of them. He does not deny objective redemption entirely. Obviously, the concept of God's demonstration through Christ is central to Abelard's argument.

We have already seen how Abelard assailed two current theories of objective redemption in this question by means of dialectics. While his position that these theories were fatally flawed was controversial enough, he made some additional statements in his criticisms that only inflamed the controversy further. First, he argues that Christ's death was not essential for conveying forgiveness to humanity; Christ could and did forgive simply by speaking a word. Then, in vivid terms, he asks what need there was for Christ to suffer for the sake of human redemption. This would lead William and Bernard to state that Abelard taught

---

Abelard is not an exemplarist, that exemplarism is incoherent without the objective transaction of Christ's death, which Abelard does affirm.

190. Bond, "Another Look," 11–31. Bond closely analyzes the text of 3.26, with special attention to what Abelard meant by *exemplum:* not only Christ's death, but his life. He draws no conclusions about Abelard's supposed exemplarism, but points out that Abelard was doing exegesis, engaging the text of Romans, and not developing a doctrinal system.

that Christ died for nothing. Abelard's emphasis here, however, is not so much on whether Christ's death was redemptively efficacious, but on whether God had no other means by which he could redeem humanity. He argues that God is under no compulsion to choose any particular means of redemption.[191]

In the same vein, Abelard argues against the morality of asserting that Christ's death achieved justification and reconciliation, since his murder was far more serious a crime against God than Adam's eating of an apple. In so doing, Abelard seems to challenge the Apostle's own words: "How does the Apostle say that we are justified or reconciled to God through the death of his Son, who should have been all the more angry with man because men forsook him so much more in crucifying his Son, than in transgressing his first commandment in paradise with the taste of one apple?"[192]

Finally, the style and tone of Abelard's attack on the morality of the ransom theory likely contributed to the ensuing controversy. In this attack he asks whether Christ's death could indeed make us more righteous than we were before his death, and to whom the ransom must have been paid: certainly not to the devil, who was a mere torturer; it must have been to God, and Abelard quickly demonstrates the immorality of God's demanding innocent blood as a means of atonement. Though logical in the light of his just-finished criticism of the devil's rights, his thinking challenges traditional views of redemption, not to mention Scripture.[193] The concept of ransom was too fully ingrained in western theology for Abelard to attack it in the way that he did and avoid the criticism of William and Bernard. While a simple criticism of the devil's rights might have passed the test of these two critics, an all-out assault on ransom could not.

Abelard's own subsequent positive statement on redemption might not have been quite so controversial had he not attacked

191. Weingart, *Logic,* 90–93.

192. Buytaert, 116:210–14: "Quomodo etiam nos iustificari vel reconciliari Deo per mortem Filii sui dicit Apostolus, qui tanto amplius adversus hominem irasci debuit quanto amplius homines in crucifigendo Filium suum deliquerunt, quam in transgrediendo primum eius in paradiso praeceptum unius pomi gustu?"

193. For example, Mk 10.45.

these two other positions so vehemently. Critical readers read
his subsequent declaration in the light of these criticisms, and
came to the conclusion that Abelard in fact did not believe in
any kind of objective action by Christ that achieved salvation.
Had Abelard presented this statement by itself without any criticism of the devil's rights or ransom, it might have passed with
little notice either in its own time or ours. It is those criticisms,
however, that have made Abelard's words about Christ's life and
death being a demonstration of grace and love so famous, because they have led to the belief that Abelard was an exemplarist and only an exemplarist.

In the latter part of the question at 3.26, having disposed of
the theories of the devil's rights and ransom, and wanting to
show just how Christ's death achieves redemption, Abelard returns to the Apostle's statement that Christ's death was a demonstration of grace and righteousness:

Nevertheless it seems to us that in this we are justified in the blood
of Christ and reconciled to God, that it was through this matchless
grace shown to us that his Son received our nature, and in that nature,
teaching us both by word and by example, persevered to the death and
bound us to himself even more through love, so that when we have
been kindled by so great a benefit of divine grace, true charity might
fear to endure nothing for his sake....Each one is also made more
righteous after the Passion of Christ than before; that is, he loves God
more, because the completed benefit kindles him in love more than a
hoped-for benefit.

Therefore, our redemption is that supreme love in us through the
Passion of Christ, which not only frees us from slavery to sin, but gains
for us the true liberty of the sons of God, so that we may complete all
things by his love rather than by fear. He showed us such great grace,
than which a greater cannot be found, by his own word: "No one,"
he says, "has greater love than this: that he lays down his life for his
friends." Concerning this love the same person says elsewhere, "I have
come to send fire on the earth, and what do I desire except that it
burn?" He witnesses, therefore, that he has come to increase this true
liberty of charity among men.[194]

194. Buytaert, 117.242–118.269: "Nobis autem videtur quod in hoc iustificati
sumus in sanguine Christi et Deo reconciliati, quod per hanc singularem gratiam
nobis exhibitam quod Filius suus nostram susceperit naturam et in ipsa nos tam
verbo quam exemplo instituendo usque ad mortem perstitit, nos sibi amplius
per amorem adstrixit, ut tanto divinae gratiae accensi beneficio, nil iam tolerare

Abelard places Christ's death in the context of his entire life, which was a demonstration of grace that kindled love in the hearts of humanity. Christ's sufferings kindle love, or charity, which, as we have seen, Abelard equates with justice/righteousness, and therefore Christ's death can legitimately be said to justify a person and reconcile him to God—not on the basis of having satisfied legal necessities, but on the basis of love.

If one should read this question only from among Abelard's statements on redemption, it would be hard to regard Abelard as anything other than an exemplarist. He sharply criticizes two objective theories and speaks of redemption in terms that clearly suggest an exemplarist stance; there is no mention of Christ dying for sin or other language commonly associated with objective redemption.[195] Abelard's language is similar to that which Augustine used in describing the exemplary nature of Christ's work,[196] and to that of some of his own contemporaries, William of St. Thierry included,[197] but unlike them, Abelard does not affirm the objective effects, at least not here, and for this reason

ipsum vera reformidet caritas....Iustior quoque, id est amplius Deum diligens, quisque fit post passionem Christi quam ante, quia amplius in amorem accendit completum beneficium quam speratum. Redemptio itaque nostra est illa summa in nobis per passionem Christi dilectio quae nos non solum a servitute peccati liberat, sed veram nobis filiorum Dei libertatem acquirit, ut amore eius potius quam timore cuncta impleamus, qui nobis tantam exhibuit gratiam qua maior inveniri ipso attestante non potest. Maiorem hac, inquit, dilectionem nemo habet, quam ut animam suam ponat pro amicis suis. De hoc quidem amore idem alibi dicit: Ignem veni mittere in terram, et quid volo nisi ut ardeat? Ad hanc itaque veram caritatis libertatem in hominibus propagandam se venisse testatur."

195. Weingart lists several things missing from Abelard's declaration: "we have no mention of the scriptural ideas of repentance, forgiveness of sins, and justification" (*Logic*, 95; Abelard does mention justification, however, at the very beginning of the *solutio*). Weingart does allow that the entire question is "a summary statement of Abailard's soteriology," but quickly adds that "it is not a complete elaboration of Abailard's teaching on redemption, since it suffers from self-evident and unaccountable omissions, such as the lack of any attention to the person of the Redeemer and the means of his work, to forgiveness and justification as benefits of that work, and to man's appropriation in faith, hope, and love of the gifts offered by Christ" (ibid., 95–96).

196. For example, *Io ev. tr.* 110.6; *cat. rud.* 7; and *f. et symb.* 6.

197. See William's comments on Rom 5.7–11 in his own commentary, *Expositio super epistolam ad Romanos.*

this question on redemption stands apart from the mainstream of twelfth-century thought on redemption; and it is for this reason that William accused Abelard of ignoring Christ's death as the sacrament of redemption.

Abelard does speak in objective terms elsewhere in the Romans commentary, almost in support of the theories he had previously rejected. For example, at 4.25, he speaks of how Christ "swept away the penalty for sins by the price (*pretium*) of his death," not long after he had denied the concept of ransom (*pretium*). In the same passage, he also speaks of Christ bearing the penalty of human sin,[198] a concept he uses again elsewhere to describe the means by which sins are forgiven.[199] He also describes Christ's death as a sacrifice for us that achieves remission of sins,[200] of Christ dying for our sins,[201] of Christ's blood being given for us,[202] and of that blood cleansing the stain of our sins.[203]

Abelard would again use exemplarist language in the commentary, sometimes combining it with the objective language. At 5.6, he says that Christ "died for us, not for the sake of anything else, unless it was on account of that freedom of charity to be enlarged in us, namely, through this highest love which he showed to us, just as he says, 'No one has greater love than this,' etc." At 5.9, Abelard speaks of how we are "*now justified in his blood,* that is, now through the love which we have in him, on account of this highest grace which he showed to us, namely, in dying for us while we were yet sinners."

Abelard uses the objective language in a convincing way that, if it were not for the question of 3.26, would lead a reader to think of Abelard as a staunch traditionalist. How does one rec-

---

198. Buytaert, 153.992–1000: "Duobus modis propter delicta nostra mortuus dicitur, tum quia nos deliquimus propter quod ille moreretur et peccatum commisimus cuius ille poenam sustinuit, tum etiam ut peccata nostra moriendo tolleret, id est poenam peccatorum introducens nos in paradisum, pretio suae mortis auferret et per exhibitionem tantae gratiae, quia ut ipse ait majorem dilectionem nemo habet, animos nostros a voluntate peccandi retraheret, et in summam suam dilectionem intenderet."

199. 5.19.	200. 5.21 and 8.3–4.
201. 6.9 and 14.9.	202. 7.14.
203. 8.32.	

oncile these apparent contradictions? Should one ignore them
and create a unified, carefully categorized soteriology, as Weingart does?[204] Should one see Abelard's objective statements
as attempts to demonstrate his orthodoxy, as Murray does?[205]
Should one see his passionate arguments of 3.26 as rhetorical
statements, as Luscombe implies?[206] Or should one accept these
contradictions as such, common to all the theological writers of
his time, the result of trying to explain complex questions rationally, as Clanchy argues?[207] The latter two options are by far the
best. Abelard was a vigorous debater, and in the heat of argument over redemption, he could forcefully reject concepts and
language that he might later return to use. He either denies
or affirms ransom and a legalistic conception of the God-man
relationship, depending on the situation. They are logically and
ethically untenable on the one hand, but useful expressions of
the work of Christ on the other.

Original sin

The doctrine of original sin as developed by Augustine in the
fifth century became one of the defining doctrines of medieval
Christendom, shaping views of both God and man. Redemption is necessary because of original sin. Because of the guilt
acquired by humanity in the sin of Adam and Eve, humanity is
separated from God and en route to eternal punishment. The
redemption described above was the divine response to this
guilt and punishment. It was Abelard's alteration of the Augustinian teaching on original sin, by denying the guilt but affirming the punishment, that led to one of William of St. Thierry's
criticisms of Abelard in his *Disputatio*.[208]

Abelard's views on original sin have been much discussed by
modern scholars, who largely agree about what Abelard taught
concerning it, in contrast to the ongoing difference over his
doctrine of redemption. The general consensus is that Abelard,
while trying to appear Augustinian in terminology, deviated sig-

204. See p. 45, n. 184, above.   205. See p. 45, n. 181, above.
206. See p. 45, n. 183, above.   207. *Abelard*, 274.
208. *disp.* 11.

nificantly on key points.[209] Some have noted inconsistencies in his thought on this subject, and they are in fact significant.

Indeed, Abelard's teaching on original sin in his Romans commentary, found mostly in his exposition of chapters four and five, does follow Augustine on many points. Abelard speaks of original sin as something which human beings are born with, and which they contract from the first parent, that, is, Adam.[210] Through Adam's sin, death and original sin passed into all humanity,[211] and human beings were made sinners and handed over to eternal punishment.[212] Original sin is propagated through concupiscence;[213] parents introduce concupiscence to their children, who are conceived in the sin of carnal concupiscence, which itself conveys sin, and so children already have severe judgment against them.[214] Original sin is pardoned through the sacraments of the Church, particularly baptism;[215] children require the absolution of baptism; those who die without it are condemned.[216] Abelard even quotes Augustine

---

209. See J.-B. Kors, *La justice et le péché originel d'après S. Thomas*, Bibliothèque Thomiste, Vol. 2 (Paris: Librairie Philosophique J. Vrin, 1930), 36–39, who argues that while Abelard was under Augustine's influence, and while trying in vain to appear in accord with him, he could only give a skillful transposition of his views; Weingart, *Logic*, 42–50, who argues that Abelard accepted Augustine on his own terms, but yet gave a new meaning of original sin; Sikes, *Abailard*, 200–204, who argues that while Abelard rejected the traditional doctrine of original sin, he was not Pelagian; Paul C. Kemeny, "Peter Abelard: An Examination of His Doctrine of Original Sin," *Journal of Religious History* 16.4 (1991), 374–86, who argues that Abelard appeared to be Augustinian in some respects, departed from him in many ways, and redefined the nature of original sin in a Pelagian direction; Julius Gross, "Abälards Umdeutung des Erbsündendogmas," *Zeitschrift für Religions- und Geistegeschichte*, 15.1 (1963), 14–33, who argues that Abelard deviated significantly from Augustine, and that for Abelard, there was in fact no original sin, but rather a collective punishment; and Peppermüller, *Auslegung*, 105–6, 112–14, 119–20, who follows Gross on the question of collective punishment, and who argues that Abelard ultimately failed to integrate his teaching on original sin with his sacramental teaching. For very brief summaries, see Odo Lottin, "Les théories du péché originel au XIIe siècle," *Recherches de théologie ancienne et médiévale* 11–12 (1939–40): 17–32, 78–103, 236–74, at 12.78–103, and Luscombe, *School*, 140, *passim*.

210. 5.19.   211. 5.12.
212. 5.19.   213. 4.11.
214. 5.19; see also 8.10.   215. 4.11 and 5.19.
216. 5.19.

INTRODUCTION

53

on original sin twice, and Fulgentius of Ruspé, whose work he thinks to be Augustine's, once.[217]

On the other hand, Abelard does depart significantly from Augustine's teaching when he defines original sin in his question at 5.19. After noting that sin can be defined both as guilt and as punishment, he presents his famous definition of original sin:

Since, therefore, we say that men are begotten and born with original sin and also contract this same original sin from the first parent, it seems that this should refer more to the punishment of sin, for which, of course, they are held liable to punishment, than to the fault of the soul and the contempt for God. For the one who cannot yet use free choice nor yet has any exercise of reason, as though he recognizes the author or deserves the precept of obedience, no transgression, no negligence should be imputed to him, nor any merit at all by which he might be worthy of reward or punishment, more than to those beasts, when they seem either to do harm or to help in something.[218]

Here Abelard makes fine distinctions between inherited liability to punishment and inherited guilt.[219] Original sin is not about guilt, since, to Abelard's mind, guilt can only come from a person's own free actions. As we have seen above, Abelard cites numerous patristic authorities to buttress his argument: there is no sin without freedom of choice, which children do not have; therefore they cannot sin, and do not have guilt, inherited or earned.

---

217. 4.11 (*nupt. et conc.* 2.11.24), 5.19 (Fulgentius, *fid.* 70), and 5.19 (*ench.* 93).

218. Buytaert, 164.368–78: "Cum itaque dicimus homines cum originali peccato procreari et nasci atque hoc ipsum originale peccatum ex primo parente contrahere, magis hoc ad poenam peccati, cui videlicet poenae obnoxii tenentur, quam ad culpam animi et contemptum Dei referendum videtur. Qui enim nondum libero uti arbitrio potest nec ullum adhuc rationis exercitium habet, quasi eum recognoscat auctorem vel obedientiae mereatur praeceptum, nulla est ei transgressio, nulla negligentia imputanda nec ullum omnino meritum quo praemio vel poena dignus sit magis quam bestiis ipsis quando in aliquot vel nocere vel iuvare videntur."

219. I translate *obnoxii* as "liable" rather than as "subject." Abelard uses the term some ten times in the commentary, mostly in the first sense, as the context here clearly demands.

At the end of the question, Abelard restates his definition of original sin:

It is therefore original sin with which we are born, that debt (*debitum*) of damnation with which we are bound, since we are made guilty of eternal punishment on account of the fault of our origin, that is, our first parents, from whom our origin derived. For in him, as the Apostle mentioned above, we sinned, that is, we are consigned to eternal damnation on account of his sin, so that, unless the medicines of the divine sacraments should come to our aid, we would be eternally damned.[220]

The language is again largely legal in tone: debt, binding, liability, commitment. The use of *debitum* is especially interesting, since it can mean guilt as well as debt or obligation.[221] Abelard thus talks around original sin as guilt, denying it on the one hand but using similar terms to define it on the other. He also again speaks of the inherited nature of original sin and of the presence of humanity in Adam at the time of his sin. Even though he clearly denies that this disobedience transmitted *culpa,* in these two passages he affirms the significance of Adam's disobedience.

It is not so elsewhere, where Abelard, unlike Augustine, seems to make Adam's sin of little consequence. We have already seen that he considers it morally less serious than the murder of Christ. At 5.16, he says that Christ's actions did far more good than Adam's "great offense" did harm, and in the question at 5.19 he calls the sin of Adam and Eve a "perhaps ordinary transgression." Still, Abelard for the most part asserts its ongoing effect of transmitting sin and punishment to humanity. Adam incurred guilt through the act of his own free choice, and passed down the punishment to his descendants.

As one reads Abelard's statements on original sin in his Romans commentary, one cannot help but think that he is try-

220. Buytaert, 171.594–601: "Est igitur originale peccatum cum quo nascimur, ipsum damnationis debitum quo obligamur, cum obnoxii aeternae poenae efficimur propter culpam nostrae originis, id est priorum parentum a quibus nostra cepit origo. In illo enim, ut supra meminit Apostolus, peccavimus, id est peccati eius causa aeternae damnationi ita deputamur, ut, nisi divinorum sacramentorum nobis remedia subveniant, aeternaliter damnemur."

221. J. F. Niermeyer, *Mediae latinitatis lexicon minus* (Leiden: E. J. Brill, 1993), "debitum."

ing to have it both ways: that he is trying to deny the portions of the traditional doctrine that conflict with his views of what sin really is, namely, the use of free choice to consent to evil, while retaining the portions that do not, and, in fact, affirming them as strongly as William does, arguing for punishment even of unbaptized children and justifying this not with logic but with the faith position that God only does what is best. In spite of the careful dialectic of the question at 5.19 which we have described above, this leads Abelard into the illogic of affirming the punishment of original sin without the guilt. How, one might ask, could someone be punished for something of which one is not guilty? This question did not occur to Abelard or any of his contemporaries, but it begs to be asked.[222]

Intention and consent

Abelard denies the guilt of original sin because he held that guilt is incurred only through actual sin; and actual sin is the result of intention and consent. William of St. Thierry would summarize the problems he saw with Abelard's position as follows:

He says that there is no sin except in the sole consent to evil, and in the contempt of God, which man has in the consent to sin. He says that sin is not a desire, not an evil pleasure, not an evil will, but a nature. "To desire someone else's wife," he says, "or to lie with someone else's wife is not a sin, but is only a sin in this consent and contempt of God." And

222. Gross and Peppermüller ask similar questions, though they do not directly address this one. The former finds Abelard's theory simpler and more lucid than Augustine's, though he notes that it has its contradictions, namely, that of a God who willingly condemns unbaptized children (Gross, "Umdeutung," 32). The latter argues that Abelard did not successfully integrate his teaching on the sacraments into his new conception of soteriology via his teaching on original sin. Salvation is an individual affair for Abelard, while original sin involves a "collective punishment," which no one can control, and so a person must look to Christ as an objective intercessor through his sacrifice. Peppermüller also argues that the collective punishment theory is not a satisfactory solution to the problem of original sin, because he must defend God against the charge of injustice for condemning children who have no guilt of their own. Individual salvation clashes with collective punishment, and if Abelard had been able to pursue his soteriology further, he would have had to reject original sin as inherited punishment (*Auslegung*, 113–14, 119–20).

just as he says that in the desire and pleasure no sin is perpetrated, thus he says that the sin of consent is enlarged by no act of sin.[223]

That is, William believes, Abelard says that the act or the desire is not a sin, but only the giving in to desire, which reflects contempt for God and his commandments. Similar to a passage in Abelard's Romans commentary,[224] this summary of Abelard's position does not reflect the more complex reality of his teaching, which contains both careful logical thought and psychological insight. Yet Abelard's position was not in itself controversial or new, as we shall see, but it was the extent to which Abelard would take it that would incur his condemnation.

Abelard's teaching on consent and intention is well known and well studied, precisely because it broke with the stricter contemporary teaching on some points, and because it was one of the bases of the accusations against him. Several scholars have discussed this teaching, and they largely agree on its major points: that Abelard defines sin in terms of consent and intention; that is, sin is an interior decision, rather than an exterior act; consequently, actions are morally indifferent. They also generally note Abelard's ambiguous vocabulary and equivocal arguments, and agree that his *Ethica* presents this teaching in its final and most comprehensive fashion.[225]

Though it is only an early statement on the topic, Abelard's

223. *disp.* 12: "Dicit nullum esse peccatum, nisi in solo consensu mali, et in contemptu Dei, quem habet homo in consensu peccati. Etenim nullam concupiscentiam, nullam delectationem malam, nullam voluntatem malam dicit esse peccatum, sed naturam. 'Concupiscere,' inquit, 'alienam uxorem, sive concumbere cum alterius uxore, non est peccatum, sed solus in hoc consensus et contemptus Dei peccatum est.' Et sicut in concupiscentia et delectatione nullum peccatum committi, sic peccatum consensus nullo actu peccati dicit augmentari."

224. It cannot be identified exactly, but it is quite similar to what Abelard says at 7.16; most likely it is a conflation of two passages from the *Ethica*, ed. Luscombe, 24.14–16, and 16.6–8. Possibly a student adapted those passages for the *Liber sententiarum*, which may have been William's source.

225. See Robert Blomme, *La doctrine du péché dans les écoles théologiques de la première moitié du XIIe siècle* (Louvain: Publications Universitaires de Louvain, 1958), 103–294 (Blomme devotes over half the book to studying the thought of Peter Abelard and his school on this doctrine); Weingart, *Logic*, 50–65; Peppermüller, *Auslegung*, 127–44; and Marenbon, *Philosophy*, 251–64.

teaching on consent and intention in his Romans commentary is significant for both its dependence on and its bold independence of contemporary teaching. He borrows from the traditional Augustinian theory of sin, which emphasizes willing consent to evil as a condition of sin,[226] as well as from theories then current, particularly the stages theory of Anselm of Laon, which emphasizes the movement from thought to action in sin,[227] though it is hard to know to what extent he was drawing on the general Augustinian theory or on what he learned while studying in Laon. Sin begins, Abelard argues, by making carnal suggestions to the mind; if unrestrained by reason,[228] the incitements of carnal pleasure follow.[229] Suggestion and pleasure are followed by consent to the concupiscence and the sin. Two passages from the commentary summarize these stages neatly. At 7.24, Abelard asks, "*Who will free me...from the body of this death?* that is, from [a body] thus inclined and prepared for killing the soul, lest carnal suggestions prevail over me and the spirit yield to the flesh, that is, lest conquered reason succumb and consent to pleasure." Shortly thereafter, at 8.2, he says that "*The law of the spirit of life...in Christ Jesus...has freed me from the law of sin and* therefore *of death,* that is, from the commandments or suggestions of carnal concupiscence, lest I obey them, namely, by consenting."

Abelard concentrates his discussion of consent, which may

226. On this, see James Wetzel, "Sin," in *Augustine Through the Ages* (2000), 800–802; Marianne Djuth, "Will," in *Augustine Through the Ages*, 881–85; A. Thouvenin, "Intention," in *DTC*, 7.2, 2267–80; H. J. Fischer, "Intention," in *DS*, 7.2, 1838–58; Blomme, *Doctrine*; and Risto Saarinen, *Weakness of the Will in Medieval Thought: From Augustine to Buridan*, Studien und Texte zur Geistesgeschichte des Mittelalters, Vol. 44 (Leiden: Brill, 1994).

227. On the "stages" view of Anselm of Laon, as well as the "defect of justice" view of Anselm of Canterbury, see Marenbon, *Philosophy*, 253–55; Odo Lottin, *Psychologie et morale aux XIIe et XIIIe siècles* (Gembloux, Belgium: Éditions J. Duculot, 1948–60), I.11–28, and V.9–142 (Anselm of Laon's writings, also cited by Marenbon); Blomme, *Doctrine*, 1–87; and Saarinen, *Weakness*, 43–51.

228. See 6.12, 7.24, 7.25, 8.2, and 8.13.

229. See 7.24 and 7.25. Abelard usually regards these incitements negatively, although he is famous for his statement that no guilt belongs to the pleasure of a sin, in particular that of adultery (7.16; we will consider this passage more fully below). See also 7.7, 7.14, 7.16, 8.8, and 12.3.

be either to the law or to sin, in his comments on Romans 7 and 8.[230] In most cases he seems quite Augustinian in his language, but in one case he speaks of consent in terms similar to that which his opponents would throw back at him a few years later. At 7.16 ("If I do what I do not wish"),[231] he notes that a person can consent to the law in his mind and still do what is evil; it is the inner conflict between the law and sin. Abelard uses dialectics to determine what a willing act of sin is. First noting the old dictums "Every sin is voluntary" and "No one sins unwillingly,"[232] he distinguishes between concupiscence and an act of sin. His primary assumption is that sin involves will,[233] an assumption he was to drop in the *Ethica;* if there is no will in the action, there is no sin. Abelard gives the example of one person who kills another accidentally and unknowingly by throwing a stone recklessly. The will lies in the throwing of the stone, not the killing. He then gives a thornier example, that of one person who kills another in self-defense. He does so under compulsion, unwillingly, from the desire to escape death rather than to kill. From this, Abelard argues that while every act of sin proceeds from the will, not every killing is voluntary. What was voluntary in the man's throwing the stone that killed the other man was the throwing, not the killing. Abelard then moves to the controversial part of his argument. The man who kills another in self-defense wills to avoid death, but does not will to kill; he sins through compulsion, and is a perfect example of the Apostle's words. Augustine did not consider this a sin;[234] Abelard did.

230. In addition to 7.24, 8.2, and 7.16, see 5.19, 7.15, 7.17, 7.21, and 8.13.

231. On this passage, see Marenbon, *Philosophy,* 259; Peppermüller, *Auslegung,* 128, n. 696; 136, n. 758; Blomme, *Doctrine,* 177–79, 185; and Weingart, *Logic,* 54, n. 1.

232. The first is certainly Augustinian in origin; the second could come from either Augustine or Anselm of Canterbury, depending on the context. See the passages of Saarinen, *Weakness,* cited above, for the discussion of whether a person can sin unwillingly, according to Augustine and Anselm.

233. For Abelard, the will (*voluntas*) is that function or disposition of the soul that judges and chooses prior to an action. God judges these decisions of the will rather than a person's actions. Free choice (*liberum arbitrium*) belongs to the will, and Abelard defines sin as a deformed will. See 1.18, 2.6, 2.9, 2.13, 2.15, 3.15, 3.27, 4.5, 4.8, 5.19, 7.16, 7.18, 9.21, and 13.9.

234. See *lib. arb.* I.4.

On the subject of adultery he is less harsh, perhaps not surprisingly. A man who sleeps with another's wife takes pleasure in it, on the one hand, but commits a crime and incurs guilt, on the other. Intercourse is pleasing; the guilt brings the torment to the conscience.

Did Abelard not consider adultery sinful? William of St. Thierry thought he did not. Yet Abelard did not here say what William paraphrases him as saying in his *Disputatio*. He says not that the act of adultery is not a sin; while the adultery does lie in the consent, he also speaks of committing fornication, that is, the actual act and crime, the accomplishment of the desire; here, at least, the act is not morally insignificant.[235] What is insignificant for determining sin is the pleasure of the intercourse. He distinguishes this pleasure from the guilt that the act of adultery brings to the conscience; one may physically, and legitimately, enjoy the intercourse of adultery while simultaneously suffering the moral and psychological consequences of intercourse with another's wife. This pleasure also seems different from the pleasure that a person takes in a carnal suggestion prior to consenting to sin.

Regarding this discussion of adultery as a work of scriptural exposition, it is apparent that Abelard has addressed the Apostle's words concerning doing what we do not will, and not doing what we do will; we do not wish to commit adultery; we do will pleasure. It is on this basis that Abelard distinguishes between willing and not willing, between guilt and pleasure, and it is there that a person's interior conflict lies. By using dialectics to analyze the entire act of consent, he clarifies Paul's meaning, though not to the liking of his opponents. Strictly speaking, however, in his emphasis on consent, he does not depart from Augustine, though he differs subtly, yet significantly, from his contemporaries. As Marenbon has argued, his contemporaries taught that one could consent to desire, temptation, or appe-

235. Contrast this with the passage of the *Ethica* cited above as the possible source of William's quotation: "Non est itaque peccatum uxorem alterius concupiscere uel cum ea concumbere sed magis huic concupiscentiae uel actioni consentire" (ed. Luscombe, 24.14–16). Abelard here seems clearly to have taken the opinion of the Romans commentary further.

tites; Abelard, by contrast, defined consent in terms of readiness to perform an action.[236]

In this entire argument, Abelard nowhere mentions intention, but given his conviction that intention is what makes a work good or evil, this issue certainly underlies his discussion. One consents to an act with a particular intention, that is, a purpose or reason for acting that informs the will, or desire; the intention to have intercourse with someone else's wife and violate the commandment against adultery constitutes contempt of God, and makes adultery sinful.

Abelard uses the term *intentio* throughout his commentary, and in several passages in particular we find his distinct emphasis on intention apart from the work itself. In his exposition of 1.16–17, where Paul speaks of the Gospel as the power of God for salvation, Abelard criticizes the Old Testament as inadequate for salvation, since it corrected works rather than intention.[237] Shortly after this, Abelard considers the righteousness of God that is revealed in the Gospel; he defines righteousness, *iustitia*, as God's just recompense, *iusta remuneratio*, both punishment and reward. God determines this by considering

all the things which happen according to the root of intention...And this indeed is the weighing of true righteousness, where all the things which happen are examined according to the intention rather than according to the quality of the works. The Jews paid more attention to these works than to the intention . . .[238]

By equating the Gospel with *iustitia* and then defining *iustitia* as reward, Abelard introduces to the exposition of the text his doctrine of intention to show by what means God judges people.

At 2.6 ("who will render to each one according to his works"), Abelard clarifies what Paul means by works: "that is, according to the nature of the works, which consists in the intention more

236. Marenbon, *Philosophy*, 260–61.
237. 1.16.
238. Buytaert, 65.637–38, 640–43: "...ubi dominus cuncta quae fiunt secundum radicem intentionis examinat...Et hoc quidem est examen verae iustitiae, ubi cuncta quae fiunt secundum intentionem pensantur magis quam secundum operum qualitatem. Quae quidem opera Iudaei magis quam intentionem attendebant..."

than in the action." He says that "with God the will itself is reckoned as a work performed." That is because "the works are indifferent in themselves, that is, neither good nor evil,...except according to the root of the intention, that is, the tree producing good or evil fruit." Here Abelard balances his exposition of the catalog of vices of 1.21–32, in which he described many sinful actions, with another proclamation that what is truly important are the intentions. He could not say any more clearly that actions by themselves are morally neutral, apart from any intention. The action and the intention here are completely separate.

Certainly Abelard's exposition of 2.6 is bold; it is a big leap from works to the nature of the works, and a large assumption that that is what Paul really means. Abelard would continue to expound the Apostle in this way, however, at 2.15 and 16, where Paul speaks of people's thoughts accusing or defending them, of conscience giving a good testimony, and of God judging the secrets of men. Abelard defines this testimony as "good conscience and right intention" making these people "secure in the righteousness of their works. It is according to this intention that God considers the works." This same conscience "does not stray in the discernment of works, examining them according to the very thoughts, that is, the intentions, of the rational soul; these thoughts, rather than exterior works, shall accuse or defend before God." At 2.16, Abelard would largely repeat these statements: God judges and rewards intentions, which are thoughts, rather than works.

Also significant is Abelard's comment on 14.23 ("But everything which is not of faith"), where he considers the intention of those who killed the saints, believing completely that they are doing good, whereas in fact they do wrong. He gives the specific example of those who, acting on conscience, persecuted the saints, believing them to be heretics. Do good intention and ignorance excuse these persecutors from sin? No, since sin can come from ignorance; Christ forgave those who killed him in their ignorance. Thus, intention cannot always be separated from action, and even good intention, the intention to do God's will, can be sinful. Abelard interprets the Scriptures dialectically, showing how they do not always excuse evil acts done with good intention.

Abelard obviously takes intention much further than Augustine or Abelard's contemporaries did or would have allowed. For him it is the basis of sin, and so he felt compelled to analyze it in careful detail and clarify its nuances. In so doing, he rejects the idea that acts are sinful in themselves, on the one hand, while, on the other, apparently continuing to support that idea in other passages. Again, Abelard seems inconsistent when analyzed closely; here, one must accept, as modern scholars have argued,[239] that the doctrine of sin in the Romans commentary is a transitional one, not complete, and consequently contains incompatible statements.

On consent, Abelard is certainly Augustinian, in the narrow sense, though his language at 7.16, where his Augustinianism is most evident, could easily give false impressions of teaching moral laxity. It is another case of Abelard's occasional carelessness when making a strong point.

Faith

William of St. Thierry and Bernard of Clairvaux both accused Abelard of defining faith as an opinion.[240] Some modern scholars believe William and Bernard misunderstood what Abelard meant by *existimatio,*[241] and Abelard's Romans commentary presents a very orthodox and carefully nuanced doctrine of faith.

Perhaps the most striking statement that Abelard makes in the commentary about the nature of faith, especially in the light of the accusations made against him, is that to believe is to "hold firmly with the mind."[242] Here, obviously, there is nothing uncertain or hesitant about faith. Equally prominent, if by number of times mentioned more than by importance for assessing the accuracy of the accusations against Abelard, is Abelard's dis-

---

239. Blomme, *Doctrine,* 209–12; Peppermüller, *Auslegung,* 141–44; and Marenbon, *Philosophy,* 258–64.

240. William of St. Thierry, *disp.* 1; Bernard, *Ep.* 190.4. Both use the term *aestimatio,* though Abelard actually uses the similar term *existimatio* (*Tsch.* I.1).

241. Luscombe, *School,* 112.

242. 6.8, "*credimus,* id est id mente firmiter tenemus . . ."

tinction of the various ways a person can believe. He first makes the distinction at 3.22, where he defines the faith in Christ which we hold concerning him as either "believing in him or believing him or believing on him."[243] He would repeat this distinction, rooted in Augustine's thought,[244] at 4.5 and 4.23–24, and refer to it several more times thereafter.[245] For Abelard, as for Augustine, putting faith in God and Christ is the most important aspect of believing, more so even than believing that what they say is true.

Faith being one of the three theological virtues, Abelard naturally connects it with hope and love or charity, most frequently with the latter virtue;[246] faith is the foundation of the other two, and leads into them. Additionally, Abelard is quite orthodox in connecting faith with justification and righteousness.[247] Faith is the foundation of righteousness for Abelard; through faith, apart from works, righteousness is imputed to a person.[248] This justifying faith is the faith of a lover.[249]

Overall, there is nothing even remotely questionable in Abelard's commentary about its teaching on faith. Even the distinctions he makes concerning faith are appropriate, and add to the understanding of what faith is and what it does.

The Trinity

One of the central doctrines of the Christian faith and a major point in the accusations against Abelard in both 1121 and

243. ". . . eum sive ei vel in eum credendo."

244. See, for example, *Io ev tr.* 29.6, where Augustine contrasts "credere in eum" with "credere ei." William of St. Thierry would also make this same contrast in his commentary on Romans in one of the same passages as Abelard, 4.5. On the threefold distinction in Augustine's thought, see Eugene TeSelle, "Faith," *Augustine Through the Ages,* 347–50.

245. E.g., 9.33, 10.11–12, and 10.14.

246. 3.22, 3.26, 3.27, 3.30, 4.3, 4.5, 4.18, 5.2, 8.30, 9.21, 11.17, 12.6, 12.12, 15.13, and 16.24.

247. 1.17, 1.18, 3.22, 3.25, 3.26, 3.27, 3.28, 3.30, 4.3, 4.4, 4.5, 4.9, 4.10, 4.11, 4.13, 4.16, 4.17, 4.20, 4.22, 5.1, 6.13, 9.30, 9.32, 10.3, 10.4, 10.5, 10.6, and 10.10.

248. 4.22.

249. 4.4.

1140, the Trinity looms large in Abelard's works, his Romans commentary included.[250] In his *Disputation* against Abelard, William of St. Thierry, a thorough-going Augustinian on this doctrine, devoted two long chapters to outlining and refuting the errors concerning the Trinity he had found in Abelard's works, specifically the *Theologia Scholarium*.[251] Specifically, William accused Abelard of both Sabellianism and Arianism, because he first diminished the Persons of the Trinity by making them less than subsisting persons and then made them unequal to each other. By assigning particular characteristics to each Person— power, wisdom, and goodness—rather than to all the Persons, Abelard divided the Trinity's unity, and made the names of the Trinity's Persons simply references to these qualities. By comparing the relationship of the Father and the Son to the impression made in wax by a matrix, Abelard made the Son unequal to the Father.

Abelard's doctrine of the Trinity has been much studied because of its controversial nature, though few scholars have paid much attention to what he teaches in his Romans commentary, including those who have concentrated on this work.[252] This is

250. The Trinity is the major subject of Abelard's various *Theologies*, the works that caused the most concern for critics such as Bernard and William. William would give full attention to the Trinity as a result of the Abelardian controversies, in works such as the *Aenig.*, though the Trinity is by no means absent from his earlier works.

251. Chapters 2 and 3; there he quotes from the *TSch*, 1.28–29 and 2.112. See also Bernard's attack, *Ep.* 190.1.1–3.8.

252. Even Peppermüller gives scant attention to it (*Auslegung*, 46–47, 75–78, and 96). Other discussions and analyses of Abelard's doctrine of the Trinity and contemporary reactions to it are numerous, and include Sikes, *Abailard*, 145–67; Murray, *Abelard*, 89–117; Jolivet, "Critiques," 7–51; Jaroslav Pelikan, *The Growth of Medieval Theology (600–1300)*, vol. 3, *The Christian Tradition: A History of the Development of Doctrine* (Chicago: University of Chicago Press, 1978), 264–66; Cottiaux, "Conception," 810–22; Martin Anton Schmidt, "Zur Trinitätslehre der Frühscholastik: Versuch einer problemgeschichtlichen Orientierung," *Theologische Zeitschrift* 40:2 (1984), 181–92, at 181–85; E. M. Buytaert, "Abelard's Trinitarian Doctrine," *Peter Abelard: Proceedings of the International Conference*, 127–52; David N. Bell, *Many Mansions: An Introduction to the Development and Diversity of Medieval Theology West and East*, Cistercian Studies Series, no. 146 (Kalamazoo: Cistercian Publications, 1996), 141–46; Luscombe, *School*, 115–20; Marenbon, *Philosophy*, 153–56; and Clanchy, *Abelard*, 109–11, 269–72. Their general consen-

because his discussion of this doctrine in the commentary is occasional at best, is never as extensive as it is in his various *Theologies*, and in many ways simply summarizes the discussions of those works, as Abelard himself admits.[253] We will give full attention to it here, however, to see how Abelard's exegesis leads to his views of the Trinity and to compare his views with those of Augustine.[254]

Abelard explicitly mentions the Trinity only three times in the commentary, at 1.19, 1.20, and 8.11. Since the first two of these are the more controversial passages, we will return to them in more detail after discussing the more clearly orthodox references to the Persons of the Trinity and their relations with each other; as with Abelard's doctrine of redemption, the more orthodox passages will provide the necessary context for understanding the controversial ones. He gives much attention to the relations of the Father and the Son, but less so to the Holy Spirit's relations to them.

Abelard addresses these relations of the Father and the Son in a number of passages, and in them he adheres closely to Augustinian orthodoxy, though he does not quote Augustine. In three passages, 1.3, 1.4, and 8.32, he is careful to note

---

sus is that Abelard used less caution than he should have in expressing his views, but that he was no heretic, and that he was misunderstood by both William and Bernard.

253. 1.20.

254. To summarize his views briefly, Augustine proclaimed the oneness of God and the threeness and equality of the Persons, Father, Son, and Holy Spirit. Each Person, though distinct, is fully God. They share the same nature and characteristics, e.g., power, wisdom, or love; no Person can be categorized by any one attribute. Though these Persons are equal, they have differing relations with each other. The Father is Father in relationship to the Son, whom he generates. The Son is Son in relationship to the Father; he is the Son because he is generated or begotten. The Holy Spirit is the mutual love between the Father and the Son, the gift of each one to the other; in turn they send forth the Holy Spirit as their gift to creation. Human beings are created in the image of this Trinity; one may find vestiges of the Trinity in the human memory, intellect, and will. See J. N. D. Kelly, *Early Christian Doctrines*, 2d ed. (New York: Harper and Row, 1960), 271–79; Rowan Williams, "De Trinitate," *Augustine through the Ages*, 845–51; G. Bardy, "Trinité," *DTC* 15.2, 1681–92; and William J. Hill, *The Three-Personed God: The Trinity as a Mystery of Salvation* (Washington, DC: The Catholic University of America Press, 1982), 53–62.

that Christ was Son of the Father in substance, and that he was
not adopted. In the first of these passages, Abelard interjects
these comments immediately after Paul's words, "Concerning
his Son," and then goes on to note that according to his divine
nature, Christ was begotten only by God the Father. Like most
medieval commentators, Abelard discusses Christ's paternity at
1.4;[255] Christ is Son of the Father only and not of the Holy Spirit, by whom he was conceived. In the subsequent discussion and
question, Abelard allows that Christ may be called Son of God
in the human sense, that is, in the sense of being subject to the
Father through filial fear, like all the other faithful. He reiter-
ates that Christ does not have two fathers, namely, the Father
and the Holy Spirit, because of any alleged diversity of Persons
in the Godhead; there is, he asserts, no diversity of things or difference of number therein. By contrast, Abelard does not allow
the human nature received by the Word to be considered the
"adoptive Son of God." Rather, that humanity was Son of God
through grace. At 8.32, commenting on Paul's words, "He did
not even spare his own Son," Abelard again interjects the comment that the Son was consubstantial and not adopted; and if
God did not spare his own Son, neither did he spare his adoptive sons, the prophets.

Elsewhere, Abelard speaks of Christ as the image of God and
the express likeness of the Father, "equal to him in all good
things according to divinity," and quotes Christ's words at John
14.9 ("He who sees me also sees the Father").[256] Christ continues at the Father's right hand in eternal blessedness according
to his renewed humanity, where he intercedes for humanity to
the Father.[257] It is through the Son that the Father judges;[258] and
it is the Son who sends the Holy Spirit.[259]

We have already seen Abelard equate the Holy Spirit with
grace several times. Commenting on 1.7 ("Grace to you, and
peace from God our Father and the Lord Jesus Christ"), Abelard says that he is the gift of God, the grace of the Father and

255. See, for example, the comments on this passage by Haymo of Auxerre,
Atto of Vercelli, and William of St. Thierry.
256. 8.29.
257. 8.34.
258. 2.16.
259. 10.9.

the Son, from both of whom he proceeds. Similarly, at 8.27 ("He intercedes for the saints according to God's will"), Abelard says that the Holy Spirit causes the saints to pray according to what he receives from God, because he is from God and proceeds from him, and is ordered in God's very disposition. He also speaks of the Holy Spirit as the love and bond between Christ the head and his members,[260] and of the Holy Spirit's power as "the love of God in us."[261] Abelard does consider the Holy Spirit in relation to the other Persons, but not in as much detail as the relation of the Father and the Son, or in as much detail as William describes these relations. Nevertheless, what Abelard has thus far said about the three Persons of the Trinity has been quite Augustinian and beyond reproach.

We turn now to the more controversial passages. First, at 1.19 ("For what is known about God"), he argues that what could be known about God and the nature of divinity was made known to Gentile philosophers through natural reason. Thus, Abelard says, one can find "many clear testimonies" to the Trinity in the books of the philosophers, which the holy fathers later used to defend the faith. He does not cite them in this passage, but refers his reader to a list of them in his *Theologies*.[262] This would not be a major focus of the criticism leveled against Abelard, but it would raise eyebrows among those who asserted the primacy of the revelation given to the Old Testament prophets over the natural knowledge of God obtained by pagan philosophers; Abelard seemed almost to be making them equal.[263]

Much more significant is the comment that immediately follows at 1.20. There Abelard twice makes his famous distinction of the Persons of the Trinity according to the attributes of power, wisdom, and goodness, qualities which Abelard believes were evident in "the visible works of God," and therefore were the basis of his belief that knowledge of the Trinity was available to the pagans. The second time, Paul's words, "His eternal power and divinity," as well as "Christ the power of God and wisdom of God,"

260. 8.9.   261. 15.13.
262. See Abelard's *TSch*, 1.94–2.1 for a lengthy discussion of the philosophers and their natural knowledge of God and the Trinity.
263. See, for example, Bernard, *Ep.* 189.3.

give Abelard a scriptural basis for this assertion of pagan knowledge of the Trinity. He equates power with wisdom, and says that divinity is especially suited to express divine power. That power, along with wisdom and goodness, is clear in the structure of creation made from nothing, in its skillful and rational governance, and in its moderation, things noted by both Plato and Cicero.

Abelard then offers an alternative interpretation of the words, "for his invisible things were understood from the creation of the world by the things that were made." Paul, he says, was able to describe both the unity of God and the Trinity of Persons by means of likenesses. Here Abelard presents his analogy of the bronze seal, in a form much condensed from that found in his *Theologia Scholarium*, to which he refers.[264] Unlike the use of the analogy in the *Theologia Scholarium*, where it is irrelevant to Abelard's argument,[265] in the Romans commentary the analogy serves to illustrate Paul's statement that visible, created things give an understanding of the invisible Trinity; it is a form of exposition, by which Abelard explains the procession of Persons.

To summarize this analogy: Abelard postulates a matrix or seal of bronze, in which an image is made. The bronze and the image are in essence the same thing without number, but diverse in qualities; the bronze has its own characteristics, and the image has its own. Additionally, the bronze cannot be said to come from the image, but the image from the bronze. Likewise, in the Trinity there is identical substance among the three Persons, but diversity of qualities; each Person has his own characteristic. Further, the Son is from the Father, just as the image is from the bronze, and the Holy Spirit is from the other two. Obviously Abelard leaves much out of this version of the analogy. He does not mention the act of sealing, which corresponds to the Holy Spirit, or the image in the wax, as is found in the *Theologia Christiana*.[266] Still, there is enough here for a critic of Abelard to ac-

264. 2.112–16.

265. Murray, *Abelard*, 104–5, has argued that the analogy as found in the *TSch* "is neither relevant to Abelard's argument, nor is it consistent with his main position, nor are the various uses of the analogy consistent with each other." Additionally, it illustrates a duality more than a Trinity, because the Holy Spirit is left out. That is, Abelard could have made his point just as well without it.

266. Books 3 and 4.

cuse him of Arianism, as William did: the concept of the image being formed in the bronze, and having a period of time when it did not exist, could lead a critic to such an objection, even though Abelard describes the analogy simply as a "likeness," not an exact explanation, and uses it primarily to demonstrate the procession of persons and only secondarily to describe the persons as they are in themselves and in relation to each other. Abelard would not use this image of the seal again in the Romans commentary, but he does refer to the divine Persons as power, wisdom, and goodness three more times: at 4.23–24, 8.3, and 8.11.

Certainly one may understand from these passages how Abelard could be accused of Arianism and Sabellianism. His language gives the strong impression that there was a time when the Son was not, that the Son is less than the Father, and that the Persons can be characterized by certain attributes. William criticized Abelard for using the names of the Trinity simply as representations of these attributes, rather than as the actual names of the Persons.[267] If we consider Abelard's statements at 1.20 and 8.11 by themselves, this criticism appears to have some validity. One must ask, however, whether Abelard understood "Father" as *only* designating power, in the Sabellian sense which William accused Abelard of maintaining, or whether Abelard also understood the names as pointing to actual persons with genuine relations with each other. Looking at all Abelard's references to the Persons of the Trinity in the Romans commentary, one must argue the latter.

It is also true that Abelard's language goes beyond that of Augustine. Quite possibly he believed that Augustine's emphasis on the relations of the Persons of the Trinity strained the development of the characteristics of each Person, and that it was necessary to develop those characteristics further through the use of dialectic.[268] Additionally, his emphasis on power, wisdom, and goodness reflects his belief in an ethical, perfect God.[269]

267. *disp.* 2, also cited by John D. Anderson in his notes to his translation of William's *Enigma of Faith*, Cistercian Fathers Series, no. 9 (Kalamazoo: Cistercian Publications, 1973), 81, n. 208.

268. As Schmidt argues, "Trinitätslehre," 181–83.

269. Marenbon, *Philosophy*, 54–61, 324.

He pushed beyond traditional concepts in order to give each Person his full due and to present the most morally consistent picture of God, but in so doing gave the strong impression of heresy.

Finally, Abelard was not the only person of his time who ascribed these attributes to the particular Persons of the Trinity,[270] and William of St. Thierry was aware of this.[271] He likely saw Abelard's ascription as particularly offensive when combined with what he regarded as his Arian statements.

Spirituality

Abelard was not known as a spiritual writer in his time, nor has he usually been considered one in modern times. Little has been said about his teachings on devotion and interior experience, although a number of his sermons and hymns, intended for the edification of the nuns of the Paraclete, survive.[272] Far more has been said about his ethical teaching; virtually every

270. Ascription of power, wisdom, and goodness to the Trinity in general was quite common among twelfth-century writers, as was the ascription of these attributes to the specific Persons of the Trinity. The latter tendency seems to have been common among the Victorines; both Hugh and Richard of St. Victor did it, and the latter even wrote a treatise to Bernard concerning it. See, for example, Hugh's *sac. chr.* 1.3.27; *didasc.* 7.26–27; the *sum. sent.* 1.10; and Richard's *stat.* 2.3; *trib.*; and *Trin.* 6.15. Additionally, Cistercians such as Adam the Scot could also make this ascription: *S.* 28.11; and Bernard's student Peter Lombard would do so in his own Romans commentary, 1.23. Modern scholars generally acknowledge that Abelard drew his inspiration for these attributes from Augustine's *De Trinitate*, specifically 7.2–3. See Sikes, *Abailard*, 156–57; Raymond M. Martin, "Pro Petro Abaelardo: Un plaidoyer de Robert de Melun contre S. Bernard," *Revue des Sciences Philosophiques et Théologiques* 12 (1923): 308–33; Schmidt, "Trinitätslehre," 181–82; Luscombe, *School*, 116; and Clanchy, *Abelard*, who says that Abelard "seems to have got the germ of this idea from his own master, William of Champeaux" (270).

271. *Enigma fidei* 49. William himself ascribes these same attributes to the Trinity as a whole in his own comment on Romans 1.20–21, which does not differ greatly from Abelard's in its use of philosophical concepts and its appeal to natural knowledge.

272. See François Châtillon, "Sur la place de l'expérience dans la théologie d'Abélard," *Revue du Moyen Age Latin* 45.3–4 (1989): 88–91. This is the sole discussion I have found on this subject.

major study of Abelard addresses it. This is unfortunate, as an examination of his Romans commentary shows him to be a devout man of genuine religious experience. He wrote for scholars, not for monks, but in the midst of his comments and questions on Romans, he commended to his students an experience of divine love, and with it an ethic of love of neighbor.

To be sure, Abelard expounds no particular plan of spiritual development or ascent in his Romans commentary, and does not articulate a complex explanation of the inner experience of divine love. Nevertheless, he is profuse in referring to the love of God in this work, and affirms that one may directly experience that love. He speaks of a certain illumination or enlightenment, by faith, grace, or the Holy Spirit, though never of an enlightened love or reason.[273] He speaks of friendship with God,[274] and frequently mentions clinging or adhering to God.[275] Though he has no plan of progress, he does speak of perfection and of those people more complete and less complete.[276] He is aware, of course, of the contemplative life and of how contemplative monks "burn ardently with the fire of divine love."[277] And, as we will see, Abelard speaks of being kindled by love or grace.

We have already seen a prime example of direct experience in Abelard's question on redemption at 3.26, where he speaks of Christ's death as a demonstration of the love of God that binds us to him through love and that kindles love and causes us to love God more. There are three other major passages as

273. See 1.14 (illuminated by Christ the wisdom of God), 2.2 (by divine grace), 3.27 (the spiritual illumination of Jeremiah and John the Baptist), 4.18 (Jews illuminated by faith, and preachers who illuminate others with their teaching), 8.30 (the elect are those illuminated by faith and prepared for eternal life), 8.36 (by faith), 9.11 (Jacob and Esau illuminated by faith in the womb, like Jeremiah and John the Baptist), 10.21 (Paul's preaching illuminates the world), 11.10 (holy men illuminated by the Holy Spirit), 11.25 (some Jews illuminated by faith in Christ, and the illumination of wisdom), and 13.12 (the illumination of the day of salvation, and by faith).

274. 1.7, 7.6, and 9.25.

275. See 1.4, 3.22, 4.5, 5.19, 7.6, 8.9, 8.30, 8.36, 9.3, 9.27, and 14.10.

276. See 3.26, 4.7, 12.19, 14.1, 14.3, 14.19, 14.20, 15.7, and 16.3.

277. 4.18, ". . . id est contemplativorum, qui divini amoris igne vehementius fervent . . ."

well that we should examine as examples of Abelard's spirituality of love: 7.6, 7.13, and 13.9–10. All three of these passages contain questions either on the commandments or on love, and all three interrelate love of God with love of neighbor.

In the first passage, Abelard discusses the Old Testament commandment to love one's neighbor as a way of demonstrating the imperfection of the Mosaic Law and its inability to save apart from Christ. Explaining how Christ expanded the meaning of "neighbor" from friend or benefactor to one who acts mercifully, Abelard argues that the fullest meaning of the term is found when one understands the Good Samaritan as Christ himself, who was a neighbor to the Jews both through blood and through his acts of charity toward them. To love one's neighbor, then, is to love Christ, to cling to him and his commandments.

After adding witnesses to this effect from Ambrosiaster and Augustine,[278] Abelard then turns to "the two branches of love"—God and neighbor. He interrelates them by arguing, as he would again in 13.10, that love of neighbor includes the love of God, "since we should understand no one more rightly as neighbor or friend than our Maker and Redeemer, from whom we have both ourselves and all good things," most significantly charity. Therefore, since "neighbor" includes God, the law is fulfilled through love of neighbor and through love of God; whoever truly clings to God through love keeps his commandments. Abelard argues that love is true only when referred to God, and that one must love God for his own sake and one's neighbor for God's sake. Whoever clings to God through charity must fulfill the commandments pertaining to strangers as much as those pertaining to one's neighbor.[279] Finally, Abelard addresses briefly the question of love of self, included in the commandment to love one's neighbor. All the previous discussion, he says, is of no consequence, unless we love ourselves; and this we cannot do if we act unjustly and despise God's commandments, thus demonstrating self-hatred.

Not much later, in his comments on 7.13—comments that

278. See Ambrosiaster, *Rom.* 13.8, and Augustine, *doc. Chr.* 1.30.31.
279. Abelard quotes Augustine, *doc. Chr.* 3.10.16.

have been much discussed by modern scholars[280]—Abelard approaches love of God and neighbor from a different angle, that of its intention and genuineness. The true and genuine love that Christ taught and demonstrated, he argues, sought no ad-

280. See Marenbon, *Philosophy*, 300, n. 10, who provides the major citations. The discussion has focused largely on whether this teaching of selfless love for God came under criticism by other teachers, such as William and Bernard of Clairvaux, as argued by Étienne Gilson, and continued by Weingart. Both believe that in fact William and Bernard considered Abelard's theology misguided, and that one should love God for hope of blessedness. Gilson regards Abelard's definition as rooted, at least in dialectic, as purely theoretical, and as having no basis in "the realities of mystical experience to which he remained a stranger," and finds his relation with Heloise to be an additional source of his teaching. He cites a passage from William's *cont.* as evidence that William opposed Abelard's teaching of love without hope for blessedness or reward (Étienne Gilson, *The Mystical Theology of St. Bernard*, trans. A. H. C. Downes, 1940, repr., Cistercian Studies Series, vol. 120 [Kalamazoo: Cistercian Publications, 1990], 158–66). The passage of *cont.*, to which we shall return, is section 11, p. 56, in the English translation (*On Contemplating God, Prayer, Meditations*, trans. Sister Penelope, Cistercian Fathers Series no. 3 [Kalamazoo: Cistercian Publications, 1970]). See PL 184:375D: "Quod autem est absurdius uniri Deo amore et non beatitudine?"). Weingart agrees that Abelard's teaching was opposed by William and Bernard, and cites the same passage from William's *cont.*, as well as the whole of *nat.*, along with several works of Bernard and Hugh of St. Victor (*Logic*, 173, n.1). I will not argue about Bernard and Hugh; I will state that both Gilson and Weingart are wrong about William. A close examination of the passage from *cont.*, of the whole *nat.*, and of William's teaching on love in the Romans commentary, shows no significant conflict between William and Abelard on the topic of love. While William does not explicitly take up selfless love, he could hardly have opposed it, either on theoretical or practical grounds. While William's mystical experience was much deeper than Abelard's, as Gilson rightly argues, he was equally theoretical and speculative, and was hardly mercenary in his approach to loving God. While William certainly hoped for beatitude and the vision of God, he did not see these as a reward for loving God, but as graces given to those ascending to him to restore them to the divine image—to what they were supposed to be in the first place. Marenbon also differs from Gilson by pointing out that Abelard, following Augustine, makes this selfless love not so impracticable after all, by using the example of the father who loves his useless son or the wife who loves her useless husband. One can apply this same love towards both humans and God. Marenbon also shows how Abelard subtly adapted Augustine's concept of charity, presented in *doc. Chr.*: rather than enjoying God for his own sake, one loves God for his own sake. See *Philosophy*, 298–303. See also Peppermüller's brief discussion, under the heading of charity as the fulfillment of the law, *Auslegung*, 159–61.

vantage of its own, but only ours, with the desire for our salvation. While there is indeed a reward for love, one who loves perfectly loves without the intention of that reward. In fact, if we love God only for our own sake and advantage, we cannot truly call that love "charity."

Abelard then quotes Augustine at length on loving God for his own sake and not because he gives us something; one must love God willingly and freely, simply because God exists, and because he is good. To love God for what he can give is not to love God freely.[281] One must love God for his own sake and not one's own, not even because God loves the lover first; one may calculate one's advantage in love, but this will not gain the reward of righteousness. After considering the selfish, mercenary motives with which most people love God, Abelard counters that to love God for himself alone, and not our own advantage, is true love for God, considering not what he gives us, but what he is in himself; considering God only in the motive of love, and allowing him to act in us truly and for the best. Such a love is comparable to that of a father for a useless son and of a wife for her husband, who recognize that there is no advantage to be had from them. Such should be our affection toward God, to love him for what is good in himself rather than for our advantage, because he is good in the highest degree. Still, Abelard allows that we may begin to love God imperfectly, out of hope for reward or of fear rather than love, and incline toward a more perfect charity.

Abelard's teaching on selfless love, for both God and neighbor, reaches its apex in his comments on 13.8–10, where Paul considers love of neighbor. At 13.8, Abelard initially, and briefly, defines this latter love as "to wish well to him for his own sake."[282] He takes this up again at 13.9, where Paul mentions the specific commandment to love one's neighbor as oneself. Abelard makes the distinction between "as" (*sicut*) and "as much as" (*quantum*): the first demonstrates similarity, the second equality. Abelard favors the former, and expresses an *ordo caritatis*: since no one is to be loved except for God's sake, a person is worthy of being loved more the more dearly he is held by God

281. Abelard quotes from Augustine's *div. qu.*, q. 35.1, and *en. Ps.* 53.10.
282. "Diligere alterum est ei propter ipsum bene optare."

and the better he is. God is to be loved above all, then those who are better. Those whom we love more, we wish to be happier; but here intention is important. To wish that one's enemy were dead and in heaven is not to love with proper intention, because the intention is to be rid of that enemy. One must intend that person's happiness for his own sake. Love of neighbor works no evil, commits no adultery, and commits no murder, as David did.

Like most other medieval commentators on Romans,[283] Abelard interjects a discussion of the love of God into Paul's discussion of love of neighbor at 13.10, as a way of explaining how Paul can say that this latter love fulfills the law. He first defines the love of God, taken as both an objective and a subjective genitive:

Love of God from the whole heart is in us that best will toward God, by which, the more we strive to please him, the more we know we must please him. But we do that from the whole heart or rather the whole soul, when we direct to him the entire intention of our love, that we may consider not so much what is useful for us as what is pleasing to him. Otherwise we might make ourselves rather than him the object of our love, that is, the final and supreme cause. The love of God toward us is that disposition of divine grace for our salvation. Truly he loves his neighbor as himself who, for God's sake, has so good a will toward him, that he may thus strive to conduct himself for [the neighbor's] sake, lest the other be able justly to complain about him, just as the first does not wish anything to be done to himself by the latter concerning which he might justly be able to complain.[284]

283. See, for example, the comments on 13.10 of Haymo of Auxerre, Atto of Vercelli, Herveus of Bourg-Dieu, and Peter Lombard.

284. Buytaert, 290.163–291.175: "Dilectio Dei ex toto corde in nobis est optima illa erga Deum voluntas, qua ei tanto amplius placere studemus quanto amplius ei placendum esse recognoscimus. Ex toto autem corde seu ex tota anima id agimus, quando sic ad eum penitus nostrae dilectionis intentionem dirigimus, ut non tam quid nobis utile sit quam quid ei placitum sit attendimus. Alioquin nos potius quam ipsum dilectionis nostrae finem, id est finalem et supremam institueremus causam. Dilectio vero Dei erga nos est ipsa divinae gratiae de salute nostra dispositio. Proximum vero tanquam se diligit qui propter Deum tam bonam erga eum voluntatem habet, ut sic se propter eum gerere studeat, ne ille de se iuste conqueri possit, sicut nec ipse sibi ab illo vult fieri, de quo iuste conqueri queat."

Again, intention becomes important: does one love God more for what will benefit oneself, or to please God? Abelard recognizes that the former motive is in fact self-love, improperly understood. Love for neighbor takes its model from God's love for us: just as God provides grace for our salvation, acting with a good will toward us, so we act toward our neighbor with a good will for his sake.

After defining love of neighbor in terms of the negative and positive versions of the Golden Rule ("Do not do to others"/ "Do to others"), Abelard relates this love to love of God: first, God is to be loved only for his own sake, but the neighbor for God's sake. This means that the love of God is included in love of neighbor, since the latter cannot exist without the former. Conversely, however, love of God does not necessarily include love of neighbor; God can both be loved and exist without the neighbor. Therefore, Paul could rightly say that love of neighbor fulfilled the law.

In these three passages, Abelard has outlined a comprehensive ethic of love, defining its ideals, its proper conduct and intentions, and its *ordo*. He has analyzed both the love of God and the love of neighbor, separately and together, showing what each is in itself and how the latter depends on the former. The love of God is paramount; love of neighbor is secondary, and founded upon love of God. Though Abelard defines "neighbor" universally, he does not assert that one must love all neighbors equally.

One might argue that Abelard's discussion of loving God, while profound, lacks the convincing experiential language that so characterizes other writers on this topic, such as William of St. Thierry and Bernard of Clairvaux. This is not to say that Abelard knows or says nothing of interior experience. His frequent references to love and charity as fire and warmth, though common among spiritual writers, show that he had a certain level of experience: the ancient fathers were kindled in the love of God by hope, and those perfected are kindled in that love even more; contemplatives burn ardently with the fire of divine love; Christ's death kindled the most high love of himself; the apostles preached the ardor of charity; those who live according to the

Spirit are inflamed with spiritual desires; the richness of the olive signifies the fire of charity; those who have received grace are kindled by its love; and by heaping coals on our enemy, we kindle him to love.[285] Additionally, when Abelard mentions the Holy Spirit, he often does so in an experiential way, speaking of how we experience the gifts of the Holy Spirit or the powers and gifts of God, or of Christ indwelling us through the Holy Spirit.[286] The Holy Spirit is himself "the life of souls, because he is love."[287] The experience of that love is such that, as Abelard is fond of noting, when that love is perfected, it casts out fear.[288] And, as we noted above, he also frequently speaks of clinging to God. It is obvious that Abelard is genuinely devout and that his spiritual rhetoric is more than just theory, even if, as Étienne Gilson points out, he is no mystic,[289] or at least does not talk like one.

The love of God and neighbor is built on a moral foundation. Underlying Abelard's experience of love are penitence, virtue and obedience, self-discipline and restraint, and the imitation of Christ. Penitence to Abelard is a key component both of initial conversion and of the ongoing life of faith. On the one hand, God waits long for sinners to return to him through penitence, and gives to them his kindness, hoping that will lead to penitence.[290] It is a means of seeking after God, if a person understands God and his ways and promises, and of gaining peace and reconciliation with him.[291] On the other hand, penitence becomes an essential discipline for the converted, a means by which to amend their lives. Without it, sin can build a dwelling within a person and become a habit.[292] Performing penance does not eliminate the need to die to sin, however; one must strive to die to it once, and not wish to sin again.[293]

---

285. 3.26, 4.18, 4.25, 8.2, 8.5, 11.17, 11.22, and 12.20.

286. See 8.5–6, 8.9, 8.10, and 8.11.

287. 8.2, "*Spiritus uitae,* id est Spiritus Sanctus qui est vita animarum, quia amor est."

288. 1.7, 3.26, 6.17–18, 8.14, 8.16, 9.25, and 12.11. Cf. 1 Jn 4.18.

289. See p. 73, n. 280, above.

290. 2.4 and 3.26. In both these passages, Abelard links God's patience (*patientia*) with human penitence (*paenitentia*).

291. 3.11 and 10.15.   292. 6.12.

293. 6.3. See also 4.7 and 4.8.

Hand in hand with penitence goes the quest for virtue, the avoidance of vice, and death to sin. For Abelard, virtues are not just moral ideals, but are, according to the ancient Latin meaning, powers or qualities, in particular of the soul.[294] Abelard regards them as the substance of the true life of the soul.[295] To seek virtue, therefore, is not merely to live a moral life. Virtues are conferred and multiplied by the grace which Christ gives to build in us a kingdom of righteousness that governs all longings and checks illicit impulses.[296] They are the steps of newness of life which a person takes to leave behind the vices that kill the soul, to imitate Christ in the likeness of his death and burial by dying to sin, and to arrive at the glory of Christ's resurrection.[297] They are akin to the gifts of the Holy Spirit, by which Spirit Christ is present in his people; virtues are a sign of Christ's indwelling presence, and they are the means by which the human spirit avoids damnation and is justified.[298] Abelard admonishes his readers to put on these virtues of Christ, equating this with putting on Christ, himself the fullness of all virtues;[299] to become perfect in these virtues, by always growing into better things and in the heavenly life of perfect happiness;[300] to cling to virtue by imitating good; and to hate vices by withdrawing from the conduct and habits of the perverse.[301] One must use virtues to put to death evil suggestions and fight against vices and temptations of the devil,[302] because these vices in turn assault us. To defend against this assault is to suffer with Christ.[303] Abelard goes to great lengths urging his readers to die to sin and not to persevere or remain in it. Baptism means that a person has crucified his old man and mortified his members, and so is no longer a slave to sin, that it should reign over him; rather, he is now a slave to righteousness, and by the Holy Spirit puts to death the deeds of the flesh.[304]

Part of the quest for virtue includes obedience to God and

294. "…id est uirtus quae est optimus animi habitus…" (7.18).
295. 8.13.   296. 5.21.
297. 6.4–5.   298. 8.10.
299. 13.14.   300. 12.2.
301. 12.9.   302. 8.13 and 13.12.
303. 8.17.
304. See Abelard's lengthy comments on Rom 6 and 8.1–14.

his will. Abelard defines this obedience in several ways: to act according to faith, to serve Christ, to fulfill his will, and to fulfill with a work what should be fulfilled.[305] The higher form of obedience, that of sons, is rooted in love and stands in contrast to the obedience of fear performed by a slave.[306] Such obedience occurs through reason, the natural law of the mind,[307] and brings health and bears fruit.[308] Obedience is owed to Christ persistently and perpetually, and is one of the means by which we are bound to him and cling to God.[309]

All these disciplines lead toward a final goal, that of conformity to Christ and the restoration of the image of God within a person. Abelard equates the image of God, in which human beings were created, with reason, that is, rationality, which he in turn equates with the mind or the "interior man" of Romans 7.22–23. It is through reason that a person strives for good against sin. That same image, or reason, can be killed by drunkenness, which makes the drunkard like a wild, irrational animal.[310] On the other hand, there are those who try to preserve God's creation uncorrupted within themselves and reform that image in which they were created, by resisting the sins which defile and destroy that image.[311] Such people become conformed to the image of Christ, himself the image of God. They are said to "put on Christ" by laying aside the old man with his deeds.[312] We have already seen the stress Abelard laid on the conformity to Christ and death to sin that occurs through baptism in Romans 6; here he equates that conformity and imitation with being remade in Christ's image and the restoration of the original image of God within us.

Reason, understood here primarily as the capability for rational and moral thought, and secondarily as logic, plays a significant role in Abelard's spirituality and ethics in the Romans commentary. Not only does Abelard equate it with the original image of God within us, and with the mind; and not only does he say that it is reason that enables a person to strive against sin.

305. 1.5, 14.9, 14.18, 16.25–26.   306. 1.1.
307. 7.22–23 and 7.25.   308. 3.2 and 7.4.
309. 1.7, 7.4, and 7.6.   310. 13.13.
311. 8.19.   312. 8.29.

He also equates reason with our spirit, which receives and recognizes the testimony from the Holy Spirit that we are the sons of God,[313] and with the natural law that enables the Gentiles, who lack the written law of Moses, to obey God's will.[314] As such, reason is the opposite of sin and concupiscence, which are irrational and contrary to nature.[315] Reason restrains and checks the suggestions of the flesh.[316] It is the primary moral force, or virtue, within a person (though Abelard does not call it such), as well as the means by which a person ascends to the understanding of God, whether through observation of God's works in the world or through logic and inquiry. But unlike William of St. Thierry, beginning in his Romans commentary and proceeding to his later works, such as *The Golden Epistle*, Abelard does not move beyond rationality to a supra-rational, "spiritual" level. While his descriptions of love are profound, even moving, they do not move to the levels of William's descriptions of ecstatic love. Love and reason cooperate, but one does not surpass the other.[317]

Translator's Notes

I have made this translation from Eligius Buytaert's critical edition in the series Corpus Christianorum Continuatio Mediaevalis, and from Rolf Peppermüller's critical edition in the series Fontes Christiani.[318] I have attempted to follow Abelard's style as closely as possible, to include his sentence structure. Abelard writes long sentences with frequent pauses to explain words and phrases, and this style makes for awkward sentences and therefore difficult reading at points. Additionally, as pointed out above, he frequently leaves out portions of the text of Romans on which he is commenting; for the sake of clarity and continuity, however, I have supplied these portions in square brackets.

313. 8.16. 314. 1.19 and 2.14.
315. 7.17. 316. 6.12 and 8.13.
317. See for example 8.13, where Abelard speaks of love strengthening reason, and 8.16, where he speaks of our spirit, or reason, recognizing that we are sons of God, that is, we are subjected to God through love.
318. See above, p. 10, for a discussion of these two editions.

Following the procedure of Corpus Christianorum, the first citation of the text of Romans being expounded is in bold type, and subsequent citations are in italics. Supporting Scriptural citations and quotations from classical and patristic writers are in quotation marks. References to these passages are found in the footnotes; these include references to parallel passages in Abelard's other works. Abelard's later revisions, labeled *Lectiones Abaelardi* by Buytaert, are contained within angle brackets. In square brackets are the chapter and verse numbers of the passage of Romans being commented on, while the page numbers of Buytaert's edition appear in parentheses. Following Peppermüller, I have used the headings for various questions and other parts of the commentary found in the margins of manuscripts *m*, *O*, and *R*, placed there by scribes. Finally, I have indicated by footnotes those places where Abelard uses *amor/amare* or *dilectio/diligere*, which I could only translate as "love" in this text; this is a matter of interest to many scholars of early twelfth-century theology and spirituality.

COMMENTARY ON THE
EPISTLE TO THE ROMANS

PROLOGUE

(41) LL OF DIVINE Scripture aims at either teaching or exhorting in the manner of a rhetorical speech;[1] for it teaches while it proclaims what must be done or avoided, but it exhorts with its holy admonitions, either by dissuading when it turns our will from evil things or by persuading when it steers it toward good things, so that of course we may now desire to fulfill the things which we have learned must be fulfilled, or to avoid their opposites. Therefore, according to this scheme, the teaching of both the Old and the New Testament is threefold. Of course, the law of the Old Testament, which is contained in the five books of Moses, teaches the commandments of the Lord above all else. Next, the prophetic books and histories, along with the other scriptures, encourage us to complete actively those things which were commanded and arouse men's hearts to obeying the commandments. For when the prophets and holy fathers saw that the people obeyed the divine commandments less, they offered admonitions, so that through promises or threats they might lead them to obedience. It was necessary that object lessons from the histories be added, in which both the reward for those who obey and the punishment of those who transgress are placed before [the people's] eyes. But these are those old rags which were fastened into ropes to pull Jeremiah from the well,[2] namely, the examples of the ancient fathers, which were used with the holy admonitions for pulling the sinner from the depth of vices.

The teaching of the New Testament is likewise threefold, in that the Gospel, which teaches the form of true and perfect

1. Cf. Ps-Cicero, *Heren.* 1.2.
2. Jer 38.11.

righteousness, takes the place of the law, and then the Epistles with the Apocalypse, which urge obedience to the Gospel, take the place of the prophets, [and the Acts of the Apostles and the many other Gospel narratives (42) contain the sacred histories].[3]

What the general intention of the Epistles or Gospels is

From these things it is evident that, although it is the purpose of the Gospel to teach, the Epistles and the Acts of the Apostles maintain this purpose: to exhort us to obey the Gospel and confirm us in those things which the Gospel teaches us.

Let no one, therefore, slander the Epistles as though they were written superfluously, after the Gospel, which is the perfect teaching, since we mentioned that they were written as admonitions, rather than as teaching, although there are some beneficial lessons or counsels contained in them which the Gospel does not have. Thus Paul, writing to the Corinthians, says: "For I, not the Lord, say to the others: If any brother has an unbelieving wife," etc.,[4] and also teaches that circumcision and the other carnal observances of the law now ought to cease, because they were not revealed in the Gospel. Also, when writing to Timothy, he teaches many things concerning the episcopal, priestly, or levitical office which the Gospel did not describe.[5] Nevertheless we say that the perfect teaching of the Gospel was passed on as far as sufficed for the form of true righteousness and the salvation of souls, not for the ornamentation of the Church or enlargement of salvation itself. For, in respect to the property of the state, there are certain things that pertain to its safety, and certain things that pertain to its enlargement, just as Cicero recalls at the end of Book 2 of *Rhetoric*. The things which pertain to safety are those without which a state cannot endure safe and healthy, like fields, forests, and other things of this sort which are very necessary to the state. Other things are accordingly not necessary but rather exceptional, namely, as when one state acquires the things beyond what is necessary, that prove it more worthy than other states or make it more secure, such as beautiful buildings, an abundance of treasure, great mastery, and similar things.[6]

---

3. Addition of *mO*.   4. 1 Cor 7.12.
5. 1 Tm 3.1–15; 5.1; 17–25.   6. Cf. Cicero, *inv.* 2.56.

But perhaps those things which the Gospel taught concerning faith and hope and charity or concerning the sacraments could have sufficed for salvation, even if apostolic regulations were not imparted, nor any instructions or dispensations of the holy Fathers, although the canons or decretals, the rules of the monks, and the many writings of the saints are full of holy admonitions. For (43) no transgression should be charged to those neglecting these things if no commandment concerning them was given. Nevertheless, the Lord wished that certain commandments and dispensations be added as well by the apostles and the holy Fathers, by which the Church, that is, his city, might be adorned and enlarged, or by which the very safety of its citizens might be secured more completely, just as he is inclined to allot in individual cases. Therefore, the Lord reserved some of the things to be commanded and disposed by his disciples and those to come, so that, for those persons whom he permitted to do greater things in miracles than he himself had done, he reserved some authority of the commandments, by which he might exalt them further, and the more beloved he made them to his Church, the more [the Church] would recognize that they were necessary to himself.

Therefore, as was said, although the purpose of the Gospels is to teach us those things which are necessary for salvation, the Epistles maintain this purpose: to exhort us to the obedience of the evangelical teaching, and to teach some things to enlarge and to defend salvation more securely.

The purpose of the present Epistle

Truly this is the common purpose of all the Epistles. In each of them it is fitting that the particular purposes and themes and manners of treatment be sought, as in this Epistle, whose purpose is to call the Romans back to true humility and fraternal peace, who, converted from among the Jews and Gentiles, were placing themselves in front of each other with snobbish contention. It achieves that in two ways, by amplifying the gifts of divine grace and by diminishing the merits of our own works, so that no one may presume to boast about his works, but one should attribute everything to divine grace, whatever he is able to do, by which grace he may recognize that he has received whatever good he has. Therefore, the whole of all the subject matter consists in these two things: both our own works and divine grace.

Material. Manner of treatment

Indeed, the manner of treatment consists in the lessening of our works, just as has been said, and the exaltation of grace, so that now no one may presume to boast about his works, but "let him who boasts, boast in the Lord."[7] But the Gentiles boasted that they had gained the Gospel so quickly, just as it is written: "A people whom I did not know served me; in the hearing of the ear they obeyed me,"[8] and that (44) they had in no way previously trespassed in these things that they had done, who until then had known God by no law; but the Jews especially swelled with pride concerning the fleshly observances of the law.

Therefore, in order to destroy the pride of both, he attacks them, alternating his rebukes, now one, now the other, sometimes both at the same time, so that he might show that the Gentiles were without excuse in their sins, who, if they had not received the written law, had the natural law by which they were able to know God and discern evil from good; and that the Jews could not be justified by the works of the law as they thought, but that they attained the mercy by which they were justified only by the grace of the God who calls them both.

But it is asked concerning those Romans, to whom this epistle is sent: By whose preaching had they previously been converted? The *Ecclesiastical History* and Jerome and Gregory of Tours pass on the tradition that they had been converted through Peter the Apostle; Haymo is of the opposite opinion, saying that they had not been instructed in the faith by Peter first or by any of the twelve apostles, but by certain other Jewish believers coming to Rome from Jerusalem. But the *Ecclesiastical History* says in Book 2, Chapter 14: "In the time of Claudius, the mercy of divine providence led Peter to the city of Rome. The first to arrive in the city of Rome, he opened the door of the heavenly kingdom with the keys of his Gospel. Therefore, when the bright light of the Word of God had dawned upon the Roman city, the shadows

7. 1 Cor 1.31.   8. Ps 17.45.

of Simon were extinguished with their originator."[9] Jerome also says this about this epistle, concerning the passage, *That I may impart to you some spiritual gift:* "Paul says that he wants to strengthen the Romans who held the faith by the preaching of Peter, not that they had received it from Peter, but that their faith might be strengthened by the confirmation of the two apostles and teachers."[10] Gregory of Tours also mentions it in this way in Book 1, Chapter 25, of the *Histories:* "Peter the Apostle addressed Rome when Claudius was Emperor, and there, preaching openly with much power, attested that Christ is the Son of God. For from then on, Christians began to dwell in the city of Rome."[11] But Haymo says this in the introduction of his exposition of the present epistle: (45) "The Apostle wrote this epistle to the Romans from Corinth; neither Peter himself, nor any of the other twelve disciples, taught them first, but some Jewish believers who came from Jerusalem to Rome, where the Emperor of the world dwelt, to whom they were subject, proclaimed the faith to the Romans which they had taught at Jerusalem."[12]

We should note that if we carefully pay attention to the things that are said, there is no contradiction between the doctors mentioned above and Haymo. For if we entirely look over the chapter of the *Ecclesiastical History* recounted above, we will find that Peter, first of all the apostles, not of all the doctors, did preach to the Romans. Jerome also, when he says that the Romans received or acquired faith from Peter through his preaching, harms nothing, since it could have happened through the disciples of Peter coming from Jerusalem, not through Peter himself. Haymo indeed denies that it was done through the person of Peter himself; therefore, when Peter was named by him,

---

9. Eusebius of Caesarea, *Hist. eccl.* 2.14, n. 6, and 15, n. 1. "Simon" refers to Simon Magus, the villain of Acts 8.9–24, whom tradition linked to the city of Rome; see Justin, *1 Apology* 26.

10. This commentary, which Abelard attributes to Jerome, is in fact an altered version of Pelagius's commentary on Romans, which circulated under various names, such as Jerome or John the Deacon (PL 30). See Souter's edition and notes, especially on this particular passage, which Souter classifies as a later interpolation, pt. 3, p. 4.

11. Gregory of Tours, *Franc.* 1.24.

12. Haymo of Auxerre, *Rom.*, Argumentum.

he adds "himself." In addition, Haymo does not say that Peter did not instruct them, but that he was not the first to do so. What the aforesaid Gregory says is that Peter preached at Rome under Claudius: he did not add that he preached first, but that he attested openly, on the basis of many powerful miracles, that Christ was the Son of God.

But as to what he added, that from then on Christians began to dwell in Rome, we can understand that, possibly hidden at first, they then were made known by Peter.

Although it is not believed that this epistle was written first, it was nevertheless placed first in order by the holy fathers because it is directed against the first vice and root of the others, that is, pride, just as it is written: "Pride is the beginning of all sin";[13] or also because it is aimed at the church of the first episcopal seat. Concerning this, Haymo mentions, "But that epistle does not hold that rank in the body of Epistles on the basis of the order in which it was composed, but because of the dignity of the Romans, who then ruled all the nations, it gained the primacy. But this was done not by the Apostle, but rather by him who took care to gather all his Epistles into one body."[14] In the same work he again says, "But the name 'Romans' is interpreted as 'exalted' or 'thundering' because at that time, when (46) the Apostle sent this epistle to them, they ruled over all the nations and thundered their commands."[15]

But the Apostle is believed to have sent the present epistle to Rome from Corinth through Phoebe, servant of the church of Cenchreae, which is "a place near Corinth, a port of Corinth itself," just as Origen mentioned about this epistle.[16] Concerning this Phoebe, the Apostle himself says this at the end of the epistle: "I commend to you Phoebe our sister," etc.[17] Jerome, expounding on this passage, says: "The Apostle shows here that the person of a man and of a woman should not be shown favoritism, when he sends a letter to the Romans by a woman, as it is reported."[18]

13. Eccli 10.15.
14. Haymo, *Rom.*, Prol.
15. Ibid., 364C.
16. Origen, *Rom.*, Praef.
17. Rom 16.1.
18. Pelagius, *Rom.*, 16.1, Souter, 3.26.

BOOK ONE

(47)
[1.1] **P**AUL. FOLLOWING the custom of those who write epistles, he who encourages them to true salvation places the greeting at the beginning. He prefixes this greeting with certain things that he adds, as it were in place of a preface, through which he might in a few words make those who were attentive either willing to learn or well disposed. He makes them attentive both by his own person and by the person of Christ who sends him, and by that very thing, that is, the Gospel teaching which he encourages them to observe; by his own person, since he commends it as set apart for the apostleship and called by God to the preaching of the Gospel; but he also commends the person of the Lord Jesus Christ, whom he also calls "Son of God" and claims that it is he who was promised to the fathers as the Redeemer of the human race, and who was conceived by the Holy Spirit and arose as the great raiser of the dead. But he does not neglect the commendation of the Gospel, since he mentions that it was itself promised through the Holy Scriptures of the prophets of God. Their ability to learn is noted in this way, that because he says that the duty of the preaching of the Gospel was imposed on himself, he proclaims that he will write about these things that pertain to the teaching of the Gospel. He also wins them over to himself when he confesses that he is both Christ's servant and theirs, both by his humility and by the love[1] which they had for Christ, as well as by these things which he adds concerning the love which he has for them, when he thanks God especially for their conversion and longs to come to them that he might instruct or confirm them more fully.—Now let us follow the text.

---

1. *Amor,* here and in the next line.

We must note that, according to the *Exposition* of Rufinus on this epistle, which is believed to be a translation of the *Exposition* of Origen, the Apostle had two names before he was converted. He who was Paul was formerly called Saul, "just as it is written," [Origen] says, "in the Acts of the Apostles: 'Saul, who was also called Paul.'"[2] According to Jerome (48) and Augustine or others,[3] the Apostle himself changed his name because of Paul the proconsul, whom he converted with his first miracle, as is written in Acts.[4] He adopted this name, so that he might now be called Paul, just as he was called Saul before, so that after his conversion, just as he adopted a new life, or rather the new duty of preaching, so also he might choose a new name. The Lord did the same thing with the Apostle Peter, by whom he who was called Simon previously was, after his conversion, called Peter.[5] Therefore, the Roman Church also established the custom that those whom it exalts on the seat of blessed Peter, it also changes their names. But he was called Saul, as if he were named for the previous Saul from the same tribe, that is, of Benjamin, and in the persecution of the faithful he imitated the Saul who persecuted David and his own,[6] just as this Saul persecuted Christ and his members.[7] To him [Christ] said, "Saul, Saul, why are you persecuting me?"[8] But Jerome is witness, that just as "Jacob" translated into Latin is "Jacobus," and "Joseph," "Josephus;" so also "Saul" is now called "Saulus," just as if it were a name of three syllables, although we are accustomed to enlarge a bisyllabic with a diphthong.[9] It seems that Saulus is a diminutive of Saul, just as Julius is of Julus.

But just as Saul was humble at first and later became proud, on the contrary this Saul, at first proud and the great persecutor of the Church, is now called Paul, that is, "small," or "quiet" on account of humility, for according to Augustine, "Paul" means "little" in Latin. Therefore, we also say, "wait a little," that is, a

2. Acts 13.9; see Origen, *Rom.*, Praef.
3. Jerome, *Philem.* 1; Augustine, *conf.*, 8.4.
4. Acts 13.6–12.   5. Mk 3.16; Lk 6.14; Jn 1.42.
6. 1 Sm 18–30.
7. Rom 11.1; Phil 3.5–6; Acts 9.4–5; 22.4–8; 26.11–15; Gal 1.13, 23.
8. Acts 9.4; 22.7; 26.14.
9. Jerome, *Phil.* 1.

little amount of time.[10] To what extent he was humble, you may hear from the man himself: "For I am," he says, "the least of the apostles, and am not worthy to be called an apostle."[11] Ambrose says, "He calls himself Paul on account of Saul, that is, changed, and because Saul is interpreted as 'restless' or 'trial,' this one called himself Paul when he came to faith in Christ, that is, as if he were now quiet, when before he would cause trials for the servants of God in his zeal for the law."[12] To what extent (49) he became quiet and patient and always busied himself lest he scandalize someone, he also explains, he who worked with his hands, lest he burden someone, making a good living from the Gospel, not like the other apostles.[13]

In praise of Paul

"Paul" is said to be interpreted as "'marvelous' or 'chosen'" by Jerome in *The Book of Hebrew Names*.[14] It was he whom the Lord himself called a vessel of election,[15] and his life as well as his teaching performed a marvel among the apostles. It is established that he was both virgin and martyr;[16] although these merits were divided among the great apostles Peter and John, in him they are found joined, and surpassed the others in attaining the grace of preaching as well as of virtue; through him almost the whole world was converted and the very prince of the apostles was corrected by necessity from a ruinous hypocrisy,[17] so that in him that maxim of Truth might be fulfilled: "The last shall be first, and the first shall be last."[18] <We do not doubt that Benjamin was a type of him, youngest of his brothers and beloved[19] intensely by his father.>[20]

Concerning this famous standard-bearer of Christ and vigorous trumpet of the Lord, the very Peter who was corrected by him breaks out in praise of his excellence: "As also our most

10. Augustine, *en. Ps.*, in Ps 72.4; cf. *ep. Io.* 8.4.
11. 1 Cor 15.9.
12. Ambrosiaster, *Rom.*, 1.1.
13. Cf. Acts 20.34–35; 1 Cor 4.12; 1 Thess. 2.9.
14. Jerome, *hebr. nom.*, *Ad Romanos*.   15. Acts 9.15.
16. 1 Cor 7.7.   17. Gal 2.11–16.
18. Mt 20.16.   19. *Diligere*.
20. *Lectio Abaelardi*, found only in *mR*.

beloved[21] brother Paul," he humbly says, "wrote to you according to the wisdom given to him, as he speaks about these things
in all his epistles, in which there are certain things difficult to
understand, which the ignorant and unstable pervert just as
they do the other scriptures, to their own damnation."[22] <The
holy doctors have both acknowledged and stood in awe of this
difficulty proceeding from the excessive subtlety of the method
of argument. Therefore, Ambrose also says in a certain letter
which begins thus: "Although I know that nothing is more difficult than to discuss the reading of the Apostle, since Origen
himself is by far less experienced in the New than in the Old
Testament," etc.[23] Augustine says in his first book of *Retracta-
tions:* "I had begun the exposition of the Epistle to the Romans,
but if it were completed, there would have been many books of
this work, of which I have finished only one, just on the discussion of the greeting, (50) but then I stopped, discouraged by
the size and work of it.">[24] And blessed Jerome says in his *Letter
to Pammachius,* "As often as I read the Apostle Paul, I seem to
hear not words, but thunder."[25] He also says in his *Letter to Pau-
linus,* "Paul was the last in order and the first in merits because
he worked harder than all of them."[26] And again he says in his
Letter to Eustochium, "'Concerning virgins,' the Apostle says, 'I
have no command from the Lord.'[27] He said this, because he
also was a virgin, not by command but by his own will. For they
should not be listened to," he says, "who fabricate stories that
he had a wife, since, when he recommended perpetual chastity,
he concluded, 'But I wish that all were just as I am.'"[28]

How much he was esteemed among philosophers who heard
his preaching or saw his writings, Seneca, distinguished both for
his eloquence and for his way of life, testified with these words
in the epistles which he sent to him:

---

21. *Carissimus.*   22. 2 Pt 3.15–16.
23. Ambrose, *Ep.* 75.
24. Augustine, *retr.,* 24. These lines are a *Lectio Abaelardi,* found only in *m.*
25. Jerome, *Ep.* 49.13 (*Ep.* 48.13 in PL 22).
26. Jerome, *Ep.* 58.1.   27. 1 Cor 7.28.
28. Jerome, *Ep.* 22.20.

When I read your little book of many letters which you sent to certain people in a certain city or provincial capital, disregarding mortal life with a wonderful exhortation, we were continually revived. I do not consider those ideas to have been spoken by you but through you, indeed sometimes both by you and through you. And as a matter of fact, the majesty of those matters is so great and they shine with so much generosity that I think that the lifetimes of men scarcely would suffice for those things which could be taught and brought to perfection.[29]

And Jerome mentions this praise of Paul by Seneca in his book *On Famous Men*, in Chapter 12 where he writes:

Lucius Annius Seneca Cordubensis, a disciple of Photinus the Stoic and uncle of Lucan the poet, was of a most continent life. I might not place him in a catalogue of the saints, except that those epistles of Paul to Seneca or of Seneca to Paul, which are read by many, stir me. In them, although he was the teacher of Nero and the most powerful person of that time, (51) he says that he hopes he can hold the place among his friends that Paul has among the Christians.[30]

Now if you also add the praise of the prophetic authority to the philosophical panegyric, you will find that the superiority of this apostle above the others reached a special distinction of glory with regard to both the patriarchs and the prophets. For, just as he says, deriving his beginning from the tribe of Benjamin,[31] he is in the type of him whom the patriarch Jacob, as well as David, greatest of the prophets and kings, joyfully foretold. Indeed, Jacob says: "Benjamin is a rapacious wolf, snatching prey in the morning, and in the evening he shall divide the food," or, according to another translation, "in the evening he shall divide the spoils."[32] David, foreseeing in the spirit the princes of the future church, and, as it were, preferring this one to the others, says, "There is Benjamin, a young man in ecstasy of mind."[33]

For the first Benjamin, the son of Jacob, who bore the type of the latter Benjamin who was yet to come from his own seed, was

---

29. Ps.-Seneca, *epist. Paul.* 1.

30. *vir. ill.*, 12. Cf. St. Jerome, *On Illustrious Men*, trans. Thomas P. Halton, Fathers of the Church 100 (Washington, DC: The Catholic University of America Press, 1999), 26–27.

31. Rm. 11.1, Phil 3.5.   32. Gn 49.27.

33. Ps. 67.28.

last in order among his brothers, yet through grace first with the father by whom he, having been begotten in old age, was loved[34] especially. So also Paul was last in order of calling and conversion among the apostles, and first, as is said, in merits with God. Benjamin also, when he was born, killed the mother who gave him birth, who, while dying, by reason of the pain of birth, "called his name Benoni, that is, son of [my] pain; but his father," when he changed his name, "named him Benjamin, that is, son of his right hand."[35] For Paul, when he was reborn in Christ, is said to have killed, as it were, his Jewish mother, who had given birth to him and educated him in the teachings of the law, since he especially abolished the precepts of carnal observances, in which they lived, and reduced all their glory to nothing, as if in leaving his mother's womb he also withdrew from the school of the synagogue by his conversion, according to which he himself says, "who set me apart from my mother's womb and made me alive through his grace."[36] Therefore, his mother rightly called him "Benoni, that is, son of [my] pain," because the more Paul attacked her error, the more he caused her to sorrow, and the more pleasing he was to her because of the excellence of his wisdom, the more he saddened her, since he was lost. But rightly did his father wish to change his name, in order that he might call "him son of the right hand," that is, of his good fortune <or strength>[37] (52) rather than "son of pain," because this destruction of the synagogue, which, as we have said, happened through Paul, should be reckoned as the good fortune of the faithful and the common exultation of the Church rather than as pain. <The countless persecutions against him show with how much strength of soul he flourished.>[38]

The words, "he snatches prey in the morning and divides the food in the evening,"[39] mean that at first he was a persecutor of the Church, and later [by a more fortunate plunder than he had carried out before][40] administered the restoration of the

---

34. *Diligere.*   35. Gn 35.16–20.

36. Gal 1.5.

37. *Lectio Abaelardi*, found only in *m.*

38. *Lectio Abaelardi*, found only in *mR.*

39. Gn 49.27.   40. Marginal addition in *R.*

spiritual word by the doctrine of his preaching. The words "distribute the spoils" in another translation means that he, after he was converted, snatched away many souls from the devil and, as if they were spoils, when the enemy was put to flight, preserved those whom later he ordained through church offices and all the ministries of the faithful.

<Jerome, in the prologue of *The Books of Hebrew Questions on Genesis*, claims that, according to the Hebrews, "the altar, where the victims were sacrificed and the blood of the victims poured out on its foundation, lay in the region of the tribe of Benjamin."[41] Indeed, that shedder of Christian blood is more suitably understood, concerning whom it is written: "Breathing threats and slaughter against the disciples of the Lord,"[42] etc., so that he might mangle the members of Christ on earth just as a wolf mangles sheep.>[43]

That "young man Benjamin" is, as it were, last in time among the apostles, superior to the others in mind and reason, inasmuch as he "was taken up" to the third heaven "and heard secret words which a man is not allowed to speak."[44] By him the very first of the apostles was corrected from a ruinous hypocrisy[45] and the whole Church was spiritually instructed, so that, among all the writings of the saints, his epistles have deservedly obtained a privileged place as much by their usefulness as by their subtlety. Of these we have now taken up for exposition the one which is directed to the Romans, which, by the judgment of all the most learned people, is entangled as much by the difficulty of the text as by the subtlety of the reasoning.

(53) **A servant.** Since the Lord says to the apostles: "I will no longer call you servants but friends,"[46] why does the Apostle now call himself a servant? Indeed, that we may allow for distinguishing two kinds of servants, that is, of those subjected. Fear of punishment holds some of these subject. Concerning these it is said that "a servant does not remain in the house forever,"[47] and again, "when you have done everything that was commanded

41. Jerome, *hebr. quaest.*, 49.27.
42. Acts 9.1.
43. *Lectio Abaelardi*, found only in *m*.
44. 2 Cor 12.4.
45. Gal 2.11–16.
46. Jn 15.15.
47. Jn 8.35.

you, say: we are useless servants."[48] Love[49] causes the others to be
obedient, and to these indeed it is said: "Well done, good and
faithful servant," etc.[50] It is easy to answer the aforesaid question
in this manner, that in one way he is simply called a servant, and
in another a beloved[51] servant of **Christ**, or a good servant. For
in the first case, as it were, a certain compulsion from servile
fear, not a voluntary subjection, is shown; in the second, a filial
obedience through love[52] is meant. Perhaps it is not necessary
that forced and involuntary subjection always be signified simply by the mentioned term "servant," unless perhaps by some
addition the subjection of friendship is removed, just as when
it is said: "I will no longer call you servants but friends."[53] For
when "but friends" is added, as if in contrast to the word "servants," they are understood in what was said before as servants,
who are only servants, and not also friends. In other respects
they to whom the Lord entrusted his talents are all simply and
generally called servants, both the good and the bad. And so
they are generally called servants, whether or not they love[54]
those who are in charge, provided that they are thus subject
to them, so that both their property and they themselves may
completely remain in their power, so that they who are called
servants may not possess either themselves or any property. In
this way, therefore, the Apostle calls himself a servant *of Christ*
in this passage. He submitted himself to him completely, so that
he might let nothing remain by his own choice except to submit
himself totally to the will of Christ, saying to him through all
things: "Let your will be done."[55] For who would find fault, since
the Lord through grace did not even wish to call the apostles
servants, who nevertheless acknowledge through humility that
they are servants? For he does not say, "Now you will not call
yourselves servants but friends," but "I will no longer call you
servants but friends."

But the Apostle rightly declares himself obedient at the first
when he summons others to obedience, so that not only by

48. Lk 17.10.   49. *Amor.*
50. Mt 25.21, 23.   51. *Diligere.*
52. *Amor.*   53. Jn 15.15.
54. *Diligere.*   55. Mt 6.10.

word, but even more by example, he might stir up his hearers, having eagerly followed (54) him of whom it is written: "The things which Jesus began to do and to teach," first especially "to do" and later "to teach."[56]

When he had mentioned before the name *of Christ*—which is a common term for all the anointed ones, both the king and the priest, regarding which it is written, "Do not touch my christs"[57]—he brought up his personal name, that is, Jesus, so that he might distinguish this Christ from the others as much by the uniqueness of his person as by his high rank. For he alone is properly called Jesus who alone truly can save into eternity. When, therefore, he is called Christ, that is, anointed, because kings as well as priests were anointed, it shows that he was established by God both as a king and as a priest for us, through which two roles he might save us, which is what "Jesus" means. For he became a priest for us, by sacrificing himself for us on the altar of the Cross; and in truth he was called a king by virtue of his strength and power, by which he can subject all things to himself, and so to speak he binds the strong devil even more strongly, inasmuch as he is the one to whom "the Father has given all things into his hand."[58]

Called to be an apostle, that is, *called* by God and chosen to be an apostle, he comes to preach, though not by his own authority. Otherwise he would have been a thief and brigand according to that word of the Truth: "All who have come are thieves and brigands."[59] "They came," says Jerome, "who were not sent."[60] Therefore, also the word "apostle" is rightly translated as "envoy" or "ambassador." Notice the excellence of his humility, since he said *called*, rather than chosen. For a calling is a cry of the voice to those who are a long way off, that they might come near or hear. But the more distant he was from God, the more savage he was as a persecutor of the Church. Therefore, he carefully says, not "chosen" or "adopted," but *called*, as if drawn by the Lord from a great distance for the purpose of preaching his Gospel.

56. Acts 1.1.
57. Ps 104.15.
58. Jn 3.35.
59. Jn 10.8.
60. Jerome, *Osee* 2, on 7.1.

Set apart for the Gospel of God, apart and by himself, not chosen with the other apostles, not by the Christ still on earth in mortal existence, but now by the one established in heaven at the right hand of the Father[61] and glorified as much by his resurrection as by his ascension. Therefore, also, when writing to the Galatians, in order that he might render his election acceptable against those who misrepresented him as not to be numbered with the other (55) apostles, because he was not chosen by the Lord Jesus Christ on earth with the other apostles, he says: "Paul, an apostle, not of men or by man, but by Jesus Christ and God the Father, who raised him from the dead," as if he was saying: "Paul, an apostle, not by man," that is, a mortal, "but by Christ,"[62] now glorified by the resurrection and having nothing of mortal or corruptible nature.

He is called *set apart* for the preaching of the Gospel, while, when the other apostles were occupied with preaching and the resurrection of the Jews, he was appointed especially for the Gentiles as if he was their own apostle. Therefore, he was also specially called "the teacher of the Gentiles."[63] Here is that passage from the Acts of the Apostles where the Holy Spirit says: "Set apart to me Barnabas and Paul for the work" of ministry for which "I have taken them."[64] *Gospel* means "good news," namely, because the preaching of the Gospel should announce that what was promised before has been completed.

[1.2] **Which he had promised beforehand.** This is a commendation of the Gospel that he says was at one time promised to us by God. **Through his prophets.** "For no one," as Ambrose says, "announces something unimportant with great heralds."[65] The Lord says through Jeremiah: "Behold, the days are coming and I will complete a new covenant," etc.[66] He says *his prophets*, to distinguish them from the false or reprobate ones, such as Balaam,[67] or those who sometimes predict things to come through a malign spirit. For a prophet is someone who reveals things to come by predicting them. Therefore, he is called a

---

61. Cf. Eph 1.20.

62. Gal 1.1.

63. 1 Tm 2.7.

64. Acts 13.2.

65. Ambrosiaster, *Rom.* 1.2.

66. Jer 31.31.

67. Cf. Nm 22–24.

prophet, as it were, by prophesying, that is, predicting. **In the scriptures**, so that the prophets might announce this not only with words, but even confirm it in writing. **In the holy scriptures**, that is, written for the teaching of holiness and the form of devotion and composed by the dictation of the Holy Spirit.

[1.3] **Concerning his Son**, that is, his own son, substantial, not adopted, **who was made to him from the seed of David according to the flesh**, that is, according to human nature, who according to his divine nature was begotten only *to him*, namely, to God the Father, that is, for the honor of him who was always glorified and honored in the Son, since the Son himself says that he does not seek his own glory but the glory of him who (56) sent him.[68] *From the seed of David*, that is, from Mary who was from the lineage of David,[69] since the promise concerning Christ was made both to Abraham and to David,[70] so that he might be born from their seed through his mother; here, though, he mentions only David, who sometimes sinned gravely,[71] and not Abraham, who especially appeared righteous, so that the entire mystery of this Incarnation might be ascribed to divine grace and not to human merits. Indeed, it is enough to name David, and be silent about Abraham, since Scripture teaches that Christ is from the lineage of Abraham,[72] through David, who was also of the lineage of Abraham.

[1.4] **Who was predestined**, namely, according to the flesh; that is, he was prepared by divine grace according to that which was also said to his mother: "Hail, full of grace."[73] For "predestination" means "preparation of divine grace."[74] *Predestined*, I say, **Son of God in power**, that is, that he might be the power and strength of all those clinging to him through faith. **According to the Spirit of holiness.** To the two things mentioned before, he adds two others, as it were allotting one to each. To that which he said first: *Who was made to him from the seed of David according to the flesh*, he adds this: *According to the Spirit of holiness*, that is, through the working of divine grace which is called

---

68. Cf. Jn 8.50.   69. Lk 1.27.
70. Cf. Gn 18.18; 22.17–18; Rom 4.13; 2 Sm 7.8–16.
71. 2 Sm 11.1–27.   72. Mt 1.1.
73. Lk 1.28.   74. Augustine, *praed. sanct.* 10.19.

the Holy Spirit, first cleansing and sanctifying his mother from sin,[75] so that she might receive the most sacred flesh from the seed of the sinner David; and to that other passage which he mentioned before, just after the first: *who was predestined Son of God in power*, he adds this: **by the resurrection of the dead of Jesus Christ,** as if he should say: from then it happened that he was the power or strength of all those clinging to him through faith, from the time his resurrection was completed, attested by the resurrection of the dead that happened on the same day, concerning which things it is written that "they came into the holy city and appeared to many."[76] For then every uncertainty of unbelief went away which had befallen the disciples concerning the Passion, of whom some indeed, having given up hope, said: "But we hoped that he might be the one to redeem Israel."[77] He says that they are the dead *of Jesus Christ*, that is, for (57) his honor; they were dead for this reason, that they might glorify him by the testimony of his resurrection.

We can also understand a spiritual resurrection of the soul from vices, concerning which Simeon says that "he was appointed for the ruin and resurrection of many."[78] For Christ alone is the one who can free souls from death, namely, "the Lamb of God who takes away the sins of the world."[79]

We must note that, as blessed Augustine says in his *Enchiridion,* although Christ is said to have been born from the Holy Spirit and Mary, nevertheless he is not therefore said to be the Son of the Holy Spirit just as he is of Mary, since, of course, he was not born or conceived from the substance of the Holy Spirit just as he was from the substance of Mary, but rather his all-surpassing conception and birth occurred through the working of the Holy Spirit, that is, of divine grace, and therefore he is also said to have been born from him, that is, conceived through him.[80] For not everything that arises from something is called its "son," as when hairs grow from the head or lice from ourselves. Since we are born again by water and by the Spirit,[81]

---

75. Lk 1.35.
76. Mt 27.53.
77. Lk 24.21.
78. Lk 2.34.
79. Jn 1.29.
80. Cf. Augustine, *ench.* 38.12.
81. Jn 3.5.

by no means are we called sons of water. They are accustomed
to be called the sons of those from whom they were not born,
as with adoptive sons, sons of the devil, sons of Hell, or sons
through teaching. Nevertheless, if someone should say that
Christ is the Son of God or of the Holy Spirit in a human sense,
in that manner by which the other faithful are made subject
to him through filial fear, I do not judge it absurd. Nevertheless he does not therefore have many fathers, by means of God,
namely, the Father and the Holy Spirit, especially since neither
do the other elect have many fathers because of the diversity of
persons. For neither in that instance should we say that there
are many fathers nor many gods or lords,[82] since there is no diversity of things or difference of number.

   If it is asked whether that human being in Christ, received by
the Word, is the adoptive Son of God just as the other elect are,
since he also possesses this good through grace, I do not think
we should allow it. For those who are adopted and thus made
sons, at any rate were not first sons in that manner by which they
were made. But that humanity received by the Word, born and
conceived entirely without sin, (58) was Son of God through
grace immediately from that point when he came into being.
But the rest of us, who are born with sin and are called "sons of
wrath,"[83] begin to be what at first we were not, through adoption when we are reborn in baptism. He therefore, although he
is called the Son by grace according to his humanity, nevertheless did not receive this title through adoption, because he had
it from the time he came into being. <Therefore, Hilary says
in Book 12 of *On the Trinity*: "And to God we indeed are sons,
but through the working of the Son; for we were once 'sons of
wrath,' but we were made sons of God through adoption,[84] and
we deserve to be called that, rather than that we are born as
sons. And because everything that is made, did not exist before
it was made, so when we were not sons, we were made into what
we are. For beforehand we were not sons, but since we have obtained this, this is what we are. But we are not born but made,
not begotten but purchased. For God purchased for himself a

82. Cf. 1 Cor 8.5–6.   83. Eph 2.3.
84. Eph 2.3; Rom 8.15, 23; Gal 4.5; Eph 1.5.

people, and by this means he begat. But we know that the Lord never begat sons in the proper sense of the term.">[85]

[1.5] **Through whom we have received grace and apostleship.** Now that he has praised the person of Christ, he adds praise of himself and of his own office, since he maintains that he is sent to preach by such a great authority, that his preaching should be received at least by reason of the authority of the one who sent him. *Grace and apostleship,* that is, the obligation of preaching was conferred on him freely, not by his own merits. Or: at first *grace* in his conversion and the remission of sins in the conferral either of powers or of miracles or of any gifts, and later *apostleship* when he was sent to preach.

The Romans could have said to the apostle: Even if you are called to apostleship, it is not over the Gentiles, or if it is over some Gentiles, it is nevertheless not over us. Therefore, he adds **among all the Gentiles,** that is, so that I might preach to all the nations of the Gentiles. They are called Gentiles or nations as if they were "begotten"[86] or "born,"[87] that is, living without the training of the law, as if they were beasts. The term "pagans" comes from *pagus,* "country person," that is, with no house or only one outside the city, so that pagans are "rustics" and not urban people, who are not yet instructed to live properly and honestly in the laws of the city. <For a city is an assembly (59) of men for the purpose of living according to law.>[88] They, therefore, who were thoroughly foreign to the City of God, as yet instructed in none of the divine laws, are justly called pagans; they now wish to be called Saracens rather than Hagarenes, boasting that they are named by free Sara, as it were, rather than by the maidservant Hagar.[89] **For the obedience of faith,** that is, for fulfilling with a work what was to be fulfilled before they believed. For first it must be known what things are to be done before they may be completed by a work. **For his name's sake,** that is, God's or Christ's, so that he might be known and thus loved,[90] according to that which Christ himself says about himself and

85. Hilary, *Trin.,* 12, no. 3. This is a *Lectio Abaelardi,* found only in *m.*
86. *Genitae.*   87. *Natae.*
88. Marius Victorinus, *rhet.* 1.1. This is a *Lectio Abaelardi,* found only in *mOR.*
89. Cf. Gal 4.22–31.   90. *Amare.*

the Father: "That they may know you alone and the one whom you sent, Jesus Christ."[91] Whatever things he has are marked and known by his name, and therefore "name" here stands for knowledge. But truly such good cannot be recognized unless it is immediately loved.[92]

[1.6] **Among whom you also,** that is, in the calling of the Gentiles, among whom you Romans now are, **are called by Jesus Christ,** that is, called by his glorious name of Christian.

[1.7] **To all who are at Rome.** Up to this point all the preceding text of this greeting has been in suspense, as though, when all the things that have preceded are repeated, it says: *Paul, a servant,* etc., sends word, it must be understood, *to all the beloved*[93] *of God who are at Rome, called to be saints;* this, I say, is the word he sends: *Grace to you and peace,* etc. **To the beloved of God,** as if he should say: I do not say simply *to all who are at Rome,* to believers and to unbelievers, to the elect and to the reprobate, but to these only who through their conversion have now entered into friendship with God, now made subject to him in the manner of the Christians, that is, by love[94] rather than by fear. To these indeed that saying applies: "Now I shall no longer call you servants," and again, "But I have called you friends."[95] Or, *to the beloved of God,* that is, by God who loved[96] them first, so that he might choose them by his prevenient grace, not by their merits. **Called to be saints,** that is, *called* through an internal inspiration or by the grace of preaching for this purpose, that they may be holy. When he says that they were called by God rather than that they (60) called on God, he magnifies the grace of God, which sometimes manifests benefits to the unwilling or to those not seeking them.

But since this greeting applies to all those to whom the epistle is directed, how does he say *to the beloved of God* and *to those called to be saints,* since the epistle is especially directed to those or on account of those who need to be corrected, who by arrogant striving, as was said, wished to place themselves before

91. Jn 17.3. 92. *Diligere.*
93. *Dilectis (diligere),* throughout this passage.
94. *Amor.* 95. Jn 15.15.
96. *Diligere.*

each other? For how can they who act arrogantly be called the beloved of God? Was it necessary for the Apostle to lie or to write something false to win their good will? But truly this greeting applies to all, although thus far not all may be the beloved of God, so that when he greets those only who are the beloved of God, he judges them alone of being worthy of greeting, and the others he invites to imitate them, namely, so that they might strive to be the beloved of God. Fittingly then, though none there were the beloved of God, he could call them the beloved of God, according to the opinion of those who professed this concerning themselves, just as some say ironically at one time or another. For it is not called a lie, as blessed Augustine confirms, unless it is "a false meaning with the will to deceive."[97] Here, of course, the Apostle does not intend to deceive but to admonish.

Grace to you, and peace. He calls grace a free gift, that is, not bestowed as the result of previous merits. *Grace and peace*, that is, the gift of peace by which they who proudly contend are reconciled with one another and with God himself. "For how can he who does not love his neighbor whom he sees, love God whom he does not see?"[98] **From God our Father and the Lord Jesus Christ.** The gift of God, which he calls grace, is called the Holy Spirit. So, when we call the Spirit seven-form, or we name seven spirits of God,[99] we show that there are seven gifts of divine grace. Rightly, therefore, does he postulate that the gift of God, which is called the Holy Spirit, is given by the Father and the Son at the same time, from whom the Spirit must proceed at the same time. Construct it in this way: *from God the Father and the Lord Jesus Christ;* I say from God *our* Father, both the Lord Jesus Christ's Father (61) and ours. For this reason the Son himself calls God both his own Father and ours when he says, "I ascend to my Father and your Father,"[100] his indeed by nature, but ours by adoption; on account of this he especially commends the grace of God to us, by which we are made brothers and coheirs of the Lord Jesus Christ.[101] We are called sons indeed if we are subjected to him by love[102] more than by fear. He calls Jesus

97. *mend.* 4, 5.

99. Cf. Is 11.2–3.

101. Rom 8.17.

98. 1 Jn 4.20; *diligere.*

100. Jn 20.17.

102. *Amor.*

"Lord," because obedience is owed to him persistently and per-petually just as to a lord by his servants, according to which he called himself a servant above.[103]

[1.8] **First then.** Lest the preceding greeting of the epistle seem produced more by the occasion and custom of writing epistles than by the inner disposition of charity, with how much charity does he embrace them when he adds this, saying that *first*, that is, especially, he *gives thanks to God,* for the conversion and faith of the Romans, since that had to be done for all those converted. Indeed it was necessary that the Apostle first show the gratitude which he held for them, so that when he later re-proved them seriously, they might understand that it was done out of love[104] and receive his correction or warning more will-ingly. Therefore, as if flattering them in the manner of a skilled orator, he entices them first so that he might rather make them more attentive and well-disposed to hear him. **[I give thanks.]** To give thanks to someone is to praise, to bless, to glorify him for the benefit conferred freely by him. **To my God through Je-sus Christ,** that is, the one who was made merciful to me just as also to other sinners through his Son, our Redeemer and Mediator; or, *I give thanks through Jesus Christ* because I recognize that the conversion of the Romans took place through Christ, not through our power or that of other men. I also recognize that by myself I am not worthy to praise God, but by the grace of his Son whom I serve. It is for this, I say, that *I give thanks.*

Because your faith is made known; that is, it is spread abroad to the praise of God and as an example of conversion of others **in all the world,** that is, everywhere in the world or in the great-est part of it. For the more the Roman people became known as the head of all the world, the more the things which happened among the Romans became known, and the more superior they were, the more they attracted others by their example to con-version. Therefore, Quintilian says in "On the Blind Man": "The higher each stage of honor extends, (62) the clearer it is as an example to those who watch."[105] And again, "This is the condi-

---

103. Rom 1.1.   104. *Amor.*

105. Ps.-Quintilianus, *Decl.,* 3, Miles Marianus, c. 13. Abelard cites the title of the previous declamation.

tion of the powerful, that whatever they do they appear to command."[106]

By these and similar words of the Apostle with which he says that he *gives thanks to God through Jesus Christ*, the Church, unless I am mistaken, established a custom that in the celebrations of the Mass, when thanks are given to God the Father, in the very petitions of prayers either the words "Through our Lord Jesus Christ" or something similar is always added, and if we recall that everything which we do is by no means pleasing to God the Father, unless through the very Mediator who reconciled us to him,[107] then we will not obtain any good thing from him, except through the same one who has made peace with him for us.[108]

[1.9] **For [God is my] witness.** He shows, as it were, the reason that he thanks God in the highest for the grace conferred on them, because he embraces them with so much affection that he remembers them always in his prayers; that is, as often as he prays for himself he prays also that he might be able to come to them, so that he might have some fruit among them also. Therefore, he says, *God is my witness,* to whom I make that prayer, and who cannot be deceived, and who alone can examine intention. He does not say simply **without ceasing** but **without ceasing in my prayers,** so that there might be no prayer of his without remembrance of them. **Whom I serve in my spirit,** that is, with the inner man, namely, from all the affection of the heart, just as a friend, not in eye-service[109] as a servant who fears being whipped. **In the Gospel of his Son,** that is, in the preaching of the Gospel which the Lord Jesus himself both handed on to us and taught us.

[1.10] **[Always in my prayers] I am asking,** also, **if by any means,** whether through peace of mind or tribulation, whether by land or sea, I might come to you in the body. **A favorable journey,** he says, according to **the will of God,** not his own, who, whatever the perils of the saints, works for their good,[110] and who provides for them better than they can provide for themselves, since in all things every religious person repeats often, "Your will be done,"[111] not mine.

---

106. Ibid., c. 15.
107. Cf. Rom 5.10; 2 Cor 5.18–19.
108. Cf. Col 1.20.
109. Eph 6.6.
110. Rm. 8.28.
111. Mt 6.10.

[1.11] **For I desire [to see you].** The reason why he prays to come to them is that by his preaching he might bring some spiritual gift to them, namely, by strengthening them with his exhortations in that same teaching (63) which they had received. He says that this gift is to strengthen them, that he is encouraged together in them just as they also are encouraged in him; that is, he says that this consolation is common both to him who would instruct and to those who would be instructed, to them indeed because they were strengthened by his doctrines if in some things they might doubt and falter, to him indeed who, when they had been strengthened, was made more secure by their steadfastness. This is that common consolation between those who teach and those who learn, which Boethius mentions in the beginning of his *Hypothetical Syllogisms*, when he says: "Although I think that the greatest consolation in life is set forth in all the teachings of philosophy which are to be learned and investigated," etc.[112] **Of a spiritual grace,** that is, of some spiritual, and not bodily, gift, given freely by the Apostle, not in hope of temporal gain.

[1.12] **[To be comforted together in you] through that faith** which you now have in common with me, that is, to strengthen you in that faith which has already been proclaimed to you, not in something new. **Which is mutual,** that is, which we have in common between us or which is common to all believers. Therefore, it is also called catholic, that is, universal, not private or separate like that of the heretics; it can exist in any corner of the earth, and is not extended everywhere. When he adds **yours and mine,** he shows that his faith, which is that of all the believers, is as much the Romans' as the Apostle's. It can even be said that at that time faith was *mutual*, when he binds the believers to each other with vicarious charity. For this is that true "faith which," just as he himself says, "works through love."[113]

[1.13] **But I do not want [you to be ignorant, brothers, that I have often proposed . . .]** Lest the Apostle's desire to come to them seem insufficient unless he attempted to achieve it, he says that he had often attempted and made preparation, but

112. Boethius, *syll. hyp.* I.
113. Gal 5.6; *dilectio.*

thus far he was not allowed to accomplish it, since the hidden dispensation of God had so ordained. **To come,** I say, **to you** on account of this: **that [I may have] some fruit,** that is, that I may bring something useful to you. For the fruit of the tree is useful not to the one who brings it but to the one who receives it, and to the Apostle the desire of a good will is enough if the result is lacking, and nothing is diminished from his merit if the result is impeded.

(64) [1.14] **[I am a debtor] to Greeks and barbarians,** as if he should say: Indeed, it is necessary for me to wish this, because according to the duty of preaching imposed upon me, *I am* made *a debtor* to all peoples by God. Aside from the Greeks, he calls all the other Gentiles barbarians, deeply alienated both from the worship of the one God and from the law of God. Among the Greeks faith in one God became known through the philosophers, and the Law was learned through the Septuagint, translated by interpreters. **To the wise and to the foolish;** that is, both to those who believe, now illuminated by Christ, the Wisdom of God, just as you are, and to the unbelievers; indeed to the former, that I may strengthen them, and to the latter, that I may convert them.

[1.15] **And so, as much as is in me...** *I am a debtor,* I say, and willing to accomplish what I ought; and this is what he says: *so, I am a debtor, as much as is in me,* **I am eager to preach the Gospel to you;** that is, as much as I am able, I am inclined and willing to accomplish what I ought of the duty imposed upon me, namely, to preach to you just as I preached to the other Gentiles. For although they were now converted to the faith, nevertheless there was work to be done among many others with preaching and exhortation. Regarding the other Romans, it can be accepted that there were those who were not yet converted. Therefore, he says in a general way, **to you who are at Rome,** not, "you who have been converted."

[1.16] **For...** Therefore, *I am eager* because **I am not ashamed** to preach **the Gospel,** although in it certain shameful things might appear, which are proclaimed concerning the Lord Jesus according to the weakness of the humanity he assumed. Again: *I am not ashamed of the Gospel,* that is, of the preaching of the

Gospel; that is, I cannot be refuted like those who fail to give explanations. **For it is the power,** as if he should say, *therefore I am eager to preach the Gospel* and *I am not ashamed of the Gospel* on account of the weakness of the assumed humanity, because **for everyone who believes** and accepts the Gospel, **it is the power of God for salvation,** that is, a *power* conferred on us by God to save us, through which everyone progresses. *The Gospel,* that is, the good news, is called the New Testament on account of its excellence, not only, as we explained above, because it teaches that what was promised in the Old Testament was fulfilled, but also because its (65) teaching of righteousness is entirely and truly sufficient and perfect, since the old law, as the Apostle himself says, brought nothing to perfection, correcting works rather than intention. **To the Jew first** at that time, **and** later **to the Greek.** For *first* the apostles were converted from the Jews, through whom the preaching of the Gospel penetrated to the Greeks thereafter, and finally to the Latins. And so that passage, which says *first,* with regard to the Romans or other Gentiles, can refer at the same time to the Jews and the Greeks; or let us say that in the time of the Apostle Paul they were converted *first,* that is, especially, from the other peoples.

[1.17] **For the righteousness of God,** indeed *for salvation,* because there the teaching of the entire salvation is contained, namely, where *the righteousness of God,* that is, his just recompense, is plainly and perfectly contained and transmitted, either among the elect for glory or among the wicked for punishment. And this is since it **is revealed in it,** that is, the Gospel; that is, the *righteousness of God* is taught in its proclamation, that is, his just recompense to everyone, both to the elect, as was said, and to the reprobate. *It is revealed,* I say, **from faith to faith,** that is, *from faith* in punishments that directs us *to faith* in rewards. For it follows, as if from contraries, that, while we know the things which deserve punishment with God, we understand also the things which gain reward, because it is necessary that he who hates evil love[114] good, just as it is written: "You have loved righteousness and hated iniquity."[115] But I think this is especially revealed and

114. *Diligere,* here and in the quotation from Ps 44.
115. Ps 44.8.

distinguished in the Gospel where the Lord considers all the
things which happen according to the root of intention, saying:
"If your eye is single, your entire body will be full of light. If
your eye is dark, your whole body will be dark."[116] And this indeed is the weighing of true righteousness, where all the things
which happen are examined according to the intention rather
than according to the quality of the works. The Jews paid more
attention to these works than to the intention, although now
Christians, with natural righteousness awakened, pay attention
not so much to the things that happen as to the inclination
with which they may be done. We even plainly have there in the
Gospel each retribution, where it is said by (66) the Lord: "Go,
you cursed," and "Come, you blessed";[117] and elsewhere he says,
"For with the same measure," etc.[118] When it says *from faith* in
the things to be punished *to faith* in the things to be glorified,
we have a sequence for the day of judgment, where, when the
wicked have been punished, the elect shall be crowned.

Just as it is written, namely, in the prophet Habakkuk, **the
righteous lives by faith,**[119] that is, according to this revelation
made concerning these things which are to be believed, concerning both the punishments of the wicked and the rewards of
the righteous, any of the elect perseveres in his righteousness,
as long as he avoids these things which he believes will be punished and strives for the contrary things he believes will please
God.

[1.18] In order that he might strike terror in the souls of
the proud Romans, he pursues here that part of the divine righteousness by which the soul is punished, saying: **For [the wrath
of God] is revealed.**

First invective against the Jews and Gentiles
Because he said that the righteousness of God is revealed
from faith, namely, that the wicked are to be punished, as we
said, now he plainly determines that there, that is, in the Gospel, **the wrath of God** is manifested, that is, his righteous vengeance on the unjust. He speaks of the *God* **from Heaven** in

---

116. Mt 6.22–23.   117. Mt 25.41 and 34.
118. Mt 7.2.   119. Hab 2.4.

distinction to the false gods or the substitutes for God in the Church, to whom it is said: "I have said, 'You are gods.'"[120] Or, *is revealed from Heaven,* that is, by the fall from Heaven of the angels who were haughty, of those irrecoverably alienated from the eternal blessedness. For if he undertook to damn irrecoverably such precious creatures so quickly with such punishments, what should we hope concerning men, who offend him with so many sins?

<Another interpretation. Concerning that punishment of angelic apostasy, it is clearly shown why he is angry to the point of condemnation, namely, concerning a perverse will before a work. For the devil did not complete with a work what he willed by being proud, as when he said to himself, "I shall place my seat," etc.[121] Therefore, by no means did the result of the work which followed after condemn him, but the will did so. So also Simon Magus, by desiring the gift of miracles which he did not obtain, was condemned, not by a work but by unbelief, because he believed the Holy Spirit could be bought, just as Peter said to him: "Because you thought," etc.>[122]

(67) **[Above all] ungodliness,** with regard to the greater transgression of the Jews who were taught with the written law; **unrighteousness,** with regard to the transgression of the Gentiles, who used the natural law alone. **Above all** ungodliness, that is, above all with regard to punishment, etc. And rightly does it say *to be above,* as if to prevail among those who are in no way able to defend themselves from that which is superior. [*Of those*] *who hinder the truth of God in unrighteousness;* that is, they do not permit what they understand concerning the true God to bear fruit, following their own unrighteous desires and placing their own will before the divine will.

[1.19] **Because what is known about God [is manifest in them].** Note that in this epistle the Apostle, just as we mentioned above, in order to restrain the exaltation both of the Jews and of the Gentiles, who were contending arrogantly, inveighs alternately against both—now against the Gentiles, now against the Jews, now against both at the same time. But he mentioned

---

120. Ps 81.6.   121. cf. Is 14.13.

122. Acts 8.20. This whole passage is a *Lectio Abaelardi,* found only in *m.*

before an invective against both equally when he said: *Above all ungodliness and unrighteousness,* showing that God was prepared for punishment. Now particularly and especially he inveighs against the Gentiles, who seemed less reprehensible and nearly excusable in their own view, because they did not serve the true God whom they were not able to know, as they said, without a written law. He plainly blunts this excuse, showing that without anything written God was known before by the Gentiles through the natural law, which he had given to them from himself through reason, that is, the natural law, and by conferring knowledge through his visible works. And this is what he says, <*What is known,*>[123] as if he should say: I said that they hinder what they understand concerning the true God.

Second invective, against the Gentiles

And I said well "what they understand," *because what is known about God,* that is, concerning the nature of divinity, is now revealed to the world through the written law, indeed, had been **manifest in them** before without writing through natural reason, that is, not only to them, but also through them to others. Therefore, also many clear testimonies concerning the Trinity (68) are found in the books of the philosophers, who were the teachers of the Gentiles; the holy fathers even diligently gathered these in the commendation of our faith against the attack of the Gentiles. We have brought together many of these in the little work of our *Theology.*[124] **For God revealed it to them,** at least by the results of his own works.

[1.20] And this is what he adds: **For his invisible things,** etc. Here he distinguishes the entire mystery of the Trinity, that they might be able to consider not only the unity of God, but also the Trinity by the works themselves, just as we infer from the quality of any work of what kind and of what skill its maker was. And pay attention diligently to what is said: *what is known of God* was revealed *to them;* that is, they believed those things which we now believe concerning these things which pertain to divinity rather than to the mystery of divine Incarnation. For the mys-

123. *Lectio Abaelardi,* found only in *m.*
124. *TSum* 1.30–59; *TChr.* I.54–125; *tsch* 101–25; *TSch* 1.94–188.

tery of the Incarnation could by no means be conceived with human reason from the visible works of God, just as the power of God and his wisdom and benevolence were clearly perceived from these things which they saw. I believe that the entire distinction of the Trinity consists in these three things. For the term "God the Father" seems to me to express what divine power expresses, begetting the divine wisdom that is the Son; and "God the Son" as the divine wisdom brought forth from God; and "God the Holy Spirit" as the love[125] or benevolence of God proceeding from God the Father and the Son.

To continue: *God revealed it to them* because, through the reason which God conferred upon them, his divine Trinity became known by his visible works, and through his effects the Maker himself impressed the knowledge of himself on them. And this is what he says: *for his invisible things,* that is, God's; that is to say, his multiform or sevenfold Spirit,[126] who sometimes is called the seven spirits in the same way as the gifts of sevenfold grace; the sevenfold Spirit of God is himself contemplated by the intellect; that is, he is pondered not with the eyes of the body, but with the understanding of the reason. **Were understood from the creation of the world through the things that were made;** that is, he is understood by the effects of works in the world that he willed to happen and to be set in order so well.

His eternal [power and divinity]. We understand here his wisdom, that is, God's, which is, as we have said, the Son of God, concerning whom he says elsewhere: "Christ the power of God and wisdom of God."[127] (69) The evangelist calls this wisdom the Word,[128] that is, a conception of the mind, and the philosopher calls it "mind," which he affirms was born of God.[129] The **power** of God is called his wisdom because he makes all things very good and sets them in order in wisdom. It is a feeble and invalid work that is not skillfully done. **Divinity** in this passage stands for the majesty of the divine power which is especially hinted at, as I reckon, by the name of Father. For "God," *Deus,* as Isidore testifies, is interpreted as *theos,* that is, "fear,"[130] and power of any

---

125. *Amor.*
126. Is 11.2–3.
127. 1 Cor 1.24.
128. See Jn 1.1.
129. Macrobius, *somn.* 1.2.13–18.
130. Isidore of Seville, *etym.,* 7.1.5.

kind is fear for those made subject. Therefore, the divine power is especially expressed by the proper name of God or divinity, that is, deity. The bishop Maximus teaches this diligently in the *Exposition on the Creed* which is said to be *of the Apostles,* which is read on the fifth Sunday of Lent, with these words: "You believe in God the Father Almighty. In 'God' is shown a nature that cannot be born, in 'Father' the truth of the unbegotten, in 'Almighty' the fullness of power. For he is almighty through the unbegotten deity, and he is Father through omnipotence."[131] But we have diligently and sufficiently discussed these things in the first part of our *Theology,* as we were able.[132]

It is especially clear, therefore, from the entirety of the creation of the world, so wonderfully made, so properly adorned, how powerful, how wise, how good its Creator is, who was able and willing to make so great and so excellent a work from nothing, and ordered all things so skillfully and rationally; so that in individual things nothing more nor less than was necessary was done. Therefore, even Plato himself, when he discussed the origin of the world, praised the goodness of the divine power and wisdom to such an extent that he argued that God could not in any way have made the world better than he did.[133]

And not only did the philosophers of the Gentiles perceive the marvelous Creator from the very composition or marvelous adornment of the world, but also they ascribed [to him] with fitting reasons the excellent providence of divine direction on the basis of its excellent arrangement. One of them, Cicero, in the first book of his *Rhetoric,* (70) showed with strong reason that the world itself is ruled by providence and not by chance when he declared that those things which are ruled with prudence and providence turn out and are directed better than the other things, and claimed at once that nothing is directed or arranged in a better or more orderly way than the world itself, and proved this instantly with clear reason, showing how beneficially and reasonably those things which are in the world adhere to their orderly arrangement.[134]

131. Ps.-Maximus of Turin, *Hom.* 83, *De trad. symb.*
132. *TSch* 1.41–52.   133. Plato, *Tim.* 29e.
134. Cicero, *inv.* 1.34.

Not only can we also explain what the Apostle says, *for his invisible things [were understood] from the creation of the world,* etc., in this way, that from the composition and adornment of the world the power, wisdom, and goodness of the Maker could be perceived through human reason, according to which, as we have said,[135] three Persons are distinguished in God; but we can also say that human reason ascended through the likeness of corporeal things to such a degree that it might be able to prove the very unity of God and in him the Trinity of Persons, as well as the manner in which those Persons relate toward each other, with fit examples of likenesses, namely, by placing before the eyes some creature of the world such as the substance of bronze, and by observing something that happens in that substance of bronze, as for example the bronze image that was made in the bronze itself by our activity, so indeed as the bronze itself and the bronze image, which is made in the bronze itself or from the bronze, are in their essence the same thing without number, but nevertheless are diverse in their qualities, since one is characteristic of the bronze, and the other of the bronze image; and although the bronze and the bronze image are the same in essence, nevertheless the bronze image is from the bronze, not the bronze from the bronze image. And so in the divine Trinity, although there is the same substance of three Persons, that is, of the Father and the Son and the Holy Spirit, the Persons are nevertheless diverse in their qualities, since there is one characteristic of the Father, another of the Son and of the Holy Spirit. And although each Person is the same in essence as the others, the Son nevertheless is from the Father just as a bronze image is from the bronze, not the Father from the Son, just as the bronze itself is not from the bronze image, and the Holy Spirit has his being from the two other Persons, not they from him.—But we think we have discussed these things as much as was necessary in the second book of our *Theology.* (71) Let us return now to the text.

[For the invisible things of God] from the creation of the world were

135. See above, "From the mystery of the Incarnation...proceeding from God the Father and the Son." Compare the rest of the paragraph with *TSch* 2.112–16.

understood through the things that were made, that is, through some
creature of the world, in the same way as they were understood
through the bronze itself and through those things which were
made in the bronze, just as there is a bronze image or something similar.—The other things in the exposition should not
linger.

So that they may be without excuse, that is, so that the Gentiles might not be able to excuse themselves through ignorance,
namely, of the knowledge of the one God, although they did
not have the written law.

[1.21] And therefore he adds that they are *without excuse,* **because although they knew God,** namely, through human reason,
which is called "natural law," **they did not glorify him as God;**
that is, they did not show the veneration of reverence owed to
him through humility, **neither did they give him thanks,** that is,
recognize from the gift of his grace this knowledge which they
had about him, and which they had before the others (and they
praise him on account of this). **But they perished in their own
thoughts,** namely, in the manner of smoke, which rises higher
the more it fails and is annihilated. For thus the more they
swelled up by arrogance on account of the knowledge that they
gained, ascribing it to their zeal or talent, not to divine grace,
the more they deserved to be made blind and sink down into
error even more. And this is what he adds in explanation: **and
their foolish heart was darkened.** It was *foolish* because they ascribed to themselves and not to God his particular gift and believed they got it by themselves and not from him. Therefore,
their heart is deservedly *darkened,* and the natural reason in
them obscured.

[1.22] It was truly *darkened,* because **they became fools,** deprived even of natural knowledge, **claiming to be wise,** that is,
boasting that they are wiser by themselves than those made wise
by God.

[1.23] **And they exchanged the glory...** And in so much
foolishness, indeed madness, they burst forth, as much through
the error of unbelief as through ignorance of life. The Apostle
adds: *And they exchanged the glory* **of the incorruptible God;** that
is, the honor and the sacrifices which they should have shown

to the true God, who cannot be corrupted or changed in anything, (72) they showed to a false man; that is, they became
idolaters to the imaginary likeness of a corruptible and mortal
man; and not only **in the likeness of a man,** but also of any irrational animals, **of birds** as well as **of four-footed creatures and
serpents.** But perhaps they believed that certain spirits, which
they called gods, ruled over men, and certain spirits ruled over
other living beings, and therefore they worshiped them in the
forms by which they appeared to rule. Haymo says:

The Assyrians worshiped the likeness of Bel, father of the king Nin, as
God, and the Babylonians the very one whom they call Bel, the Sido-
nians Baal, the Jews Beelzebub, and the Philistines Zebet. The Romans
worshiped a goose and the Egyptians a bird of prey; furthermore, the
Egyptians worshiped Apis, that is, a white cow, the Babylonians a drag-
on, and the Egyptians a crocodile, which is an aquatic serpent swim-
ming in water like a fish, feeding on land like an ox.[136]

[1.24] **On account of which,** that is, because they acted fool-
ishly with regard to God, with the result that they worshiped
false animals, that is, likenesses of them, in place of God, **God
handed them over [to the desires of their heart];** that is, he allowed them to go after their unclean desires so that what they
conceived disgracefully with their mind, they accomplished
even more disgracefully with their action. **That they might afflict,** that is, damage, and compel **their bodies** by a certain power against nature, and dishonor them with the abusive filth of
the sin of the Sodomites committed **among themselves,**[137] so
that they might pollute themselves mutually.

[1.25] **Who exchanged.** This is a contrivance or repetition
of the reason why God allowed that concerning them, because
against him, he says, they especially trespassed when they exchanged **the truth of God for a lie;** that is, they worshiped false
gods under the name and with the honor of the true God; and
they [worshiped and] served the creature, that is, demonic spirits that they believed inhabited the idols. **[Rather than the Creator,] who is blessed,** that is, who is glorified, that is, appears

136. Haymo, *Rom.*, 1.23.
137. Cf. Gn 19.4–8.

praiseworthy from among all his creatures through all the successions of time. **Forever,** as if those successions of time were named by the term "following."[138] **Amen,** that is, "it is true"; for this is an adverb, sometimes of affirming, sometimes of desiring.

[1.26] **Therefore, he handed them over,** because nevertheless (73) they detracted from the divine excellence. It is not enough to say this once in order to deter the hearer all the more from such things. He calls their pollutions of unnatural desire **disgraceful passions.** Any substance is justly said to suffer and to bear, as it were, a certain violence, as often as something contrary to nature is done in relation to it. What the disgraceful things of this sort are, he immediately adds by assigning them both to women and to men, to demonstrate the greater vengeance of God. The women are called **their women,** whom they had made their own in this, as it were, by the teaching of the very worst example. **[. . . have changed the natural use into that use] which is contrary to nature** and therefore should be called abuse rather than use. *Contrary to nature,* that is, to the arrangement of nature, which made the genital organs of women for the use of men and vice versa, not so that women might cohabit with women.

[1.27] **[And in like manner the men also, having abandoned the natural use of women,] were inflamed;** that is, they burned **in their desires** outside the law of nature, not with natural pleasures; **and** they received **the reward,** that is, the fitting retribution **for their error,** that is, their blindness and idolatry, **in themselves,** mutually polluting each other in the body just as they had been corrupted in the soul through unbelief.

[1.28] **And just as they did not see fit [to acknowledge] God;** that is, they did not praise and choose *God* whom they knew, **to acknowledge,** that is, to preserve him in the memory by cleaving to him, **God handed them over to a reprobate mind;** that is, he allowed them to become so thoroughly blind that they became entirely shameless; they showed absolutely no signs of uprightness in themselves, about which they nevertheless had

---

138. An apparent etymology on the words *saecula* and *sequendo.*

composed many works; with the result **that they might do,** that
is, that they might fulfill with a work, **those things which are not
fit,** not only the things that are evil in God's sight, but those
that are consistent with no teaching of men, nor can they be
excused by some reasoning even among the wicked.

[1.29–31] I say that they are **filled with every filthiness,** that
is, *filled* not only with all sins together but with individual ones,
with the result that each iniquity is found full and complete in
them. Therefore, he immediately subdivides the portions of iniquity by enumerating those that he shows they are filled with:
malice, through which they are eager to bring injury on others;
fornication, which is every unlawful sexual intercourse, apart
from one's wife; **greed,** that is, an immoderate desire for earthly
things; **vileness,** with which (74) they rejoice in ruining others,
and it is not enough that these others should only die; **envy,**
aching for the goods of another; **murder,** both by work, if they
can, and by will; **disputing,** by speaking openly against the truth;
deceit, that is, pretense, when one thing is done secretly and
another is counterfeited; **ill-will,** even toward their own benefactors; they are **whisperers,** that is, secretly pulling others down,
when they cannot do so openly, and when they dare even in the
open; **disparagers,** not only of men whom they pull down or
wish to harm, but they are also **haters of God;** they are **abusive,**
through their insults; **arrogant,** striving to be above their equals;
haughty, by striving to be equal to their superiors; **inventors of
evil,** that is, contriving some new kind of sinning in which they
may delight; **disobedient to their parents,** both inhuman in this
and wilder than the wild beasts themselves; **foolish,** having no
discernment of good on account of their familiarity with evil;
dissolute, with regard to the exterior way of life, which is the
witness of a badly ordered mind; **without affection,** that is, natural kindness toward the relatives of one's own kind; **merciless,**
that is, without compassion for the misfortunes of others; **without loyalty,** that is, the mutual bond of charity with someone or
the observation of some covenant.

[1.32] It was these who had sunk down in such blindness
that they do not know how to turn around through penitence;
they no longer understand; that is, they do not pay attention

or take care **that those who do such things deserve death,** specifically eternal death, **although** at first **they understood the righteousness of God,** that is, his vengeance due for individual sins. **[And not only those who do them,] but even those who consent [to those who do them].** "To consent" means here that someone does not resist the sin of another, when he could and should. For perhaps God could resist the sins of many, by frustrating them lest they occur, though he is not obligated to frustrate our persistent sins, or when he uses the sins themselves for the better; therefore we should not in any way say that God consents to sins.

But we must note that this aforesaid blindness or malice should not be understood concerning all the philosophers or users of natural law, since most of them became acceptable to God as much by their faith as by their morals, as for example the Gentile Job and perhaps some of the Gentile philosophers, who led a most continent life before the coming of the Lord. Blessed Jerome speaks of such people (75) in his commentary on Matthew where he mentions: "From that which the evil servant dared to say: 'You reap where you did not sow, and gather where you did not scatter,'[139] let us understand also that God accepts the good life of the Gentiles and the philosophers, and in one way compares those who act justly, and in another way those who act unjustly, with him who serves the natural law, to condemn those who neglect the written law."[140] By the Lord reaping where he did not sow, according to Jerome, we understand that those who act well by the natural law reap life, among whom no word of preaching was sown. But perhaps because few among the philosophers became like this, this was said about them above as it were generally, without any exception, so that the wise might presume less on their own wisdom, which is accustomed to puff up more than to build up, as the Apostle attests elsewhere: "knowledge puffs up, charity builds up."[141]

It was enough for the Apostle in this passage to show, for the purposes of restraining the proud contentiousness of the

139. Mt 25.24.
140. Jerome, *Math.* 4 (on 25.26–28).
141. 1 Cor 8.1.

Gentile Romans and maintaining their humility, that through some of the philosophers the knowledge of or faith in God was known to the Gentiles and the same teachers of faith had seriously sinned, so that their blindness led all the way to idolatry, and with the greatest error of idolatry they sank down to the greatest dishonor of life, as he mentioned above. He teaches that all these things are the penalty of the sin of pride,[142] so that according to the purpose of the present epistle, which was written entirely to combat the plague of pride, he immediately dissuades from pride at the very beginning of the epistle. The sin that follows is called the penalty of the sin that precedes, that is, its just reward according to the penalty, since on account of the preceding sin which a person neglected to correct, he deserves to sink down into another sin, so that, according to that passage of the Apocalypse: "He who is filthy, let him continue filthy."[143]

Question One

Three questions present themselves in this passage. One of them is, what is it that constitutes idolatry, since in the worship of God we Christians also have some sculptures or pictures either of angels or of holy men?

Question Two

And another (76) question is, why is God said to hand someone over to other sins for his preceding sins and to do this by his righteousness,[144] since he who is handed over deserved this? Is God also the author or cause of sin? By withdrawing his grace he seems to compel a person to sin, who might not be able to keep himself clear from sin when grace is withdrawn, just as someone who, for whatever reason, takes the ship away from him who is between the waves and abandons him there, actually compels him to die.

Question Three

The third question is, how is it just for God to withdraw his grace from the wicked, so that when it has been withdrawn, that

142. Rom 1.26–31.   143. Rv 22.11.
144. Cf. Rom 1.28, 32.

person becomes worse and sins more, unless of course it is just for him to become worse and to sin more, that is, to offend and condemn his Creator even more? But who says that this, which is very unjust, is just, since a sinner ought rather to come to his senses than to add to his sins? For if it was just for him to sin more, how might he be judged responsible or even said to sin by doing that which was certainly just for him to do? But we reserve the answers to these proposed questions for the consideration of our *Theology.*

[2.1] **Therefore.** From a single invective, namely, against the Gentiles, he passes to a general one, as if he should thus say: Since these to whom the written law was not given cannot, through ignorance of God, excuse themselves from sin, that is, from contempt for the Creator, therefore no one can. And this is what he says: *Therefore,* **you are without excuse, O man, every one of you who judges.** *Every one of you,* I say, *who judges,* that is, you who have the discernment of reason and the ability to distinguish good and evil. Of course, little children who do not yet have this ability to distinguish are free from this contempt. For in what are you truly *without excuse?* Because you must be condemned with your own judgment, since you reprove in others things that are the same as or similar to what you do. But this especially pertains to the proud contention of the Romans, by which they desired to set themselves over one or the other, and defending themselves individually, (77) they judged others to be guilty. **For in that which,** that is, the same sin that **you judge,** that is, you reprove the other and judge him worthy of damnation, **you condemn yourself;** that is, you do what is damnable by performing those things, and you make an assertion and you carry out the sentence against yourself with your own judgment. And for what reason and in what way, he adds when he says: **for you do the same things that you judge,** that is, the things you reprove in others, namely, the bad works that you commit against your own conscience.

[2.2] I said *the things that you judge* by reproving, but you judge this well by accusing, because God judges those things by punishing; and this is what the text says: **For we know,** etc. And so: I said *you condemn yourself;* that is, you make yourself damnable by performing those things, and it is indeed true: *For we know,* we who have been illuminated by divine grace, **that the judgment of God** which **is according to the** very **truth** of the thing cannot err; it is **against those who do such things,** namely, those who are to be punished and condemned.

[2.3] And since it is so, namely, that God damns such people, **do you imagine,** you **who judge,** that is, you who denounce or accuse **those who do such things, and you do them,** *do you imagine,* I say, **that you will escape the judgment of God,** that is, his just vengeance on such people?

[2.4] And are you also unaware that the more damnable you are, the more patience God exercises in waiting for you, and by waiting for a long time his kindness invites you to penance, and you turn this kindness of his patience into contempt for him, and the less you fear him the more he bears your offenses and does not immediately punish them? And this is what he says: *Or are you unaware?* **Do you condemn the riches of his goodness,** that is, God's, the rich and abundant sweetness of his affection? Of his *goodness,* I say, **of his patience and long-suffering,** that is, of his prolonged patience. *Or* **are you unaware that the kindness of God,** that is, this display of his goodness by which he waits, **leads you** as much as it can, that is, it invites, it encourages you **to penance** for your sins rather than to contempt for him who waits?

[2.5] But you, **according to your hardness and impenitent heart you store up for yourself,** that is, you eagerly heap up **wrath** *for yourself* as if it were precious riches, that is, vengeance to be carried out on you **on the day,** that is, at the time of **wrath and revelation,** that is, of the vengeance of God to be revealed against you. And so that that wrath may be understood as righteousness rather than as cruelty, and as deliberate rather than as presumptuous, he adds **of the just judgment,** that is, I say, *of wrath,* that is, (78) of vengeance arising from the judgment of the just deliberation **of God,** who cannot act unjustly.

[2.6] How truly just the divine judgment is, he adds saying: **Who will render to each one** what he deserves **according to [his] works,** that is, according to the nature of the works, which consists in the intention more than in the action. The nature of the retribution is according to the nature of the works, because as the works are, so is the retribution, namely, good for good, evil for evil, since with God the will itself is reckoned as a work performed. Therefore, he is also said to be the tester of the heart and the kidneys and to see into what is concealed.[145] In this passage he substitutes the work for the inner disposition of the work, when the term is transferred from the effect to the cause. Otherwise, the judgment of God might not be shown to be equitable, since the works are indifferent in themselves, that is, neither good nor evil, or they seem worthy of recompense, except according to the root of the intention, that is, the tree producing good or evil fruit. Such it is, therefore, that he says *according to* **his** *works*, as if he should say, according to the will of those things that they desire to happen or not to happen. Otherwise the pride of the devil and the greed of Simon,[146] which did not obtain the effect of a work, might not appear to pertain to this judgment. But small children who, dying during the years of discretion, do not appear to have merit, do not concern the revelation of this judgment, by which it is said: "he renders to each one according to his works,"[147] that is, he will give to him what he deserves.

Diligently, therefore, did the Apostle express what should be understood as the judgment of God, since he says that it is a revelation *of judgment*. For everyone shall be judged then not with words but with an exhibition of a work; that is, it will be shown whether he was worthy of reward or punishment. While he lived, the end of this person remained hidden even to the saints, whether or not he was predestined to life.

But this judgment, that is, this revelation or inquiry of the divine judgment, both occurs individually, every day, in the deaths of individuals, and must occur generally at the end of the world, when indeed everyone shall be revealed to everyone, namely, as they were before, whether they are worthy of reward or of punishment. Truly, in that general inquiry there are said to be two orders each in the elect and the reprobate. (79) For certain of the elect, that is, of the predestined, shall only judge there and

145. Cf. Ps 7.10; Mt 6.4; 6, 18.   146. Cf. Acts 8.18–24.
147. Mt 16.27; Rom 2.6.

shall not be judged, and some shall only be judged. So also there shall be two orders of the reprobate, since some of them must be judged only, others must be judged not at all. For whoever of the elect are not found to be undefiled before the day of judgment shall be judged then, that is, revealed. Concerning such people he says elsewhere: "But he shall be saved, nevertheless as through fire."[148] Truly they who were found perfect in life, or made clean before the judgment itself, are not then to be judged, that is, revealed, but rather shall judge equally with Christ himself. Those sharing his majesty and glory shall shine so that it may immediately be clear from them, just as from Christ himself, how well they have done who cleaved to them, how badly those who condemned them. And thus they also shall sit with Christ as judges, wholly secure in themselves and judging others, that is, as was said, revealing whether they did well with them or badly against them, so that they may be worthy either of a reward on account of this or of punishment. But the reprobate who die in their own unbelief are now judged, that is, revealed, at the very end; they need not be <generally>[149] revealed farther on, according to that saying of the Truth: "He who does not believe, has already been judged."[150] But these who have faith, who led a doubtful life in secret (on account of which their end is uncertain), are to be judged, that is, revealed, then.

[2.7] **To these indeed who according....** He shows how the nature of retribution is according to the nature of the work, so that good may be rendered for good, and vice versa. And this is what he says: *To these who according* **to patience in good works** <understand: "are . . .">,[151] so that he may show that tribulations are not lacking to those who do good, through which they are purified or make progress, **glory and honor,** that is, a glorious honor, when our humanity reaches the height of the angels and we shall reign equally as heirs of God and co-heirs with Christ himself. And lest that glory be ascribed only to the soul, he adds

148. 1 Cor 3.15.
149. *Lectio Abaelardi,* found only in *mO.*
150. Jn 3.18.
151. I.e., the glory and honor that he mentions a little later. This is a *Lectio Abaelardi,* found only in *mO.*

something about the bodies to be glorified that will be incorruptible, saying, **and incorruption,** namely, of the body; *to these,* I say, (80) who seek **life,** not the transitory life that the Jews sought, but the **eternal** life that the Christians sought, so that he might show that they justly obtained that for which they panted with all their desire, that they were not cheated in their hope, just as it is written about any just person: "He sought life from you, and you gave it to him," and again, "You gave him the desire of his soul."[152]

[2.8] **But to these who by contention** ("are" is understood),[153] that is, those who knowingly oppose the divine will; he immediately expounds this, saying, **and who do not acquiesce to the truth** that they know, so that they might act in the way they believe they ought truly to act, but rather **put confidence in,** that is, they acquiesce or assent to, **iniquity** so that the evil that they conceive in the soul they complete by their work, that is, they strive to fulfill; **wrath and anger,** which they deserved ("is rendered," you should understand), that is, the punishment of God without his forbearance. The elect, if they are in any way punished at some time, namely, that they might be purified, patiently endure and thereafter are not angry, but rather rejoice and give thanks, giving heed to what is written: <"The Lord chastised me and did not hand me over to death,"[154] and again,>[155] "God corrects those whom he loves, but scourges the son whom he receives."[156] Therefore, Jerome says as well in his letter *To Castricianus,* "Wrath is great when God is not angry with sinners."[157]

[2.9] **Tribulation and distress.** He shows from what things the aforesaid *wrath and anger* arise. For *tribulation* is *distress* where he who is tormented has abandoned all hope of escaping, so that hope may not be left to him as a kind of salvation, but that he may also be tormented with despair itself. And because he had

152. Ps 20.5, 3.
153. Peter seems to understand "by contention," *ex contentione,* as an adjective: "But to those who are contentious," as the Douay-Rheims translation likewise understands this passage.
154. Ps 117.18.
155. *Lectio Abaelardi,* found only in *O.*
156. Heb 12.6; *diligere.* Cf. Prv 3.12.   157. Jerome, *Ep.* 68.1.

said *to these* imprecisely, he adds that this generally occurs in **every soul of a man who does evil,** both **of the Jew** and **of the Gentile,** that is, both those taught by the written law and those taught by the natural. He says *who does,* not who did, that is, who perseveres in malice, not who desists from it; those who will not set aside an evil will, even in the midst of torments, have been established with the devil, and they still wish to do the same things if it were allowed, (81) and therefore the punishment will justly be perpetual because the guilt will persist perpetually in the soul. Therefore also, as blessed Jerome attests, the Lord will justly say on the Day of Judgment: "Depart from me, you who do iniquity," that is, you who not only did but still *do* in your very hearts; [158] then, as we said above, the will is reckoned by God as a completed action.

Rightly does he say that punishment takes place *in the soul,* not in the body, *of a man,* because it belongs to the soul alone, and not to the body, to lament or feel and be saddened or pleased, to be angry or glad. And if we should reflect diligently, [the soul,] which alone can will, might merit with God, who recompenses the will, either reward or punishment on account of a good or bad will, and it alone can properly be said to sin in the same way as it can be said to have virtues and to be made alone blessed by the vision of the divine majesty, which is perceived only with the eyes of the mind, and not of the body. But insofar as the five senses of the soul are said to be physical, since only the soul feels, as was said, or insofar as certain sins are called carnal, and certain sins spiritual, since only the soul alone sins, because it alone has reason and can will, we should not understand that the body itself either feels or sins, but that by it either the senses are set in motion or the desires are fulfilled, as gluttony is by the throat, and lust by the genitals.

Therefore, the soul alone merits and obtains reward or punishment from God on account of a good or bad will, and alone can be a participant in blessedness or wretchedness, although its penalty or glory may be increased by a body that has been restored. [159] Therefore, we say that there is a twofold ruin for the

158. Jerome, *Matth.* 1 (7.24); Mt 7.23.
159. I.e., in the resurrection of the dead. See Peppermüller, I, 184 n. 91.

wicked and a twofold stole for the saints, with regard both to
the soul and to the body. The blessed soul shall rejoice further
and shall glorify the Creator even more when the body itself,
because it became so weak and subject to suffering here, will
see then that it has been prepared to such an extent that it cannot die any more nor incur some injury by its contact with the
soul. And this same restoration of the human body is called the
glorification or blessedness of the body. So also what the soul
itself will suffer through the corporeal members can be called
the punishment of the body. Nevertheless, although the glory
or punishment of souls is doubled on account of the bodies, we
do not therefore prefer that twofold (82) glory or punishment
to the simple glory or punishment of the angels or demons,
who do not have a bodily nature.

That it is true, as has been said, that the soul alone suffers
or feels, the saints themselves also claim. Augustine says the following in Book 22 of *The City of God:* "If we reflect more diligently, suffering, which is said to be the body's, belongs more
to the soul. For suffering belongs to the soul and not to the
body, even when the cause of the sorrow arises to it from the
body, since it suffers in that place where the body is wounded."[160] Again he says in his *On Genesis*: "Feeling belongs not
to the body, but to the soul through the body."[161] In the same
work again: "For the body does not feel, but the soul through
the body."[162] In his letter *To Dioscorus*, the one that begins, "You
ask me countless questions," he says, "The rational soul does
not receive from the body either the greatest good or any part
of the greatest good. Those who do not see this are blinded
by the charm of carnal pleasures, which charm they do not
consider to come from an unhealthy state. But the complete
health of the body will be that final immortality of the entire
man. For by so powerful a nature God made the soul, that by
his most full blessedness, which is promised to the saints at the
end of time, it might overflow as well to the lower nature, that
is, the body, not the blessedness which is proper to enjoyment

160. Augustine, *civ. Dei* 21.3.2, *ad litteram.*
161. Augustine, *Gn. litt.*, 3.5.
162. Ibid., 12.24.(51).

or understanding, but the fullness of health,[163] that is, the vigor of incorruption."[164]

Of the Jew first, and then the Greek. He calls every one learned in the written law a Jew, and a Greek every one provided with reason, that is, very well instructed in the natural law, in the manner of the Gentile philosophers, who were Greeks. Of these, where the discretion is greater, so is the transgression, and therefore he says: *of the Jew first and then the Greek,* that is, especially *of the one doing evil,* that is, of the one trespassing, <namely, in comparison with other, as it were irrational, men>.[165]

[2.10] **But glory and honor.** He mentions again the recompense of the righteous which he had mentioned before, so that he might stir us more fully and more frequently to remember it. (83) He indeed says that peace is not only the rest from the assault of exterior enemies, but also that concord of spirit and flesh, so that in nothing more might the flesh struggle against the spirit, when all the molestations of carnal suggestions have been entirely finished. **To the Jew first and to the Greek,** namely, **to the one who does good.** For the more they knew the highest good, God, either by what was written or by reason, the more they clung to his will by living temperately. Therefore, he also places *first* in this place for the greatest effect, as above.

[2.11] **For there is no…** I said *to every* generally and without discrimination, making no difference of retribution on the basis of the eminence of the persons, and justly, because *there is no* **favoritism of persons with God;** that is, the divine judgment never punishes someone there less or glorifies him more according to some eminence or superiority which he appeared to have here, but equally requites all according to their merits, both those having the law and those not having it, both those who boast that they are of the race of Israel as well as the others. And he shows that he requites only according to merits, since the quantity of the punishment is according to the quantity of

163. Peppermüller: *sanitatis*; Buytaert, however, reads *sanctitatis*, "holiness"; neither editor notes textual variants. PL 178.813A reads *sanitatis.*

164. *Ep.* 118.14.

165. *Lectio Abaelardi,* found only in *mO.*

the transgressions. Therefore, it is appropriate that we should similarly imply this concerning rewards.

[2.12] Therefore, just as the transgression of him who also received the written law is greater than of him who is instructed only in the natural, so he shows that the punishment of the first is greater and of the second is lesser, saying: **Whoever has sinned without the law,** namely, the written one, such as the Gentiles did, that is, who have no law by which they might be taught, shall indeed perish, that is, they shall be condemned, but **they shall perish without the law,** that is, they incur no punishment from the transgression of the written law but only from the transgression of the natural law. **And whoever has sinned in the law,** that is, also through the transgression of the written law, just as the Jews did, **shall be judged by the law,** that is, they will be able to be convicted as guilty openly through the profession of the law which they received but did not observe.

Question

But since the transgression is greater of those who are transgressors also of the written law (84) than of those who transgress the natural law, why did he say there *they shall perish,* and here *they shall be judged,* since those sins which are saved up for the judgment do not seem as great as those which do not await the judgment, but they immediately condemn and compel the accused to die, apart from any consideration of judgment? But indeed, as we have said, he said that they are judged instead of being convicted openly, so that the greater the sin appears, the more openly it can be convicted, namely, by the transgression of the written law which was passed on openly and publicly by God before all and confirmed with miracles. For the things that are condemned with a public judgment are openly denounced, and do not find a defender after the sentence of judgment has been approved.

[2.13] **For it is not the hearers...**

Third invective, against the Jews

The invective against the Jews begins. It continues: I said *they shall be judged by the law,* as if it were a legal action, because, although they hear the law, they are not therefore righteous unless they do the works that the law instructs. And this is what he says: *For it is not the hearers,* that is, it is not because they are *hearers of the law* that they **are righteous with God,** that is, in the divine judgment, although [they may be righteous in] human judgment, **but the doers,** that is, because they do the things that the law instructs.

But indeed, since he says elsewhere that no one is justified by the works of the law, how can he now say that *the doers of the law* are justified, unless in this passage he means that the *doers* are those who by the love[166] of God act spontaneously, according to which a good will is accounted as a work done, as we have said?[167] For we do not please God by an exterior work, but rather by the will. In this passage, therefore, he speaks of the will; in the other, of an exterior work. We can even understand here the natural law which alone the Gentiles use. Concerning these things and in the things that follow he says that we understand this about the written law of works, so that it is understood in this way, that not only they who hear the words of the natural law are righteous, but they who fulfill it by action. But the words of the natural law are those that commend love[168] of God and of neighbor, such as: "Do not do to another what you do not want done to you,"[169] and "What you want men to do to you, do also to them."[170]

[2.14] **For since the nations...** And truly the power of justification consists not in the hearing of the written law but in its doing, as was said. Therefore, it appears that the Gentiles, although they do not have a written law that they can hear, nevertheless, since they do those (85) works which the law instructs, are saved just as the Jews are. And this is what he says: *For since the nations,* that is, the Gentiles, who **do not have** the written **law, naturally do it,** that is, instructed in the natural law, that is, in the knowledge of God and the discernment of reason which *they have naturally,* that is, as a result of their creation, not as a result of somebody's written teaching; they, I say, **not having a**

166. *Amor.*
167. See 2.6.
168. *Caritas.*
169. Tb 4.16.
170. Mt 7.12.

law of this kind, that is, one written externally just as the Jews have, **they are a law to themselves,** that is, they gain the same reward by themselves without a written law that the others gain through obedience to the written law.

[2.15] For they who outwardly show in their action the good will that they have in their mind **show that the work of the law is written on their hearts.** When he says *written,* he means the perseverance of a good will. For just as blessed Gregory says, "What we speak passes away; what we write endures."[171] Therefore, those who are the hearers of the law as it were speak the law that is written on parchment, and do not hold it joined to their hearts; just as on the contrary they act **when their conscience gives them a** good **testimony,** that is, when their good conscience and right intention, which is known to them and not to others, make them secure in the righteousness of their works. It is according to this intention that God considers the works.

And within themselves alternately… The text here is accustomed to be read in different ways.[172] Sometimes genitive plurals are placed here in this way: **Of accusing or even defending thoughts;** and sometimes ablatives in this way: **When their thoughts accuse,** etc. Therefore, Augustine says in Book 20 of *The City of God*: "Just as it is written, 'the examination of the wicked shall be in his thoughts,'[173] and the Apostle says, 'When their thoughts either accuse or excuse them on the day when God shall judge the secrets of men,'" etc.[174] He says also on Psalm 118: "All works, either good or evil, proceed from thought. Everyone is innocent in thought; everyone is guilty in thought. Because of this it is written: 'A holy thought shall save you,'[175] and elsewhere: 'The examination of the wicked shall be in his thoughts'; and the Apostle says: 'when their thoughts accuse

171. *moral.* 33.4.

172. Abelard is referring to variants of this passage in the Latin texts of Romans, one of which reads, *et inter se invicem cogitationum accusantium aut etiam defendentium,* using genitive plurals, while the other reads, *et inter se invicem cogitationibus accusantibus, aut etiam defendentibus,* using ablative plurals to create an ablative absolute construction.

173. Wis 1.9.   174. 20.26.3. Literal citation.
175. Prv 2.11.

(86) or even defend them,'" etc.[176] He also says on Psalm 5: "It is said, 'Let them fall by their thoughts';[177] let them fall by their thoughts accusing them, by their conscience, just as the Apostle says: 'And of accusing or defending thoughts,'" etc.[178]

I, however, think that this textual variation resulted especially from the usage of the Greek language, since the Greeks, lacking the ablative, use the genitive in place of the ablative. Therefore, it happened that, according to the various translations from Greek into Latin, sometimes the genitive case was preserved in Latin just as it was in Greek; sometimes accordingly the meaning required that with us it be changed into the ablative. For although this epistle which is sent to the Romans is understood at first to have been written in Latin, although it was written in Greece at Corinth, nevertheless we believe that later various translators or expositors of it arose who, as was said, imitated the Greeks, since perhaps they did not have that Latin scripture at hand and therefore returned to the Greek examples. Now, therefore, let us expound the text both ways.

Since, therefore, it was said before that *when their conscience gives testimony to them,* he adds *of thoughts alternately within themselves,* etc., as if he should say, and with such a conscience that does not stray in the discernment of works, examining them according to the very thoughts, that is, the intentions, of the rational soul; these thoughts, rather than exterior works, shall accuse or defend before God. And this is conscience, I say, *of thoughts,* that is, that which considers the thoughts themselves rather than works. And he adds why he especially considers them, because they accuse or excuse [a person] with God. I say, *of thoughts,* namely, those entertained, *alternately within themselves,* so that they might reckon what is to be done concerning [the accusing thoughts] as well as the others, [the defending thoughts,] according to that rule of natural law posited above: "Do not do to another what you do not want done to you,"[179] and "What you want men to do to you, do also to them."[180]

[2.16] **On the day,** that is, at the time, **when God shall judge**

176. *en. Ps.,* Ps. 118; *serm.* 24.6.   177. Ps 5.11.
178. *en. Ps.,* in Ps 5.13.   179. Tb 4.16.
180. Mt 7.12.

through his Son, that is, Jesus Christ, according to which it (87) is written, "The Father has given all judgment to the Son";[181] **the secrets of men,** that is, the intentions rather than the exterior works, **according to my Gospel,** that is, just as I proclaim, claiming that God rewards intentions rather than works.

If indeed it is an ablative absolute in this manner: *and alternately within themselves their thoughts accuse,* etc., it will be joined to the other, previously mentioned ablative: I said that *their conscience gives testimony to them* and their *thoughts* that they entertain *alternately within themselves,* that is, through which thoughts they examine themselves in the same way as they examine others, as was said, when their very own *thoughts,* that is, when their particular intentions, understand: *give testimony to them.* And it is the explanation of it, as it were, that is mentioned before: *their conscience,* as if he should say, *their thoughts,* etc. And as to why their thoughts before God give *testimony* to them, that is, make them secure, he adds, because as was said, only their thoughts can accuse or defend them before God. And this is what he adds: *when they shall accuse or even defend,* etc.

But it is asked how, after the commandment of circumcision was given, "Every soul whose foreskin has not been circumcised," etc.,[182] the uncircumcised Gentiles such as Job and perhaps most others were saved, concerning whom it was said: *For since the nations,* etc. But if we diligently attend to the very words of Scripture and the very beginning of circumcision that was first enjoined upon Abraham, we shall see that the injunction of circumcision was not a general one but concerns only Abraham and his seed, that is, Isaac, as when the Lord said to Abraham: "Because your seed shall be named in Isaac,"[183] not in Ishmael. Therefore, since the Lord also enjoined circumcision on Abraham, he says: "This shall be the covenant between me and you and your seed after you."[184]

Origen also openly and clearly shows in the following words on this epistle, from other words of Scripture, that the sign of circumcision was a commandment to the people of Israel alone and their home-born slaves and those purchased with money.

---

181. Jn 5.22.
183. Gn 21.12.

182. Gn 17.14.
184. Gn 17.10.

For when that short verse was expounded: *If therefore the uncir-cumcised man keeps the righteousness of the law,* etc.,[185] diligently (88) discussing the commandment and motive for circumcision, he says:

It does not seem unsuitable to discuss the general rationale for circumcision. "The Lord said to Abraham: But you shall keep my testament, and all your seed after you in their generations. And this is the testament between me and you, and between the whole of your seed after you: Every male of yours shall be circumcised, and every boy shall be circumcised on the eighth day. Every male among your descendants shall be circumcised, every home-born slave and every slave purchased with money."[186]

Let us discuss whether the commandment also binds those who believed among the Gentiles. It never made mention of a proselyte, that is, of a foreigner, but it commands the home-born slave or the slave purchased for a price to be circumcised, not the freeman. Therefore, let us examine the Levitical law: it says, "Speak to the sons of Israel and say to them: If a woman bears a male, he shall be circumcised on the eighth day," etc.[187] Observe, both how Moses is commanded here to speak about the law of circumcision only to the sons of Israel and how no mention is made of foreigners. Since he speaks in some commandments not only to the sons of Israel but also to the proselytes, that is, the foreigners, a necessary distinction should certainly be observed, because just as it says there: "Speak to Aaron,"[188] and elsewhere, "to the sons of Aaron,"[189] and elsewhere, "to the Levites,"[190] it is certain that the rest are not subject to these laws; in that these things are commanded to the sons, with nothing said of the foreigner, one should not think that the commandment is a general one where there is a restriction of name.[191]

So therefore, nobody else is bound by the law of circumcision, except someone who derives his origin from Abraham or who is a home-born slave or a slave purchased with money.[192]

But do you wish to see that, wherever he wishes, he may show expressly that the alien is bound with the law? Hear what is written: (89) "Any

185. Rom 2.26.
186. Origen, *Rom.,* 2.13; Gn 17.9–12. Passage from Origen edited and paraphrased.
187. Lv 12.2–3.   188. Ex 8.16.
189. Lv 6.25; 21.1; etc.   190. Cf. Nm 18.26.
191. Origen, *Rom.,* 2.13, edited and paraphrased.
192. Ibid., edited.

man from the sons of Israel and from the foreigners who has eaten
any blood, I shall ruin his soul because the soul of all flesh is its blood,
and I have given it to you so that through it there may be propitiation
upon the altar for your souls, because the blood shall atone for the
soul."[193] You see therefore that this law, which was also given to the foreigners, is observed by us among the Gentiles who believe. Therefore,
the church of the Gentiles accepts the law concerning the regulation
of blood in common with the sons of Israel. For, understanding these
things written in the law in this way, that blessed council of apostles at
that time made a decision, and wrote to the Gentiles that they should
abstain from blood and what has been strangled. But perhaps you will
ask if the law concerning what has been suffocated was given in common to the sons of Israel with the foreigners? Listen: it says, "A man
from the sons of Israel and from the foreigners who are among you,
whoever has hunted a wild animal or bird which is eaten, must pour
out its blood and bury it in the earth, because the soul of all flesh is its
blood."[194]

In fact, among those things that we brought forth above concerning
the Levitical law, even this is asserted: "A man from the sons of Israel
or from the foreigners who are among them, whoever has made a ho-
locaust or sacrifice and did not bring it to the door of the tabernacle to
offer it to the Lord shall be banished from his people,"[195] and through
this even the Church of the Gentiles seems to be obligated to perform
holocausts. The law does not command him to do it, but if perhaps
he did, it teaches how he should do it. For it is certain that, while the
temple at Jerusalem stood and the traditional religion of the fathers
flourished, many of the Gentiles also came to the temple to worship
and offer sacrifices. But since this was commanded to be done in one
place only, concerning which it commands here that the victim should
be led to the door of the tabernacle to be slaughtered, it could legitimately be done as long as the condition of the place remained intact.
Finally, the Savior said to the ten lepers he had cleansed: "Go, show
yourselves to the priests and offer sacrifices for yourselves just as Moses
commanded."[196] Now then, why is that which is not permitted to the
worshipers themselves to show, asked for from the foreigners?[197]

We said these things so that we might show chiefly that the (90) commandment of circumcision was not enjoined on anyone other than
those who derive from the race of Abraham and their home-born

193. Lv 17.10–11.
194. Lv 17.13; Origen, *Rom.*, 2.13, edited and paraphrased. Peter would
later refer to this passage again in his comment on 14.23.
195. Lv 17.8–9.
196. A conflation of Lk 17.14 and Mt 8.4.
197. Origen, *Rom.*, 2.13, edited and slightly paraphrased.

slaves or slaves purchased with a price, that the Gentiles who believe in God through Christ are free from laws of this sort.[198]

Also: "Let them first restore the condition of the temple," etc.[199]

[2.17] **But if you...** It is the Gentiles who to you, O Jews, seem distant from the race of the holy fathers and their legacy, since the Lord says to Abraham: "Because your seed shall be named in Isaac,"[200] and moreover they were not instructed in the written law, and thus they labor well, but against you. Because the Apostle makes this known in a certain arrangement [of words] and with angry indignation, he magnifies it, saying: *if you* **call yourself a Jew,** that is, not that Jew who actually exists in imitation of the faithful fathers, but *you call yourself* one only in name, you thus call yourself, namely, after the patriarch Judah or Judas Maccabeus, etc.

Origen says the following:

He does not say "you are," but *you call yourself.* He teaches in what follows that he is truly a Jew who is circumcised *in secret.*[201] But he who is so *openly* so that he may be seen by men is not truly a Jew but is called one. And it says in the Apocalypse: "They who say that they are Jews and are not."[202] He who is truly a Jew takes his name from that Judah of whom it is written: "Judah, your brothers shall praise you,"[203] and the other things that were prophesied about the Savior.[204]

Augustine says on Psalm 71:

They are especially called Jews because Saul, the reprobate and evil king, came from another tribe; later, David came from the tribe of Judah, and the kings always from that time on came from the tribe of Judah. Therefore, they are called Jews. The foreign kings began with Herod. Therefore, when the Lord came, the kingdom of the Jews was overthrown and taken away from the Jews, because they did not wish to recognize the true king. Now see if they should be called Jews. By their own word they withdrew from that name and so they are not worthy to be called Jews, except in the flesh only. They raged against Christ, that is, the offspring of Judah, the seed of David. They said: "We have no king but Caesar."[205] O Jews, (91) if you "have no king but Caesar," then

---

198. Ibid., edited.   199. Ibid., lit.

200. Gn 21.12.   201. Rom 2.28–29.

202. Rv 3.9.   203. Gn 49.8.

204. Origen, *Rom.*, 2.11, edited and paraphrased.

205. Jn 19.15.

the ruler has departed from Judah, and he has come to whom he was
counter-promised. They, therefore, are more truly Jews who became
Christians from the Jews. The true Judea is the church of Christ, which
believes in him who came from the tribe of Judah through Mary.[206]

Haymo says: "'But if you call yourself a Jew,' meaning from
the patriarch Judah," etc.[207]

Ambrose says: "'First to the Jew and to the Greek.' They began to be called Jews from the time of Judas Maccabeus, who,
when defeated, resisted the sacrileges, and with trust in God assembled the people and defended his race."[208] We should note
that in this passage Ambrose does not say that they are called
Jews after Judas Maccabeus but were called such at that time,
particularly since in the other books of the Old Testament they
are not found to have been so named as in the books of the
Maccabees. Even if they were so named after Judas Maccabeus,
they seemed to be so named after Judah the patriarch, since
Judas Maccabeus also was so named after that Judah.

[2.17–21] **And you rest in the law,** so that you do not wear out
from errors, by inquiring what things you are to do, and you are
completely absorbed in zeal for those things, so that you do not
direct it to something else, namely, to the writings of the poets
and philosophers. **And you boast in God,** namely, by haughtily
boasting of the knowledge of God and the law given to you by
him, on account of which law **you know his will,** namely, what
actions are pleasing to him, **and you prove,** that is, you distinguish not only useful things from useless, but even **more useful** from useful. **You are confident,** namely, that you can show to
others the way of righteousness in the commandments of God.
Whether those living in darkness or the foolish and children, he
understands them alike to be blind, and similarly undertakes to
be a **guide** and **light** and **teacher** and **master** for the same, so that
there may be a certain compression of words resulting in their
confusion, not a diverse signification. But whence [the Jew] is
sure that he is a *guide* **to the blind,** that is, sufficient to teach others, he adds: I say that you **have a form of knowledge and truth
from the law,** that is, a true knowledge that can instruct and in-

206. Augustine, *en. Ps.* 75.1.   207. Haymo, *Rom.*, 2.17, *ad lit.*
208. Ambrosiaster, *Rom.*, 1.16.

form others for the purpose of acting well. You, to be sure, (92) are so distinguished and so great according to your own judgment, **you who teach another,** that is, you correct, etc.

[2.21–23] But regarding that which he ought to correct in himself, he adds the following: **You who preach,** namely, from the words of the law, etc.; **Who detest idols,** that is, the forms of likenesses, on account of what is signified, why do you not avoid **sacrilege** on account of itself, because it is evil in itself? A violation of a holy thing is called a sacrilege, especially of those things that belong to the worship of God, for example the temple and the things that pertain to it. In fact, the Jews profaned the temple of God, whether the material and figurative one or the spiritual and true one, by conducting business in the temple made with hands, on account of which they were expelled from there by the Lord;[209] or by crucifying the Lord himself, who said concerning the temple of his own body: "Destroy this temple," etc.[210] **You dishonor God,** that is, you make him contemptible to others, to the best of your ability. He uses a rhetorical device in this passage that is called a repetition, which has the same beginning in diverse passages of the discourse, such as "you who," which is repeated four times.

[2.24] **For [God's] name . . .** Although he had said above *but if you* (singular), now he says **by you** (plural), plainly making known that he introduced the generic person of the Jew as if to convict generally a rebellious people, from which those Jewish converts who were at Rome boasted that they descended. He says that in fact among this people some were accused of theft, or still are, some of adultery, etc.

To continue: I rightly say that *you dishonor,* namely, you people of the Jews, because *by you* **God's** *name,* that is, the knowledge of him that you boast you have, **is blasphemed among the Gentiles,** that is, the unbelievers. For, as Cicero mentions, knowledge is often accustomed to be blamed for a man's vice, as if knowledge teaches how to act wickedly.[211] **Just as it is written,** in the prophet Ezekiel with these words: "My holy name, which you have desecrated among the Gentiles,"[212] that is, you

209. Jn 2.13–16.
210. Jn 2.19.
211. Ps.-Cicero, *Heren.* 2.27.
212. Ezek 20.39.

have caused it to be held in contempt and derision and have cheapened it , although it was most precious in itself.

(93) [2.25] **Circumcision indeed...** Above, the Apostle removed the boasting in the law given [to the Jews] on account of this: that they do not do what the law enjoins, and therefore they are denounced by the law rather than justified. Now, on account of this very thing, that they do not obey the law, he removes the boasting of circumcision, because just as the legislation is of no use to those who receive it unless they keep it, so circumcision is of no use unless they obey the law, with the result that they fulfill the other precepts, such as the precept of circumcision. For he who "has offended in one thing," as another apostle says, "is guilty of all";[213] that is, he is a transgressor or despiser of the whole law, namely, of that which contains all the precepts of God. For since the law enjoins all things simultaneously, not only one, whoever transgresses one does not keep the law, and so through the transgression of every precept he is made responsible for having violated the law. Therefore, fleshly circumcision is of no use for salvation if the law is violated in other things, just as baptism (whose place, as blessed Gregory attests,[214] circumcision once held) does not save if we remain transgressors in other things.

But since circumcision is of no moment in this age (according to what the Apostle says, writing to the Galatians: "but if you are circumcised, Christ is of no use to you";[215] that is, Christ confers nothing useful to you from this sign), it appears that in this passage the Apostle is looking at the first state of the law, when circumcision was useful. Those Jewish converts now boasted about this state of the law, although it had passed on, and was defunct with regard to carnal observances. If the Apostle, looking at his own time, should now say: *Circumcision indeed* **is useful, if you observe the law,** it is as if he should say: circumcision now is useful if it is the spiritual kind rather than the fleshly, the kind that is equally common to the Gentile as to the Jew. Therefore, custody of the law creates a spiritual circumcision, that is,

213. Jas 2.10.
214. Greg. Magn., *moral.* 4.3; cf. Abelard, *Rom.*, 2, in 4.11.
215. Gal 5.2.

a separation from vices that is figured through fleshly circumcision. Such it is, therefore, *if* you keep *the law,* as if he should
say: if circumcision is spiritual, it is of the heart rather than of
the body, because circumcision is a superfluous sign where what
was signified is lacking through negligence.

But if you are a breaker, that is, a transgressor, etc. That small
part of the genital member is called a **foreskin** that those who
circumcise cut off from its top. And it is called a *foreskin* [216] (94)
as if from "trimming before," that is, cutting before, although
"to trim" should not be used in place of "cutting away," as if it
meant "to lop off."[217] Nevertheless, it says in Songs: "The time of
trimming has come,"[218] that is, of lopping-off.[219] But just as circumcision of the flesh signifies circumcision of the heart, that
is, separation from fleshly vices, so the *foreskin* that is retained
indicates the filthiness of fleshly desires. Therefore, the Jews
called the Gentiles who had the foreskin not "uncircumcised,"
that is, filthy ones, but the *uncircumcision* itself, that is, filthiness itself. **Your circumcision,** namely, in your flesh alone, I say,
which you approve, which you make, but which God does not; it
is made *uncircumcision* to you, that is, filthiness in some degree,
since you might rather be convicted as one accused after having
received the sacrament of circumcision and the profession of
the law that is to be observed, if you do not observe it, than if
you had not done this.[220]

[2.26] **If therefore…** He concludes, as if from contraries: inasmuch as your circumcision, that is, the fleshly one, becomes
uncircumcision for you, that is, it defiles and damns you more if
you do not observe the law, therefore **the uncircumcision** of that
Gentile, if he fulfills what is written in the natural law, **is reckoned**
to him by the Lord **as circumcision,** that is, they who have the
bodily foreskin are judged by the divine judgment to be of the
same merit of which the spiritually circumcised are as well. For
he does not repeat here "your circumcision," in order to under-

216. I.e., *praeputium.* Throughout this discussion of circumcision *praeputium*
is translated either as "foreskin" or "uncircumcision," according to the context.

217. *prae putando, praescidendo, putare, incidere, amputare.*

218. Song 2.12.   219. *putatio, amputatio.*

220. I.e, received circumcision.

stand the fleshly one, just as he asserted above, but he simply says *circumcision,* in order to indicate the spiritual one accomplished by God. He even understands the fleshly foreskin, namely, a small part of the body, not the filthiness of the heart, when he says *his foreskin* in the same way as "your circumcision" above. Otherwise he would not have said that *the foreskin* is reckoned *as circumcision.*

Read it in this way: *If the uncircumcised one,* that is, the uncircumcised Gentiles whom you, namely, the Jews, call "the uncircumcision" as if it were a dishonor, **keeps the righteousness of the law** rather than the figures, that is, they fulfill the moral precepts of charity that justify each person, (95) **will not his foreskin,** that is, the Gentiles who have their own foreskins, namely, the fleshly ones with which they were born, be **reckoned** by God as worthy of reward?

[2.27] As was said, for the truly and spiritually circumcised, **uncircumcision,** even by itself, **fulfills the law,** that is, it accomplishes it: for *the fullness of the law,* as will be said later, *is love.*[221] This fulfilling of the law happens by nature, that is, by instruction in the natural law, what we call those two precepts of restraining charity: "That which you do not wish for yourself," etc.[222] **It shall judge you;** that is, it will openly convict the one who is accused, you who neglect to do well, even though you have been instructed in the written law in which you boast; *you,* I say, O Jew, **who are a breaker of the law,** that is, a transgressor **through the letter** that kills,[223] that is, the literal sense and fleshly sign in which you trust, especially in the things that signify, not adhering to what is signified, that is, [adhering] to the figures rather than the things themselves and to the likeness rather than to the truth.

[2.28–29] **For it is not he...** Rightly do I say that *uncircumcision* is reckoned *as circumcision* through the exhibition of good works, and rightly do I say that circumcision becomes uncircumcision through evil works, for although those circumcised **outwardly** in the flesh are called Jews, nevertheless they are not truly Jews, that is, in the heart; but rather were they called pagans above, although in no way are they reckoned Jews or cir-

221. Rom 13.10; *dilectio.*   222. Tb 4.16; Mt 7.12.
223. Cf. 2 Cor 3.6.

cumcised. They are called Jews openly, who in name only and by the nation of Judah are named Jews, acknowledging God outwardly with the voice and withdrawing from him with the mind. Concerning them it is said: "This people honors me with their lips, but their heart is far from me."[224] **But he who is one secretly, is a Jew:** acknowledging God in the heart where God sees, and who tries to serve God, not in the sight of men. **Nor is that circumcision which is outward;** that is, that which is done by hand **in the flesh,** that is, in the removal of the flesh, is not circumcision; that is, it is not the true lopping-off of vices and destruction of lust, but the true **circumcision** is that which is **in the heart,** that is, through which vices and lusts are lopped off from the rational soul. (96) *Circumcision,* I say, occurred **in the spirit, not the letter,** that is, according to the spiritual and mystical sense, not the literal. **Whose praise,** namely, of a Jew or of spiritual circumcision, **is from God** because God makes it acceptable, not men, that is, fleshly men, who understand the law only carnally, not spiritually, and who consider the works rather than the disposition, looking in the face, and not in the heart.

[3.1] **What advantage, therefore...** The Apostle sets against himself the opposition which the Jews could make against the aforesaid reasoning, so that he may destroy it. For the Jews might say: You said that circumcision passes over into uncircumcision, and uncircumcision into circumcision, *therefore what advantage is there* **for the Jew** over the Gentile? That is, what greater benefits does circumcision confer to the Jews than to the Gentiles, who were called *dogs* [225] and unclean? **Or what is the advantage of circumcision,** that is, for the circumcised? This is added as if it were the exposition of what precedes. For, since he said *to the Jew,* only those people could be understood who belong to the tribe of Judah, from whom they were called Jews. And because it says *what advantage?* it could apply as much to good as to evil, and perhaps even more to evil, since he especially reproached the Jews in the preceding passage. But it is the Apostle's custom to accept the Gentiles in their uncircumcision as much as the Jews in their circumcision.

224. Is 29.13; Mt 15.8.
225. Phil 3.2.

[3.2] **Much,** plainly more, of the advantage was conferred from of old by the Lord to the Jew than to the Gentile, **in every way,** that is, in all ways, namely, by instructing them in the law, by strengthening them with countless miracles and benefits, and by rousing them to his love.[226] But this was **first,** that is, the greatest, among the gifts of God, that he gave to them the law, so that they might be instructed not only by the natural law, like the Gentiles, but moreover with the written law; and this is what he says: that that was the *first,* that is, the greatest, benefit, because **the utterances of God were entrusted,** that is, committed, **to them,** in the law or the prophets. Indeed, this gift can teach them and preserve them for eternity.

(97) Note, however, that he does not say " committed," but *entrusted,* as if for the moment this teaching was adapted for them; this indeed was about to pass over to us through the spiritual and correct understanding of it and to cease in its carnal observances, in which the Jews especially trusted. It is as if God is called a trustor of his utterances, for which he requires obedience from these to whom he entrusts them as if they were wages. He calls the words of God *utterances* as if they were outside other kinds of discourse by their excellence, on account of their fruit and health-bringing teaching, that is, of obedience.

[3.3] **For what...?** Should we be concerned, someone might say, about the divine utterances given to that people, since on account of their lack of faith God did not complete the good things promised to them, either concerning the redemption of the human race through his Son, or concerning any promise whatever? The Apostle refutes this in two ways, by showing that not all the people were unbelieving, so that the promises to that people were thoroughly denied, and that God could not break his promises, because *he is true.* Read it in this way: I said well that that is the greatest of the divine utterances, through which he draws his people to himself. For what impedes the divine purpose?**...if some of them did not believe** those utterances, that is, those which were promised and proclaimed to them then, **does not their unbelief,** clearly of those who did not believe, **nullify faith in God,** that is, through which they believed

226. *Amor.*

in God, so that it did not happen that Moses himself, Joshua, and the other faithful ones believed? **May it not be so,** namely, that their faith in these promises that he entrusted to them and which were proclaimed to them then should be nullified or made vain.

[3.4] **But God is true.** I said *may it not be so,* not thoughtlessly but prudently, since *God is true,* that is, fixed or unmoved, in these things that he promises or proclaims. **But every man is a liar,** that is, changeable in his intention, so that his judgment or will may be able to be changed easily.

(98) Perhaps someone asks if Christ's humanity, united to his divinity, might have been able to lie or sin, even though in what was said before about him, *But God is true,* and what is immediately joined to it, *every man is a liar,* the God-man seems excluded, so that *every man is a liar* should be understood only of someone purely human, not of the man who is God. But no one should doubt that the man united to God, after he is united to him or while he is united to him, can in no way sin, just as the one who is predestined, either after or while he is predestined, can not be condemned.

But truly, if it is simply said that that man who is united can in no way sin, anyone can doubt. For if he absolutely can not sin nor do evil, what merit does he have by avoiding the sin which he can in no way commit? or how, even, is it said that he avoids what he in no way can fall into? Therefore, Boethius, in his work *Against Eutyches and Nestorius,* says about the humanity God took to himself: "How can it happen that he assumed the humanity that Adam had before sin, since the will and the inclination to sin could exist in Adam?"[227] Moreover, it is written in praise of the just one: "He who could transgress and did not transgress, who could do evil and did not."[228] "He will dwell on the heights," etc.[229] And indeed this applies to man's free choice, that he may have the power to do both good and evil. Because if Christ did not have this power, it seems that he was deprived of free choice and that he avoided sin by necessity rather than by the will, and that he had this [avoidance of sin] by nature rather than

227. Boethius, *c. Eut.,* 8.   228. Eccli 31.10.
229. Is 33.16.

by grace. For what was conferred by grace to anyone, [it would seem,] came to him by a gift rather than from the property of his own nature; what we have by the gift of another rather than from ourselves should not be said to be both natural and free. Who denies that the man who is united to God, namely, in one person, consists of soul and flesh, even without that union, just as other men can exist in their own nature? Otherwise he would seem to be of lesser strength if he could not subsist by himself like the other men, and had a nature of accident rather than of substance. (99) Because if he could exist by himself, why could he not also sin like the others?

It seems to us, therefore, that in this also, just as in other things, we should carefully consider the significations of the propositions, when, for example, "possible" or "necessary" is posited with a qualification, and when it is predicated simply, that is, without any qualification adjoined to it.

Certainly it is true, given that it is stated without qualification, that it is possible for him, who is predestined and is going to be saved, to be damned, since it is entirely possible that he was not predestined nor to be saved. With the qualifier, however, it is not true to say that it is possible for him to be damned even though he is predestined or even though he is to be saved. Thus also it is possible that he who was mutilated has two feet, since every man is a biped, and it is possible for the one who is blind to see; nevertheless it is not possible after he has been mutilated or after he is blind. Otherwise, it might be possible for a regression to occur from privation to possession, which is entirely false.[230] Thus also it is perhaps not absurd for us to allow in the sense with no qualification that it is possible for that human, who is united to God, to sin, but it is not possible after he is united and while he is united. Truly it is impossible in every way for Christ, God and man simultaneously, to sin, since the very name of Christ describes the union of God and man. And thus the words *every man is a liar* seem to be a true proposition in every way.

230. Cf. Aristotle, *Categories*, 13a30, from the version of Boethius, ed. Minio-Paluello (Aristoteles-Latinus I, 1–5) 35: "change occurs from quality to privation, from privation to quality is indeed impossible."

As it is written: That you may be justified… He shows through the authority of the Psalm how God is true in keeping his promises and unwavering in his purpose. For the Lord had promised to David that his Christ would be born from his seed.[231] This promise seemed to be voided entirely after David's adultery, and it was judged entirely improper that the Son of God should receive flesh later on from the seed of such a sinful man; and so it was necessary that God, who had promised this to him, should be made a liar. Considering that this in no way (100) could happen, he who had done grave wrong said, "I have sinned against you alone,"[232] that is, against the honor of you alone who rightly set iniquity in order and turn all things to your glory, "and I have done evil in your sight," that is, you know, to whom nothing lies hidden, so that through this it may be clear how righteous you are, since you know that I do not deserve to have you keep your promises to me; nevertheless, because you are righteous and true, you cannot frustrate your own promise. For if this sin lay hidden to God, no reason would appear why he did not fulfill the promise. But now, since he knows that the sin is committed and that the sinner deserves the opposite, nevertheless he keeps the constancy of his truth unmoved, namely, by fulfilling his promises.

That you may be justified **in your words;** that is, that *you may be justified* by carrying out your words concerning the promises which you made to me; that is, that you may appear righteous and true **and may prevail,** namely, over human judgment, **when you are judged** by men, that is, you are accused of a lie as if you could not later on fulfill your promise on account of my crimes.

[3.5] **But if…** The Apostle himself introduces opposition to the aforementioned things, as if he should say: it is said that God is justified, that is, he appears righteous and true especially on account of sins, namely, since they cannot hinder that promise of his; indeed, he even converts them to his glory. But if our sins, as was said in the aforementioned example from David, **commend the righteousness of God,** that is, they contribute to the praise and glory of his truth, **what shall we say?** That is, what

231. 2 Sm 7.8–16; 11.1–27.
232. Ps 51.6 (Vg. 50.6).

could we respond to the following objection, which says: **Is God unjust, who inflicts wrath?** That is, the vengeance on account of the sins which, as was said, commend his *righteousness,* that is, do they show him to be especially praiseworthy with regard to the unchangeable purpose of his truth? And since the Apostle does not object to this in his own person, as if it did not seem to him that God acted unfairly in this, he adds: **I speak as a man,** that is, as a carnal animal, who does not taste "the things which are of God,"[233] not as a spiritual man "who judges everything," that is, who possesses the just judgment of reason both in divine things and in human.

[3.6] And therefore he says, **May it not be so,** namely, that we should accept that God acts unjustly (101) by punishing the sins which also contribute to his glory, so that, although sins are not good, nevertheless it is good that sins exist. Therefore, Augustine says in his *Enchiridion:* "Nothing happens unless the omnipotent one wills it to happen, either by allowing it to happen or by doing it himself. We should not doubt that God does well, even by allowing evil to happen. For he does not allow this except by his righteous judgment. And indeed, everything which is righteous is good."[234] Again, "For unless this good existed in order that evil things might exist, in no way would they be allowed to exist by the omnipotent good."[235] **Otherwise,** that is, if it were other than as we say, that is, if God acted unfairly by inflicting vengeance for sins, **how would he judge the world,** that is, everyone, good as well as bad, by repaying them for their merits either with glory or with punishment?

[3.7] **For if the truth...** He comes back again to the objection made above as if commending it, namely, that God rightly seems unfair in punishing sins if they commend that very righteousness of his, because they should not now be reckoned as sins but as good works that commend his truth. *For if the truth* **of God abounded to his glory by my falsehood,** that is, the immovability of his truth is made more praiseworthy by the changeability and inconstancy of my profession; although I lie to him, nevertheless he cannot lie to me. **Why am I still judged?** As long

233. 1 Cor 2.14–15.   234. Augustine, *ench.* 95–96.
235. Ibid., c. 96.

as that which I do, **as a sinner,** contributes to his glory, that is, by what reason should those things I do be reckoned as sins?

[3.8] And why **should we** not rather **do evil that good may come;** that is, why should we not sin, so that God may be glorified by our sins? **Just as we are slandered** by some, **and just as some assert that we say,** namely, myself and other spiritual men who even say that evil things are so well ordered that they contribute to the glory of God. Therefore, even that aforementioned doctor says in Book 11 of *The City of God,* when he speaks of the goodness of God and the malice of the devil: "Just as God (102) is the best creator of good natures, so is he the most righteous arranger of evil wills."[236] Again, in the same passage, he says of the devil: "When God created him, he was not ignorant of his future malice, and he foresaw the good things which he would do from his evil actions."[237] Again, a little later: "For God would not have created anyone (I do not speak of angels), even among men, whom he knew beforehand would be evil, unless he equally knew to what uses of good things he would adapt them."[238] He says in the *Enchiridion:* "For the omnipotent God, because he is the highest good, would not allow anything evil in any way in his works, unless he was even so omnipotent and good that he would even create good from evil."[239]

Whose [condemnation is just], namely, of those slandering us, that is, not so much for speaking their opinion as for blaspheming against us. For it is clear that the evil things also were so well ordered by God, that even the pagan philosopher Plato openly professed, "For nothing comes into being that is not preceded by a legitimate cause and reason."[240]

[3.9] **What then?** I said that the condemnation of those slandering us was just; from this we seem especially to have commended ourselves as if we are of such a kind by our own merits that nothing among us should be slandered. *What then?* Can it be said that **we surpass** those who will be justly condemned; that is, are we more worthy than they by our own merits and our own

236. Aug., *civ. Dei* 11.17.   237. Ibid.
238. Ibid., 11.18; Abelard, *TChr* 1.2.
239. Aug., *ench.*, ch. 11.
240. Plato, *Tim.* 28a, from Calcidius's verson; see Abelard, *Rom.,* 4 (9.21).

virtue? **In no way,** but if we have any good in us, it is from God rather than from ourselves, just as in what follows he says that *it is not of the one who wills neither of the one who runs, but of God who has mercy,*[241] because his mercy, rather than our strength, is sufficient for salvation, since by ourselves we are all together culpable, just as we showed above that all are without excuse, Jews as much as Gentiles. And this is what he says: **For we have alleged,** that is, we have ascribed, as it were, a cause by asserting that **Jews** as much as **Greeks,** whom he concludes are wiser, **are all under sin;** that is, they are accused and doomed to punishment (103) as transgressors. And here he returns to a general invective, gathering testimonies from the scriptures, from which he proves that all are equally guilty and inexcusable.

[3.10] **Just as it is written,** namely, in Psalm 13, **There is no one righteous,** etc. The Psalm where these testimonies are contained for us makes, as it were, a general invective against all who, not knowing the time of their visitation, held as an abomination [the belief] that God became incarnate and suffered for the sake of human redemption. Therefore, the same Apostle says the same thing elsewhere: "But we preach Christ crucified, a stumbling block to the Jews, and foolishness to the Gentiles."[242] Therefore, the Psalm says: "The fool has said," that is, "the natural man who does not perceive the things which are of the Spirit of God,"[243] namely, concerning that hidden mystery of our redemption, since he would examine the weakness of assumed humanity: this "God does not exist." "Has said," not with words only, as Peter did when he denied [the Lord],[244] but also with the heart, because [the fool] so believed.

[*There is no one righteous,*] that is, there are very few, almost no one, who are righteous, that is, rendering to each one the things which are his. For may it not be so that we should believe that the Church will not persevere from her first election to the very end at least among some of the faithful, which before the law [contained] many people and after the law more, such as he who composed this Psalm, and gathered numerous others under grace. Therefore, also in the advent of the Lord, when

---

241. Rom 9.16.
243. 1 Cor 2.14.

242. 1 Cor 1.23.
244. Cf. Mt 26.34–75.

Israel for the most part was held in blindness, we read that there were some remaining, such as Simeon, Anna, and the Mother of the Lord herself with her husband Joseph, and also the father and mother of John the Baptist, with him. But often when it says "all" or "none," it is not universally applicable but is said about the largest part, just as if it should say about the city in which there are few good people: All who live there are evil, or, there are no good people there.

On this account, in his letter *To Pope Damasus*,[245] Jerome says concerning the prodigal son:

"My son, you are always with me, and all that I have is yours."[246] Does that include (104) angels and thrones? By "all," understand the prophets and the divine utterances. According to what we have often expounded, "all" does not refer to the whole but to the greatest part, so that "all have turned away,"[247] and "all who came before me were thieves and robbers,"[248] and "I have become all things to all people, so that I might win over all,"[249] and "They all look after their own interests, not those of Jesus Christ."[250]

[3.11] But as to why *there is no one righteous*, he adds: because **There is no one who understands God** or **seeks after** him. *There is no one who understands God,* that is, no one who attends to his promises or to lesser things, because "the natural man does not perceive the things which are of the Spirit of God,"[251] but he is "just like a horse and mule who have no understanding."[252] And because *there is no one who understands God,* he does not know how to seek through penance after him whom he lost through negligence.

[3.12] He adds to this negligence, saying: **All have turned away;** that is, when they abandoned God, they turned their zeal to the world so that they might condemn eternal things in place of temporal ones, and so *all* alike, Jews as well as Gentiles, **have become useless** to themselves. For no one is so unjust that he becomes utterly useless, since God even uses evil people for the best, as was said, just as [he used] the wickedness of Judas or the

---

245. See Jerome, *Ep.* 21.
246. Lk 15.31.
247. Ps 13.3.
248. Jn 10.8.
249. Cf. 1 Cor 9.22.
250. Phil 2.21.
251. 1 Cor 2.14.
252. Ps 31.9.

devil. For in one and the same act, God the Father and the Son and Judas cooperated, because the Father handed over the Son, and the Son handed over himself, and Judas handed over the Lord. That handing over, which Judas brought about, brought about the common redemption of all people. Through the preaching of Peter the Apostle, some were converted and saved, and the Lord turned the wickedness of Judas into the salvation of all people. The divine grace used the evil of the one as much as the good of the other to our greater advantage. Who will also doubt that the wickedness of the devil is always disposed by God for the good, since he also does nothing without God's permission, either by punishing the guilty or testing the righteous or doing whatever? Therefore, his power can only be righteous just as his will can only be unrighteous, who has his power from God but his will from himself. "For there is no power except from God," the Apostle himself attests later on.[253] Therefore, the Truth said to the unjust governor: (105) "You would have no power over me unless it were given to you from above."[254] Therefore, those who do evil should be understood to be useless to themselves rather than utterly useless, since in the order of things the divine disposition permits nothing to be done uselessly or superfluously, as has been shown.

But how *all have turned away* or from what they have turned, namely, from what good work, he adds, saying: **There is no one who does good,** that is, who works well and fulfills what he should. For although the handing-over of the Lord that was done by Judas, and at the same time, as was said, by the Father or by the Son, may seem a good thing, nevertheless Judas did not do that deed well because he committed it with a perverse intention, that is, from the desire for money.[255] For the Lord taught that all works should be weighed by the intention when he said: "If your eye were simple," etc.[256] Otherwise, the work of Judas, in which the Father as much as the Son worked mercifully, would also have to be called a good work.

There is not even one. It is a repetition of what was said before, namely, of that which was said: *there is none who does good,*

---

253. Rom 13.1.
255. Jn 12.6.

254. Jn 19.11.
256. Mt 6.22; Lk 11.34.

so that the qualifier might be supplied lest the saying be taken generally. Therefore, it is as if he should say, *there is no one,* I say, *who does good* until he comes by believing and by joining himself through love[257] to him who truly is one and unchangeable by nature and unique through eminence, that is, to God or to Christ, who is "the one mediator between God and man";[258] through faith in whom he argues in what follows that we are saved without the works of the law. It can even be understood in this way: *there is none who does good, even one,* as if he should say: there is scarcely anyone who does good; that is, there is almost no one who does good. For there is almost no one where one only remains.

[3.10–19] **…is an open sepulcher.** These three following verses which are contained in our Psalter, are by no means read continuously in the Hebrew, according to Origen or Jerome. Therefore, Origen says about this epistle: "In some of the Latin examples those testimonies that follow are found in order in the thirteenth Psalm, but in almost all the Greek examples, no more in the thirteenth Psalm, (106) than up to, *There is no one who does good, not even one.* But what the Apostle also says: *Just as it is written, there is no one righteous, there is no one who understands, no one who seeks after God,* is not found in the Psalm with the same words, but it is written thus: *The Lord looked from heaven upon the sons of men that he might see if there is anyone who understands or seeks after God.*[259] And the words, *There is no one righteous,* I think that he takes from that passage: *There is no one who does good, not even one.*[260] And you will find the words, *Their throat is an open sepulcher, they act deceitfully with their tongues,* in the fifth Psalm.[261] *The venom of asps is under their lips,* I think has been taken from one of the Psalms, with the words changed.[262] *Whose mouth is full of cursing and bitterness,* seems to have been taken from the ninth Psalm.[263] *Their feet are quick to shed blood,* you will find either in Isaiah or Proverbs.[264] But *Sadness and misfortune are in their paths, and the way of peace they have not known,* I do not at all remember where

---

257. *Amor.*
258. 1 Tm 2.5.
259. Ps 13.2.
260. Ps 13.1.
261. Ps 5.10.
262. Ps 139.4.
263. Ps 9B.7.
264. Is 59.7; Prv 1.16.

it is written;[265] I suspect nevertheless that it can be found in one of the prophets. But in the Psalms it is written: *There is no fear of God before their eyes.*[266] But he seems to have assembled these witnesses so that he might show that what he alleges, that *Jews and Greeks are all under sin,*[267] he proclaims not so much as his own view as that of Scripture." "*All are under sin* should be understood to have been said concerning those who certainly are taught either by the natural or by the written law not to sin."[268]

Jerome, in the preface of Book 16 of his *Commentary on Isaiah,* says to Eustochium:

You brought a minor question about the eight verses of Psalm Thirteen that the Apostle adopted, which are read in the churches and are not contained in the Hebrew: [*Their throat is*] *an open sepulcher,* etc. . . . I considered this witness both from the Psalms and from Isaiah to be (107) woven together. For the first two verses, [*Their throat is*] *an open sepulcher,* etc., are from the Fifth Psalm. But that which follows, *The venom of asps is under their lips,* is from the One Hundred Thirty-Ninth Psalm. Again, the saying *Whose mouth is full of cursing and bitterness,* is taken from the Ninth Psalm. But the three little lines which follow, *Their feet are quick to shed blood, sadness and misfortune are in their paths, and the way of peace they have not known,* I have found in Isaiah. The last verse, that is, the eighth, *There is no fear of God before their eyes,* is at the beginning of the Thirty-Fifth Psalm.[269]

Again he says:

Finally, all the Greek commentators, who left to us commentaries consisting of their learning on the Psalms, observe and pass by these lines, acknowledging with certainty that they are not contained in the Hebrew nor are they in the seventy translators,[270] but in the common edition which is called "koine" in Greek, and which has spread into all the world.[271]

But now let us follow the text.

[3.12] It is said: **All have turned away,** and **there is none who does good,** and not only have they *turned away,* but they

---

265. Is 59.7–8.   266. Ps 35.2.

267. Rom 3.9.

268. Adapted from Origen, *Rom.* 3.2.

269. Jerome, *Is., Praefatio libri XVI, ad Eustochium.*

270. That is, the translators of the Septuagint.

271. Jerome, *Is., Praefatio libri XVI, ad Eustochium.*

even strive so that they might cause others to turn away and especially cause injury, as if it is not enough that they alone are condemned but they seek a multitude as a partner as if for self-defense.

[3.13] **Their throat,** because it is an instrument for forming or extending the voice, signifies a word which is emitted through the throat. Therefore, their word, inducing to evil, is like **an open sepulcher** on account of a wickedness conceived by the mind, as if from the stench of a shut-up corpse corrupting others and offending the noses of those standing nearby, that is, confusing and infecting their natural discernment. **With their tongues.** It is, as it were, a parabolical exposition of what was said before, since he says that they speak deceitfully, that is, against their conscience to commend those things to which they persuade, or to reproach those things from which they dissuade. **The venom of asps,** which Moses himself also calls "incurable,"[272] and through this witnesses that it is worse than the others, deadly, that is, mortally sinful; he means the sins which like (108) venom inflict others with their persuasions. But these, namely, the sins to which they persuade, are said to be **under their lips;** that is, they are so hidden in their shrewd words that they might not be able to be noticed by the hearers.

We can even understand by "incurable venom of asps" that unforgivable sin against the Holy Spirit,[273] when someone, through envy or desire, attributes to the devil some of those works which he does not doubt are done by God, just as some of the Jews did, who, so that they might turn the people away from Christ, censured [Christ's] works as diabolical; which [works] they did not doubt were done by the Spirit of God, that is, divine grace, and therefore they were said to sin against the Spirit of God, that is, the gift of divine grace, since they knowingly attributed to the devil something for which they should have glorified God, lying against their own conscience. Indeed, this sin, even if it could be blotted out through penance, nevertheless is an award of punishment by divine judgment, so that no one may be restored in this fall by coming to their senses, and

272. Dt. 32.33.
273. Mt 12.31–32; Lk 12.10.

therefore it is called unforgivable. But this sin lay hidden *under their lips;* it did not appear in their lips because, while they thus offended against their own conscience, they held something else in the heart than what they revealed with their mouth.

[3.14] **Whose mouth,** that is, both for himself and for those who acquiesce, he gained from the Lord cursing and bitterness, namely, that concerning which it is said through the prophet: "The voice of that day is bitter; the strong man shall face tribulations then."[274] Such a mouth is **full of cursing and bitterness,** as if it should be said, [full] of that bitter cursing with which it is said to the reprobate at their condemnation, "Away, you cursed, to the eternal fire."[275] There is indeed another cursing, as it were sweet and paternal, when we throw a curse upon the anathematized for their correction rather than for condemnation.

[3.15] **Their feet are swift to shed [blood];** that is, they have a strong inner disposition toward murder, even if they are not allowed to complete the work. For the foot with which we march signifies the inner disposition, or will, with which we are led to the work.

(109) [3.16] **Ruin and misery,** that is, miserable ruin, is **in their paths,** that is, in the works through which one is prepared[276] for eternal death, even destroying others with themselves and even corrupting them through their examples, so that they may be destroyed like the dust which the wind casts out from the face of the earth; that is, diabolical temptation drives here and there and casts them out from the steadfastness of the land of the living.

[3.17] **And the way of peace;** that is, they are utterly destroyed by condemnation in their ways because **they have not known** the way of God, that is, Christ, through whom, as mediator between God and men, we have received peace and been reconciled to God,[277] who "is our peace," so that, as the same Apostle says, "he made both into one."[278] He also said about himself: "I am the

---

274. Zeph 1.14.   275. Mt 25.41.
276. Buytaert; Peppermüller reads "hastened."
277. Cf. 1 Tm 2.5; Col 1.20; Rom 5.10; 2 Cor 5.18–19.
278. Eph 2.14.

way";[279] "I am the door; if anyone enters through me, he shall be saved."[280] Indeed, *they have not known* this *way,* that is, Christ, and they disdained him in accordance with the weakness of his flesh or believed him to be mere man, and on account of this they did not revere him as God. Neither did they believe John, who warned about him and said, "Now the axe is laid at the root of the tree. For every tree that does not produce fruit," etc.[281]

[3.18] And this is what he adds: **There is no fear of God [before their eyes],** that is, before their fleshly eyes, with which they perceived his weakness. It was done so that they might not fear him as God, since only the weakness of his humanity appeared, not the majesty of his divinity.

The first book ends; the second begins.

279. Jn 14.6.   280. Jn 10.9.
281. Mt 3.10.

BOOK TWO

  UT WE KNOW [that whatever the law says, it says] ... The Apostle returns to the invective against the Jews, so that just as he took away from them boasting in circumcision, he also takes away boasting in the law or any carnal observances, lest perhaps he seem to have especially commended the law when he said, *First because the utterances of God were credited to them.* First, he takes away their boasting in the law by proving that they are accused by the law rather than justified.

To continue: I introduced testimonies from the law, <that is, from the Old Testament,>[1] through which I might demonstrate that all are guilty, namely, both Jews and Gentiles. But we know that the Jews are especially accused by these things which the law says to them alone, not concerning them alone, although it was given to and imposed upon them alone. And this is what he says: *But we know,* etc., as if he should say: although we might also gather the aforementioned testimonies against the Gentiles from the law, nevertheless we know that the law was not spoken to those to whom it was not given, although it was spoken concerning them; but **to these** only **who are in the law,** that is, they are bound and held fast by the profession of the received law.

We must note that sometimes only the five books of Moses are properly comprehended by the term "law," and sometimes the entire Old Testament, as in this passage. Therefore, Augustine says in Book 15 of *On the Trinity,* "Sometimes all the utterances of the Old Testament [are meant] by the term 'law,' but other times the law which was given through Moses is properly meant."[2]

So that every mouth may be closed; that is, it is restrained

---

1. *Lectio abaelardi,* found in *mOR.*
2. Augustine, *Trin.* 15.17.30, paraphrased and edited.

and it falls silent from its self-glorification and is not opened except to glorify God, since of course we understood that the greatest glory of that peculiar people[3] of God, which they used to have from the law, believing that they are justified through their works, should be reckoned of no account. And thus it is **subjected to God;** that is, it humbles itself, (111) taking nothing for granted from its own boasting, which was even taken away from those who appeared great before God.

[3.20] **Because by the works of the law,** that is, its bodily observances, which that people especially paid attention to, for example circumcision, sacrifices, the observance of the Sabbath and of the other figural commandments of this kind, **no one,** that is, no one who fulfills those things carnally only, and not spiritually, **shall be justified in his sight,** that is, with God, although in the sight of men, that is, the human judgment that judges concerning exterior and visible things, such people are counted as righteous.

For through the law [comes the knowledge of sin]. This refers to two things said earlier. To that passage that says, *So that every mouth may be closed and [the whole world may be] subjected,* etc., he adds *For through the law;* to that other passage, *because by the works,* etc., he adds, *But now, without [the law],* etc. Continue in this way: Why should men be restrained from self-glorification through the law? Because through it they are especially rendered inexcusable concerning their sins, which they recognized through it rather than part with them, indeed they even increased, as shall be said further on: *So that through the commandment sin might become sinful beyond measure.*[4]

[3.21] **But now...** I said that no one shall be justified before God through the particular works of the written law, that is, those figurative commandments that the natural law does not know. But *now,* that is, in the time of grace, **the righteousness of God,** that is, what God approves and through which we are justified with God, that is, charity, **is made manifest,** namely, through the teaching of the Gospels, **without the law,** that is, those carnal and particular observances of the law. Neverthe-

3. Cf. Dt 7.6; 14.2; 26.18.
4. Rom 7.13.

less, that *righteousness,* I say, **was testified to by the law and the prophets,** which also anticipated it.

[3.22] On what this righteousness truly depends he immediately adds, saying, **But the righteousness of God...** He says that it is **faith in Christ** which we have from him, either by believing in him or believing him or believing on him.[5] Therefore, when he also added **[to all and upon all] who believe,** he did not add any of these [distinctions], so that it may apply to all equally. By the faith that we have concerning Christ, charity (112) is increased in us, because through this which we hold fast, that God has united our nature to himself in Christ, and by suffering in that nature, he has shown us that greatest charity, concerning which he himself says, *No one has greater love than this,* etc.;[6] for his sake we cling both to him and to our neighbor by the indestructible bond of love.[7] Therefore, it is also written further on, *Who therefore shall separate us from the charity of God? Tribulation?* etc.; and again, *For I am certain that neither death,* etc.[8] *Righteousness,* I say, dwells **upon all** the faithful, in their higher part, that is, in the soul, where only love[9] can exist, not by the exhibition of exterior works.

For there is no [distinction]. Rightly did I say *upon all* equally, namely, both Gentiles and Jews, because there is no difference between them by virtue of this *righteousness of God through faith in Christ,* just as there once was by virtue of the works of the law, because, just as all have sinned, so they are justified indiscriminately through this most high grace shown to us by God.

[3.23] And this is what he says: **For all have sinned and need the glory of God;** that is, they have a need as if from an obligation to glorify God.

[3.24] **They are justified freely,** that is, because they are justified, not by their preceding merits, but **by his grace,** that is, God's, "who first loved us."[10] What that grace may be, that is, his free and spiritual gift, he adds, saying, **through** our **redemption** made through Christ.

---

5. "...eum sive ei vel in eum credendo."
6. Jn 15.13; *dilectio.*　　　7. *Amor.*
8. Rom 8.35, 38.　　　9. *Dilectio.*
10. 1 Jn 4.10; *diligere.*

[3.25] **Whom God** the Father **put forth** for us **as an atonement,** that is, a reconciler, **in his blood,** that is, through his death. And because this atonement is put forth, that is, established, by God not for everyone but only for those who believe, he adds **through faith,** because this reconciliation extends only to those who believed and waited for it. **To demonstrate his righteousness,** that is, his charity, which, as was said, justifies us with him, that is, to show us his love or to teach us how much we ought to love him,[11] *who did not spare his own Son* for us.[12] **On account of the forgiveness,** that is, that through this righteousness, that is, charity, we may obtain the forgiveness of sins, (113) just as also the Truth said through itself concerning the blessed sinner, "Her many sins are forgiven, because she loved much";[13] I say that forgiveness was obtained, even, I say, of preceding offenses.

[3.26] **In the forbearance of God,** that is, on account of the patience of God, who does not immediately punish the guilty and destroy sinners but waits long that they may return through penance and cease from sin, and thus they may obtain leniency. **To demonstrate . . .** First, he had simply said *to demonstrate his righteousness;* now he adds **at this time,** namely, in the time of grace, that is, of love[14] rather than of fear. When, therefore, he says **his righteousness,** that is, God's own, *at this time,* through that which is added: *at this time,* namely, of grace, he teaches openly how he first understood righteousness, that is, the charity which is applicable to the men of our time, that is, the time of grace, as if it were our own.

The words *in the forbearance of God* can refer to what follows, that is, to that which is added, *to demonstrate his righteousness at this time,* so that the sense may be that God held back or delayed in the preceding time for this purpose, that he might manifest his righteousness, which we have mentioned, that is, his charity, *at this time* **so that he may be righteous** by his will **and the one who justifies** by what he does, that is, that he may also wish to fulfill through Christ what he had promised, namely, concern-

---

11. "show us his love . . . ought to love him": *dilectio, diligere.*
12. Rm 8.32.   13. Lk 7.47; *diligere.*
14. *Amor.*

ing our redemption or justification, and that, just as he wished, he may complete the work. [...who justifies] **him who by faith belongs to Jesus Christ,** that is, who believes in him as Jesus, that is, the Savior, through this: that he is the Christ, that is, God and man.

Question

The greatest question in this passage imposes itself, namely, what is that redemption of ours through the death of Christ? or, how does the Apostle say that we are justified in his blood, we who seem worthy of a greater punishment, because we, unjust servants, committed that deed on account of which the innocent Lord was murdered?

First, therefore, it seems we must ask by what necessity God (114) assumed humanity in order to redeem us by dying according to the flesh, or from whom he redeemed us who held us captive either by justice or by power, and with what justice he freed us from that one's power, or if you will, what price did he give which the other wished to receive, so that he might relinquish us?

And indeed it is said that he redeemed us from the power of the devil who, through the transgression of the first man (who subjected himself to him by obeying voluntarily), also possessed all his posterity by a certain right and always would, unless a liberator should come. But since he freed only the elect, how did the devil possess them either in this age or, more than now, in the future? Did the devil torment that poor man who rested in Abraham's bosom, just as he did the condemned rich man, although he tortured him less?[15] or did he even hold absolute power over Abraham himself and the other elect? How did that wicked torturer hold absolute power over him who was mentioned to have been borne by the angels into the bosom of Abraham? Abraham himself testifies concerning him, saying, "But now he is comforted here, and you are tormented," and moreover he asserts that "a great abyss has been established" between the elect and the reprobate, so that in no way can these pass over to those; still less does the devil, more vile than all,

15. Lk 16.19–31.

have power there where no unjust person has place or even passage. What right, even, could the devil have to possess a man, unless perhaps because, with the Lord allowing it or even handing him over, he had received him for the purpose of tormenting him? For, if a servant wished to desert his lord and subject himself to the control of another, is he permitted to do this, so that the lord may not seek him and bring him back by right? Who doubts that if the servant of a certain lord should lead his fellow-servant astray with his persuasions and cause him to turn away from obedience to his own lord, how much more (115) should the one leading astray be accused before his lord than the one led? and how unjust is it that he who led another astray should, from that time on, deserve to have an advantage or authority over the one he led astray, who, even if he first had rights in respect to him, deserved to lose that right by this very wickedness of his act of leading astray? For it is written, "He deserves to lose his advantage who abuses the authority entrusted to him."[16] Because if one should be set over another by these fellow-servants and should be about to receive power over him, by no means would it be proper that the more worthless one be put in charge, who has no right to preference at all, but it might be more agreeable to reason that he who is led astray might employ the chastisement of vengeance against him who injured him by leading him astray. Furthermore, the devil could not give the immortality which he promised to man as a result of his transgression,[17] so that by this he might be able to hold him fast by some right.

Therefore, by these reasons it seems to be proved that the devil, through his seduction, obtained no right over man, whom he seduced, unless perhaps, as we have said, as far as it concerns the permission of the Lord, who had handed man over to the devil for punishment as if to a jailer or torturer. For he had not sinned except against his Lord, whose obedience he had forsaken. If, therefore, the Lord wished to pardon sin for him, just as was done for the Virgin Mary and as Christ did for many before his Passion, as was said concerning Mary Magdalene,[18] and

16. Gratian, *Decret.*, cap. 63, causa XI.
17. Gn 3.5.   18. Cf. Lk 8.2.

as was written when he said to the paralytic, "Believe me, son, your sins are forgiven";[19] if therefore, I say, the Lord wished to forgive a man's transgression without the Passion and to say to his torturer, "I do not want you to punish him any more," how could the torturer justly complain who, as was shown, had received no right to torture except by the Lord's permission? If, therefore, the Lord had ceased to permit this, no right would have remained for the torturer; to him who complains or mutters against the Lord, it would be fit that the Lord answer him immediately, "Or is your eye bad because I am good?"[20]

(116) The Lord did no injustice to the devil when he received clean flesh from the sinful mass and humanity devoid of every sin. This man did not obtain this by merits that he might be conceived, born, and persevere without sin, but through the grace of the Lord who receives him. Could this same grace free other men from punishment if he wished to forgive their sins? For when their sins were forgiven, on account of which they were being punished, no explanation appears to suffice to punish them further. Therefore, he who showed such grace to man that he united him to himself in a person, could he not surpass the lesser, namely, by forgiving sins for him? What necessity, therefore, or what reason or what need was there, since his divine compassion could free man from the devil by a command alone? What need was there, I say, for the Son of God, for the sake of our redemption, when he received flesh, to endure so many great fasts, reproaches, lashes, spitting, and finally the most violent and shameful death of the cross that he might even endure the cross with sinners?[21]

How does the Apostle say that we are justified or reconciled to God through the death of his Son,[22] who should have been all the more angry with man because men forsook him so much more in crucifying his Son, than in transgressing his first commandment in paradise with the taste of one apple?[23] For

19. Mt 9.2.   20. Mt 20.15.

21. Cf. William of St. Thierry, *disp*.7; Bernard of Clairvaux, *Ep*. 190.8; Mt 27.38, 44; Mk 15.27; Lk 23.33, 39.

22. Rom 3.24–25.

23. Cf. William of St. Thierry, *disp*. 7; Bernard of Clairvaux, *Ep*. 190.8; Gn 3.16–19.

where sins were multiplied the more by men, the more just it
was for God to be angry with men. Because if that sin of Adam
was so great that it could not be atoned for except by the death
of Christ, how shall that murder which was committed against
Christ be atoned for? (117) or so many great crimes committed
against him or his followers?[24] Did the death of the innocent
Son please God the Father so greatly that through it he is reconciled to us, we who perpetrated this by sinning, on account
of which the innocent Lord was murdered? Unless this became
the greatest sin, could he forgive it much more easily? Unless
evils were multiplied, could he do so great a good?[25]

Are we also made more righteous in this through the death
of the Son of God than we were before, that we should now
be freed from punishment?[26] To whom was the ransom of his
blood given that we might be redeemed, unless to him in whose
power we were, that is, as was said, God, who had delivered us
to his torturer? For it is not the torturers but their lords who fix
or receive ransom for captives. How did he release the captives
with this ransom, if he himself beforehand demanded or established this ransom so that he might release the captives? How
very cruel and unjust it seems that someone should require the
blood of an innocent person as a ransom, or that in any way it
might please him that an innocent person be slain, still less that
God should have so accepted the death of his Son that through
it he was reconciled to the whole world.[27]

These and similar things seem to us to inspire a not insignificant question, namely, concerning our redemption and justification through the death of our Lord Jesus Christ.

Answer

Nevertheless it seems to us that in this we are justified in the
blood of Christ and reconciled to God, that it was through this
matchless grace shown to us that his Son received our nature,
and in that nature, teaching us both by word and by example,
persevered to the death and bound us to himself even more

---

24. Bernard of Clairvaux, *Ep.* 190.8.
25. Ibid.   26. Anonymous, *cap. haer.* 4.3.
27. Bernard of Clairvaux, *Ep.* 190.8; cf. 2 Cor 5.19.

through love,[28] so that when we have been kindled by so great a benefit of divine grace, true charity might fear to endure nothing for his sake. We do not doubt that this benefit kindled the ancient fathers, expecting this through faith, in the supreme love[29] of God just as it kindled the men of the time of grace,[30] (118) since it is written, "And they who went before him and they who followed him cried out, saying, 'Hosanna to the son of David,'" etc.[31] Each one is also made more righteous after the Passion of Christ than before; that is, he loves[32] God more, because the completed benefit kindles him in love[33] more than a hoped-for benefit.

Therefore, our redemption is that supreme love[34] in us through the Passion of Christ,[35] which not only frees us from slavery to sin, but gains for us the true liberty of the sons of God,[36] so that we may complete all things by his love[37] rather than by fear. He showed us such great grace, than which a greater cannot be found, by his own word: "No one," he says, "has greater love[38] than this: that he lays down his life for his friends."[39] Concerning this love[40] the same person says elsewhere, "I have come to send fire on the earth, and what do I desire except that it burn?"[41] He witnesses, therefore, that he has come to increase this true liberty of charity among men. Carefully considering this, the Apostle says later on *that the charity of God is poured out in our hearts, through the Holy Spirit who was given to us. For why did Christ, etc.;*[42] and again, *But may God commend his charity in us, in that while...,* etc.[43] We will expound this more fully in its own place.

But now briefly, as far as it pertains to the brevity of the exposition concerning the means of our redemption, this seems to us to suffice. If anything is missing, however, we reserve it for our more thorough treatise, *The Tropologies.*[44]

28. *Amor.*					29. *Amor.*
30. Anon., *cap. haer.* 4.4.			31. Cf. Mk 11.9; Mt 21.9.
32. *Diligere.*					33. *Amor.*
34. *Dilectio.*					35. Bernard of Clairvaux, *Ep.* 190.9.
36. Cf. Rom 8.21.				37. *Amor.*
38. *Dilectio.*					39. Jn 15.13.
40. *Amor.*					41. Lk 12.49.
42. Rom 5.5–6.				43. Rom 5.8.
44. This work has not come down to us, although parts of it may be found in the anonymous *cap. haer.,* ch. 4.

[3.27] **Where, therefore, is...** I said that without the law the righteousness of God is now manifested through faith in Christ equally upon all who believe. Therefore, O Jew, *where is* **your boasting** any more, namely, that one thing which you had from the law and its bodily observances? Now **it is excluded;** that is, it was taken away from you and annulled. **By what law,** namely, *is it excluded?* By the law **of works,** (119) that is, of some exterior works? **No, but by the law of faith,** as was said, *in Jesus Christ,* that is, by the charity coming from faith in our salvation through Christ. For if someone already believes and loves[45] before he is baptized—just like Abraham, concerning whom it is written, "Abraham believed God, and it was counted to him as righteousness,"[46] and perhaps Cornelius, whose merciful acts were accepted by God[47] when he had not yet been baptized—and truly repents of his previous sins, just like the tax collector who went down from the temple justified[48]—I do not hesitate to say that he is righteous or has righteousness, which renders to each person what is his.[49] Therefore, we say that Jeremiah and John were sanctified from the womb,[50] where, having been spiritually illuminated, they already knew and loved[51] God, although it was still necessary for them to receive the sacrament of circumcision which then held the place of baptism.[52]

Why therefore, you will say, was it necessary that they be circumcised or baptized later who before were already righteous by the faith and charity they had, and who, if they then died, would have had to be saved? For no one who is damned can die a righteous man or having charity. Again, no one without baptism or martyrdom, after the decree of baptism was given, can be saved. Nevertheless, since he had charity before baptism or martyrdom, he could then have died, at that time when, you will say, if he died, he would have had to be both saved and damned. But we believe that everyone who loves[53] God sincerely

45. *Diligere.*
46. Rom 4.3; Gn 15.6; Gal 3.6; Jas 2.23.
47. Acts 10.4. 48. Lk 18.14.
49. The common definition of *iustitia.*
50. Jer 1.5; Lk 1.15. 51. *Diligere.*
52. Cf. Gregory the Great, *moral.* 4.3; see above on 2.25.
53. *Diligere.*

and purely for [God] himself is already predestined to life, and he is not at any time to be hindered by death until the Lord should reveal to him either through prophecy or through the Spirit whatever was necessary for him concerning the sacraments, and should give the capability for understanding this from above.

Certainly this can be said in opposition: that he who was already righteous before baptism, namely, by believing in and loving God, (120) existed at that time in which, if he died, it would have been necessary both that he be saved and damned; this can be said in opposition concerning anyone who commits mortal sin who is predestined to life, such as the adulterer David. For just as it was necessary that the former, who was righteous, be saved, so also the latter, because he was predestined; and just as it was necessary that the person not baptized be damned, so was it for the adulterer.

And so it was for David at the time when, if he died, it was necessary that he be both damned and saved. But again, there was no time when he could not die well, no time when he could not die badly, as long as he had the free choice of the will. Therefore, there was not any time when it was necessary that he die both well and badly; on the contrary, at no time was it necessary that someone die well, or die badly, but at the several times when someone can die well, he can die badly at the same time. Nevertheless at no time is it true to say in a combined statement that he could die simultaneously well and badly.

The same is true of him who has charity before baptism and because of this is righteous. We assent that there was no time when it would have been necessary that he be simultaneously saved and damned, if he were to die. For he who has charity before baptism, can be without charity at that time and thus die and only be damned; the one baptized could die at that time when he was not yet baptized, and thus be saved.

But if you should say in a combined statement that he can simultaneously have charity and not have been baptized, I do not admit this any more than if you said that someone could die both an adulterer and predestined. Indeed, just as it is necessary that he who is predestined should act well that he may be saved, so should he who is already righteous by believing and loving be baptized on account of the previously established sentence of the Lord concerning baptism or on account of the perseverance of righteousness.[54] For if he who has charity before he is baptized, should finish his life before he is baptized, by no means would he persevere in that charity, since (121) he would despair thoroughly of the eternal blessedness and would perceive in advance that at his death he is immediately to be damned forever.

But just as we say that someone is righteous by faith and love[55] before baptism, nevertheless his sins are not yet forgiven in baptism, that is, their punishment [not yet] thoroughly remitted, so we say that after baptism small children and those who have no power of discernment, although they have obtained the forgiveness of sins, are nevertheless not yet righteous, although they are clean in God's sight, who nevertheless are not yet capable either of charity or of righteousness nor able to possess any merits. If they die in this weakness, when they begin to depart from the body and see the glory prepared for them by the mercy of God, at that time the charity of God is born in them with discernment.

Therefore, lest someone of the Jews be able to object to us, indeed to the Apostle, that we are also justified *through the law of works,* that is, of external works such as baptism, let it suffice that we have alleged this concerning our justification, indeed the justification of all people, which depends on charity, and before the sacraments are received, whether ours or theirs. When the prophet saw this, he said, "At whatever hour the sinner bemoans his sins, he shall be saved."[56]

[3.28] **For we testify,** namely, we whom the Lord set over his Church, that is, we hold or declare. "Therefore," Haymo says, we call those who testify "judges or witnesses."[57] **That a man,** everyone, namely, both Jew and Gentile, **[is justified] by faith** as if it were necessary for himself, because "without faith it is impos-

54. Cf. Jn 3.5. 55. *Dilectio.*
56. Cf. Ezek 33.12, 19.
57. Cf. Haymo of Auxerre, *Rom.* 3.28.

sible to please God."[58] *By faith,* I say, without the works of the law, namely, those exterior and bodily observances.

[3.29] **Or [is he the God] of the Jews [only?]** *We testify,* and rightly, that even the Gentiles attain the grace of God *through faith,* who nevertheless do not observe the works of the law, just as the Gentile Job once did, and now even the Gentile converts. And this is what he shows, saying: *Or is he the God of the Jews only* through grace?

[3.30] **Since indeed [God is one],** as if he should say that he is the God of both through grace, because **he justifies** both **through faith,** which, as we have said, leads to charity. [He justifies] **the circumcision, that is, the Jews,** (122) **and the uncircumcision, that is, the Gentiles.** The words **by faith—through faith** are a diversity of speaking, not of meaning. Therefore, Augustine says in his book *On the Spirit and the Letter,* "This was not said for the purpose of distinguishing, as if one person is *by faith* and the other is *through faith,* but for the purpose of variety in the way of speaking."[59]

[3.31] **Therefore, [do we destroy] the law [through faith?]** Since, of course, we say that men can be saved *through faith without the works of the law,* **do we therefore destroy the law through faith;** that is, do we teach that it is invalid through the commendation of faith? **In no way! Rather, we establish the law;** that is, we wish that the law might be fulfilled in every way. For he now truly fulfills even the figural precepts, who does or believes that which they now only must represent by figures, not accomplish, who pays attention not so much to the sound of the voice as to the sense and intention of the one commanding. Finally, as the Apostle himself says, *The fullness of the law is love.*[60] Concerning this, when he mentions its commands, the Lord says to the rich man, "Do this, and you shall live."[61]

[4.1] **What therefore...** Seeing that those exterior works of the law cannot confer righteousness, *what therefore* **shall we say that Abraham found** of righteousness or usefulness **according to the flesh?** that is, through those carnal observances such as

---

58. Heb 11.6.
60. Rom 13.10. *Dilectio.*

59. Augustine, *spir. et litt.,* 29.50.
61. Lk 10.28.

circumcision or sacrifices? As if he should say, Nothing. When he says, **Our father,** that is, the one whom we ought to imitate as if we were his sons through the teaching, he makes his question more difficult, as if we should follow him in those things.

[4.2] **For if...** And truly, by the divine judgment, he did not obtain righteousness through those exterior things, because through those things he has no reward with God. This is what the Apostle says: *If* **he was justified by works,** that is, he practiced those exterior works which seemed to men to belong to righteousness, he indeed **has glory, but not with God;** that is, he is held on account of this to be great among men, who judge from visible things, *not with God,* who observes the heart[62] and tries the kidneys[63] and sees what is hidden.[64]

(123) [4.3] **For what...** And rightly do I say that Abraham was justified with God not *by works* but by faith, because we have this from the testimony of Scripture. And this is what he says: *For what* **does Scripture say?** Let us pay attention to what is written in Genesis, namely, to what follows: **Abraham believed God,**[65] that is, the divine promises, however incredible or great they seemed, whether by leaving his own land that he might be multiplied in a foreign one,[66] or the promise of a son,[67] or whatever he promised to him. But this is that true "faith which operates through love."[68] Therefore, when he says that *he believed God,* he means: by believing he willingly carried out the commands of the Lord, **and it was reckoned to him** by the Lord **as righteousness;** that is, this obedience of faith made him righteous with God, not circumcision or the other bodily observances that were later written in the law.

[4.4] **But to him,** as if he should say, Not without reason do I say that Abraham, if he were justified by works, would have *glory,* that is, the greatest praise among men, *but not with God;* but on account of this I say that *to him* **who works, wages are reckoned** by men **according to what is owed;** that is, what is owed is said to be his acquisition and of its own virtue, not to be conferred

---

62. Prv 24.12.
64. Mt 6.4; 6, 18.
66. Gn 12.1–3.
68. Gal 5.6; *dilectio.*

63. Jer 11.20; 17.10.
65. Gn 15.6.
67. Gn 15.4.

by an alien grace, since with God only the faith of the one who loves[69] suffices for righteousness.

[4.5] And this is what follows: **But for him who does not work,** that is, who does not perform the legal works, but who truly clings through faith to him *who justifies the ungodly;* **for the one who believes on him who justifies the ungodly, his faith is reckoned [to him] as righteousness,** namely, by him *who justifies the ungodly,* that is, by God; that is, he rewards him for this faith as if he were righteous. Here the Apostle openly defined what kind of faith he understood when he said *to the one who believes on him.* For it is one thing to believe in God,[70] namely, that he exists; it is another thing to believe God,[71] that is, that his promises and words are true; and another to believe on God.[72] This is what it means to believe on God, as Augustine says in his treatise on John: "By believing to love,[73] by believing to esteem,[74] by believing to strive that he may be made his member."[75] The reprobate and the demons therefore believe (124) in God, they believe God, but they do not believe on God because they do not love[76] nor by loving are they incorporated to him, that is, do they make one body through devotion to the Church, which is his body.

But how it is reckoned he adds: **according to the purpose of the grace of God,** that is, according to that which consists in the purpose of the divine goodness, which rewards inclination more than works. In other respects many who do not have the capability of working, although nevertheless they have the will, are condemned.

[4.6] **Just as David terms,** that is, expounds for us, **the blessedness of the man who has been accepted,...,** that is, who receives through his mercy when he is not able to rise by himself to him, **to whom God confers righteousness,** which he to whom it is conveyed could not lay hold of by himself. *He confers it* **without the works of the law,** namely, legal works.

---

69. *Amare.*

70. *Credere Deum.*

71. [*Credere*] *Deo.*

72. [*Credere*] *in Deum.*

73. *Amare.*

74. *Diligere.*

75. Augustine, *Io. ev. tr.* 29.6, "By believing to love, by believing to esteem, by believing in him to go and be incorporated into his members."

76. *Diligere.*

[4.7] For what he says: **Blessed are those whose iniquities are forgiven,** etc., he means generally, whoever they may be, either Jews or Gentiles. Iniquity is forgiven when its penalty is pardoned through the grace which could be required by righteousness, and through this Scripture now establishes this grace as a foundation, so that whatever may be built upon it subsequently, it may be reckoned to prevenient grace. But just as divine grace leads man to perfection when sins have been forgiven, he continues, when finally he adds that sins are covered over and finally not imputed. Sins are forgiven through the sigh of penitence, concerning which it is said, "At whatever hour the sinner groaned,"[77] because before, iniquity truly displeases him and every evil will of his disappears; now, in this way the sinner is reconciled with God, so that he may be freed from the pains of Hell and not ever fall into it, and that, if in this sigh he dies, he is ready for every satisfaction which he might accomplish. Then, however, **his sins are covered over** when in this world satisfaction follows penance. This satisfaction indeed even abolishes the purgatorial punishments of the other world, since penance has first blotted out the condemnatory punishments, that is, those of Hell. At that time, therefore, *his sins are covered over* before the eyes of the judge when he now sees nothing in front of them to punish.

(125) [4.8] **Blessed is the man...** Since he first set forth "the blessed" in the plural when he said, *Blessed are those,* etc., what is it that he now says by the singular "blessed," and mentions "the man," saying, *Blessed is the man,* etc., except that he extends the benefits of divine grace as far as the individual person who is united to God in the one person of Christ? The same prophet depicts the blessedness of this person immediately at the very beginning of the book where it is written, *Blessed is the man who has not departed.*[78] "Man" is therefore said to derive from "powers"[79] because he who has acquired no weakness from the corruption of sin, who, being stronger, has bound the strong man and seized his weapons,[80] is particularly spoken of as a man on account of his superiority; but all others are, as it were, effemi-

---

77. Ezek 33.12, 19.
78. Ps 1.1.
79. *Vir...viribus* (from *vis*).
80. Mt 12.29; Mk 3.27.

nate and weak by comparison with him, submitting to earthly pleasures. But **the Lord has imputed** no **sin** to this one, since he is entirely immune from sin, because he has judged him worthy of no punishment for any sin, whether original sin or his own, who was not conceived in sin nor committed any sin.

We can even understand by the thrice-named blessedness the three kinds of men to be saved. One kind consists of the small children sanctified by baptism or martyrdom and of anyone truly performing penance, to whom it is not allowed to fulfill the satisfaction of penance in this life; another kind, to be sure, consists of those who correct sins through suitable satisfaction; the third kind remains in the uniqueness of the one Savior, as was expounded. Since, therefore, he says, *Blessed are they whose iniquities are forgiven,* he understands forgiveness alone, which no satisfaction follows here. But for the little children who, according to the psalmist, were conceived in sins,[81] those sins in which they were conceived and born are forgiven as long as they do not incur the condemnation of original sin for them, as we have said. But others, just as we also mentioned above, (126) covered over past sins by the satisfaction of good works. And the peculiar nature of the construction seems to require this, so that when it says "whose" and "whose,"[82] let us not understand the same people but different. For it is one sense if "whose" is quoted once, in this way, *Blessed are they whose iniquities are forgiven and sins are covered over,* another if it is repeated twice as the text presently has it. For he mentions the same people when it is said once, and different people when it is said twice.

Question

A question about the grace of God and human merits imposes itself in this passage: Namely, what our merits are in God's sight, since all good things should be ascribed only to the grace of him "who works in us," the same Apostle attests, "both to will and to perfect according to his good will."[83] Therefore, he says elsewhere, "But what do you have that you did not receive? But if you received it, why do you boast as if you did not receive it?"[84]

81. Ps 50.7.   82. See Ps 31.1.
83. Phil 2.13.   84. 1 Cor 4.7.

It should also be asked in what our merits consist, namely, in the will only or also in the [meritorious] act, that is, why does God reward us with glory or punishment; and whether virtue is sufficient for blessedness even if it does not break out in a [meritorious] act; and whether an exterior work which follows a good or evil will should increase merit; and since every virtue belongs to the rational soul and stands established in it, whether every sin in like manner belongs to the rational soul; and what difference is there between the vice of the rational soul and sin, and in how many ways may we speak of sin? But because this pertains especially to ethical consideration, and should be dwelt upon at greater length in these things to be explained than the brevity of exposition demands, let us reserve it for discussion in our *Ethics.*[85]

[4.9] **Therefore, does blessedness...** Seeing that it has been shown in how many ways blessedness can be named or possessed, let us also see by whom it is had, that is, by the circumcised only or also by the uncircumcised. And this is what he says, by way of a question: Therefore, does this blessedness, (127) which we of course attain by believing on God also without the works of the law, **abide in circumcision only,** that is, among the circumcised, **or also in the uncircumcision,** that is, among the uncircumcised? He establishes what this blessedness is by saying that it is what Abraham attained to when he was justified by faith. And this is what he adds: **For we say,** that is, we demonstrate from the testimony referred to above, **that Abraham's faith,** by which, as was expounded, he believed on God, *was reckoned to him by God* **as righteousness;** that is, God reckoned him righteous and judged him worthy of the reward of the righteous.

[4.10] I said that *it was reckoned.* Therefore, let us ask about Abraham **how,** that is, when, his *faith* **was reckoned** to him *as righteousness,* namely, whether it was before he was circumcised or after, so that through him of course we can also judge concerning other people, whether or not only the circumcised attain this blessedness of righteousness. And this is because he

85. *Ethica,* 1–3, 5–6, 8, 13–14.

says, *how?*—namely, by asking and immediately explaining, **in circumcision,** that is, after he was circumcised, **or in uncircumcision,** that is, before he was circumcised, namely, while he still retained his foreskin.

[4.11] **And he received the sign.** Perhaps someone might ask why Abraham superfluously received circumcision, since he was justified before and had received nothing in it of justification. And therefore, anticipating this question, he says that Abraham did not receive this sign exteriorly for some justification, but for the signification and demonstration of the righteousness that he possessed interiorly while he was still uncircumcised. And this is what is said: *And he received the sign* of **circumcision; that is,** he received circumcision as a sign. As a sign of what thing, he immediately adds, **a seal,** that is, as a seal, that is, as a sign **of the righteousness of faith while he was uncircumcised,** that is, among the uncircumcised just as much as among the circumcised, so that by such a sign he might rather define righteousness (128) than obtain it. He uses the term "righteousness of faith," which is interior, to distinguish it from that which men are accustomed to call righteousness,[86] which they administer exteriorly in vengeance on the evil and in paying out some favors. Therefore, it is written, "Beware, lest you perform your righteousness before men, in order that you may be seen by them."[87]

We can even vary *sign* and *seal* so that circumcision may be a sign of one thing, and a seal of another; a sign may be of the carnal sons of Abraham, and a seal of the spiritual sons, since he was made father both of the Jews according to the flesh and of the Gentiles through faith. For a "seal," *signaculum,* according to Haymo, is like a signet, *sigillum,* "which is pressed upon something so that it may be concealed,"[88] and therefore it seems rightly to refer to the spiritual sons of Abraham who were to come from the Gentiles, and who had not yet appeared. Therefore, the circumcision which began in him, and was reserved in his fleshly posterity, was as much sign as seal, because the fleshly sons of Abraham were distinguished by it from the other

---

86. *Iustitia* can be translated either as "justice" or as "righteousness."
87. Mt 6.1.   88. Haymo, *Rom.,* 4.11.

peoples, and his spiritual sons yet to come were prefigured by the Gentiles, who imitated him, of course, through faith. Therefore, Ishmael, whom he begat according to the flesh, not according to the power of a miracle, is rightly read to have been circumcised: through this one the exterior circumcision of the fleshly sons of Abraham is indicated, through which, as was said, the fleshly Israel is known. But Isaac, who was born later, represents the spiritual circumcision, cutting away the vices of the Gentile people who were called later, which the proselytes also prefigured.

Rightly, therefore, did the Apostle, distinguishing *sign* and *seal* with regard to the Jews, the fleshly sons of Abraham, and the Gentiles, Abraham's spiritual sons, say at first the *sign of circumcision,* that is, the sign of the fleshly Israel, through which indeed that people was distinguished from the others, and later the *seal of the righteousness of faith* which is in the foreskin, that is, the mystery of spiritual circumcision which alone the faithful gathered from the nations have.

A seal can also be understood as a clear sign, according to which it is said in praise of the apostate angel, "You [were] the seal of (129) likeness," etc.[89] For through this sign of circumcision the righteous and spiritual man is especially designated, who renounces the pleasures of the flesh on account of God, and by himself cuts away those pleasures which especially dominate in the kidneys and are exercised through the genitals.

"Seal" can also be understood as a diminutive of "sign,"[90] that is, a small sign of the righteousness of Abraham. For it was not a great thing to cut away that skin for the kingdom of God, in comparison with what later the spiritual sons of Abraham, both martyrs and the other saints, later endured for Christ's sake.

Sign and *seal* can also be distinguished so that what is a great sign in the flesh, common to both good and bad, is a small sign of the righteousness of Abraham, because there are few who cling closely to Abraham through righteousness just as they do through the flesh. Therefore, it is a sign according to the flesh, but a seal, that is, a small sign, according to righteousness, be-

89. Ezek 28.12.
90. *Signaculum, signum.*

cause it is enlarged among the many descendants of Abraham according to the flesh, but narrowed among the few according to righteousness. Therefore, he rightly says *a sign of circumcision,* namely, of something exterior, which applies to all people equally, and *a seal of righteousness,* which is for the few.

But now a few things should be discussed concerning the virtue and sacrament of circumcision, namely, what it might confer or signify, and why it was ordained rather for the male genital member and not the female, and commanded to take place on the eighth day for infants.[91] For among adults, no time was fixed to be circumcised, except when they were converted to Judaism.

Nevertheless it is known that among the ancients circumcision had the power that baptism now works with us. Therefore, Augustine says in Book 1 of his work *On Marriage and Lust,* "For from this time circumcision was ordained among the people of God, because it was then *a seal of the righteousness of faith,* it effectively signified cleansing, and in small children it began to have power against the old original sin just as baptism did for the restoration of man from the time when it was ordained."[92] Gregory says in Book 4 of his *Moral Teachings,* "What the water of baptism effects among us, among the people of old either faith alone did for small children, (130) the power of sacrifice for the elders, or the mystery of circumcision for those who were descended from the line of Abraham."[93]

Therefore, from these things it is clear that circumcision obtained the same power for the forgiveness of sins among the ancients that baptism now has; and nevertheless those who now die immediately upon having been baptized immediately enter the Kingdom of Heaven. This did not happen then, namely, because the victim was not yet sacrificed, namely, in the pouring out of the blood of Christ, just as those who were baptized with the baptism of Christ and perhaps died before his Passion, could still have had no access to the heavenly gate. For only through the Red Sea did the Israelites have passage to the promised land;[94] that is, baptism, which is designated by the sea,

91. Gn 17.10–12.
92. Augustine, *nupt. et conc.* 2.2.24 (not Book 1).
93. Gregory, *moral.* 4.3.   94. Ex 14.21–25.

could not send anyone across to the true promised land, that is, the heavenly Jerusalem, without the redness, that is, the pouring out of the blood of Christ. But just as the sacrifice of Christ, later joined to baptism, conveyed the Kingdom of Heaven, so, when it followed the circumcision of those who went before, it assured the Kingdom to them.

But circumcision of the flesh is a sign of the interior circumcision of the soul, just as the exterior washing of baptism is a sign of the interior cleansing of the soul through the forgiveness of sins. But it was especially fitting that this sacrament take place in the genital member, where the sin of original guilt is propagated through fleshly concupiscence together with offspring, so that that member might justly be punished through which sin itself was transmitted to those who came after. But the woman to whom it was said, *In pain shall you bear children,*[95] was not to be afflicted with a punishment of this sort, for whom the most grievous pain which she endured in giving birth should have been enough for a punishment in her genitals, through which sin likewise was transferred. For this sex, unless I am mistaken, the sacrifice offered on behalf of it[96] suffices for an indulgence, and as a cure for original sin.

Moreover, on account of this it seems to us that the genital of the man especially should have been circumcised rather than that of the woman, so that it might be pointed out to everyone among that people who were begotten through that member that the cure of this sacrament was necessary, through which they were cleansed from the contamination of the old man. It is not so (131) with the woman, since the Lord Jesus was born from a woman apart from every sin.[97]

Circumcision of the man can also spiritually designate the same blessed man, who alone was conceived without concupiscence, and who received pure flesh and was completely without the uncircumcision of uncleanness. In the type of this, Abraham's servant, in an oath,[98] put his hand under his thigh which

---

95. Gn 3.13.   96. Lv 12.6–8.

97. Cf. Heb 4.15.

98. Here *sacramentum* has the sense of an oath rather than a ritual or mystery of faith.

was first circumcised, as if he was swearing an oath to him who was first promised to be born to him from his seed, that is, to Christ.[99]

A certain day, the eighth, was rightly fixed beforehand for the circumcision of infants,[100] so that in this there might plainly be prefigured the brightness and blessedness of that eighth day which is promised to the saints,[101] which is owed to them alone who lived innocently in the manner of little children, but the sacrament of purification does not suffice for this if the innocence of life is not guarded. The Lord exhorts us to this, when, having set a small child in the midst [of his disciples] he said, "Unless you be converted and become as this little child," etc.[102]

The eighth day, on which the small child was circumcised, signifies the future brightness of the saints on the day of resurrection, when the truth of the renewed flesh shall endure without the superadded corruption of sin; this shall be the true circumcision, in the stripping of the old man "with his deeds,"[103] when, with no pricks of carnal concupiscence still remaining, we should live angelically, where, Truth says, "they do not marry nor are given in marriage, but they shall be like the angels of God."[104] But because the whole time of the present life is completed in seven days, the perpetual brightness of future life is rightly understood by the eighth day. Therefore, it is certain that the Psalms which are entitled *for the eighth day*[105] pertain to the day of resurrection.

But it is asked whether infants dying before the eighth day are damned, since they are not yet allowed to be circumcised according to the commandment of the Lord, and we do not read that sacrifices are to be offered for them before the day of maternal purification, that is, (132) forty days from the birth of a male child.[106] And truly, since it is written, "Every soul whose flesh of his foreskin has not been circumcised shall perish from

---

99. Gn 24.2–9.
100. Gn 17.12.
101. Cf. Augustine, *Gn. litt.* 4.13; Abelard, *Hex.; Allegoria.*
102. Mt 18.3.
103. Col 3.9.
104. Mt 22.30.
105. Pss 6.1; 11.1.
106. Lv 12.1–5.

his people,"[107] and again, since by the commandment of the Lord boys are forbidden to be circumcised before the eighth day, the divine sentence of damnation for such persons seems severe: he both made circumcision necessary for these and did not allow them to be circumcised when they could. For it was not right that anything be taught or established by the Savior which might oppose salvation; the cure which could help many should not be weakened, such as the faith of the parents or the ritual of the sacrifices by which it is determined that small children or adults be cleansed beforehand, according to that passage of Gregory that we just discussed. But indeed this objection to the institution of our sacrament, that is, of baptism, seems to be excessive, since on account of an absence of water only does it happen that some lack baptism, which the Lord ordained in water alone;[108] nevertheless we do not establish that they shall be saved apart from baptism, unless martyrdom intervenes, even though they may strive for this or others may strive on their account.

Therefore, trusting his every disposition of divine providence—he alone knows why he chose this person and rejected that one—let us hold immovable the authority of the Scripture which he himself gave us, so that we may lightly claim that at the time of circumcision no one of Abraham's seed who died without it was saved, unless perhaps they were murdered for the Lord just as it is believed concerning the innocents.

But note that it says, *of Abraham's seed,* since some of the faithful who died uncircumcised after the institution of circumcision and before the coming of Christ were saved by the natural law no less than the circumcised, such as Job and perhaps some of the other Gentiles, who were content with the natural law; and by the ritual of the sacrifices which Job is said to have offered on behalf of his sons, they were purified from original sin or their own sins just as Abel or Noah were before the law or the institution of circumcision.[109] The Apostle mentioned such things above, saying, *For when the Gentiles who do not have the law,* etc.[110] Therefore, Isidore says in *On the Highest Good,* Book 1, Chapter

107. Gn 17.14.
109. Gn 4.4; 8.20.

108. Jn 3.5.
110. Rom 2.14.

15, (133) "Not only did the saints of the Jewish people prophesy and long for the coming of Christ, but there were even many holy men among the nations who had the gift of prophecy, to whom Christ was revealed through the Holy Spirit and by whom he was awaited, such as Job and Balaam, who assuredly proclaimed the coming of Christ."[111]

But although Job is also believed to have been descended from Abraham and from Isaac through Esau, nevertheless not anyone should be counted as the seed of Abraham or Isaac who is begotten from the sons of the patriarchs, who in no way remains in the worship of God. Therefore, the Lord also said to Abraham, alleviating his distress, namely, concerning Hagar the maid-servant who was to be driven away at Sara's command, and Ishmael her son, "Do not be troubled about the boy and your maid-servant. All the things that Sara said to you, hear her voice, because in Isaac shall your seed be named. But I shall make the son of the maid-servant into a great nation, because he is your seed."[112] The Apostle follows this up below in the present epistle and expounds it, as it were, spiritually, saying, *For not all who are of Israel are Israelites, nor are all they who are Abraham's seed his children, but "in Isaac shall your seed be named," that is, it is not those who are children of the flesh who are the children of God, but they who are the children of the promise are considered his seed.*[113]

Therefore, according to the truth of the history, neither Job nor the many others should be called the seed of Abraham, although they are from the line of Abraham, because they were born, as was said, from unbelievers. Nevertheless, the fathers of such people, although they were unbelievers such as Ishmael or Esau, are the seed of Abraham because they were not born from unbelievers, according to which the Lord said to Abraham above concerning Ishmael, "because he is your seed," but nevertheless the seed of Abraham was not to be designated in them as it was in Isaac. Therefore, it is one thing that Isaac or Ishmael "is" the seed of Abraham, and another that the seed of Abraham "be named" in Isaac or Ishmael. For such is the meaning:

111. Isidore of Seville, *sent.* 1.15.9.
112. Gn 21.12–13.
113. Rom 9.6–8.

"In Isaac shall your seed be named," as if it should be said: in Isaac's posterity, joined to him both in the flesh and by faith, (134) and not to some of the intervening fathers who withdrew from the worship of God.

For I believe that this is signified, when the Lord, beginning the covenant of circumcision with Abraham and his seed with these first words: "I shall establish my covenant between me and you and your seed after you in their generations," added directly, "with an everlasting agreement, that I may be your God and the God of your seed after you." For such is the meaning: "in your generations with an everlasting agreement, that I may be your God," etc.,[114] as if it should be said: in your posterity, allied to me continually through obedience, not those separated from my worship through the interposition of unbelieving fathers.

But in this way neither Job nor the other Gentiles, descended from Ishmael or Esau, should be considered Abraham's seed, and nothing, neither circumcision nor the other figural precepts of the law, pertains to them, since these things were imposed only on Abraham and his seed, as we determined above. For it is written concerning circumcision, when the Lord enjoined it upon Abraham for the first time, "I will establish my covenant between me and you and your seed after you in their generations, with an everlasting agreement, that I may be your God and the God of your seed after you, and I shall give to you and your seed the land of your sojournings, all the land of Canaan, for an eternal possession, and I shall be their God. And you shall therefore keep my covenant, and your seed after you in their generations. This is the covenant which you shall observe between me and you and your seed after you: Every male from among you shall be circumcised, and you shall circumcise the flesh of your foreskin, that it may be as a sign of the covenant between me and you. The eight-day-old infant among you shall be circumcised. Every male in your generations, both the slave born in your house as well as the slave purchased by you, shall be circumcised, and whoever was not of your lineage, and my covenant shall be in your flesh as an eternal covenant. The male whose foreskin has not been circumcised, his soul shall perish

114. Gn 17.7.

from his people because he made my covenant invalid."[115] And
a little later, "I have also heard you concerning Ishmael, and
I shall multiply him greatly. But I shall establish my covenant
through Isaac, whom Sara shall bear to you."[116]

Augustine says in Book 1 of his work *On Marriage and Lust*,
(135)

God ordered this concerning infants to be circumcised: "The male
who is not circumcised in the flesh of his foreskin on the eighth day,
his soul shall perish from his line because he destroyed my covenant."
Let him say, if he can, how that boy of eight days "destroyed the covenant," to what extent an innocent infant properly relates to that? He
therefore "destroyed the covenant" of God at that time, not in the matter of the commandments concerning circumcision, but in the matter
of the prohibition of the tree,[117] when *through one man sin entered into
the world and death through sin, and thus it passed into all men, in whom all
men sinned.*[118]

Behold, Blessed Augustine expounds how each one of the
first parents transgressed the testament or covenant of the
Lord, that is, the first law given to them by the Lord in paradise, so that in any event they are held in the chain of original
sin; so that even the small child, when he has been born from
Abraham and the other believing parents of his people, that is,
by lot and the blessedness of his believing parents, should be
excluded, unless he should be helped by the remedy of circumcision, as was said.

But that which is added in the precept of circumcision:
"Both the slave born in your house and the slave purchased by
you shall be circumcised, and whoever was not of your lineage,"
should be understood in this way, that the Lord commands this
for their domestic slaves or those purchased, whether they were
Hebrews, that is, from their lineage, or not; he does not command it for the other nations. Therefore, it is thus: "Both the
slave born in your house and the slave purchased by you [shall
be circumcised], and whoever was not of your lineage," as if he
is speaking of domestic slaves and those purchased, even all
who were not "of your lineage."

115. Gn 17.7–14.   116. Gn 17.20–21.
117. Gn 2.17.
118. Augustine, *nupt. et conc.* 2 (not 1).11.24; Gn 17.14; Rom 5.12.

Therefore, there is not a general precept of circumcision just as there is of baptism, as found in the Gospels, but it was handed on to the people of Israel alone, not to the Gentiles. Origen diligently shows this in later passages, distinguishing on the basis of those testimonies in the text (136) the things which are general precepts of the law pertaining both to Jews and to Gentiles from those which are not. Therefore, it is certain that this is not a general tradition of law. Moses himself diligently distinguishes this in Deuteronomy when he says, "And now, Israel, hear the precepts and judgments which I am teaching you, so that by doing them you may live and enter and possess the land which the Lord is about to give you."[119] Again, "For what other nation is so famous that it has ceremonies, righteous judgments, and all the law which I shall set forth before your eyes today?"[120] Again, "You shall teach it to your sons and grandsons."[121] And somewhat later, "The Lord your God chose you, that you may be to him a special people from all the peoples who are on the earth."[122] And the Psalmist says, "He makes his word known to Jacob, his righteousness and judgments to Israel. He has not done so for every nation, and he has not made his judgments known to them."[123] The Apostle also openly stated above that the law was not spoken or given to everyone, saying, *But we know that whatever the law says, it says to those who are in the law.*[124]

But having mentioned these things before concerning circumcision, we are not allowed to pass by briefly the sayings of the ancients pertinent to it.

Origen, in his commentary on this epistle of Paul, where it said above, *If therefore the uncircumcision,* etc., says on this passage:

God said to Abraham: "But you will keep my covenant, and all your seed after you in their generations. And this is the covenant between you and me and your seed after you: Every male of yours and every boy shall be circumcised on the eighth day. Every male among you shall be circumcised in your generations, the home-born slave and the slave purchased with money."[125]

Let us discuss whether the commandment also binds those who be-

---

119. Dt 4.1.   120. Dt 4.8.
121. Dt 4.9.   122. Dt 7.6.
123. Ps 147.19–20.   124. Rom 3.19.
125. The following quotations all come from Book 2, ch. 13, of Origen's

lieved among the Gentiles. It never made mention of a proselyte, that is, of a foreigner, but it commands the home-born slave or the slave purchased for hire to be circumcised, not the freeman. Therefore, let us examine the Levitical law: it says, "Speak to the sons of Israel and say to them: If a woman (137) bears a male, he shall be circumcised on the eighth day," etc.[126] Observe, both how here Moses is commanded to speak about the law of circumcision only to the sons of Israel, and no mention is made of foreigners. Since he speaks in some commandments not only to the sons of Israel but also to the proselytes, that is, the foreigners, a necessary distinction should certainly be observed, because just as it says there: "Speak to Aaron,"[127] and elsewhere "to the sons of Aaron,"[128] and elsewhere "to the Levites,"[129] it is certain that the rest are not subject to these laws; so one should not think that the things commanded to the sons of Israel, with nothing said of the foreigner, are also a common commandment where there is a restriction of name. So therefore, nobody else is bound by the law of circumcision, except someone who derives his origin from Abraham or their home-born slave or slave purchased with money.

Again,

We said these things so that we might show chiefly that the commandment of circumcision was not enjoined on anyone other than those who derive from the race of Abraham and their home-born slaves or slaves purchased with money, that the Gentiles who believe in God through Christ are free from laws of this sort.

Again,

Let us see what should be understood about circumcision from allegorical principles. Circumcision is the cutting-off of a certain part of a genital organ, through which fleshly offspring is provided. By this I reckon it is indicated figuratively that if any impurity adheres by cohabitation with the flesh it should be cut off from the soul. Therefore, that cutting-off is thrust on the genitals because these kinds of vices do not come to the soul by their own substance but by the excitation of the flesh. A week is allotted to the present age, but the eighth day contains the mystery of the age to come. (138) Therefore, the spiritual circumcision belongs to those who serve in the future world in which

Romans commentary, and were heavily edited and paraphrased by Abelard; Abelard used portions in his commentary on 2.16. The biblical quotation is Gn 17.9–12.

126. Lv 12.2–3.
127. Ex 8.16.
128. Lv 6.25; 21.1; etc.
129. Cf. Nm 18.26.

"they neither marry nor are given in marriage,"[130] and it belongs to those "who have made themselves eunuchs on account of the kingdom of God,"[131] and whose "conversation is in heaven"[132] even while they walk on earth.

But the Lord says to Ezekiel, "No foreign son who is uncircumcised in heart and in flesh shall enter my holy place."[133] But let us see whether it perhaps could not be attributed to two general sins, so that it may be the uncircumcised in heart who does not have faith, and the uncircumcised in flesh who does not have works. For one without the other is reproved, because it is said both that "faith without works is dead" and "without faith no one is justified."[134]

Again,

And it is said that they are circumcised in the ears when, according to the counsels of Solomon, they do not listen to empty sound;[135] and he is called uncircumcised in the lips[136] who would not circumcise blasphemy, vulgarity, and foul speech from his mouth, who did not place a guard on his mouth.[137] Similarly, why should not he be called uncircumcised in the foreskin of his flesh who immoderately flows toward the natural impulse of sexual intercourse? Is he truly regarded as circumcised who uses legitimate functions for this sort of business, as much as posterity requires?

Truly, since we have discussed the reason for circumcision, it will not seem incongruous to add that the son of Nun is said to have circumcised the sons of Israel a second time with stone knives, by the command of the Lord.[138] By all means, this seems impossible as far as the letter is concerned. For when the foreskins have been circumcised in the flesh once, what can a second circumcision achieve? Indeed, it is evident how our Joshua,[139] who truly led the sons of Israel into the Holy

130. Mt 22.30; Mk 12.25.

131. Mt 19.12. Note that Origen is said to have done this very thing, and also that Peter Abelard was castrated for his affair with Heloise a number of years before writing this commentary.

132. Phil 3.20.

133. Cf. Ezek 44.9.

134. Jas 2.17, 20, 26; cf. Gal 2.16.

135. Cf. Eccli 28.28.

136. Cf. Ex 6.12, 30.

137. Ps 38.2.

138. Jos 5.2–9.

139. The Latin name is *Iesus,* which can be translated as either Joshua or Jesus. In this sentence the phrase "our Joshua" (*Iesus...noster*) refers to Jesus Christ.

Land after Moses, circumcised the nation of believers a second time. For the first circumcision is that by which he cut off from the people either the worship of idols or fabrications of philosophical persuasion, (139) but in the second he cut off the habit of the old man and vices of the flesh. And at that time what was written in Joshua son of Nun was fulfilled: "Today I have removed from you the reproaches of Egypt,"[140] the ways of the Egyptians and savage impulses of the mind.

The Stoics say: Circumcision may indicate something mystical, and may comprehend an allegorical symbol. Thus, was it necessary that the form of symbols and the enigmas of the law be established with the pain and danger of small children, with the torments of a tender and innocent infant? Did the law-giver not have any place where he might place mystical forms except in the shame of modest places, and the seal of God except in obscene parts of the body? Did God, Creator both of the soul and the body, thus indicate that he had created that part of the body superfluously, which he later commanded to be cut off, so that through the pains of the wretched he might correct his own error? Or what he made beneficially, did he wrongly order to be removed? Moreover, if it is God's concern that many be brought to the practice of sound religion, a very great obstacle arises from circumcision. For this reason, not only does each one turn from this pain, but he also flees the disgrace of mockery.[141]

I think that it is necessary to respond to these things. No wise man denounces in others what he regards as honorable and great with himself. For circumcision is regarded as so plain[142] among you Gentiles that it is not entrusted generally to the common and those of low birth, but only to the priests and to those among them who were devoted to more excellent pursuits. For among the Egyptians, who are held to be most ancient and learned in your superstitions, from whom nearly everyone else borrowed sacred rituals and ceremonies, among these, I say, no one studied either geometry or astronomy, which is regarded as special among them; certainly no one examined the secrets of astrology and horoscopes, (140) than which they considered nothing more sacred, unless they had received circumcision. Every priest among them or the soothsayer or servant in any of their temples, or, as they call them, prophet, was circumcised. No one learned the priestly writings of the ancient Egyptians unless he was circumcised. No one was considered to be a seer or an initiate and partaker of heaven, as they think of it, and of hell unless he was circumcised. Therefore, do you judge that we consider disgraceful what you hold so noble and great, that you may believe that the secrets of heaven and hell can be dis-

140. Jos 5.9.
141. Origen, *Rom.*, 2.13, edited.
142. Abelard's text has *manifesta*, whereas Origen's text reads *magni*, "great," which of course makes far more sense.

closed to us only by signs of this kind? Therefore, if you open your histories, you will find not only that the priests of the Egyptians received circumcision, but also the Arabs and Ethiopians and Phoenicians and others whose zeal for superstitions of this sort was regarded more excellent.

These things were said against the Gentiles. Now a word should be directed to those who believe Christ, but do not receive the law and the prophets. It is written in the epistle of Peter that we have been "redeemed...with the precious blood" of the Only-begotten,[143] and without a doubt we were purchased from someone whose slaves we were, who also demanded a ransom which he wanted in order to release those he held. But the devil held us, to whom we were sold by our sins. He therefore demanded as our ransom the blood of Christ. Truly, until the blood of Jesus was given, it was necessary for those who were established in the law that each one give his own blood for himself as a kind of imitation of the future redemption. And therefore we, for whom the ransom of the blood of Christ was paid, do not hold it necessary to offer the blood of circumcision for ourselves as a ransom. If it seems reprehensible that God commands that this be inflicted on infants, you will also condemn this thing done in Christ, who was both circumcised and shed his own blood with the punishment of the cross. Because entrance to religion indeed seems difficult with the dread of circumcision, advancing to the Gospel will seem by far more difficult, (141) where a person is commanded to offer not a small part of his body but his very life.[144] But according to you the examples of the martyrs also will hinder men from approaching the faith. Or is a religion believed to be all the more constant because it offers nothing slack, nothing soft or luxurious? Because if there is nothing sacramental about circumcision, why would it be incongruous if, to distinguish itself from the other nations, the people who are instructed under the law of God should wear some sign of their own? And if the cutting-off of some part seemed necessary, what was so appropriate as to find that [part] which seemed obscene, and to remove those things whose diminishment hindered nothing of the body's functioning?

Because they say that if that part of the body was not necessary, it should not have been made by the Creator, [and] if it was necessary, it should not have been removed, let us ask ourselves also if they say that the procreation of children is necessary? Without a doubt they will respond that it is necessary. Therefore, they will be blameworthy who, by the preservation of continence and virginity, do not attend to the necessary duties of nature.[145]

In short, we should say that, just as many sacrifices were necessary

143. 1 Pt 1.18–19.
144. Cf. Mt 10.39, 16.25.
145. Cf. Mt 19.12; 1 Cor 7.25–38.

before a single sacrifice, Christ, the spotless Lamb, offered himself to the Father,[146] so many circumcisions were necessary until the one circumcision was passed on to all in Christ, and the shedding of the blood of many was the precursor until the redemption of all took place through the blood of one.

Ambrose, in his *Epistle to Constantius,* especially agrees with what Origen says above about circumcision when he says,

The question troubles many people, for what reason circumcision is enjoined as useful by the authority of the Old Testament and rejected as useless by the instruction of the New Testament. What, therefore, shall we say: that Father Abraham obeyed, so that he might first teach that which his descendants would not obey?[147]

Again he says,

But we discover in ancient history not only that the Egyptians, but even some of the Ethiopians, Arabs, and Phoenicians (142) used circumcision with their own people. And they still think that they keep this as a way of conduct to be approved, because having been initiated by the firstfruits of their body and blood, they think that the snares that the demons arouse in our race should be destroyed with the consecrations of a very small part. I now think we should consider that for no idle purpose, in this small piece of a member, a boy should be circumcised on the eighth day, when the mother, who is required before the eighth day to sit in filthy blood, begins to be in pure blood.[148]

Jerome says in his commentary on Romans,

It is asked why circumcision was given if nothing was gained through it. First, so that the people of God might be recognized among the nations. When they were alone in the desert, they were not circumcised. Or, so that their bodies might be recognized in war. This is the reason why they are marked in such a member: first, lest another member, which might be seen publicly, become either disabled or filthy; again, on account of the promise of grace in which it could be pleasing through chastity, or that Christ might be made known as the one to be born from [Abraham's] seed. Until Christ, that fleshly [circumcision] was to exist which had to bring about a spiritual one. Bearing his type, Joshua was ordered to circumcise the people a second time.[149]

146. Cf. Jn 1.29, 36; 1 Pt. 1.19.
147. Ambrose, *Ep.* 72.1–2.
148. Ibid., 6–7.
149. Pelagius. *Rom.,* 2.26.

There used to be, I remember, some question about how
Joshua circumcised the sons of Israel a second time by the command of the Lord with stone knives, as if they who had been
circumcised before could be circumcised again. But blessed Augustine, in his book *Questions of the Old and New Law,* removing
every error of this perplexity, teaches that this second circumcision was not done to the same [individual] persons, but to the
same people.[150]

Concerning this, the histories of the Book of Joshua clearly
contain these very words:

At that time the Lord said to Joshua, "Make for yourself knives of stone
and circumcise for a second time the sons of Israel." He did what (143)
the Lord had commanded and circumcised the sons of Israel. But this
is the reason for the second circumcision. The entire people who had
gone out of Egypt, all the warriors, the men, had died in the desert
during the very long journey, and they had all been circumcised. But
the people who were born in the desert during the forty years of the
journey in the very broad wilderness were uncircumcised, while those
who had not listened to the voice of the Lord were annihilated. The
sons of these fathers followed in their place and were circumcised by
Joshua, because, just as they had been born uncircumcised, no one
had circumcised them on the way. But after they were all circumcised,
they remained in the same place in their camps until they were healed.
And the Lord said to Joshua, "Today I have taken away from you the
reproach of Egypt."[151]

So I am amazed that Origen, so scholarly a man, erred to
such a degree in this second circumcision performed by Joshua
that he claimed above that this could have been done in no way
according to the letter; nevertheless, the history made by Joshua adds this immediately, saying, "And he did what the Lord
had commanded, and he circumcised the sons of Israel." Now,
let us return to the exposition of the epistle.

That he may be father of all... He had said two things: namely, that while he was uncircumcised, that is, while he had a foreskin, Abraham's faith was reckoned to him as righteousness, as
if he were spiritually circumcised, and that he was also later circumcised in the flesh, so that through these two things he might

---

150. Cf. Ambrosiaster, *quaest. test.,* q. 81.
151. Jos 5.2–9.

be set before others as father and author in example and teaching, as much in the spiritual circumcision as in the fleshly one. And this is so that **through uncircumcision,** in which he was justified before he was circumcised, *he might be father* **of those who believe,** so that because they are believers, this **may be counted to them as righteousness,** although the exterior sign might be lacking.

[4.12] **And that he may be the father of circumcision,** namely, of the exterior one, that is, set before all as the first in the spiritual as well as the fleshly circumcision, in example and authority, the father, namely, **not only to these who are circumcised,** that is, those to whom circumcision of the flesh was commanded, **but also to these who follow,** etc., that is, who have faith along with a foreskin. Construct it in this way: (144) ... **the footsteps of the faith of our father Abraham, which,** namely, faith, **is in uncircumcision,** that is, among the uncircumcised as much as the circumcised.

[4.13] **For [the promise to Abraham] was not through the law.** Since he had shown above that man is justified by faith *without the works of the law* and through this had taken away from the Jews their boasting in the law, he interposed the clear example of Abraham their father. Therefore, he now returns to emptying the boasting in the law as if repeating the things said above in order to prove them, and says, I said above that I judge that *a man is justified through faith without the works of the law,* which is clear in Abraham himself, who, receiving the greatest work of the law, that is, circumcision, was justified rather *through the righteousness of faith* than through that work of the law. And rightly, *for not through the law,* that is, through any work of the law or through the obedience to the law which had not yet been given, did he deserve to receive the promise of inheritance, **but through the righteousness of faith,** that is, through justifying faith or through the righteousness coming from faith; **or to his seed,** that is, those instructed with his example, **that he might be the heir of the world,** that is, perpetual possessor of all good things, which are figured by the fertility of the promised land. For he possesses all good things who has all necessary things, and it is said that nothing is lacking to him who needs nothing. Therefore, the Apostle says concerning those who strive for heavenly things by despising earthly ones, by the example of Abraham the sojourner: *As if having nothing and possessing everything.*[152] Or, *he might be heir of the world;* that is, they alone are chosen from the whole world to be heirs.

[4.14] **For if they [who are of the law are heirs]...** I rightly say that what was promised to the faithful as an inheritance is not attained through the works of the law. In another way **faith is emptied;** that is, the merit of faith is weakened, since unbelievers as well as believers can have those works of the law and become heirs through this, and **the promise is annulled,** that is, made ineffectual and invalid. Through this promise in the seed of Abraham the nations who do not have the works of the law are to be blessed. (145) *For if they who are of the law are heirs,* that is, they who have the works of the law, through this they deserve the inheritance.

[4.15] **For the law [works] wrath.** Again he shows that the inheritance is not obtained through the law, that is, the exterior works of the law that the law orders. What is more, men are judged guilty through the law, with the result that they lose the inheritance. For many works of the law are so burdensome that they crush those by whom or in whom they are done to such a degree, so that scarcely, or, more accurately, never, are their precepts pleasing to them, nor can they be fulfilled voluntarily, for example, to destroy "tooth for tooth and eye for eye,"[153] and to inflict death on some. For who gladly carries these out among those whom he loves[154] or gladly incurs them on himself? Therefore, Peter in the Acts of the Apostles, refuting those who wished to impose the works of the law on Christians, so that of course they also might keep [the works], said, "Men, brothers, why do you test God by imposing a yoke upon the neck of the disciples which neither our fathers nor we could bear? But we believe that we are saved by the grace of the Lord Jesus, just as they are."[155] Therefore, the law made a carnal and

152. 2 Cor 6.10.
153. Ex 21.24; Lv 24.20; Dt 19.21.
154. *Diligere.*
155. Acts 15.10–11.

stiff-necked people guilty on account of its works, instead of pu-
rifying them. It conveyed no righteousness to spiritual people
through its own peculiar exterior works. And this is what he
says: *For the law,* that is, those legal works, *works the wrath* of God
among them rather than kindness or some justification. And
why wrath? Because it makes them, certainly not others, transgressors of itself; and this is what he says: **For where there is no
law, [there is no transgression];** that is, those people to whom
those legal precepts were not given do not incur the guilt of
duplicity, that is, of transgression, through it, since they do not
obey them voluntarily.

[4.16] **Therefore, by faith,** certainly they are heirs, since it
is not by law. Or continue it in this way: I said that the promise
of inheritance was made not through the law but through the
righteousness of faith; therefore, they are heirs *by faith.* And this
is what he says: **So that the promise,** namely, of inheritance, **may
be steadfast,** that is, brought to completion, **for all the seed** of
Abraham, that is, the one imitating his faith, Gentile as much as
Jew. And this is what he adds: **Not only to him who lives by the
law,** (146) that is, to the Jew who submits to the law, **but also to
him who lives by Abraham's faith,** that is, to the Gentile who
imitates Abraham by faith alone, **according to grace,** namely,
God's, his *promise is steadfast,* not according to the merits of legal
works. **Who is the father** (namely, Abraham) **of us all,** of Jews
as much as of Gentiles; that is, he is put forward to all as an example to be imitated.

[4.17] **Just as it is written,** namely, in Genesis,[156] as if he
should say, he is father in that way and is put forward to all as an
example by which the Lord promised that he would be **father
of many nations,** that is, of diverse peoples, namely, by believing, rather than by implementing the works of the law. This he
openly teaches when he adds, **before God, whom you believed.**
These are the words of the Lord when he spoke to Abraham:
Because [I have made you] a father [of many nations]. For thus
it is written: "Your name shall not be called Abram, but you shall
be called Abraham, because I have made you a father of many

---

156. Gn 17.4.

nations."[157] Therefore, the interpretation of Abraham's name is intimated by these words, because it means "father of many," but because *nations* is added, it is an explanation of what we should understand these many things to be rather than an interpretation.

But also, what the Apostle said: *before God, whom you believed,* either was removed from our translation or added on the part of the Apostle, so that he might indicate that Abraham was put forward as father to all by faith more than by circumcision. He is regarded, that is, established as father *before God,* that is, in [God's] plan. He sought to produce sons not for himself but for God, not by having intercourse to satisfy his pleasure but to prepare sons of God more by the example of faith than by the propagation of the flesh. He teaches this openly when he adds *whom you believed,* concerning all his promises, as if he should say, "I have set you as a father before God, whom you believed," that is, so that through this belief in him you might produce many sons similar to you by the example of your faith.

What God says, when speaking to Abraham: "I have made you a father of many nations before God," and he does not (147) say, "before me," but speaks in this way about himself as if about another—this is a custom of Hebrew style. Therefore, the very law-giver who wrote this was always accustomed to speak about himself as if about another, as when he says, "The Lord said to Moses,"[158] and again, "And Moses was very meek."[159] This, however, does not seem to have been done without reason, namely, that one person speaks as if about another. For it is established among the saints and especially among the prophets that God speaks, rather than they. Therefore, the prophets, when they are about to say something, frequently say, "Thus says the Lord," and the Truth says to his disciples in the Gospel, "For it is not you who speak."[160] The Lord, appearing and speaking to Abraham or to others now and then, since he showed it through an angel, cautiously distinguished the truth of the angel appearing

157. Gn 17.5.
158. E.g., Ex 3.14–15; 4.19; etc.
159. Nm 12.3.
160. Mt 10.20.

and speaking from himself, so that by that kind of speaking another person may be understood, who forms the words, rather than the one from whom the words came, that is, the angel [is distinguished] from the Lord.

Who gives life. And justly did you believe in him concerning his promises, because such is he *who gives life to* **the dead;** that is, he converts the unbelievers to faith just as he wishes. "Dead" is what unbelievers are called; "wounded" is what sinners are called. For the life of the righteous is called faith according to that passage, "The righteous shall live by faith."[161] The unbeliever has nothing good inwardly by which he might be able to please God, because, as the Apostle says, *without faith it is impossible to please God.*[162] **And he calls [those things which are not as if they are];** that is, he causes things not existing to obey with his words, for "he spoke and they were made, he ordered and they were created,"[163] just as if they were existing things.

[4.18] **Who against hope...** Having commended the power of the Lord so that in no way might there be doubt about his promises, he commends also the constancy of Abraham's faith, to whose imitation he urges us. When Abraham had first despaired of Sara, he hoped that he would have his heir from Hagar. But later, on the contrary, he believed and hoped through the promise of the Lord. And this is what he says: **he believed in hope** *against hope;* that is, by trusting the divine promises, he was led *in hope,* namely, of bearing an heir, contrary to the first hope. It can be understood in another way: when he married Sara, he believed that she was fertile and likely to bear sons for him in her youth, according to nature. But later, (148) frustrated in this hope, on the contrary he believed deeply and hoped on account of the Lord's promise, that is, that his sterile wife would bear in her old age, against nature. It was a marvelous thing, that he could believe according to that rule of dialectic: "For if what seems to be contained more completely is not, what seems to be contained less will not."[164]

161. Rom 1.17.
162. Heb 11.6.
163. Ps 32.9.
164. Cf. Abelard, *Dial.* 3.1.

That he might become the father [of many nations], that is,
that he might deserve to be put forward as an example through
such constancy of faith concerning the promises of God, even
to the Gentiles; **according to what was said to him,** namely, by
the Lord in Genesis: **Thus will your seed be,** that is, the men to
be begotten for me by the example of your faith, as uncountable **as the stars,**[165] etc. By stars and sand we can also distinguish
the Jewish and Gentile peoples, from whom the spiritual sons of
Abraham are equally gathered, so that not only a great number
of sons, but also a diversity of peoples is indicated. The Jews are
compared to the stars, now illuminated through faith by the law
and restrained from the flow of worldly desires through the law
and made, as it were, celestial in their hope, while on the contrary, the Gentiles, bound by no law, flowed freely through every
desire, gazing only at earthly desires.

But because the words of the promise concern the Gentiles
only, among whom Abraham's faith was especially to be fruitful, we can perhaps distinguish more suitably three orders of
the church in the stars and sand of the sea. By the stars, which
are both burning and shining, two more lofty orders, namely,
of continent men, that is, of contemplatives who burn ardently
with the fire of divine love,[166] and of preachers who illuminate
others with their teaching; by the sand of the sea, the order of
married people who dwell as if in the sea, that is, in wet places, indulging in luxury, who both fluctuate in the concerns of
worldly anxieties and endure their sadnesses with difficulty.

[4.19] *He believed,* I say, **and he was not weak in his faith;** that
is, his faith was not slack or infirm in anything, as much as the
promise was deferred and seemed impossible, but in like manner he steadfastly believed that which he thoroughly knew was
contrary to nature, (149) just as before he had waited for that
to happen through nature. **Nor did he consider his dead body;**
that is, he did not give heed to the impossibility of his own nature or of his wife's, but to the power of the one promising. He
says, *his dead body;* that is, it was now entirely powerless through
nature for producing the son who was promised. **Although**

165. Cf. Gn 22.17; 26.4.
166. *Amor.*

Abraham himself **was almost one hundred years old,** that is,
ninety-nine, **and Sara's dead womb** likewise for the work of producing children, on account of old age as much as sterility.

Pay attention: When he says that Abraham was *almost one hundred years old,* he intimates that he was not at all able to produce
children on account of age alone, not on account of sterility;
nevertheless we should not believe that Abraham was entirely
powerless to produce children, because after Sara died, he married Keturah, from whom he produced sons.[167] For the nature
of the old man accomplished in the young woman what it could
not in the old and sterile woman. The very words of the Apostle
determine this sufficiently. For he does not simply say *Abraham's
dead body,* but he immediately adds, *and Sara's dead womb,* so that
through the addition of Sara, he might show that Abraham was
powerless with Sara specifically, and not with someone else. He
did not repeat the negative conjunction but inserted a copula-
tive. He did not say, he did not *consider his dead body* **nor** *Sara's
dead womb,* but rather he added, **and** *Sara's dead womb.* From this
he intimates that we should not understand that each one was
thoroughly powerless individually for producing children, but
jointly with each other.

In fact, we should note that this promise, "Thus shall your
seed be, as the stars of heaven and the sand of the sea,"[168] is not
found to have been made to Abraham when Isaac was promised
to him, but after he wished to sacrifice him to the Lord according to the Lord's command. For thus it is written, "I have sworn
by myself, says the Lord, because you have done this thing and
not spared your only-begotten son on account of me, I shall
bless you and multiply your seed as the stars of heaven and the
sand on the shore of the sea."[169] Indeed, we know that even before Ishmael was born, the Lord promised Abraham (150) that
his seed would be uncountable "as the dust of the earth,"[170] and
other things later on such as the stars of heaven, but he added
nothing at that time about the sand of the sea.[171] But we have

167. Gn 25.1–2.
169. Gn 22.16–17.
171. Gn 15.5.

168. Gn 22.17.
170. Gn 13.16.

for that reason noted these things, because the Apostle seems to adjust the last promise and the conception of Isaac, so that it might appear that the promise was made before Isaac was conceived. For so he said above, *Who believed in hope against hope, that he might become the father of many nations according to what was said to him, "And your seed shall be as the stars of heaven and the sand of the sea"*; and he immediately added, *And he was not weak in faith, nor did he consider his body,* etc. Therefore, the present text of the epistle should be combined in such a way that what was said before, *who believed in hope against hope,* might refer to this: *And he was not weak in faith,* etc.; to that which alone was inserted, *that he might become the father,* etc., what is added might relate, *according to what was said to him: "Thus shall,"* etc.

I think we must ask in what way Abraham was not weak *in faith* with regard to the promise of Isaac, since he also, like Sara, is reported to have laughed and spoken, without confidence as it were, concerning this promise. For thus it is written in Genesis: "Abraham fell on his face and laughed, saying in his heart, 'Do you think that a son will be born to a hundred-year-old man and that Sara, a ninety-year-old woman, will give birth?' And he said to the Lord, 'O that Ishmael might live before you.'" But actually when this comes before, "Abraham fell on his face," that is, by worshiping and supplicating he showed gratitude for the promise, it is clearly intimated that he did not despair about it. We read that Sara in no way did this when she laughed. It is said also concerning Sara that she laughed privately, behind the door; concerning Abraham that he laughed in the heart rather than with the mouth, so that the laughter of the heart might be understood as the joy of the mind, not mocking of the promise; and those words which follow, "Do you think that to a hundred-year-old man," etc., are words of admiration rather than of desperation. And because he adds, "O that Ishmael might live before you," he shows that Abraham's humility did not so much presume concerning (151) the goodness of divine grace to the extent that God himself does not offer it to the one who asks for it, but rather that it was enough for Abraham if Ishmael should live to him in place of his seed.[172]

172. See Gn 17.17; 18.10–15.

[4.20] **Also in the renewed promise [of God].** Promises were made to Abraham concerning two things: namely, concerning the giving or multiplying of seed to him, and concerning the giving of the land of Canaan to him or his seed.[173] But more often we read that each promise was made to him at the time when their completion was delayed. But that [promise] concerning the possession of the land received the greatest delay, which was promised to be completed long after his death. Therefore, the Apostle calls this second promise a "renewed promise," as if he should say, not only in the first promise, namely, concerning the seed, did he not doubt, but not even in the second one concerning the possession of the land, although it was a long time off, later, in the future, namely, in the fourth or fifth generation of the sons of Jacob departing from Egypt.[174]

He did not hesitate in distrust; that is, he did not have doubt in his heart, just as he seems to have had words of doubt in his mouth and did not immediately believe, except when he had first received a sign in a vision, just as he immediately believed the first promise concerning the seed. For thus it is written concerning the Lord and Abraham, "'You shall have an heir who shall go forth from your own womb.' And he led him outside and said to him, 'Look up at the heavens and number the stars, if you can.' And he said to him, 'Thus shall your seed be.' Abram believed the Lord, and it was reckoned to him as righteousness. And he said to him, 'I am the Lord, who led you from Ur of the Chaldeans, that I might give this land to you and you might possess it.' And he said, 'Lord, whence can I know that I shall possess it?' And the Lord responded, saying, 'Bring to me a three-year-old cow,'" etc.[175] Therefore, we believe that Abraham added these words of doubt, which were asking for a sign, for a confirmation for later generations more than for his own, just as John the Baptist asked the Lord not for himself but for his disciples, saying, "Are you the one who is to come?" etc.[176] **But he was strengthened in faith,** that is, in the expecta-

173. Gn 12.7; 13.15–17; 15.7.
174. Gn 15.16.
175. Gn 15.4–9.
176. Mt 11.3.

tion, not by the thing itself, which was to be a long time after his death, **giving glory to God,** that is, showing gratitude to him for these things, not attributing anything to his own merits.

(152) [4.21] **Knowing fully,** that is, believing steadfastly, **that whatever [he promised, he was able to do]:** He shows that the promise of God is provident and reasonable, that he promises nothing except what he can or even must fulfill. For it is certain that he cannot do anything except what he must, that is, what is appropriate for him.

[4.22] **Therefore, it was reckoned [to him as righteousness],** namely, because *he was strengthened in faith, giving glory to God, knowing fully,* etc.; that is, even this steadfastness of faith, if the exterior works ceased, is imputed to him by the Lord as righteousness, so that it might suffice for him to be justified.

[4.23–24] **But it is not [written],** as if someone should say, What is the report of such great praise of Abraham to us? He responds that this praise of him is not written **for his sake alone,** that is, to commend him, **but also for our sake, to whom,** namely, to those taught by his example, **it shall be reckoned** *as righteousness* **to those believing on him,** etc., that is, if by believing on God we might imitate Abraham. Believing *on him,* he says, not "believing in him" or "believing him," just as we explained above.[177] **Who raised [Jesus Christ],** that is, who has now fulfilled in the seed of Abraham through Christ what Abraham expected was yet to be and what he understood to have been figured to himself in the promise of land or the blessing of his seed. For all Abraham's exultation should be understood to have been concerning the figured Isaac, that is, Christ, rather than the figurative Isaac. Therefore, the Truth also said through himself, "Abraham your father rejoiced to see my day; he saw it and was joyful."[178] But in this passage the Apostle expressed in a few words the sum total of human restoration and salvation, both in the head and in the members, saying that Christ rose again **from the dead,** *who was handed over,* etc.

But note that while the Apostle says that God the Father raised Christ, and what he especially assigns to God the Father

177. See comments on 3.22 and especially 4.5.
178. Jn 8.16.

is of power, he teaches that the divine power most particularly belongs to the Person of the Father, just as the divine wisdom belongs to the Son, and the goodness of divine grace to the Holy Spirit. (The text of our *Theology* explains this more fully.)[179]

(153) *From the dead,* that is, of the body among the dead, of whom he was one.

[4.25] **Who was handed over.** He leads the cause of Christ's death as well as his resurrection back to us. He is said to have died **on account of our transgressions** in two ways: at one time because we transgressed, on account of which he died, and we committed sin, the penalty of which he bore; at another, that he might take away our sins by dying, that is, he swept away the penalty for sins by the price of his death, leading us into paradise, and through the demonstration of so much grace—by which, as he says, "No one has greater love"[180]—he drew back our souls from the will to sin and kindled the highest love[181] of himself. **And he rose for our justification.** He calls the perseverance of righteousness which makes just, *justification.* For he is not called just who sometimes acts justly, but he who has this as a practice. Therefore, what is said, *He rose for our justification,* means that by the hope of the glory of the resurrection, which he showed to us in himself, he might cause us to persevere in righteous works.

[5.1] **Therefore, having been justified by faith...** Seeing that the justification of Abraham through faith was written about for our sake as well, namely, that we might similarly be justified by his example, *therefore having been justified by faith* rather than by the works of the law, **let us have peace with God;** that is, let us thus be reconciled to him. And because, however righteous we might be, we need Christ the mediator, he adds **through our Lord Jesus Christ,** from whom every good thing extends to us as if from the head to the members, at one time by the example of his life, at another by the preaching of doctrine.

[5.2] And this is what he says: **Through whom we have ac-**

---

179. *tsch* 62, *TSch* 1.55 (resurrection of Christ); *tsch* 36–39, *TSch* 1.29–32 (three divine Persons).

180. Jn 13.13; *dilectio.*

181. *Dilectio.*

cess to the grace in which we stand, and we glory... And what
that glory is, (154) he adds, saying, **in the hope of the glory of
the sons of God,** that is, by that hope which we have of obtaining that inheritance of the highest blessedness, which is owed
to sons, not to slaves, and this is *through faith,* which precedes.
For hope is born from faith, since the elect rise up by the faith
which they have to the hope mentioned above, and no one can
hope anything except what he first believes. He says that grace
is "freely given," not conferred for merits, because *the sufferings
of this time are not worth comparing to the future glory.*[182]

[5.3] **And not only this,** namely, that *we glory in the hope of the
glory of the sons of God,* **but we also glory in tribulations;** that is,
we reckon that we are afflicted with great honor in God's service
according to what is written in the Acts of the Apostles: "They
went rejoicing from the presence of the council," etc.[183] **Knowing** also, that is, observing great fruit in these things, therefore
we glory, namely, **that tribulation works patience;** that is, in labor
it shows the virtue of patience, and the very exercise of tribulation renders us stronger for enduring those things.

[5.4] **And patience works testing** according to what is written: "The Lord tested his chosen ones like gold in a furnace";[184]
that is, he showed their worth, their steadfastness, both to themselves and to others; **and testing works hope,** that both we and
others might trust him concerning our merits through the
grace of God.

[5.5] And lest that hope seem useless, just as it is said concerning the wicked, "But the hope of the wicked shall perish,"[185]
he adds, **But** this **hope does not confound;** that is, it does not acquire shame for us in the future, because we shall possess what
we hoped for. And as if someone might ask how we can know
this, he adds that we have charity through which we hope for
what we deserve. And this is what he says: **Because the charity of
God [is poured out in our hearts].** He says [*the charity*] *of God;*
that is, it is chastely disposed on account of God, in contrast to
fleshly love.[186] He says that charity, that is, love, has been poured

---

182. Rom 8.18.   183. Acts 5.41.
184. Wis 3.6.   185. Prv 10.28.
186. *Dilectio,* equated with *caritas* here and in the next sentence.

out, which embraces the enemy, concerning which it is written, "I have seen an end of every perfection; (155) your command is exceedingly broad";[187] that is, I have considered and understood that your broad command concerning charity is the end of every perfection; that is, it is that command to which the intention of all your commands is directed. **Through the Holy Spirit who has been given to us,** that is, through the operation of the divine grace bestowed upon us.

Augustine says in Book 4 of his *Christian Doctrine,* concerning the words *Tribulation works patience,* "It is acknowledged here as a figure which by certain people is called in Latin *gradatio,*[188] since the words or perceptions are joined the one after the other, just as here we see patience immediately following tribulation, testing immediately following patience, and hope immediately following testing."[189]

[5.6] **For why...** I justly said that charity was poured out in our hearts, for why else **did Christ die,** unless, of course, so that the charity of God might be spread abroad in us? **According to the time,** that is, as if at the hour and in passing over from death he was detained who soon rose again; *he died* **for the wicked,** so that he might free them from damnation, **when we were as yet weak.**

We should note, however, that in this passage the Apostle clearly describes the manner of our redemption through the death of Christ, since he says plainly that he died for us, not for the sake of anything else, unless it was on account of that true freedom of charity to be enlarged in us, namely, through this highest love[190] which he showed to us, just as he says, "No one has greater love than this," etc.[191] I think that we have spoken sufficiently above concerning this manner of redemption.[192]

[5.7–8] **For scarcely [does someone die]...** I said that Christ died for the wicked so that charity might be poured out in our hearts, as if this was the great thing that he did. And truly this was great and salutary, namely, that God died for the wicked, because *scarcely* does a man undertake to die **for a righteous man.**

---

187. Ps 118.96.
189. Augustine, *doc.Chr.* 4.7.11.
191. Jn 13.13; *dilectio.*

188. *Gradatio* = "climax."
190. *Dilectio.*
192. See comments on 3.26.

I said *scarcely,* and I did not deny totally, because perhaps, although very rarely, it can be found out who might die for love[193] of a good, that is, righteous, man. (156) And this is what he says: **For perhaps someone,** that is, anyone, **might dare to die for a good man,** knowing that he will be rewarded for it by God. When he says *perhaps* and *dare,* he proclaims a difficulty. But Christ did not only dare to die; indeed, he also died for sinners. And by the manifestation of so much grace **God commends,** that is, he builds or confirms, **his charity towards us,** since **Christ** the Son of God **died for us while we were yet sinners.**

[5.9] If he thus took care in this, *while we were sinners,* by handing over his only Son to death for us, **therefore, how much more,** that is, how much more easily or gladly or commendably, does he now take care of us for salvation, we who are **now justified in his blood,** that is, now through the love[194] which we have in him, on account of this highest grace which he showed to us, namely, in dying for us while we were yet sinners. And this is what he says: **we shall be saved from wrath,** namely, the wrath to come, that is, from vengeance on sinners, **through him,** namely, through Christ dying once for us, frequently praying for us, and continually teaching us.

[5.10] **For if when [we were enemies]...** I said that *Having been justified in his blood, we shall be saved from the wrath* of God *through him,* and rightly, because now **we are reconciled to God through the death of his [Son],** although at first he considered us as enemies to be punished. And if his death alone was able to justify or reconcile us, **how much more** will his life be able as well to protect and save us *from his wrath.* For it is certain that every one can do more alive than dead. **[...having been reconciled, shall we be saved] in his life,** that is, the life of the one who was raised and now lives.

[5.11] **But not only this,** namely, that *we shall be saved,* that is, we shall achieve salvation through him, but also we have obtained the greatest glorying and we ascribe the greatest honor to ourselves, because God has given to us such a **reconciliation.** And this is what he says: **We glory in God,** not in ourselves, that

193. *Amor.*
194. *Dilectio.*

is, concerning such a great benefit on account of his grace, not on account of our merits, bestowed on us through Christ.

[5.12] **Therefore, just as...** Here the text seems to be defective, unless we try to join it to what is above or below in some way. (157) But perhaps it will thus be joined to the words above, as if we were to say, *we receive reconciliation through Christ, therefore,*[195] that is, on account of what was said above, because, of course, *he died for us,* just as on the other hand we incur damnation through Adam. And this is what he adds: *just as* also **through one man,** namely, Adam, **sin entered,** because, when he sinned before, he gave to sin an entrance **into this world,** that is, into this part of the world, namely, the earthly part in which human beings dwell, not where the angels dwell who sinned before. **And through sin death,** namely, bodily death, **and thus,** namely, by beginning with Adam, both **death** and sin, in any case original [sin], **passed into all men;** *one man,* I say, that is, Adam, **in whom all** the others **sinned;** that is, they incurred the penalty of sin.

Perhaps the verse could also begin, *Therefore,* and the construction be directed to things below, long afterward, namely, that passage: *So also through the righteousness of the one man, to all men,* etc.,[196] as if it should thus be said, *Therefore,* namely, because *we have received reconciliation through Christ,*[197] *so also through the righteousness of the one man,* ("one enters" should be understood) *into the justification of life to all men, just as through one man sin entered into this world,* etc.[198] But the other things which are interposed keep the text in doubt.

[5.13] **For up to the law...** I say rightly that sin entered into all, since they who lived before the law were not immune from sin; it might appear more so concerning them. Although as yet the transgression of nothing written made them guilty[199] *up to*

195. Rom 5.11; not fully quoted by Peter.
196. Rom 5.18.
197. Rom 5.11.
198. Rom 5.18.
199. Peppermüller: "...although as yet the authority of nothing written made them guilty of transgression." Peppermüller follows the reading of manuscript A, which includes the word *auctoritas,* not noted either by Buytaert in his critical apparatus or by Peppermüller in his; see Peppermüller, "Zur kritischen

the law, that is, in all that time before the law was given through Moses, **sin was in the world,** although it was not imputed, that is, charged or punished by men through some law, **since the law,** of course, **was not** yet written but only natural, through which nevertheless they had some discretion of good or evil by which they could recognize sin. (158) Sin before the law can even thus be said not to be imputed by men; that is, what sin was, was known by none or by few, before the law forbade concupiscence as sin, and taught that sin exists in the heart rather than in the work. Indeed, the Apostle openly teaches this in what follows, saying, *Is the law sin? May it not be so! But I do not know sin except through the law. For I did not know concupiscence,* etc.

Therefore, **sin was not imputed,** either original or one's own; that is, it was not recognized by men until the law described it. For that sin of the first parents was in concupiscence, as it is written: "Therefore, the woman saw that the tree was good for eating and beautiful to the eyes and delightful to see, and she took of that fruit and ate it."[200] And although sin was not imputed by men before the law, as was said, nevertheless even then it was imputed by God since he inflicted the penalty of bodily death on all for it, proclaiming to us through this that we should especially be on guard against our own sins, while we endure this on account of another's sin.

[5.14] And this is what he says: **But death reigned,** namely, bodily death; that is, it obtained quiet dominion even before the law, that is, **from Adam to Moses, even in those who did not sin [in the likeness of Adam's transgression]** by transgressing knowingly just as Adam did, that is, in children or any innocents. **Who,** namely, the old Adam, **is the form of the one yet to be,** that is, the likeness of the new Adam, that is, of Christ, who was to be after him. "Adam," just like "human being," is the common name both of man and of woman. Therefore, when he is called the new Adam, it is as if the new human being is said to be entirely contrary to the old human being through obedience.

Ausgabe des Römerbrief-Kommentars des Petrus Abaelardus," *Scriptorium* 26:1 (1972): 90.

200. Gn 3.6.

The Apostle himself reveals the likeness of Adam and Christ, showing that Christ is the father of all spiritual people, just as Adam is of fleshly people; that is, Christ thus rules over all to beget in God just as Adam begets in the world, and thus Christ is the author for life and rest just as Adam is for death and punishment. It can even be brought back to this likeness, namely, of Adam and of Christ, because elsewhere the same Apostle, (159) understanding this, says, "I say that this is a great mystery in Christ and in the Church."[201] But the previously mentioned likeness is enough for the present text. The Apostle himself follows this likeness, namely, concerning the fleshly and spiritual generation.

[5.15] **But the offense** of Adam **is not like the gift** of Christ; that is, they are not equal in those things which they transmit to their descendants, and more things are transmitted through Christ to his descendants for salvation than are transmitted through Adam for damnation; and justly, because it was more appropriate for divine righteousness or piety that through Christ it might do more good than do harm through Adam, that is, to give more advantages through Christ than troubles through Adam. For God is by far more inclined to bestowing good than to inflicting evil. And this is what he says: **For if by the offense of one,** namely, Adam, and one offense, not many, **many died,** that is, were damned, such as children who have not been baptized, who are not lost on account of something else, **how much more towards the many,** that is, in the same way, towards many, not only towards one person, as it should absolutely—and not comparatively—be understood, ought **the grace of God and the gift in the grace of Christ** to abound, that is, through the gifts of God bestowed upon that man, "from whose fullness we have all received,"[202] and who obtained for us with his merits whatever good we have.

[5.16] **And not as through the one,** namely, the man Adam, **did sin,** namely, one sin, that is, original [sin], *pass into* (understood as he said above) all, **so also the gift,** similarly one [gift]

201. Eph 5.32.
202. Jn 1.16.

passed through one man, Christ of course, indeed many gifts to many people. And this is what the Apostle understood in the above verse, but he repeated it so that he might demonstrate it, saying, **For the judgment indeed,** that is, **on account of the one** sin, namely, Adam's, is the *judgment* of God **for condemnation** of his descendants; that is, he convicts them to hand them over to eternal punishment. But the **grace** of God, that is, the free gift of forgiveness, **from the many offenses** forgiven by Christ, both original and personal, is given to us **for justification,** that is, for the absolution of punishments. Therefore, it appears that more things are bestowed on us by Christ for salvation than by Adam for condemnation, since he, (160) Adam, of course, brought the one sin to the world, that is, the punishment of the one sin, namely, the original sin, but [Christ] brought forgiveness both of that sin and of the others. And justly, because it was fitting that so many great benefits of Christ provide more help than the harm which the one offense of Adam did, which was not great by comparison with the others.

Therefore, Jerome says in his letter *To the Daughter of Maurice,* diminishing this sin, "Adam should be spared more, who was still young and was not influenced by the example of someone sinning beforehand and dying on account of his own sin. But I do not know how it can be allowed to you, after so many examples, after the law, after the prophets, after the Gospels, after the apostles, if you wish to transgress."[203]

[5.17] Expound it thus: since through the offense **of one,** namely, Adam, and **through one,** namely, [one] offense, **death reigned** also over the soul, that is, it quietly obtained descendants, much more fittingly and justly **through one Jesus Christ,** perfected with the fullness of all good things, did his spiritual descendants rule, **receiving the abundance of** divine **grace;** that is, many good things were bestowed on them beyond their merits, I say good things, **of the gift and of righteousness.** Only those gifts are said to belong to *the gift* to which there is no merit joined, just as in children; but they belong to *righteousness* (*iustitia*), where something is given for merits. For righteous-

---

203. Ps.-Jerome (Pelagius), *Claud., Ep.* 13.6; see below on 5.19.

ness (*iustitia*)[204] is said to be that which renders to each what is his.[205] **They shall reign in life,** namely, eternal life; that is, they shall obtain an enduring life, a kingdom as it were, not a consulship. You should not wonder that the Apostle mentions this notion more frequently, since he is especially careful to commend Christ in this, and wishes with valid reasoning to demonstrate to all that Christ is to be trusted more than Adam is to be feared. What he firmly commends to memory, he more often repeats.

[5.18] **Therefore, just as through [the offense] of one...** Since through Adam we incur damnation and through Christ we attain justification, that is, the forgiveness [of sins], therefore through one the former is bestowed, and through one the latter. And this is what he says: *Just as through the offense of one* (161) **[all men]** ("are brought" should be understood) **to condemnation,** so that they also might be subject to eternal death on account of it. **To all men,** both *those who did not sin in the likeness of Adam's transgression,* as he mentioned above,[206] and the others; or both those who lived before the law and the others, as he also mentioned above.[207] Thus **through the righteousness of one** they are brought **to the justification of life,** that is, to the forgiveness of sins, which bestows eternal life **upon all men** in the same manner, not to specific individuals, but to both the indicated races of men.

[5.19] What follows immediately proclaims that the Apostle does not speak about individuals, where only **the many** and not "all" are mentioned. And the Apostle plainly describes, as he said above,[208] how the first Adam is the form, that is, the likeness, of the second, that is, of Christ, in this way: namely, that just as Adam transferred what was his, that is, sin, to his descendants, so [Christ transferred] what is his, namely, the grace of justification, to his [descendants]. **For just as...** Indeed, it was done through offense and righteousness, because **through the disobedience [of the one man many were made sinners, so also through] the obedience....** And this is what he says: *For just as,* etc. He says that many, not all, were made sinners through the

204. Or "justice."
206. Rom 5.14.
208. Ibid.

205. Cf. Augustine, *civ. Dei* 19.21.
207. Rom 5.12.

sin of Adam; that is, they were handed over to eternal punishment. For if we disregard that Christ the man was always immune from every sin, there are many for whom original sin was
pardoned through the sacraments of the Church, and who later
were condemned by their own sins. In no way did Adam make
them sinners in the manner in which it was said, but they made
themselves sinners, because it does not now seem that the sin of
Adam is punished in them—for this was pardoned to them—
but their own sins only. Some, though, according to the parable
of the Lord about the two fellow-slaves,[209] might wish that the
sins forgiven would return to the damned and ungrateful and
be joined to the punishment, so that that for which a person
now receives pardon is again punished; although the Apostle
contradicts that plainly in what follows, saying that the gifts and
calling of God are without repentance.[210] We will discuss this
more diligently in its place.

Perhaps we can even say that none of those to be saved were
made sinners by Adam, as was determined, (162) that is, made
subject to eternal death, but were only damned without the sacrament.

Through the obedience of one, who of course "was made
obedient unto death,"[211] **they shall be made righteous,** that is,
thoroughly immune from every sin even through punishment.

Note that he says that in Adam **they were made,** in Christ
they shall be made. That sin of Adam was conveyed into us as if it
existed right now and it was fixed through his own punishment;
but that justification through Christ is as yet to be, since it is
hidden, and those who are Christians especially are subject to
afflictions in this world. Therefore, John the Apostle says, "We
are sons of God, and it has not yet become evident what we shall
be. We know that when he shall appear, we shall be like him,"
etc.;[212] and Paul himself says, "Our life is hidden in God with
Christ."[213]

But we should not lazily pass by what the Apostle so often
repeats in this passage concerning sin and grace, conveyed

209. Mt 18.23–34.
210. Rom 11.29.
211. Phil 2.8.
212. 1 Jn 3.2.
213. Col 3.3.

through Adam and Christ, and that, as if necessary reasoning and manifest righteousness required it, he demonstrated that more good things should be bestowed through Christ, although not to more, than evil things through Adam, as if Christ had more power to help than Adam had to hurt; this is clear. But from this, unless I am mistaken, the Apostle has left it to us to consider that God also devised this for himself in the Incarnation of his Son, so that he came not only with mercy, but also with righteousness to aid sinners through him, and by his righteousness what had been impeded by our offenses was completed. For when God made his Son man, he actually established him under the law which he had given in common to all men. Therefore, it was necessary that by the divine precept that man love[214] his neighbor as himself and exercise the grace of his charity among us, first by teaching us, then also by praying for us. Therefore, by the divine precept, he was driven to pray for us and especially for those clinging to him through love,[215] just as in the Gospel he interceded with the Father for his own very often. Indeed, his highest righteousness required that his prayer be denied in nothing; (163) the divinity united to him permitted him nothing except what was necessary to will or to do.

The Apostle himself diligently taught this in two other places: when he wrote to the Galatians concerning the following: "Born of a woman, born under the law, so that he might redeem those who were under the law";[216] and to the Hebrews: "Who in the days of his flesh, offering prayers and supplications, with a loud cry and tears, to him who could save him from death, was heard by virtue of his reverence," etc.[217]

He was therefore made man; he is bound by the law of love[218] of neighbor so that he might redeem those who were under the law but could not be saved through the law, and that he might supply from his own merits what was not in our own. And just as he was unique in sanctity, he became unique by expediency regarding the salvation of others. Otherwise, what great thing

214. *Diligere.*
216. Gal 4.4–5.
218. *Dilectio.*

215. *Dilectio.*
217. Heb 5.7.

does his holiness deserve if it suffices for his salvation only, and not for someone else's? Did Adam save himself by obeying? Each of the saints obtains this through the grace of God. Much more should divine grace have accomplished something in that unique righteous person. The riches of a powerful man are not abundant which do not suffice to enrich others.

Questions, or objections, regarding original sin

Now we must come to that old complaint of the human race and endless question, namely, concerning the original sin, which, as the Apostle mentions in the present passage, overflows from the first parent to the descendants, and we must labor for a solution as we shall be able.

First, therefore, it is asked what we should call original sin, with which individual humans are begotten. Next, it is asked by what righteousness is the innocent son made guilty for the sin of the father before God, the most merciful judge, which would not be approved before judges in the world; and what we now believe was forgiven for him who committed it, or was abolished in others through baptism, is punished in the sons who were not yet able to consent to sin; and those whom their own sin does not make guilty, another's condemns, and the iniquity of the first father draws them into damnation more than the iniquities of their neighbors, however more serious. How very cruel this would be, (164) and contrary to the most high goodness of God, who desires to save rather than destroy souls, that for the sin of the parent he would condemn the son whom he might by no means save by virtue of his righteousness.

Investigation of solutions, and in how many ways sin is described

But in more ways Holy Scripture interprets the term "sin": indeed, in one way, and especially so, for that fault of the soul and contempt for God, that is, by our perverse will, with which we are established as guilty before God; but in another way sin is called that punishment for sin which we incur through sin itself, or for which we are held guilty on account of that sin. Indeed, according to this signification sins are said to have been dismissed, that is, the punishments of sins are forgiven, and the

Lord bore our sins, that is, he endured the punishments of our sins. And when someone is said to have sin or to be as yet with sin, who nevertheless does not sin through an evil will, for example an unjust person asleep, it is such as if we should still acknowledge that he is liable for the punishment of his own sin. But in the third way Christ himself is called "sin" by the Apostle, that is, a sacrifice for sin.[219]

He briefly touches on what original sin is.

Since, therefore, we say that men are begotten and born with original sin and also contract this same original sin from the first parent, it seems that this should refer more to the punishment of sin, for which, of course, they are held liable to punishment, than to the fault of the soul and the contempt for God. For the one who cannot yet use free choice nor yet has any exercise of reason, as though he recognizes the author or deserves the precept of obedience,[220] no transgression, no negligence should be imputed to him, nor any merit at all by which he might be worthy of reward or punishment, more than to those beasts, when they seem either to do harm or to help in something.

Therefore, Augustine, discussing the soul of irrational animals, says in his book *To Peter on Faith*, "Therefore, neither eternity is given to irrational spirits, nor is any judgment prepared for them, in which either blessedness is rendered to them for good works or damnation for evil works. Therefore, no discernment of works is required in them because they received no faculty of understanding from heaven. (165) Therefore, on that account their bodies will not be resurrected, because those animals had neither justice nor iniquity, for which either eternal blessedness or punishment should be repaid to them."[221]

In Chapter 26 of his book *Eighty-Three Questions,* he says, "The just God who governs all things permits no punishment to be inflicted on anyone without cause, no reward to be given undeservedly. But the merit of the punishment is sin and the merit

219. 2 Cor 5.21.
220. So read most of the manuscripts. Peppermüller follows the *Abbreviatio,* which reads: "…as if when he does not recognize…"
221. Not Augustine, but Fulgentius of Ruspe, *fid.* 41.

of the reward is the thing rightly done. Neither the sin nor the thing rightly done can justly be imputed to anyone who did nothing by his own will."

On free choice
"Therefore, both sin and the thing rightly done exist in the free choice of the will."[222]

But Boethius, diligently explaining what free choice is, says in the third book of the second edition of *On Interpretation,* "For we assert free choice, with no outside compulsion, in that which seems to us who judge and examine what we should do or not do; we come to accomplish and do this thing when the knowledge was first anticipated, so that what it becomes takes the beginning from us and from our judgment, with no outside or violent compulsion or hindrance."[223]

Again, "But we do not call 'the free choice of the will' that which each one wished, but what each one has considered by judgment and examination. Otherwise, many animals also will have free choice of the will. For we see that they willingly flee certain things, to flock together willingly with certain others. Who does not know that if to wish something or not to wish this thing was rightly comprehended by the name of free choice, not only can a man do this, but also the other animals to whom this power of free choice is lacking? But it is free choice which those words make known, a free judgment by us from the will. For as often as imaginations flock to the rational soul and excite the will, (166) reason examines them and makes judgments concerning them, and what seems better to it, it does, when it examines with choice and considers with judgment. And therefore we despise certain pleasant things and things giving the appearance of usefulness, and certain bitter things; although we do not wish them, nevertheless we bravely endure them. To such a degree free choice exists not in the will but in the judgment of the will, and consists not in the imagination but in the assessment of the imagination itself; and therefore we are not

222. Augustine, *div. qu.* 24; Abelard (or a later scribe) breaks up the quotation from Augustine with the header "On free choice."
223. Boethius, *in Per.* 3.9.

eager for the beginnings of certain actions. For this is to use reason, to use judgment."[224]

What free choice is

Therefore, from these words of Boethius it is clear that free choice is nothing other than that faculty of the soul for deliberating and judging that which it wants to do, whether what it chooses should be done or should not be followed. Therefore, he who does not deliberate anything relevant to action, does not lack free choice, because, all the same, he is able to deliberate. No one with a sane head will contradict that this faculty is lacking in children or in the mad or the insane, who do not have the judgment of discernment. He will not concede that they deserve something, either punishment or reward, whether in these things which they do by will alone or when set in motion by an impulse of the mind, and have not been shaken by some deliberation of the soul; nor do they lie under the laws of men so that they might be thought guilty by human judgment for something.

Therefore, Augustine himself also says in his book *Questions on the Old and New Law,* "How is he decreed guilty who does not know what he did?"[225] And Jerome says in his commentary *On Ezekiel,* "As long as the soul is in childhood, it is free of sin."[226] And again you will set against me that saying of blessed Augustine cited above, that "God permits no punishment to be inflicted on anyone without cause, no reward to be given undeservedly"; that is, neither reward nor punishment is conferred on anyone who does not deserve it. This seems reprehensible not only in children, both in those damned on account of original sin and in those baptized and saved through grace alone, (167) but also even in most other people, for example Job, when he was struck, and the man blind from birth whom the Lord healed, not, as the Lord says, because he had sinned or "his parents, but so that the works of God might be manifested in him."[227] Blessed Gregory diligently considers this, and distinguishes

224. Ibid.
225. Cf. Ambrosiaster, *quaest. test.* q. 67. See above on 4.11, n. 145.
226. Jerome, *Ezech.* 4 (16.8); cf. Abelard, *Ethica* 3, ed. Luscombe, 22–23.
227. Jn 9.1–3.

the different kinds of promises[228] in Book 1 of the *Moralia*.[229]

Indeed, who does not know that God not only promises but even commands that we should repay our enemies good for evil, not according to their merits, just as we obtain many things from God through grace, which precedes and follows us, and not through merits. Therefore, the Apostle says, *But if by works, then not by grace; otherwise, grace would not be grace*.[230]

Therefore, I do not see that what the passage of Augustine asserts, which we first set forth and later opposed, namely, that God allows punishment or reward to be given to no one without cause, can easily be allowed unless we note in it a certain meaning, that when he said "God" he added "righteous" (*iustus*), so that he might note that God does not allow by righteousness (*ex iustitia*) that which he nevertheless allows by a certain provision, or else he orders it to be done from the abundance of charity rather than from the equity of righteousness. For it is righteousness (*iustitia*)[231] which renders to each one what is his own, not more or less than what is his own; that is, that thing only which he deserved, is rendered to him. But if one person bestows more good to another than he deserved, or inflicts less evil, it is of grace more than of righteousness, just as conversely it seems to be unjust if one person renders less good to another or more evil than he deserved.

Therefore, returning to the principal subject, how great should we deem that harshness which God seems to exercise in children, where, since he finds no merit, he nevertheless introduces that most oppressive punishment of infernal fire. On this account is that passage of Augustine, in the book *To Peter on Faith*: "Hold very firmly, and (168) in no way should you doubt that not only those men who now use reason, but even children, who either begin to live in their mothers' wombs and then die, or who, after they have been born, pass from this world without the sacrament of baptism, which is given in the name of the Father and of the Son and of the Holy Spirit, are to be punished with the perpetual suffering of eternal fire; because, although they had no

---

228. So Buytaert and *m*; Peppermüller reads "permissions."
229. Cf. rather Gregory, *homil.* 2, hom. 32.6.
230. Rom 11.6.   231. Or "justice."

sin of their own doing, nevertheless they acquired the damnation of original sin by their carnal conception and birth."[232]

First solution

Should it not be judged most unjust among men if someone should hand over his innocent son to transitory flames on account of the father's sin, much less to the perpetual ones? I say that by all means, it might be unjust among men, to whom vengeance for one's own injury is forbidden. But it is not so with God, who says, "Vengeance is mine, I will repay,"[233] and elsewhere, "I will kill, and I will cause to live."[234] For God causes no injustice to his creature in whatever way he should treat him, to assign [his creature] either to punishment or to rest. Otherwise animals, which were created to labor in service to humans, could justly complain and murmur against their Creator. To these murmuring about him, that passage of the Gospel responds, "Can I not do what I wish?"[235] Or that passage of the Apostle: *O man, who are you to answer God? Does the creature say to the one who fashioned it, "Why did you make me like this?" Or does the potter not have the power to make from the same mass of clay one vessel for honor, and another for disgrace?* [236] Certainly for no reason could you contend with him.

For this reason indeed I plainly declare that in whatever way God wishes to treat his creature, he cannot be accused of any injustice. That which happens according to his will cannot in any way be called evil. For we cannot otherwise distinguish good from evil, unless it is in accordance with his will and is in his plan. Therefore, also no one presumes to blame those things which seem by themselves worst and for that reason to be blamed, since they happen by the Lord's command. Otherwise the Hebrews plundering the Egyptians might seriously be accused of theft,[237] and they who killed their neighbors who committed fornication with the Midianites (169) might be judged not so much as punishers but as homicides or parricides.[238]

---

232. Fulgentius of Ruspe, *fid.* 70.
234. Dt 32.39.
236. Rom 9.20–21.
238. Nm 25.1–6.

233. Rom 12.19; cf. Dt 32.35.
235. Mt 20.15.
237. Ex 12.35–36.

To such a degree the discernment of good or evil consists in the disposition of the divine will, attending to which we cry daily: "Your will be done,"[239] as if we should thus say, Let all things be best arranged so that according to his command or prohibition the same thing that happens at one time is good and at another is evil, since by virtue of the difference of the times some observances of ancient and modern peoples may seem completely contrary to each other. For who does not know that it was first commanded to the people of old that someone should take his wife from his own tribe,[240] which is now entirely prohibited? And that then they were joined principally by marriages, now they enjoy the freedom of continence? And that circumcision and the other sacraments of the law which then were in the most high veneration by the precept of the Lord are now abominable?

It stands, therefore, as we said, that the entire discernment of good or evil consists in the plan of divine dispensation which disposes all things in the best way for us ignorant people, so that nothing should be said to happen well or badly, unless it is in accordance with or contrary to his excellent will; so that, just as we have set forth, in whatever way God wishes to treat children as well as his other creatures, we should not doubt that that happens in the best way, even if, as he might wish, he might order them all to punishment, and neither can he be accused of injustice in whatever way he might order them, either to glory or to punishment.

But because it does not suffice for the commendation of divine dispensation to absolve God from injustice in this damnation of children, unless we are able to demonstrate in some degree the grace of his goodness, it seems to us that that also is done by the dispensation of his manifold grace that abounds both to those children and the others. For we know that this is the most lenient punishment, as blessed Augustine confirms in the *Enchiridion:* "Truly, the punishment shall be the most lenient for all who, beyond the original sin which they contracted, added nothing else besides."[241] I do not think that this punishment

---

239. Mt 6.10.   240. Nm 36.7–8.
241. Augustine, *ench.* 93.

is anything other than to endure darkness, (170) that is, to lack the vision of the divine majesty without any hope of recovery. Unless I am mistaken, blessed Augustine previously named this torment of conscience the perpetual fire.[242]

We even believe that no one who dies in childhood is assigned to this most lenient punishment, unless God foresaw that this one was to be most evil if he were to live, and, on account of this, was to be afflicted with greater punishments. Therefore, children do not seem without cause to take possession of some grace of the divine goodness in this remission or alleviation of punishment.

God even uses well this most lenient punishment of children for our correction, so that of course we are made more cautious to avoid our own sins, since we should believe that such innocents, from whom neither burial nor the prayers of the faithful are withdrawn, are damned daily because of another's sins; and we should return thanks to him more fully since he frees us through his grace from that perpetual fire after the many crimes we have committed, from which [fire] he saves those [innocents] not at all. He even wished to show immediately in the first and perhaps ordinary transgression of our first parents, which he avenges in the descendants who as yet deserve nothing, how much he abhors every iniquity and what punishment he reserves for greater and frequent faults, if, in the descendants, he thus does not defer punishing this deed, which was committed once in the eating of one reparable fruit. Therefore, Jerome, in his *Epistle to the Daughter of Maurice* or *To the Virgin Consecrated to God,* says, "Adam should be spared more, who was still young and was not influenced by the example of someone sinning beforehand and dying on account of his own sin. But I do not know how it can be allowed to you, after so many examples, after the law, after the prophets, after the Gospels, after the apostles, if you wish to transgress."[243]

There are also certain peculiar and intimate reasons in the damnation of individual children, although they are hidden to us, reasons which he knows who disposes nothing except for the

242. Ibid. 68.
243. See note above on 5.16.

best. And we can indeed infer some [reasons] of this kind from these things which we frequently see happen. For it often happens that divine grace converts the death of such small children into the life of their parents, since they especially inquire[244] about their damnation, (171) which they introduced through their own concupiscence to those whom they produced, they assign it totally to their own fault and ascribe it to themselves; and, seeing this, both they and others become more fearful toward God and more pricked concerning their own sins, and come to their senses, since they have seen such a severe judgment against the children on account of concupiscence, in which they begot them.

Because of this we are invited to the good of continence rather than to indulge in such dangerous concupiscence, through which so many souls are incessantly carried down below. For these and similar reasons I judge that it is clear that God should not only not be accused of injustice concerning that most lenient damnation of children, but should even be praised on account of some conferring of his grace both on children, as was said, and on others.

Full definition of original sin

It is therefore original sin with which we are born, that debt of damnation with which we are bound, since we are made guilty of eternal punishment on account of the fault of our origin, that is, of our first parents, from whom our origin derived. For in him, as the Apostle mentioned above, we have sinned; that is, we are consigned to eternal damnation on account of his sin, so that, unless the medicines of the divine sacraments should come to our aid, we would be eternally damned.

And we should note that, although we say that children sinned in Adam, as was explained, we do not therefore simply declare that they sinned, just as when we say that some tyrant still lives in his sons, we do not therefore concede that he simply lives. Therefore, they are damned, you will say, who have

---

244. So Buytaert and *m* in the PL edition, which read *quaerentes;* Peppermüller states that all the manuscripts read *querentes,* "lament," but notes that manuscripts often render the *ae* and *oe* dipthongs simply as "e."

not sinned, which is most unjust; they are punished who have
not deserved it, which is most cruel. But perhaps this should
be conceded as far as men are concerned, not as far as God is
concerned. Otherwise, how is God not also accused for striking down children with the punishment of the flood[245] or the
burning of the Sodomites?[246] Or how did he permit blessed Job
or the holy martyrs to be afflicted or killed? Finally, he handed
over his only Son to death. He did that, you will say, well and
impressively, with a most favorable dispensation of his grace.
So also, I say, can men afflict the innocent as well as (172) the
guilty by some dispensation of most sound wisdom, and not sin
in this, as, for example, when good princes, on account of the
malice of some tyrant, are compelled to do harm to good, faithful people who are subject to him and joined to him by property, not by mind, by pillaging and plundering their lands, so that
by the harm inflicted by the select few the welfare of the many
might be provided.

It can also happen that some false witnesses, whom nevertheless we cannot refute, charge someone, who we know is innocent, concerning something. Indeed, after their testimonies
accomplished that which was adjudged regarding them, we are,
against our conscience, compelled even to oppress the innocent, so that, what is wonderful to tell, as long as we obey the
laws, we justly punish him who is not justly punished and we
justly do what is not just, when a fitting deliberation has been
held about this, lest by sparing one we should do harm to many.

So also, in the damnation of children, when they suffer what
they did not deserve, many causes of most sound divine dispensation can exist, in addition to these which we have identified,
so that it is not unjust that they are punished in this way, even
though they did not deserve it. [God] uses such punishment
not unprofitably both for them and for others, as we have ascribed above to some not improbable opinions, so that it seems
that this most lenient punishment of children should be attributed to the grace of God rather than to his righteousness, and
in what seems the greatest harshness of God, the dispensation
of great grace should be preached.

245. Gn 7.21–23.   246. Gn 19.24–25.

This is not contrary to reason if what was forgiven the parents is punished in the children, although the children do not contract this here from the fault of the parents. For a certain satisfaction intercedes for the parents and is sufficient for them only, and not for the children. For instance, when Adam and Eve were expelled from paradise, they did penance in the sweat of the face and the sorrow of birth or other afflictions because of the transgression they committed, and God was appeased with regard to them by their particular satisfaction. Finally, when they were punished with bodily death for that transgression which they committed, (173) by no means were they to be reserved for eternal death on account of that [transgression], according to that prophetic passage, "The Lord shall not judge twice against the same person, and there shall not arise a double tribulation";[247] that is, no one shall be punished with both bodily and eternal death for one and the same sin of his own. But for the children of the first parents, with all of whom God is just as angry for the fault of their fathers, as with those conceived in the sin of carnal concupiscence, which the fathers themselves incurred by the first transgression, a peculiar absolution is necessary for each one; this was established for us very lightly in baptism, so that for the sin of another with which they are bound, another's faith and confession, that of the godparents, intercedes. For he who is born bound to sin cannot yet make satisfaction for himself for that sin with which he is held fast, but he is cleansed by the sacrament of divine grace.

It should not seem astonishing if what is conceded to the parents should be exacted from the children, since that wicked generation of carnal concupiscence conveys sin and deserves wrath. Therefore, the Apostle says, "Children of wrath by nature."[248] From this wrath the first parents were indeed freed by a personal satisfaction. But it can happen in practice that, when some poor man subjugates himself and his children to the dominion of some lord, he nevertheless later gains freedom for himself by some deed of his own power or price, and not for his children.

In the very natures of things the Lord stamped a not incon-

gruent likeness of this thing on us which might in a way seem
to satisfy an objection of this sort, since only a wild olive tree is
born both from the seed of an olive tree and from the seed of a
wild olive tree, just as only a sinner is born both from the flesh
of a righteous man and from the flesh of a sinner; and from the
grain purged of chaff, grain is produced, not purged, but with
that same chaff, just as from parents cleansed from sin through
the sacrament no one is born except with sin.

But it is asked by some whether we contract sins from our immediate parents as well as from our first parents, and whether
the later someone is born, the worse off he is with multiplied
original sins. (174) To be sure, Blessed Augustine, in Chapter
46 of the *Enchiridion,* agrees that this is probably said so that the
children may also be bound with the sins of their immediate
parents, where he says,

It is not improbably said that the children are also bound with the sins
of their parents, not only of the first men, but even of their own, from
whom they were born. For that divine judgment, "I will pay back the
sins of the parents to the children,"[249] includes them especially before
they begin to belong through regeneration to the New Testament. This
Testament was prophesied when it is said through Ezekiel that the children will not receive the sins of the fathers nor will there be any longer
that parable in Israel, "The fathers have eaten sour grapes and the children's teeth became senseless."[250]

Likewise,

Regeneration was only put in place because the generation is wicked,
to so great an extent that he who was begotten from a legitimate marriage may say, "I was conceived in iniquities, and my mother conceived
me in sins."[251] He did not say here "in iniquity" or "in sin," because in
that one sin that passed into all men, and was so great that human nature was changed and converted to the necessity of death, many other
sins of the parents, as I discussed above, are found out, which also bind
the children with guilt, unless divine grace should help....But concerning the sins of the other parents from Adam himself up to one's
own father, it can be disputed whether he who is born is entangled
with the evil acts and the many original offenses of them all, so that the
later he is born, the worse off he is.[252]

249. Ex 20.5
250. Cf. Ezek 18.2; Jer 31.29; Augustine, *ench.* 46.
251. Ps 50.7.   252. Augustine, *ench.* 46–47.

It seems that these words of blessed Augustine should refer to the probable opinion of the others, just as he himself intimated, rather than to his own assertion. For who would think that Jeremiah and John the Baptist, sanctified in the womb, and born long after Cain, were worse than he?[253] Finally, the Lord Jesus, drawing his origin according to the flesh from many fathers who were sinners, was born from the Virgin long after Cain, and although he had more ancestors who were sinners than Cain did, the large number of such fathers whose flesh he received in the Virgin did him no harm.

(175) But we should not wonder that, although original sin is pardoned, the state of immortality, which through it was dismissed, is not recovered. For it ought to be enough for us, in consequence of the abundance of divine grace, if perhaps we should escape the most grave and eternal death which we incur in both ways[254] through that sin. But God's pardoning of sin is nothing other than the relief from his eternal punishment. But that punishment of bodily and transitory death is reserved for this, as I think, so that the less we strive for this temporal life, the more easily we discern that it ends and is subject to hardships, and we should love[255] that life more which is truly blessed and has no end.

Let it suffice for the present for us to have said these things about original sin less as an assertion than as an opinion. Now let us return to the exposition of the text.

[5.20] **But the law entered in,** as if someone might ask, what did the law do before the coming of Christ, if afterwards Christ removed sin when he arrived? He answers that the law not only did not remove sins, but increased them, so that Christ inevitably came down for the purpose of also removing the abundance of sins. And the *law,* namely, the written one, *entered in* after the natural one, **so that the offense might abound.** But this was said as if it should be said concerning a person: he went out that he might die; that is, he went out, and therefore death followed

---

253. Jer 1.5; Lk 1.15.

254. As Peppermüller notes (v. 2, 438, n. 121), both temporally and eternally.

255. *Diligere.*

closely, not that he went out with this intention. So, because the law was given to a rebellious people, sin abounded through a very great transgression.

But where . . ., that is, in the same people in whom **sin abounded** through the transgression of the written law, the **grace** of Christ **superabounded;** that is, good things were bestowed freely by him, not by virtue of our merits, because at that time, on that occasion, he worked our salvation in a special way, both by being born and by preaching (this is why he said, "I was sent only to the lost sheep of the house of Israel"),[256] or by forgiving sins or performing miracles, or suffering, rising again, ascending, or sending the Holy Spirit, with the result that he gathered the apostles and the first elect, through whom afterwards the entire world was won to God.

[5.21] He says that sin abounded and that grace superabounded, (176) which not only removed sin, but also conferred and multiplied the virtues, both visibly in miracles and spiritually in the interior goods of the soul, **so that just as [sin reigned unto death];** that is, this grace abounded to this end; that is, the gift was conferred freely by Christ so that it **might reign through righteousness,** that is, that it might build a kingdom of righteousness in us, [righteousness] which governs all longings and checks illicit impulses, by preparing us **for eternal life,** and this **through Christ,** who offered himself as a sacrifice for us. *Just as* formerly *sin reigned,* that is, it had its kingdom and dominion in us, leading us *unto death,* namely, of eternal damnation.

[6.1–2] **What, therefore, shall we say? Shall we remain . . .** Seeing that *where the offense abounded, grace superabounded,* someone might say, *What shall we say,* except that we should persevere **in sin, so that grace may abound** in us just as in them? **May it not be so,** the Apostle says on his part, that we should concede this: namely, that we should ever persevere in sin on some occasion. **For we who . . .** or, *For if we . . .*, as if he should say, We should not persist in sin, because we should not remain [in sin] in any way, since **we have** now **died** to it, namely, through the grace bestowed on us with respect to the forgiveness of sins.

256. Mt 15.24.

[6.3] **Or do you not know,** as if he should say, in that sacrament and likeness of the death of Christ which you received in baptism, you are admonished that after you have been made dead to sin, you should not live in it. For just as once [Christ] died in the body, once he rose again from death, not to die any more, so you also who have been freed from the death of the soul, that is, from sin, through the grace of the baptism of Christ, not of John, should not return to sin. And this is what he says: You who thus object, *Do you disregard* the sacrament, that is, the sanctification, of the baptism of Christ? *Do you not know* this, that **all we who have been baptized in Christ Jesus,** that is, with his baptism, rather than John's, **we were** (177) **baptized into his death,** that is, into the likeness and into the sign of his bodily death? Just as it was said, that just as he died once in the body and rose again, so also we should strive to die to sin once and not wish to sin again, even if we can rise again through penance.

[6.4] **For we have been buried [with him through baptism]...** After the likeness of death and burial, he also adds that of resurrection, saying that for this purpose we have been buried with Christ in baptism, **in the death** of sin, that is, in the likeness of his three-day burial through which we die to sin; we have received it for this purpose, I say: **so that as Christ** once **rose again,** once, not again to fall into death, **through the glory of** God **the Father,** that is, through the power of the divinity which is especially expressed in the name *Father,* **so also should we walk [in newness of life]** by the steps of virtue, which make a man new, not returning to the vices which are the death of the soul.

[6.5] **For if...** I said that we have received the likeness of the death and burial of Christ in baptism, so that we might possess the likeness of his resurrection through newness of life. And justly, because **if we were planted together in the likeness of** Christ's **death,** that is, if we were firmly rooted in the grace of baptism, which is the likeness of the death of Christ, just as he was immovable in the obedience of death imposed upon him by the Father (this death of his was, as it were, the planting of a seed to be fruitful and multiply, just as he himself says: "Unless a grain of wheat," etc.),[257] **we shall also be in the likeness of his resurrection;** that is, we shall arrive through the steps of virtue at the glory of his resurrection, or rather, at that newness of life which is a certain likeness on earth of the future life, which Christ first declared by rising again.

As Origen says, "Newness of life is where we put aside the old man with his acts and put on 'the new man who is renewed in the knowledge' of God.[258] That newness should be renewed daily, if it can be said. For thus he says, 'For although our outer man (178) is wasting, our inner man is renewed from day to day.'[259] They who make progress in faith always add better things to their good works."[260]

[6.6] **Knowing this,** that is, paying attention to and considering that this is signified in that genus of the death of Christ: that **the old man** in us, that is, the transgressor Adam, **was crucified together** with Christ, so that just as the crucified Christ died bodily, so we should believe that *the old man* in us dies and is crucified spiritually through baptism; that is, every transgression through which we imitate the old and first Adam is pardoned. And expounding it, this is what he adds: **so that the** entire **body of sin might be destroyed** in us, not one member, that is, that all sins, both original and one's own, might be pardoned, not just the one or the other. Anyone who is crucified has his entire body stretched out so that he cannot move his members, just as if they all were deadened. This means that all sins have been blotted out for the baptized. **So that any more,** that is, the grace of forgiveness is bestowed on us for this purpose: that as much as we are able, clinging to it and dwelling in this cleanness, **we might not serve sin** *any more;* that is, our long habit of sin will not rule over us. This habit, contrary to our wishes, holds us fast as if we were slaves in perpetuity, and not as if we were attendants made temporarily subject.

[6.7] **For he who [has died]** ... I said rightly that the old man in us was crucified and died, so that he might not serve sin in us any more, because anyone who **has died,** as Jerome says,[261] **is**

---

257. Jn 12.24.
259. 2 Cor 4.16.
258. Cf. Col 3.9–10.
260. Origen, *Rom.*, 5.8, edited.
261. Pelagius, *Rom.* 6.7: "For he who has died does not sin in any way."

justified from sin; that is, he is now alien from the work of sin, although he does not completely lack the will to sin, just as he lacks free choice for working.

[6.8] **But if [we have died with Christ],** that is, if by the death of sin we imitate Christ's death, **we believe,** that is, we hold firmly with the mind, **that we shall also live together with him,** having been glorified forever, both in body and in soul.

[6.9] He adds the perpetuity of this life, saying, **we know,** at that time through experience, what we now believe, namely, **that Christ rising from the dead,** that is, from among the dead, of which he was one, **does not now die,** either in this present age, or in the future; **death will no longer rule over him.** (179) But why does he say, ... *will no longer rule,* as if it did rule over him at first and oppressed him as if he were reluctant? Perhaps he seemed to have dreaded death to so great an extent that he said, "Father, if it is possible," and again, "Nevertheless, not as I will," etc.;[262] he did not wish in any way to die, but allowed it. But according to his divinity, just as he is indeed one with the Father, so also he is of one will, according to what he says concerning himself: "No one takes my life from me, but I lay it down," and again, "I have the power to lay down my life and to take it up again."[263] And Isaiah says, "He was offered, because he wished it."[264]

Indeed, the soul of that man desired our salvation, which it knew consisted in its death, and on account of that which it desired, it suffered this; just as someone weak or hurt tolerates many bitter things on account of the health he desires, under compulsion, not freely, through which things he thinks that he will obtain health. But whatever someone endures under compulsion, we should not say at any rate that he wishes but rather suffers it. For nothing oppresses, that is, afflicts, someone unless it is done against his will. And no one suffers in something unless it opposes his will. Therefore, we should not say that Christ's soul so much desired the afflictions of the Passion as it suffered them; but, what even Christ himself elsewhere professes, that he did not come to do his own will but the will of the

262. Mt 26.39.   263. Jn 10.18.
264. Is 53.7 (Vg).

Father.[265] Therefore, it should also be reckoned as great merit and virtue, when someone thoroughly renounces his own will for the love[266] of God, and indeed, as Christ himself elsewhere says, also hates his own life.

Therefore, in a certain way, death itself ruled over Christ's humanity, when [that humanity] shrank from death on account of its distress and wished it to pass over rather than to come. As if unwilling, he endured on account of the obedience imposed on him by the Father. He was also born under the law although he owed nothing at all to the law.[267] Therefore, such is what the Apostle says: *Death will no longer rule over him,* as if he should say, it will not oppress the unwilling, nor violently afflict the innocent. For death, as it were, worked violence against him, since (180) it oppressed an innocent man and one who submitted to absolutely no sin, and it was only inflicted on man because of sin.

But what was said, *He does not now die,* and, *Death will no longer rule over him,* can be distinguished more suitably, so that it might refer first to the death of the body, and second to the death of the soul. For such is the meaning: *He does not now die,* as if he should say, he will not incur the present death of life, namely, the death of the body; truly such is the meaning, *Death will no longer rule over him,* as if he should say, that later death, which follows bodily death in the wicked and rules over the disobedient after the resurrection, will in no way oppress him. This death rules over all whom it seizes, because it can hinder no one except against their will. But following this distinction, the text seems to prove what he says: *For because he died,* etc. For he proves here that that death which is beyond, that is, the eternal one which follows after this transitory one, *will not rule over him* because *he died once,* that is, in the body only.

[6.10] **For inasmuch as,** that is, because **he died to sin,** that is, at no time was he ever thoroughly in sin, either actual or original, by virtue of which that tyrannical death is owed to sin, therefore he could die **once** only, as was said, in the body only, and not in the soul. **But inasmuch as he lives…** He died, I say,

265. Jn 6.38.
266. *Amor.*
267. Cf. Gal 4.4.

but he now lives, having been raised, and *inasmuch as he lives,* **he lives to God.** Just as he died to sin, indeed, because he was in this present age dead to sin, it is inevitable that in the future he should live to God. He is alive to sin who sins while alive; he is alive to God who is not out of harmony with [God's] will. This is truly assigned to Christ alone, either in his very head or in his glorified members.

[6.11] **So you also...** He brings back what he said before concerning the head through a certain likeness to the members, so that they might die to sin and live to God. And because they could say that they did not know when they might be alive to sin or when to God, he says, anticipating and sweeping away this excuse, that they might at least be zealous to fulfill that according to (181) their own consideration and the capacity of their understanding. And this is what he says: **Consider [yourselves to be dead to sin, but alive to God in Christ Jesus our Lord];** that is, you should at least live in such a way that your conscience does not reprove you, if you do not yet know fully how you should live, because, as the Apostle himself elsewhere says, "If you discern otherwise, God will reveal" that "to you" also,"[268] namely, by correcting the by no means learned opinion of your simplicity. **In Christ Jesus,** that is, through the grace bestowed on you in Christ, since all things were bestowed on you by him, not through your own merits.

[6.12] **Therefore, let not...** He turns back to what was said above, *What, therefore, shall we say? Shall we remain in sin, so that grace may abound?* And when many considerations have been introduced, he concludes that we should not remain in sin, that is, it is not fitting that sin should reign in us for any reason. To continue, seeing that you should live in such a way that you consider yourselves dead to sin, **Therefore, let not sin reign in your mortal body;** that is, let it not persevere in the frailty of your fleshliness. He does not say, "let it not exist," but *let it not reign,* that is, let it not persevere by ruling. But he teaches why he does not say, "let it not exist," when he says, *in your mortal body,* that is, in the frail substance of human nature that is inclined to

268. Phil 3.15.

sin. For it is difficult, indeed in some degree impossible, that at some time this mortality of ours should not be inclined to sin; but although it is human to sin, it is diabolical, not human, to persevere in it.

But he indicates how sin might reign and obtain dominion over us by adding, **that you may obey its concupiscences.** Sin passes through us and does not reign when reason restrains what concupiscence suggests. At that time, as though ruling and dominating, it builds an immovable dwelling in us when the evil we conceive with the mind we perform in deed, or, which is worse, turn into a habit, not wishing to amend it through penance. It is the case, therefore, that obeying the concupiscence of sin leads in this way to the result, just as the soul's perverse concupiscence, which is sin's, persuades.

(182) [6.13] **But do not [give up]...** Not only should you not obey the evil concupiscence, but also let your foresight be zealous thus to anticipate it, so that when it wishes to dominate, it cannot. You shall do this, if you do not give up **your members to sin as tools of iniquity;** that is, you will not prepare those instruments for iniquity conceived with the soul, that is, for evil concupiscence, to accomplish sin with a work. But at that time we prepare our members according to the evil concupiscence to lead to the act, when we indulge excessively in food or drink whereby the flesh can easily frolic, or when we prepare and adorn ourselves in such a way as to be able to please women, or when we persist in boxing or sword fights so that through those things we may overwhelm whomever we wish, or in lawsuits when we exercise the tongue so that we may thereby gain money, and by whatever means we cause some part of our body to do some easy or convenient evil thing.

But give yourselves up, that is, prepare yourselves, **to God;** that is, devote yourselves to the divine will, inasmuch as you have been raised by him through faith, spiritually, from the death of the soul. And this is what he says: **as those made alive from the dead.** And because faith without works is dead,[269] he adds, *and give up* **your members as tools of righteousness to God,** that

269. Cf. Jas 2.17, 26.

is, as instruments which God uses for righteous works, just as if someone subdues the appetite with abstinence so that what he removes from himself he bestows on another, or keeps his hands busy in labor, *so that he may have the means to give to him who suffers need*,[270] or applies his ears to preaching or his eyes to sacred reading so that he may also be able to teach others, and so forth.

[6.14] **For sin...** I said that you should give up *your members to God,* and that you owe this chiefly on account of the grace of the Gospel, which has been brought near, and the most serious punishment of the law, which has been removed. And this is what he says: *Sin,* that is, the law of sin, that is, of punishment rather than of grace, **shall not rule over you** who have now been converted to Christ; that is, it shall not oppress and distress with those rods of intolerable punishments. Therefore, he adds the reason why, saying, **For you are not under the law;** that is, you are not now obliged under the legal institutions, as if repressed by that most heavy yoke of the law, "tooth (183) for tooth, eye for eye," etc., **but under grace,** namely, of the Gospel. We should call this, namely, the Gospel, a covenant of love[271] and mercy, just as the former was a covenant of fear and vengeance. Therefore, the Psalmist predicts in praise of Christ, "Grace is poured out on your lips";[272] that is, charity is extended as far as his enemies, according to what he says elsewhere: "Your commandment is exceedingly broad,"[273] and all your preaching resounds. He thus admonishes that all these things should be forgiven or persuades us that we toil in vain for the forgiveness of sins from God unless we forgive everyone all injustices.[274]

[6.15] **What then? Shall we sin...?** Using the opportunity of what was said before, he interposes a question and answers it saying, *What then?*—namely, what should we say or maintain? That is, we meet this question rationally, as it were: *Shall we sin* **since we are not under law but under grace?** That is, do we pervert this liberty of grace, which we have received, for the purpose of sinning, because we should not here fear bodily vengeance? **In no way,** because this is not liberty but slavery.

270. Eph 4.28.
271. *Amor.*
272. Ps 44.2.
273. Ps 118.96.
274. Cf. Mt 6.12; 18.21–35.

[6.16] And this is what he adds: **Or do you not know…;** that is, are you so dull that you do not know **that you are slaves to the one to whom you give yourselves for obedience as slaves,** that is, to whom you freely hand yourselves over, without coercion, so that you may follow what he commands, not considering whether it should be done but because it was commanded by him? **Either of sin,** that is, of a perverse will leading **to death,** that is, damnation, as it were, of the one who commands and prompts perverse works; **or of obedience,** namely, slaves, that is, of a good will or command which should be obeyed, **to righteousness,** that is, to some righteous work.

[6.17–18] **But thank…** I said *either of sin or of obedience,* as if I questioned whose slave you are, but (I, understood) *thank* **God** that, although previously **you were slaves of sin,** now you have become *slaves of obedience.* And this is what he says: **but you obeyed** (184) **from the heart,** that is, from love[275] rather than from fear, **in that form,** that is, according to that manner **of doctrine in which you were instructed** by preachers. And so, **having been freed** from the slavery of sin, which previously you obeyed, **you became slaves of righteousness,** that is, of the righteous or upright will or divine commandment, which is not only called righteous, but also righteousness.

The second book ends; the third begins.

275. *Amor.*

BOOK THREE

 (185)
[6.19]

SPEAK IN a human way, as if he should say: And now, because you have been freed from the yoke of sin and have been handed over to the obedience of righteousness, I speak by exhorting you to persist in it. And because I observe that you are still weak and carnal, that is, inclined to return to your sins, I speak to you after the manner of men, that is, more gently than is just, so that if not more, at least to the extent that you strive to fulfill the works of righteousness, you strove to serve iniquity. And this is that human saying, **on account of the weakness** of their fleshliness, that is, that [weakness] which they draw from fleshly desires. He immediately adds this, saying, **For just as...,** as if he should say, I truly speak to you in a human way because of this: that just as once **you delivered,** that is, you openly and shamelessly prepared **your members to serve filth,** that is, fleshly foulness such as excess or appetite, **and iniquity,** that is, spiritual vices such as wrath or hatred towards someone or desire for an unsuitable thing; *you delivered* [*your members*] *to serve* those things, namely, **for the purpose of** committing **iniquity,** so that a perverse desire of the mind might be guided into execution; **so now** prepare them **to serve righteousness,** that is, righteous desires **in sanctification,** that is, in the execution of a holy work.

Those who sin not so much by weakness as by zeal prepare their members for the purpose of iniquity, just as some people enjoy warm water so that they can be free more continually for dissipation or salty food, or for drink, and they often drive the very members of their body to disgrace against their nature. He also prepares his own hand for committing iniquity, if he provides to it the sword which he uses against him whom he hates. On the contrary, he prepares his members for righteousness if he tries to govern them and hold them in check lest they burst forth to unlawful things, but so that they may make progress toward the crown; since "he had the power but did not transgress"[1] those things; indeed, he courageously destroyed every impulse of improper suggestion in them and supplied them with whatever he could for doing well, such as sacred texts for the eyes, readings for the ears, the works of mercy or the tools of religious labor for the hands.

(186) [6.20] **For when…** I said rightly that now, *having been freed from sin, you became slaves of righteousness*, because on the contrary, being at that time **slaves of sin, you were free for righteousness,** that is, you were strangers to the slavery of righteousness. A consideration from contraries: just as he is called a slave of righteousness who serves it, so on the contrary he is called free of it who is far from its slavery, that is, who does not take care to fulfill it.

[6.21] **What fruit, therefore…** that is, seeing that at one time you were slaves to sin, complete strangers to righteousness, *what fruit,* that is, benefit, **did you then have,** from the things referred to above, namely, filth and iniquity? **Of which,** that is, the committing of which things, **you are now ashamed.** And this is what he says: **The end of those things,** that is, to which the particular consequence owed to them leads, **is death,** namely, of the soul, that is, the torment of everlasting punishment.

[6.22] **But now, having been freed from sin,** that is, from the burdensome yoke of evil habit, **[you have become slaves to God, and] you have,** here and now, **your fruit in sanctification;** that is, you have the very forgiveness of sins by which you are sanctified as a reward. **And the end,** that is, the conclusion to which this sanctification leads, you have now prepared for you, **eternal life.** He justly says that *the end* is both the eternal *life* and the eternal death of the soul. These extremes follow when the life of the body and temporal death have ended.

[6.23] **For the wages [of sin is death]…** To those two things said before, *For the end of those things,* etc., and *But now, having been freed,* etc., he adds these two: *For the wages,* etc., and: **But the grace of God [is eternal life in Jesus Christ our Lord],** showing

1. Sir 31.10.

how he arrives at the two ends that he specifies, namely, death and life, at death on account of righteousness, but at life on account of the grace conferred previously through Christ. *For the sufferings of this time are not to be compared with the future glory which shall be revealed in us.*[2] Therefore, he rightly calls the reward of sin proceeding from death "wages," but he names the reward for obedience to God proceeding from eternal life, not "wages," but "grace." For the term "wages," *stipendium*, comes from the noun form *stipe*, "gift," and the verb *penso-pensas*, "to compensate." But gifts or a gift is called the wage that is granted to soldiers when their work is compensated or their usefulness to their commanders is examined. (187) But Haymo says this: Wages, "that is, reward," "is called *stipendium* from the gift to be weighed (*stipe pendenda*), that is, the substance to be weighed. For in ancient times money was weighed out rather than counted out."[3]

Continue in this way: I said that *the end of those things,* that is, of filth and iniquity, *is death,* and rightly because they are the *wages* of every sin; that is, death is the righteous and due reward for those, namely, who persevere in it. But **eternal life** should be called the *grace of God* rather than our *wages;* that is, it is freely bestowed upon us rather than owed to our merits, and this is through Christ Jesus, through whom we are reconciled to God.

[7.1] **Or do you not know...** The Apostle had said above, *For you are not under the law but under grace,*[4] and again he added here most recently that we obtained this grace of eternal life *through Jesus Christ* our Lord, rather than through the law. Therefore, because someone could ask, After the law was given, how could anyone be saved without observing it? Is any grace at all added? The Apostle anticipated and explained such a question in a suitable likeness, showing that just as a woman whose first husband has died can pass over to another without blame, so the people of God, bound once to the yoke of the law like a woman to a man she is bound to obey, can pass to the liberty of the Gospel without blame, now that the law has died. For "the law and the prophets [were in effect] up to John,"[5] whose name

2. Rom 8.18.   3. Haymo, *Rom.*, 6.23.
4. 6.15   5. Lk. 16.16.

is interpreted as "the grace of God," that is, up to the time of the singular grace of the coming of Christ. The Lord promised this time when he said through Jeremiah, "Behold, the days are coming, says the Lord."[6] The Apostle himself mentions this in the Epistle to the Hebrews, concerning the change of the Testament, the death of the Old and the birth of the New.[7]

To continue: I said that you are no longer under the law, and I taught that after Christ it was no longer necessary for you. Indeed, this should not seem extraordinary, because *Do you not know,* **brothers,** (188) that is, I do not believe that you do not know, **that the law rules in a man,** that is, it is to be obeyed by the man **as long as he lives,** that is, for the whole time determined beforehand and granted to him by the Lord, so that its obedience might prevail and be kept purely even in those figural precepts. But he interposes this: **for I speak to those who know the law,** that is, to you who once learned the law. He shows that this scolding especially is directed to those who had believed among the Jews, concerning whom he here alleges as a cause, in regard to what he says, that they are not ignorant, because they learned the law which teaches this: that it has a time fixed and determined for itself by God, so that it might not always live, as was said, just as is confirmed in the testimony of Jeremiah cited above or in other passages of the Old Testament.

[7.2–3] **For the woman who...** He shows with a suitable likeness that the law exercises domination over a subject people only in the time when it lives, because a husband does not have dominion over the wife bound to himself except while he lives. And this is what he says: *For the woman who* **is under the husband,** that is, joined to him as if to a superior, **while he lives, is bound to** his **law,** that is, the marital law, so that she might not be able to marry anyone else. **Therefore, while he lives [she will be called an adulteress if she should be with another man; but if her husband dies, she is freed from the husband's law, so that she is not an adulteress if she is with another man],** because she is thus bound to the law of matrimony.

[7.4] **Therefore, brothers...** He now adapts the previous like-

6. Jer 31.31; Heb 8.8.
7. Heb 8.6–13.

ness, saying, And so, that is, to this extent, **you,** who at first lived to the law, subjected to it through obedience, **you have now become dead** to it **through the body of Christ,** that is, through the very presence of the truth delivered to you in Christ. The shadow of this truth preceded in the law. For after the reality itself came, which is adequate by itself, those figures are no longer needed which preceded in the sign of the reality yet to be, and were worthy of worship only in the hope of that reality, lest, even if those figures persisted up to this time, the reality might be expected in a future which has now passed; and the Jews, still boasting in their antiquity, might scoff at our newness, and some might trust more in their own works than in faith in Christ, which they believe by no means suffices without works.

(189) In truth, we should note that although, according to the likeness introduced, it might seem more appropriate to say that the law died to us than we to the law; nevertheless, because the meaning is the same, it matters nothing whether it is said in this or that way.

So that you may belong to another, that is, Christ, bound only to his precepts of obedience and of the teaching of the Gospel. And lest someone object that Christ himself also died and so his own have now been set free from his yoke, he providently added, **who rose from the dead;** that is, he raised himself up from among the dead into perpetual life by his own power, **so that we,** having been kindled with the hope and desire for the same glory, **might bear fruit,** not to the world, but **to God;** that is, that we should abound with spiritual goods, with which God is delighted, rather than with mundane and worldly things, which the Jews always eagerly desired; of these, according to the letter which they pursue, no promise is obtained except a worldly one, so that by the promise of the law they thus may be said to bear fruit to the world rather than to God. For God promised to that stiff-necked people what he knew they desired more, so that he might thus attract more to obedience those who were carnal, that is, those who were eager for carnal goods rather than for spiritual ones. And consider that—since to that which he said before, *that you may belong to another who rose from the dead,* he added, *that we may bear fruit to God*—he did not say, "that you might bear fruit," but that we and you equally, that is, everyone, *may bear fruit,* either by preaching or by obeying.

[7.5] **For when we were [in the flesh]**...He said, *that you,* namely, disciples and imitators, *may belong to another,* as you did, up to that point, *that* you may bear *fruit to God,* that is, that you may be spiritual through desire rather than carnal as you once were, following the temporal promise of the law. And so he justly advises, Because, at that time through that promise of the law, you, lovers of carnal desires, could by no means render spiritual fruit to God, but rather, to death, you had mortal and damnable fruit, always adhering more and more to earthly things through concupiscence, according to what is written:

Care follows growing wealth. [8]

And elsewhere,

The love of money grows as much as wealth itself grows.[9]

Read it in this way: **When we were in the flesh,** that is, gazing eagerly at fleshly desires, (190) not at spiritual ones, the **passions of sin,** that is, the diverse concupiscences causing us to sin, so that "passions of sin" may be, as it were, an intransitive saying, that is, they were sins, just as it is said, "creature of salt" or "substance or body of stone,"[10] that is, a creature which is salt, or a substance or a body which is stone. **Which,** namely, *passions,* **were through the law,** which praises and promises the great abundance of those things which they greatly desired, namely, the best land, flowing with milk and honey, and the greatest peace and prosperity in it and long life and whatever pertains to earthly happiness, which they especially desired. By praise, promise, and hope of these things they were kindled more in the desire of them than if they in no way hoped for them or learned that they are so great. For we are not controlled greatly or continually by desire for those things we despair of. **They worked in our members so that they might bear fruit for death;** that is, they gained for us the mortal death of

8. Horace, *Odes,* 3.16.18.
9. Juvenal, *Satires* 14.139.
10. Cf. *Rituale Romanum,* the blessing of salt or stone.

damnation. Concupiscences work *in the members* when we fulfill with a work through some member the desire conceived with the mind, such as lust through the genitals or theft or pillage through the hand.

[7.6] **But now we have been set free** from that obedience to the law, which was used as a reward of temporal things, as was said, **so that in the same way we should** now **serve** God, with the mind rather than with a work, fulfilling those figures of the law spiritually rather than bodily, just as it is said elsewhere, "For the letter kills, but the Spirit gives life."[11] **In the newness of the Spirit,** that is, in spiritual desires and the understanding which did not exist before, **and not in the oldness of the letter,** that is, in ancient works which were done only according to the letter, such as fleshly circumcision, the observance of the sabbath, sacrifices, and innumerable other things.

Question

Perhaps someone might ask why even the law did not contain the promise of eternal life, so that the people might be attracted to obedience not only with desires for earthly gifts but even more for heavenly ones. But because it contained imperfect precepts, (191) just as the same Apostle mentions elsewhere, saying that "the law brought nothing to perfection,"[12] and the Truth says through himself, "You have heard that it was said to the ancients," etc., and, "Unless your righteousness abounds," etc.,[13] its reward could not be perfect; neither were heavenly things suitable for earthly desires, nor can someone be fit for God who serves as much for earthly things as for heavenly ones. Therefore, the Truth warns through itself, saying, "Let not your left hand know what your right hand is doing";[14] that is, do not mix an earthly intention with a heavenly one in any work of yours, so that you obey God for transitory and eternal goods at the same time.

11. 2 Cor 3.6.
13. Mt 5.21, 20.
12. Heb 7.19.
14. Mt 6.3.

Question

But perhaps while we desire to loosen the knots of the proposed question, we run into greater ones by this solution. For since there is a command in the law concerning the love[15] of God and neighbor, and since these two commands are enough for life—therefore, the Lord responded to the rich man who asked what he must do to possess eternal life that he must keep these two commands and they would be enough,[16] and Paul himself acknowledges that love is the fullness of the law[17]—it seems extraordinary that the law should bring nothing to perfection and that it should not be enough for life, so that justly the righteousness of the Gospel should have abounded on account of this. In fact, the commands of the law, whether concerning love or concerning other things, did not bring to perfection; that is, they could not be enough for salvation; but it was necessary that Christ should come, who is the end and the completion of the law, since without him, promised in the law, the law could in no way be fulfilled.

But if we also diligently examine the words of the law, nowhere does the law extend the term "neighbor" except to the men of his people, that is, the Jews; nor at any place in the entire law of Moses is it found written among us, "You shall love your neighbor," but "You shall love your friend."[18] The Lord himself diligently considered this when the rich man, being questioned, recited the commandments of the law to him and said, "You shall love your neighbor as yourself,"[19] and openly taught that "neighbor" be used instead of friend or benefactor on account of the added parable, showing by this discernment regarding the rich man that he only who applied mercy (192) to him who had fallen among thieves was his neighbor.[20] And through this it is clear, since the love of neighbor is applied to a friend only according to the letter of the law, that by no means is the command of love which is in the law perfect, as is that command of the Gospel in which we are commanded to love

---

15. *Dilectio*, here and throughout this question on love of God and neighbor.
16. Cf. Mt 19.16–22; Mk. 10.17–22; Lk 18.18–20.
17. Rom 13.10.   18. Lv 19.18.
19. Mt 19.19.   20. Lk 10.29–37.

our enemies and to do good to them also, so that we may be perfect just as the heavenly Father is, "who makes his sun to rise on the good and the evil."[21] The Apostle himself, noting this, does not say, *he who loves his neighbor* fulfills righteousness or the Gospel, but *fulfills the law.*[22]

Question

And again we run into the serious knot of the question of the rich man who asks what he must do to possess eternal life, and after he recited the two commands concerning love[23] of God and neighbor, the Lord answered him, "Do this and you shall live";[24] especially since he says elsewhere, "For if you love those who love you, what reward will you have?"[25] But certainly no one was to be understood better either as neighbor or as friend than he whom he designated a Samaritan, the one who applied mercy to the wounded person, that is, Christ, who certainly was a neighbor to the Jews both by blood-relationship and by the disposition of true charity or uncounted benefits,[26] whether by preaching or by performing miracles. If, therefore, that rich man then loved every neighbor or friend, and Christ, by all means, he also thus deserved eternal life by clinging to him and to his commands.[27]

Nevertheless, the command which the law had given concerning love of neighbor, that is, of friend or benefactor, had not been perfect, since by no means did it comprehend every person, both friend and enemy, although in the time of Christ it seemed to be enough on account of Christ, indeed through Christ himself, who had come and had been made a neighbor, as was said; but the commandment or law had perfection at that time, if by itself it was enough that nothing at any time should be lacking to those obeying it for the integrity of righteousness, and that it was not necessary for anything else to be added. This is by no means true, since before the coming of Christ, the love

---

21. Mt 5.44–45.   22. Rom 13.8.
23. *Dilectio*, here and throughout this question.
24. Lk 10.28.   25. Mt 5.46.
26. Cf. Lk 10.33–35.
27. Cf. Mt 19.16–22; Mk 10.17–22; Lk 18.18–20.

of those neighbors and friends who lived at that time (193) was imperfect, and was not extended as far as one's enemies, just as, later on, it was extended through Christ.

What we said above, that not every man is understood as the neighbor in the law according to the letter, can be demonstrated not only from the law itself, but also from some testimonies of the doctors of the Church. Thus Ambrose says in his commentary *On the Epistle of Paul to the Romans,* where it is written, "*Owe nothing to anyone,* etc. He wishes us to have peace with all, if it can happen, but love with the brothers."[28] And this will be to owe nothing to anyone, to render service to all people according to their respective ranks. Likewise, he says later, "*Love of neighbor works no evil.*[29] It works no evil because love is good; sin cannot be committed through that which is the perfection of the law. But because in the time of Christ it was necessary that something be added, he commanded that not only neighbors but enemies be loved. Therefore, *the fullness of the law is love,* so that it may be righteousness to love one's neighbor, and indeed, an overflowing and perfect righteousness to love one's enemies. This is heavenly righteousness, this brings about the resemblance to God the Father, who bestows yearly gifts upon those who do not worship him."[30]

It does not escape our notice that most of the holy fathers understand "neighbor," in the commandment concerning love of neighbor, as every person, and they assert this with likely reasons. Therefore, Augustine says in Book 1 of *On Christian Doctrine,* "It can be asked whether love of angels is relevant to those two commandments. For both the Lord and the Apostle Paul show that he who teaches that we should love our neighbor has left out no one."[31] Likewise, "He made known the two commandments and said that all the law and the prophets depend on them." Likewise, "The Lord said, 'Go and do likewise,' so that we may understand that he is our neighbor to whom the duty of mercy should be rendered if he requires it, or was to be

---

28. Ambrosiaster, *Rom.* 13.8, literal citation.
29. Rom 13.10.
30. Ambrosiaster, *Rom.* 13.10, literal, edited.
31. Augustine, *doc. Chr.* 1.30.31, literal, edited.

rendered if he required it. From this it now follows that he also by whom it is to be shown to us in turn (194) is our neighbor. For the name of neighbor is in relation to something, and one can only be a neighbor to a neighbor." Likewise, "Paul says, *For you shall not commit adultery, you shall not murder, you shall not steal, you shall not covet, and if there is another commandment, it is summed up in this word: 'You shall love your neighbor as yourself.'"*[32] Likewise, "Whoever, therefore, thinks that the Apostle did not command concerning every man, is compelled to confess what is most shameful, that it seemed to the Apostle not to be sin if someone committed adultery with the wife of a non-Christian or of an enemy," etc. Likewise, "Now, if the one to whom the duty of mercy is to be offered, or by whom it is to be offered to us, is rightly called 'neighbor,' it is clear that this precept, by which we are ordered to love our neighbor, even includes the holy angels, by whom the duties of mercy are employed."[33]

These [teachings] of our most scrupulous teacher Augustine according to the words of the Apostle seem to show clearly in every way that the neighbor in the law should be understood as everybody. Otherwise, the law would seem to be in no way fulfilled through the love of neighbor, which law commands many things concerning foreigners, against whom offense is to be avoided, just as offense against neighbors is.

But since there are two branches of love, namely, love of God, whose Truth says that this is "the first and greatest commandment,"[34] and love of neighbor, in the manner that the law is fulfilled through love of neighbor only if the latter love also includes the former, since we should understand no one more rightly as neighbor or friend than our Maker and Redeemer, from whom we have both ourselves and all good things, just as the Apostle himself says, "But what do you have which you did not receive?"[35] Concerning his ineffable charity surrounding us he elsewhere says, *But God commends his charity towards us in that while we were still sinners, Christ died for us.*[36] Likewise again, (195) *He did not spare his own Son, but handed him over for us all.*[37] And

---

32. Rom 13.9.   33. *doc. Chr.* 1.30–31, 32–33.
34. Mt 22.38.   35. 1 Cor 4.7.
36. Rom 5.8.   37. Rom 8.32.

the Son says through himself, "No one has greater love than this, that he [should lay down] his own life," etc.[38]

Therefore, Origen specifically understands this neighbor in this commandment of love when he says in the following parts of this epistle, "If you more scrupulously ask who is our neighbor, you will learn that in the Gospel he is the one who brought us who were lying wounded to the stable of the Church, and granted to the stable-keeper, either Paul or him who is in charge of the Church, the two denarii of the Old and New Testaments for the expenses of our care. If we love this neighbor, we fulfill the law. *For Christ is the end of the law,* etc."[39]

Since, therefore, the term "neighbor" includes even and especially God—for love of neighbor would not otherwise fulfill the law—it is established that the law is fulfilled through it and through the love of God, because he who truly clings to God through love, disregards none of his commandments, just as it is written, "If someone loves me, he will keep my word."[40] How can the love be true which is called charity, unless it refers to God? Therefore, Augustine also says in Book 4 of *On Christian Doctrine:* "I call charity the movement of the soul for enjoying God for his own sake, and himself and his neighbor for God's sake."[41] He also says in his book *On the Customs of the Church, Against the Manichees,* "*It is written, 'On account of you we are afflicted all day long.'*[42] Charity could not be marked more clearly than by the words *on account of you.*"[43] Whoever, therefore, clings to God by charity, by which alone the sons of God are distinguished from the sons of the devil, and therefore tries to obey his commandments, desires to fulfill those things which pertain to strangers as much as they concern neighbors; and in relation to each one he strives to follow the divine will equally.

Therefore, it is of no consequence that we speak with sound reverence of the fathers or the brothers and acknowledge that the law leaves off far from the perfection of the Gospel, (196) and moreover preserve every authority, apostolic as well as evan-

---

38. Jn 15.13.
39. Origen, *Rom.,* 9.31, literal, but considerably edited.
40. Jn 14.23.   41. Not *doc. Chr.* 4, but 3.10.16.
42. Rom 8.36; Ps 44.22.   43. *mor.* 1.9.15.

gelical. It is of no consequence, I say, whether we understand that the neighbor in the law is every man or, at least, provided that, as was said, God should be comprehended in the neighbor, and the love of neighbor includes also the love of God. For when it is said, "You shall love your neighbor,"[44] and "as yourself" is added, how could we fulfill that, unless we also love ourselves? But how can we love even ourselves, if, despising the commandments of God, we act unjustly? "For he who loves iniquity hates his own soul."[45]

[7.7] **What, therefore, shall we say? Is the law sin?** To continue: I said that once *the passions of sin* worked through the law, so that it might be useful for us to be set free from the law as if from sin. *What therefore shall we say?* That is, what should we think concerning the law which we held as good? Does it not now seem that it should be called evil rather than good? And this is what he says, as if opposing himself: *Is the law sin?* That is, does it draw to damnation rather than to salvation, so that it may earn damnation for us rather than salvation and only be able to do harm and not help, and have no more good in it than sin? **By no means,** namely, in order that we may believe this. **But sin...,** that is, [the law] is by all means more contrary to sin, by thoroughly teaching that it should be avoided and forbidding it, so that not only does it restrain deeds, but also concupiscences, just as the Gospel does; but less by far, since it confines them to those things only which are the neighbor's, saying, "You shall not covet your neighbor's property nor desire what belongs to him."[46]

But he asks previously why it was inevitable that sin be taught by the law, saying that before the teaching of the law, in which sin was especially committed, it was not known, that is, in the heart rather than in the work. And this is what he says about himself in the general person of men whose mind was darkened through the transgression of the first parents, so that they might condemn works rather than desires: **I did not know sin,** that is, I did not have discernment for true knowledge of sin, **except through** the teaching of (197) **the law,** because that in

44. Mt 22.39.   45. Ps 10.6.
46. Ex 20.17.

which sin is merely or especially committed, that is, concupiscence, I did not know to be sin. And this is what he adds: **For [I did not know] concupiscence,** that is, the depraved desire of the soul, namely, in the striving for earthly or fleshly pleasures; **I did not know** that this was sin, **except that the law,** by teaching it, **said, You shall not covet,** that is, except that it forbade concupiscence, although not generally, but concerning the property of the neighbor, as was said.

Note that when it is said, *You shall not covet,* sin is simultaneously both taught and prohibited, so that it might be avoided.[47] Therefore, he shows that the law is thoroughly good, because whatever belongs to it is good, whether in teaching or prohibiting; if sin abounded after the law, it should be reckoned not to a defect of the law, but of men, and we are made worse and more inexcusable after the teaching of the commandments and the negligence of them than before, according to what is written: "The slave who knows and does not do his lord's will shall be beaten with many strokes,"[48] and again, "It is better not to know the way of truth than to go back after having known it."[49] Therefore, it is rightly said, *by no means* is the law sin, that is, useless and evil by itself. But nevertheless we received from the law the opportunity for sin, which before did not exist, just as we often run into concupiscence on account of some good things which God creates, if we are without these things, or into pride, if we have them. Therefore, those things should not be called evil, if we desire or use them badly.

[7.8] Read it thus: **Sin,** that is, the punishment and the affliction of this temporal life, which we endure because of the sin of the first parents, **worked every concupiscence** in us, namely, for all earthly goods, so that through their abundance we might avoid every anxiety of earthly hardships. And he shows the way it worked, saying, **when the opportunity was received...through the commandment,** that is, through the obedience of the law that promises these earthly goods. For because the law prom-

47. So Peppermüller and *m*/PL (*vitetur*). Buytaert reads *videtur,* "understood" or "perceived," but notes no textual variants.

48. Lk 12.47.

49. Cf. 2 Pt 2.21.

ised these things on account of obedience to itself, we did not appear to sin, (198) however much we might covet those things, if we devoted the required obedience. But that which he calls *sin* in this passage, he teaches is the kindling wood, that is, the fuel, of sin; we did not pass this by in the previous book when we discussed original sin.[50] **For without the law,** that is, before the law conveyed commandments and promises, that **sin,** that is, that kindling wood of sin, as was said, though at that time it existed, it was as though dead, because it had fewer powers for arousing concupiscence than later. For we hope for what we desire the more certainly, the more we are kindled in concupiscence for it, just as we mentioned above.[51]

[7.9] **But at one time I lived [without the law];** that is, in some way, not totally, I lacked the death of that kindling wood, and I was, as it were, without concupiscence in comparison to the concupiscence that followed after the law. **But when the commandment came,** when the law was given, **sin revived;** that is, after the commandment concupiscence became strong, or *revived* in the offspring, in that it went before in the parent; that is, concupiscence was thus awakened in us after the commandment, just as it was begun in the first parents after the commandment, especially since what is prohibited is often desired even more ardently, according to what the poet says,

We always strive for what is forbidden and desire the things that are denied.[52]

[7.10] **But I died.** At first I was, as it were, weak, not dead, and I was to be, as it were, corrected, not condemned; scourged, not killed; and roused with a lesser reward, if it was by that concupiscence; **and [the commandment which was for life] was found for me [to be death];** that is, by the opportunity of the law, as was said, by which I should have been better, I was made much worse, and therefore the sin I should have avoided, I incurred more.

[7.11] And this is what he adds: **For sin, when the opportunity was received,** that is, when a reason was found for arousing us

50. See above on 5.19.   51. See above on 7.5.
52. Ovid, *Amores* 3, *eleg.* 4.17.

to concupiscence **through the commandment,** that is, the law, the obedience of which we took too much for granted, **led me astray;** that is, it deceived me, reckoning that I was particularly dear to God on account of the law which he had given me and on account of the obedience to the law which I showed to him, so that whatever I might do, scarcely or never might I be fearful of my condemnation; and I especially did not think concupiscence toward the promises, (199) however strong it might be, to be damnable, since we obeyed on account of the other [commandments], for the obedience of which they were promised. **And through it [sin] killed me,** that is, condemned me.

[7.12] **Therefore, the law . . .** Since the law is the knowledge of sin and was given for life rather than for death, therefore *the law indeed* **is holy,** that is, defective or culpable in nothing, and his **commandment is holy,** commanding and prohibiting nothing except what is necessary, and therefore **righteous** in itself **and good,** that is, useful and salutary to those who obey.

[7.13] **Therefore, did what is good . . .** He said two things: both that the commandment is good and that through it, nevertheless, *when the opportunity was received,* he was killed. Therefore, as if objecting rationally, he asks, therefore, *did what is good* in itself, namely, the very commandment, **become death for me,** that is, condemnation? **May it not be so.** For the commandment should be called damnable of no one, unless obedience of it is pernicious, just as the commandment of the devil was to Eve.[53] **But sin . . .** I said that because the commandment *is good,* it should not be said that it was *death,* that is, what is damnable, to me or to anyone. But nevertheless it somehow became a cause of condemnation to me, by itself, as was said, *when the opportunity* of concupiscence *was received,* according to what the historian said, "All bad things rose from good beginnings."[54]

Read it in this way: *But sin,* that is, the kindling wood, as we said, of sin, **worked the death** of the soul, that is, every concupiscence, **through what is good,** the commandment of the law or

53. Cf. Gn 3.4–5, 16.
54. Not yet identified, though Peppermüller points out similar passages in Ambrose, *Isaac* 7.60; Augustine, *ench.* 14 and *c. Jul. imp.* 1.37 (*Römerbrief,* 2.512, n. 33).

through the law itself being understood, as we showed above, **so that it may appear as sin,** that is, that that fault of concupiscence may be manifest and inexcusable, and that it may be the greatest. And immediately he shows that it is so great, saying, **so that sin,** that is, the kindling wood of sin as was said above, **might become sinful beyond measure,** that is, inclining us especially to sinning **through the commandment,** that is, *when the opportunity was received* from the law, as was said.

Question

Perhaps someone may ask how the commandment of the law, or the law itself, is called good or given for life, or even why it was given by God, (200) if it could not save those obeying it? To this we respond that the law was given for life in this way, that it might initiate, not accomplish, the merit of eternal life for the people of God; and therefore it is good only because all his commandments are righteous according to the letter, if not perfect, as has been said, and whatever things God commands have rational causes, even if we do not know them. But it was a dispensation of great providence to give some commandments, for a beginning, not for perfection, to a still thoroughly rude and undisciplined people, always stiff-necked and rebellious, so that at least in something this people might learn to obey who attempted no or almost no obedience, as the poet says, "One may go so far, if he is not permitted beyond."[55]

When we subdue beasts, we do not impose great burdens on them at first, but we employ disciplined novelty with their young at first, for the purpose of bearing great burdens gradually.

Nevertheless, we believe that all those who comply with the imperfection of the commandments more by the love[56] of God than by fear, what was lacking to them of perfection through ignorance, because the law was silent, is revealed to them either through some spiritual teacher or through some internal inspiration of divine grace before the day of their departure. For that people before had many spiritual men [who were] already through inspiration instructed in the teaching of evangelical

55. Horace, *Ep.*, bk 1, ep. 1.32.
56. *Amor.*

preaching, who even taught love of enemies not only in their writings but especially in their deeds. Therefore, the psalmist says, "If I rendered to those paying me back evil," etc.,[57] and again, "With those who hated peace I was peaceable."[58] David not only did not kill his greatest enemy, Saul, when the Lord put him into his hand, but even lamented deeply when he was killed and immediately punished with death the one who professed to be his killer.[59] Solomon also commends kindness towards enemies when he says, "If your enemy is hungry, feed him," etc.[60]

On the charity of God

Nevertheless, the teachings of the law as well as of the prophets are far removed from evangelical perfection. (201) The Truth, exhorting his disciples to this perfection, said, "A new commandment I give to you, that you should love[61] each other just as I have loved you."[62] This is that true and genuine love which the Apostle describes, saying, "It does not seek its own; it endures all things, believes all things, hopes all things, bears all things,"[63] so that it may even be ready to lay down its life for the brothers,[64] to use not only what belongs to it for them but its own self. And if we diligently consider what the Truth says, "just as I have loved you," and what the Apostle says, "Charity does not seek its own," we will in fact find a singular and new evangelical commandment concerning love of neighbor. For the love of Christ towards us was so genuine that not only did he die for us, but even in all the things he did for us he sought no advantage of his own, whether temporal or eternal, but our own. He did this not with any intention of his own reward, but entirely with the desire for our salvation.

In fact, this true and genuine love, which the Apostle diligently considers, he commends to us both in writing and by example when he says, "Just as I please everyone in all things,

---

57. Ps 7.5.   58. Ps 119.7.
59. 1 Sm 24.1–22; 26.1–25; 2 Sm 1.1–16.
60. Prv 25.21.
61. *Dilectio/diligere* throughout this question except where noted.
62. Jn 13.34.   63. 1 Cor 13.5, 7.
64. Cf. Jn 15.13.

seeking not what will profit me, but what will profit many people, that they may be saved."[65] Nevertheless he who acts thus ought to be certain of the very full reward of such great love. He does not do this with this intention, however, if he loves perfectly. Otherwise he seeks his own and is, as it were, a hired servant, although in spiritual things.

It should not even be called "charity" if we love him for our own sakes, that is, for our own advantage and for the happiness of his kingdom which we look for from him, rather than for his own sake, establishing the end of our own intention in ourselves, and not in him. Indeed, such men should be called the friends of fortune rather than of a man, and were made subject through avarice more than through grace.

Blessed Augustine diligently considers this in Chapter 35 of his book of *83 Questions*, where he says, (202) "To love[66] is nothing other than to desire something for its own sake."[67] Again, expounding that passage of scripture, "I will sacrifice to you willingly and I will confess your name, because it is good,"[68] he says,

What shall I offer, except what he says: "The sacrifice of praise will honor me"? Why "willingly"? Because I love freely what I praise, what is loved and praised is free. What is free? He is, on account of his own self, not on account of another. For if you praise God because he gives you something, you do not now love God freely. You would be ashamed if your wife loved [you] on account of wealth, and perhaps considered adultery if you fell into poverty. Since you wish to be loved freely by your wife, will you love God on account of something else? What reward will you receive from God, O grasping man? He reserves for you not the earth, but himself, "Who made heaven and earth."[69] "I will sacrifice to you willingly"; do not sacrifice by necessity! For if you praise on account of something else, you praise by necessity. If what you love were present to you, you would not praise.[70]

Again he says, "Disregard everything; consider him. The things which he gave are good on account of the giver."[71] Likewise, "Love[72] him freely, because you will not get something better

65. 1 Cor 10.33.

66. *Amare* and *amor* throughout the quotation from Augustine, except at the end.

67. Augustine, *div. qu.*, q. 35.1.   68. Ps 53.8.

69. Ps 113.24.   70. Augustine, *en. Ps.*, in Ps 53.10.

71. Ibid., 654.   72. *Diligere.*

from him which he gives than himself; or if you do find a better, seek this one. 'Willingly'? Because it is free. Why is it free? 'Because it is good,' for no other reason except that 'it is good.'"[73]

Therefore, by these words of blessed Augustine it is declared openly what true and genuine love towards someone is, namely, to love him for his own sake, not for what he has. Finally, if I love God because he loves me, and not because, whatever he does for me, he is someone who should be loved above all things, then that saying of the Truth is spoken against me, "For if you love those who love you, what reward will you have?"[74] Certainly not the reward of righteousness, because I do not consider the equity of the thing loved, but my advantage. And I might love another equally or more, if it profited me equally or more; indeed, I might not love him if I did not look for my own advantage in him.

Therefore, many and nearly all people have sunk down into such a reprobate understanding, (203) that they plainly acknowledge that they in no way adore or love God, if they believe that he will be of minimal use to them, since, nevertheless, he is not to be loved less if he should punish someone, since he would only do this justly and because of the person's preceding merits or with some rational motive, which should please everyone because it is just. Finally, who determines that someone is worthy of thanks who, he knows, serves for reward, not freely for itself, but with the desire for repayment? If thanks should be given for any deed in repayment for this servitude, they should be given more for our deeds, for which we are served, than to these who serve for reward, just as when the hireling whom I hired for myself serves and succeeds greatly for a great reward, or when someone serves me by love[75] for another, and not for me, thanks should be rendered for these things which happen, and not bestowed on those who act.

---

73. Augustine, *en. Ps.*, on Ps 53.10. "It" refers to "your name" (*nomen tuum*) in Ps 53.8 (Vg).
74. Mt 5.46.
75. *Amor.*

Objection

Perhaps you say that God will repay us with himself, not some other benefit, and he will give us himself, than which there is nothing greater, as blessed Augustine also mentions.[76] Therefore, when you serve him for reward in expectation of something from him, that is, for the eternal blessedness promised to you, you especially act purely and genuinely on account of that, and for that reward with which you are obligated, just as he himself advises, calling those blessed who have made themselves eunuchs for the sake of the Kingdom of Heaven;[77] and the psalmist says, "I have inclined my heart to performing your justifications on account of reward."[78] And then, truly we would love[79] God purely and genuinely for himself, if we were to do this for himself alone, and not for our own advantage; we should not consider the kinds of things he gives us, but what he is in himself. But if we consider him only in the cause of love, to whatever extent he would truly act, either in us or in others, since he would only do that in the best way, we would love him in like manner, as was said, because we would always find in him the cause of our whole love, who always perseveres purely and in the same way is good in himself and worthy of love.[80]

Such is the true affection of the father's love[81] toward the son, or (204) of the chaste wife toward her husband, since they love[82] them, even if they are useless by themselves, more than anyone they might be able to consider more useful. If in any way they[83] do not endure troubles for their sake, love[84] can be diminished, since the entire cause of love[85] abides in those whom they love[86] while they have them, not in their advantages which they have through them. The conquered and exiled Pompey relates this well in the consolation of his wife Cornelia, when he says, "You weep over that which you loved."[87]

76. Cf. Augustine, *doc. Chr.* 1.7.7; *en. Ps.* on Ps 49.14.
77. Cf. Mt 19.12.
78. Ps 118.112.
79. *Diligere/ dilectio* to the end of the paragraph, except as noted.
80. *Amor.*   81. *Dilectio.*
82. *Diligere.*   83. Or, "it," i.e., love (*amor*).
84. *Amor.*   85. *Amor.*
86. *Diligere.*   87. Lucanus, *Pharsal.* 8.85; *amare.*

Often, those men are of a liberal soul and follow honor more than advantage, if they embrace those who they perceived by chance were just like them, from whom they nevertheless expect no benefit, with an affection of greater love[88] than they have for their own servants, from whom they receive advantages every day. If only we also would have so genuine an affection toward God that we would love him according to what is good in himself, more than according to what is advantageous for us, and that our righteousness would wholly keep for him what is his, so that, because he is good in the highest degree, he may be loved in the highest degree by all!

But in that the faithful soul said above in the psalm that it was inclined to good works "on account of reward," he shows the beginning of a good working, not the perfection. For someone imperfect at first is attracted to doing good, that is, to fulfilling God's commandments, by hope of reward and by fear rather than by love,[89] just as it is written, "The beginning of wisdom is the fear of the Lord."[90] Charity is the completion or end, that is the perfection, of this, just as it is said elsewhere, "I have seen the end of all completion; your commandment is very broad."[91] He rightly said, therefore, "I have inclined," that is, at the beginning of his working, he approached it with the hope and desire for reward. Because the Truth praises those blessed ones "who have made themselves eunuchs for the sake of the Kingdom of Heaven,"[92] that is, who lived continently for the sake of eternal blessedness, I think that we can understand that they accomplished this through that continence, just as when we say concerning someone that he went out that he might die, that is, that he went out and therefore death followed, not with the intention that it might happen to him.[93]

(205) [7.14] **For we know [that the law is spiritual].** He proves what he had said, namely, that the law of Moses is good, although he received the opportunity for sin from it, because the law is indeed spiritual, not worldly, as if written by the finger

---

88. *Diligere/ dilectio* throughout this paragraph.
89. *Amor.*
90. Ps 110.10.
91. Ps 118.12.
92. Mt 19.12.
93. Cf. 5.20.

of God, that is, composed and given by the dictation of the Holy Spirit, not contrived by men. **But I am carnal;** that is, I gaze eagerly at carnal pleasures and earthly desires; and *I am* so very *carnal,* that I am **sold under sin;** that is, I freely submit myself to sin and its slavery for the price of earthly goods, exercising every concupiscence for the sake of acquiring and obtaining them; or even in the first parents I am sold with them under sin, on account of the love[94] and taste of the fruit for which Eve longed. Behold whence we were made captives! We were able to sell ourselves, we cannot redeem ourselves. Innocent blood was given for us; we can free ourselves from the dominion of sin not by our own strength, but by the grace of the Redeemer.

[7.15] **For that which I do...** He shows to what extent he is made carnal and weak and with what great yoke of perverse habit he is weighed down, saying that he knowingly does that evil which he does not will, as if someone, by the Lord's compulsion, does that which he does not desire. And this is what he says: *For that which I do,* **I do not understand** that it must be done; that is, I do not believe that it should be done; indeed, undoubtedly I know that it is evil and therefore must not be done. **For [the good] that [I will to do]...** He shows that he acts badly against his own conscience, because he both renounces what he recognizes is good, and does what he does not doubt is evil. And this is what he says: **I do not do the good I will to do;** that is, I approve what should be done and I consent to it through reason; **but the evil which I hate, [that I do];** that is, as was said, not what I will, but rather what I reject and condemn with the judgment of reason.

[7.16] **But if [I do what I do not will]...** He returns to the commendation of the law so that he may show clearly that by our judgment also it is good; indeed, it prohibits what we discern through reason to be evil, such as to covet, when it says, "Do not covet." And this is what he says: **If I do what I do not will,** that is, what I do not approve, **I consent to** and am in harmony with **the law** concerning this **because [the law] is good,** since I see that it (206) prohibits those things which I judge

94. *Dilectio.*

to be evil, such as concupiscence, concerning which he spoke above, or wrath, hatred, or envy. Indeed, though we do not will concupiscence, we have it, because certainly we do not wish to covet, although we accomplish what we covet willingly and with delight.

Some qualifications

Since, therefore, it is said, "Every sin is voluntary," and since it is said, "No one sins unwillingly," we should understand this concerning the act of sin, not concerning concupiscence. For every act of sin is thereupon said to be voluntary rather than necessary which results from a preceding will in whatever way, whether it occurs through ignorance or through some necessity. For example, someone throws a stone recklessly; and he kills a man accidentally, not knowingly. This killing arises from the will to throw the stone, not to kill the man. And there is another who, under compulsion, kills the enemy who is rushing in upon him, lest he be killed by him; and he is said to sin unwillingly since he does that also from the desire to escape death rather than from the previously-held desire to kill the man. Therefore, every act of sin is said to be voluntary and not necessary which results from the will in whatever way, as was said.

Nevertheless, if someone should say that that killing of the man through the throwing of the stone was voluntary, I do not concede it, since I call the throwing of the stone voluntary. For terms frequently change their meanings on account of their attendant circumstances, so that when we concede every substance, we nevertheless do not therefore concede every man. And so when we say that every sin is voluntary, that is, that every act of sin proceeds from some will, as was said, nevertheless we do not concede that that killing is voluntary, that is, that it was committed from the will which someone may have to kill that person.

In this way, therefore, when we commit a sin through compulsion, we accomplish at the same time both what we will and what we do not will, as in the example cited above: when we kill a man by compulsion, we avoid death through this which we will, and we perform the murder (207) which we do not will.

And so in intercourse with someone else's wife, the intercourse itself pleases us, and not the crime of adultery or the guilt that we incur. Therefore, we are pleased with the intercourse only, not with the adultery, because nothing of the guilt belongs to the pleasure of adultery but more to the torment of the conscience, and, that we may not sin and avoid adultery, we in no way will that she with whom we commit fornication be a married woman.

Since, therefore, it is said, *I do not what I will, but what I do not will,* it hinders nothing if we use "not to will" and "to will" in a proper and customary way, namely, as "to please" and "to displease," because frequently, as was said, we find both what pleases and what displeases in the same act, just as in intercourse there is carnal pleasure and the sin of adultery. We can also understand "to will" and "not to will" as "to approve" and "disapprove" according to the above rationale, just as God is said to will and not to will some things. For there cannot be in him an agitation of the soul which in us is called will or pleasure, that is, delight, but when we say that God wills something, we mean either his approval or disposition. Otherwise, when the Truth says, "How often have I willed to gather your sons and you did not will it?"[95] or the Apostle, "Who wills that all should be saved"[96] and that none should perish," and again the Psalmist, "Whatever he willed, he did,"[97] or the same Apostle, *For who resists his will?*[98] we would run into the greatest controversy. Therefore, it is said in the first two passages above that God's willing is his approval, so that he may be said to will the thing which he approves or resolves that it may be done, and which, if it is done, he rewards as if it is pleasing to him; in the remaining two passages, his willing is called disposing and "confirming with himself" what he will do. This will will never lack effect nor be resisted by anyone.

[7.17] **But now…** So, after I consent to the law through reason and differ from myself on account of the same reason and carnal concupiscence, while the spirit desires against the flesh

---

95. Cf. Mt 23.37.
96. 1 Tm 2.4.
97. Ps 113.3.
98. Rom 9.19.

and the flesh against the spirit, **it is no longer I who do that** evil, **but sin,** that is, perverse concupiscence. He does not simply say, *I do not do that,* but he says *not I, but sin,* which is to say, I am not enticed to this by means of nature (208) but by means of the defect of nature now dominating it; indeed, by means of nature, through which I am created rational by God, I struggle against concupiscence and I condemn it rather than consent to it. Since he says **sin which dwells in me,** and not "which is in me," he designates, as it were, an immigrant who comes, and not a natural citizen, and one who has an abode in him through long custom, and not a temporary dwelling.

[7.18] **For I know…** As was said,[99] sin now **dwells** in me who have been made carnal; that is, it remains continually, so that now, as it were, for me it has turned into a habit, **because good,** that is, the virtue which is the best habit of the soul, does not now remain in me who have been made carnal; he indicates this when he says, **that is, in my flesh. For to will…** He shows that he is destitute of virtue when, through the weakness of carnal concupiscence, he is not able to fulfill the good which he wills, that is, which he approves to be done through reason. **To perform the good** is to join the act to a good will, [the good] which, he says, **I do not find** in myself if I properly look at and diligently examine myself. Therefore, **to will** naturally **lies near to me,** because by myself and my own creation I possess reason, through which I approve the good that must be done, but I am not able to perform it by myself, except of course by the grace given to me.

[7.19–20] **For the good which I will…** As if he should say, I do not find that I perform **the good which I will,** because, on the contrary, I forsake it and I do the evil, and so, as he also mentions above,[100] **If I do what I do not will, I do not do it, [but the sin which dwells in me].**

[7.21] **I find, therefore,…** Since the law, as was said above,[101] conveyed the knowledge of sin to me, through which knowledge I will to do the good which it teaches, and I consent to it through reason, although sin thereupon received the opportunity; *I find, therefore,* that is, through myself I find out by the judgment of my own reason that **the law** is good; that is, it is a useful thing for me, or servant of great good, since through its teaching I acquired the discernment of good or evil, **when I will to do** it, that is, the **good** which it commands me to fulfill. For in this very thing, that I will to do that which it commands and to strive through reason, in fact I recognize that it is good, namely, in its precepts. But why he said *will*, rather than "do," he adds, saying, (209) **because evil lies near to me;** that is, I am pressed by the burden of a perverse habit which impedes a good will.

[7.22–23] **For I am delighted...** Because he said that he wills to do the good which the law commands and nevertheless does not do it, he expounds the source of each occurrence, saying that he is delighted **with the law according to the interior man,** that is, what the law teaches pleases him, and that he strives for it through reason, which he calls in this passage the *interior man,* that is, the spiritual and invisible image of God,[102] in which man was made according to the soul when he was created rational and through this was exalted over the other creatures; and again he says that he sees **another law in his members,** that is, that he perceives that the kindling wood of sin or the stimulus of concupiscence, which he obeys as if it were a law through the weakness of the flesh, reigns *in the members* of his body and dominates him just as gluttony does in the throat, excess in the genitals, and the other vices in the other parts of the body through which they are exercised; I say that that *law* of concupiscence **fights,** that is, it is contrary to the natural **law of my mind,** that is, to the reason which ought to rule me as if it were the law. For I strive for good through reason, for evil through concupiscence. **And holding me captive,** that is, as if a prisoner, and drawing me unwillingly **in the law, that is, in obedience of sin** conceived by the mind, so that I may fulfill it by a work. **Which law is in my members,** as was said, holding me captive and turning me from God my proper Lord. Therefore, also it is called "the lust of the eyes"[103] through which we desire things that are seen; and it can similarly be said of the other members, accord-

102. Cf. Gn 1.26–27.
103. 1 Jn 2.16.

ing to the exercises of the five senses in the carnal pleasures. What he repeats, *which is in my members*, he does to exaggerate and commend to our memory our weakness. As many members as we have, we continuously bear almost as many enemies in them, and we carry them with us inseparably.

[7.24] Therefore, stricken with terror, he exclaims vehemently and laments, **I am an unhappy man**—understand: I am truly—who am surrounded by so many enemies in my own body, to whom, as I said above, I was sold by my own self, and, handed over as a captive, I cannot now be freed or redeemed from this slavery by myself. And because it is so, [he asks] **Who will free me,** that is, who will be so powerful and so (210) kind to me that he should free me, **from the body of this death?** that is, from [a body] thus inclined and prepared for killing the soul, lest carnal suggestions prevail over me, and the spirit yield to the flesh, that is, lest conquered reason succumb and consent to pleasure.

[7.25] **The grace of God,** that is, not the law, not one's own powers, not any merits, but the divine benefits freely conferred on us **through Jesus,** that is, the Savior of the world. But when he adds **Christ** and **our Lord,** he shows the power and righteousness by which he can save us. For Christ, that is, "anointed one," expresses the royal power which he has. Indeed, when he says *our Lord,* he demonstrates the right which he has over us, his servants, so to speak, so that he could draw us out justly from the dominion of sin or of the devil and bring back his own, so to speak, from the aforesaid captivity.

Therefore, I . . . Since through reason, as was said,[104] I will the good that the law teaches, but through the sin which dwells in my flesh I do the evil, **therefore with the mind,** that is, reason, **I serve the law of God,** namely, the Lord, so to speak, in order to obey him through reason. But **in the flesh,** when the desire of carnal pleasure incites, **I serve the law of sin;** that is, I obey the suggestions of perverse concupiscence as if they were a law.

[8.1] **Therefore . . .** Because, as was said,[105] the grace of God frees his own through Christ, **therefore there is no condemna-**

104. Rom 7.22.
105. Rom 7.24–25.

tion for those who [are in Christ Jesus], that is, who have been built on this foundation. But he settles how we can know these things, **who do not walk according to the flesh;** that is, if at some time they commit a fault through some weakness of the flesh, just as Peter did, fearing bodily death,[106] they do not persist after their concupiscences by going from vice to vice.

[8.2] **For the law...** He said that the grace of God will free him through Christ. And how that happens he now reveals, because **the law of the spirit of life,** that is, the law of charity and divine love[107] rather than that of fear, just as the old law was, **in Christ Jesus,** that is, the [law] given to us and displayed through him, **has freed me from the law of sin and** therefore **of death,** (211) that is, from the commandments or suggestions of carnal concupiscence, lest I obey them, namely, by consenting. *The spirit of life,* that is, the Holy Spirit, who is the life of souls, because he is love. Therefore, *the law* of this *spirit* is called "the law of love," begetting sons, not shackling slaves, that is, the Gospel, because it is entirely filled with charity. Therefore, it is also said to Christ, "Grace is poured out on your lips,"[108] because his entire preaching was filled with charity. Therefore, the Spirit also filled the apostles with knowledge just as the Son had promised, when he said, "He will teach you all things";[109] this teaching is mentioned when it is said, "Suddenly there was a sound from heaven";[110] that is, a word of discernment was made to them through inspiration in the mind; it was justly demonstrated in tongues of fire, since their tongues were to preach nothing except the ardor of charity.

[8.3] **For what [was impossible for the law, since it was weakened through the flesh]...** He explains how in Christ he was freed from the law of sin. For **God** the Father, that is, the majesty of divine power, **sent his Son in the likeness of the flesh of sin;** that is, he caused wisdom, co-eternal with himself, to be humiliated to the point of assuming passible and mortal humanity, so that through the punishment of sin, to which he submitted,

106. Cf. Mt 26.69–75.
107. *Amor,* here and in the next two sentences.
108. Ps 44.2.   109. Jn 14.26.
110. Acts 2.2–3.

he seemed to have the flesh of sin, that is, flesh conceived in sin. And **with respect to sin,** that is, with respect to the punishment of sin, which he endured for us in the flesh, that is, in the humanity he assumed, not according to divinity, **he condemned sin;** that is, he took away the punishment of sin from us by which the righteous were formerly held fast, and he opened the heavens.

[8.4] **So that the justification of the law [might be fulfilled]...** He does not mean the works of the law which in no way justify, but what the law teaches concerning these things which relate to justification, without which we cannot be justified, such as the charity for God and neighbor; the law contains this imperfectly, as we showed above,[111] but it is perfected in us through Christ. And this is what he says: that the perfect charity for God and neighbor **in us,** which the law teaches, justifies us. For that greatest kindness, which he showed to us, compels [us] truly to love[112] Christ in the same way as God, in the same way as our neighbor. This [kindness] is the condemnation of sin in us, that is, the destruction of all guilt and defect through charity, generated in us by this greatest kindness.

(212) [8.3–4] Origen says, "It may more truly be held among the Greeks: *he condemned sin for sin*"; that is, he "was made a sacrifice for sin. Through this sacrifice of the flesh, as it is called, he condemned sin for sin"; that is, he obliterated it.[113] Because he also worked reconciliation and the forgiveness of sins for us in his blood,[114] of sin committed either by the devil or by the Jews against him, *he condemned sin* in us, as was said, even using evil things for the best and converting them to the good.

Two things said before should be referred and joined to two things added on. To the words *with respect to sin he condemned sin*, he joins **what was impossible for the law,** namely, to condemn or take away sin. To the words *so that the justification of the law* **might be fulfilled,** there should be added **in that it,** namely,

111. See 7.6.

112. *Diligere.*

113. Cf. Origen, *Rom.,* 6.12, highly edited. The distinction here is between "with respect to sin" (*de peccato*) and "for sin" (*pro peccato*).

114. Cf. Rom 5.11; 2 Cor 5.18–19.

the law itself, **was weakened through the flesh;** that is, for the purpose of having a full and perfect justification, the law was weak on account of the carnal people to whom it was given, as we showed above,[115] concerning the imperfect performance of its commandments. Therefore, it was impossible for the law to take away sin through obedience to it, since it did not have perfect commandments, as was said. In regard to this perfection, it was chiefly *weakened,* that is, hindered, on account of the carnality of an insolent people.

[8.4] **Who do not [walk] according to [the flesh]**... *In us,* I say, *it was fulfilled* through Christ, in us who by his teaching and example and that supreme display of charity were made spiritual, not carnal, through desire. And this is what he says: **who do not walk according to the flesh;** that is, we are not now persuaded by carnal desires, but by the grace of God, that is, the Holy Spirit, we are ruled and advanced from power to power.

[8.5] **For they**... I said that they are justified who walk not according to the flesh but according to the Spirit. And justly, because **those who are according to the flesh,** that is, who have been ensnared in carnal desires, **mind** those things; that is, they utilize the experiences of those things **which are of the flesh,** that is, which belong to carnal pleasures. **But those who are according to the Spirit,** that is, who are inflamed with spiritual desires, **perceive** by experiencing the gifts of the Holy **Spirit.**

(213) [8.6] **For the prudence [of the flesh is death].** Truly *those who are according to the flesh mind the things of the flesh,* because we obtain the death of the soul, that is, condemnation, through those experiences of carnal desires which entice us; just as on the contrary **the prudence of the spirit,** that is, the experience of the powers and gifts of God, becomes **life and peace** for us; that is, they confer a life undisturbed by any disturbance.

[8.7] **Because the wisdom [of the flesh is hostile to God].** Therefore, *the prudence of the flesh* obtains death, because it is contrary to God and displeasing to him in every way. And he immediately adds why it is displeasing: because **it is not subject to the law of God;** that is, it does not allow obedience to the divine

115. Cf. 7.6 and 7.13.

commandments. **For it cannot,** namely, maintain obedience to God.

[8.8] **But they who [are in the flesh cannot please God].** He explains why he says that the wisdom of the flesh is hostile to God: that is, they are **in the flesh;** that is, they are charmed by carnal pleasures and through this displease God.

[8.9] To continue: I said that the wisdom of the flesh is hostile to God, and not without reason, but for this reason: that *those who are in the flesh* [*cannot please God*]. **But you...** Lest the Romans, to whom he was writing, despair when they hear that *those who are in the flesh cannot please God,* as if it had been said on account of them, he consoles them, saying, *But you,* by the grace of God, **are not in the flesh but in the Spirit,** that is, not in carnal but in spiritual desires. And lest they become too confident and be aroused even more to pride in this thing which he attests as if he were certain, he writes to them especially to restrain their exaltation, and teaches them, as if with some doubt, that he professes this, saying, **But if** you have **the Spirit,** that is, the Spirit **of God,** as a resident rather than as a guest, that is, abiding **in you** through his indwelling grace, not withdrawing from you or passing through you. But to what extent there is a danger of lacking the Spirit of God he adds, saying that **If someone does not have the Spirit of Christ, he is not his,** namely, a member, because his Spirit is himself the love[116] and the bond by which his members are united to this head. Indeed, concerning this Spirit it is especially said that "God is charity."[117] But since he first mentioned the Spirit of God and later of Christ, he demonstrates that Christ himself, (214) of whose divine Spirit he speaks, is God.

[8.10] **But if,** as if he should say, but if we have *the Spirit of Christ,* which is to say **If Christ is in us** through his Spirit, that is, through the grace of his gifts, namely, the forgiveness of sins and the gathering together of virtues, **our body is dead,** that is, liable to bodily death, **on account of sin,** namely, that of our first parents, or on account of the stain of carnal concupiscence in which it was conceived. But **our spirit lives because of justifi-**

116. *Amor.*
117. 1 Jn 4.8.

cation; that is, it avoids the death of damnation by means of the virtues which justify it, as if he should plainly say that, although we obtain the forgiveness of original sin in Christ, whose death to sin is the punishment of the flesh, nevertheless he who removed the cause did not remove for us this punishment.

Question

Therefore, a not insignificant question is usually asked: namely, why is this punishment retained when sin, which is its cause, is pardoned, so that they who obtain the full forgiveness of sins in baptism may not immediately recover that immortality which they had in paradise before sin? Isidore answers this question in his work *On the Highest Good,* Book 1, Chapter 23: "If men were freed from the present punishment through baptism, they might think it was the reward of baptism, and not eternal. Therefore, when the guilt of sin has been removed, nevertheless a certain temporal punishment remains, so that that life may be sought more fervently which shall be alien from all punishments."[118]

Indeed, who does not know that nearly all men strive after temporal life more than eternal life, since they labor much more for the life which they cannot keep than for eternal life, and fear the death of the body more than the death of the soul, and are disturbed more by the hardships of the present life than of the future life? If, therefore, they are confident that they possess the happiness of this animal life, they might hasten to the sacraments of the Church more on account of that life than on account of eternal life; and content with whatever kind of consolation of this life, (215) they might, in this very consolation of evil, either wholly condemn or strive less for the perfection of that glory [of the other life], because they might prefer a lower thing to the highest good.

[8.11] **Because if the Spirit...** I said that our *body is dead;* that is, it remains subject to temporal death even after the forgiveness of all sins. But it itself shall be freed from this mortality in the resurrection, so that divine grace may glorify not only the

---

118. Isidore of Seville, *sent.* 1.22.3.

soul but also the body. And this is what he says: **If the Spirit of him,** that is, of the Father, by which Father the divine power is especially designated; *of him,* I say, **who** through his own power has now **raised** our head, that is, **Jesus, from death,** who dwells, as was said, in us, the very same one who *raised Jesus,* not from weakness, but from death. Therefore, [Paul] returns to the resurrection of Christ so that, recounted often, it may render us more secure. **He shall also give life to our mortal bodies,** so that the members may participate in the same glory of the resurrection in the head; *he shall give life,* not like the bodies of the wicked, which shall be passible and suitable for torment, but **on account of the Spirit dwelling within,** that is, accordingly, reverence is owed to the Spirit of Christ, who dwells in those bodies as if in a temple and is quiet when the impulses of the flesh have been restrained through his grace.

Question

It is not a small question—since the divine substance united human substance to itself in the one person of Christ, and the individual substance of the Father and the Son and the Holy Spirit is through and through the same—why the Son, rather than the Father or the Holy Spirit, is said to have been made incarnate; or since the works of the Trinity are undivided, inasmuch as whatever one of the Persons does, the others also do, how is the Son said to have assumed flesh, and not the Father or the Holy Spirit? But this is drawn from our *Anthropology.*[119]

[8.12] **Therefore, brothers…** Since *they who are in the flesh cannot please God,*[120] therefore **we are not debtors to the flesh;** that is, we should not obey carnal desires, we who (216) owe nothing contrary to God to anyone, who are rightly commanded to lay down our soul for God's sake. Let worldly powers consider this: that no obedience is owed by those subjected to them when they enjoin upon them something which God prohibits, even if they bound them to themselves in this by an oath of fealty or promise.…**that we should live according to the flesh.** He expounds what he said before, namely, how we should under-

119. Lost.
120. Rom 8.8.

stand that *we are not debtors to the flesh,* lest by chance someone should understand this as having been said concerning the substance of the flesh; to which we are debtors to the extent that it relates to its necessary care, in food and clothing, so that we may supply this to it. Therefore, such is the meaning, *We are not debtors to the flesh so that we should live according to the flesh,* although we are in the flesh, that is, [not] so that we may pursue carnal desires.

[8.13] **For if [you live according to the flesh];** that is, you are not subject to the flesh because obedience to it would condemn you. And this is what he says: **you will die;** that is, you will incur the death of the soul, which is sin, by consenting to it, if, when it arouses, you do not struggle as much as you are able. **But if by the Spirit,** that is, by some gift of divine grace more than by your own power, **you put to death the deeds [of the flesh],** if you cannot yet thoroughly root out its suggestions, **you will live,** on the contrary, with the true life of the soul, either here in virtues or in eternal blessedness. *The deeds* are put to death as if a small child conceived in the womb should be killed before it is born, while we hinder the evil things which we conceive with the mind lest they proceed as far as works, destroying every opportunity as much as we are able; just as it is written, "Blessed is he who will grasp and dash his children against a stone";[121] that is, he will put to death and kill sins conceived with the mind through some suggestion, while they are as yet children, by dashing them against a stone, that is, by crushing and destroying them on that stable foundation of all good things, which is Christ, while reason, strengthened through the love[122] of Christ, strives, lest that for which the human mind lusts, through the weakness of the flesh, be carried out. Just as the same Apostle relates elsewhere, "The flesh lusts against the spirit, and the spirit against (217) the flesh";[123] that is, reason checks the suggestions of the flesh, lest they proceed as far as works. And Solomon says, "The patient man is better than the strong man, and he who rules his own soul than he who storms a city."[124]

[8.14] **For all who...** Rightly do I say that *you will live, if you*

---

121. Cf. Ps 136.9.
123. Gal 5.17.

122. *Amor,* here and in 8.14.
124. Prv 16.32.

put to death the deeds of the flesh by the Spirit, because **all who are led by the Spirit of God,** rather than compelled, that is, they are persuaded by love rather than constrained by fear, **are sons of God,** rather than slaves; that is, they are subjected to him through love rather than through fear.

[8.15] **For [you did] not [receive the spirit of slavery to fall back into fear].** As if someone should ask, Does God have many sons, since Christ is called his Only-Begotten? The response is that he indeed has many, but through adoption, not through nature, because you yourselves also **received the spirit of adoption** in which the sons of God are made. Therefore, he also says elsewhere *that the charity of God is poured out in our hearts through the Holy Spirit who has been given to us.*[125] Therefore, he says that the *spirit of adoption* is a gift of charity through which we are adopted by God as sons. **In whom,** namely, the Spirit, that is, in the profession and the recognition of his gift, **we cry** to God intently, and we exultantly say, **Abba, Father;** that is, we profess him as Father rather than as Lord, and through this we recognize that we are sons rather than slaves. For thus did the Truth also frequently teach in the Gospel, that we call God "Father" rather than "Lord,"[126] so that he might also encourage us by this to filial subjection. Therefore, when he passed on that spiritual prayer to the disciples, he said, "When you pray, say, 'Our Father, who art in heaven,'" etc.[127] Therefore, do we also rightly call the abbots of monasteries "Father," so that by that name they are plainly admonished more to be loved[128] as fathers than to be feared as lords.

He says that *we cry,* we Hebrews, *Abba;* you Gentiles, *Pater;* since the former name is Hebrew or Syriac, the latter Greek or Latin. Augustine says in his commentary *On the Epistle to the Galatians,* "*Abba, Pater,* are the two words which he used so that he might interpret the first with the last. (218) For *Abba* means *Father,* on account of the entire people who were called from the Jews and Gentiles, so that the Hebrew word might refer to the Jews and the Greek word to the Gentiles."[129] He also says

125. Rom 5.5.
127. Mt 6.8–9; Lk 11.2.
129. Augustine, *ex.Gal.* 31.

126. Mt 6.8–9 and 14–15.
128. *Amare.*

in Book 3 of his *Harmony of the Evangelists,* "This is the Hebrew word *abba,* which is *pater* in Latin."[130] Haymo says on this passage, "*Abba* is Hebrew and Syriac; *Pater* is Greek and Latin. The Apostle, foreseeing that both peoples were to be gathered to the faith, placed two names under one signification, so that believers among the Hebrews and Syrians might say, '*Abba,* have mercy,' and believers among the Greeks and other peoples might say, '*Pater.*' This is what is found in the Gospel of Mark, where the Lord says, '*Abba, Pater,* if it is possible, let this cup pass from me.'"[131]

...**the spirit of slavery in fear.** He calls that a gift of servile fear, by which we are restrained not from an evil will but from evil action, from the terror of punishment, just as the Jews were before, through the bodily punishments of the law. *You did not receive the spirit of slavery* through the Gospel, as the Jews once did through the law.

[8.16] **For the Spirit himself,** *of adoption,* whom we mentioned and have, causes **our spirit,** that is, our reason, to recognize **that we are sons of God,**[132] that is, that we are subjected to him through love.[133] For everyone recognizes that nothing is better than his own conscience, and whether he should be called a slave or a son.

We should indeed note that in these things which the Apostle says to the Romans, some of whom were to be strongly censured, a person representative of the faithful is understood in this passage, and he explains not so much what they were like as what they should be.

[8.17] **But if they are sons,** namely, *of adoption,* and by all means **heirs,** because they are adopted for this purpose; that is, they are freely chosen, that they may attain the inheritance; **heirs indeed of God,** that is, of the Father, and **co-heirs of Christ,** that is, of his natural Son, in that perpetual possession of blessedness. He shows how great it is to attain that inheritance

130. Cf. Augustine, *cons. Ev.* 3.4.14.

131. Haymo of Auxerre, *Rom.* 8.15; Mk 14.36.

132. Full text: "For the Spirit himself bears witness to our spirit that we are sons of God."

133. *Amor.*

of God through which we become like Christ his Son: **If, however...** I said that we are *heirs*, with this intention, however: **if we suffer** with Christ, because no one shall be crowned unless he has struggled legitimately, against the assault of enemies or vices. And because, as Cyprian says, (219) it is not punishment but cause that makes a martyr,[134] he adds, **that we may also be glorified with him,** that is, if we suffer to such an extent that we may be worthy to be glorified with Christ. This happens at that time when charity prepares [us] for suffering, for Christ as for ourselves, and necessity does not draw us, so that we may thus pay off the loan to him. Therefore, all suffer for him to the extent it is in them, whoever, as we said, are prepared to suffer for him, if they are not lacking to a persecutor, although a persecutor is lacking to them.

[8.18] **For I consider,** as if someone should ask, Is that inheritance so great that one should suffer to merit it, to the point of death, just as Christ suffered? The response is that indeed, I consider it to be so great that it exceeds by far all the merits of men, however greatly they may be deserved by suffering. And this is what he says: **the sufferings of this time are not to be compared,** that is, those temporal and transitory tribulations, however severe they might have been, are not of such great importance that that unspeakable and eternal glory of the future life **which shall be revealed in us** should be owed to them, because now indeed, "We are the sons of God," as it is written, but "it does not yet appear what we shall be."[135] For perpetual good is rendered to nothing transitory by obligation, although it may be good; but through the grace of God, superadded to our merits, we obtain that for which we were in no way adequate by our own merits.

And if we diligently pay attention, nothing transitory is worthy of the reward of eternal good. For only charity, which never passes away,[136] merits eternal life; and those who are equal in charity are held as equals before God in reward, even if another

---

134. Peppermüller points out that this is in fact Augustine, *S.* 327.1. Cf. Cyprian, *eccl. cath.* 14; *Ep.* 31.4.

135. 1 Jn 3.2.

136. 1 Cor 13.8.

is deprived of the operation of charity, entangled by some failure. Therefore, justly, blessed Augustine claims that John, who did not suffer, has a crown of martyrdom equal to that which Peter has, who did suffer, so that God may consider not so much the effect of the suffering as the inner disposition.[137]

[8.19] **For the longing...** I rightly spoke of **the future glory** *which shall be revealed in us,* namely, the sons of God, because (220) *the longing* of all the faithful **longs for** this **revelation,** that is, of the glory due to the sons of God. As if he should say, "Longing, each one longs," just as it is said, "Going, they went";[138] that is, they long perseveringly and boldly for *the revelation* **of the sons of God,** meriting it with good works, that is, the reward in which shall be revealed who the sons of God are, who are predestined for the life which is still hidden. He calls a **creature** those who try to preserve God's creation uncorrupted in themselves, and to reform the image of God in which they were created,[139] by resisting as much as they are able the sins which obliterate and defile it.

[8.20] And truly the faithful long for this revelation because on account of it they despise the vanity of the present life, and, not wanting it, they endure; they now desire rather "to be released and be with Christ."[140] And this is what he says: **the creature was subjected [to vanity] unwillingly;** that is, to the extent that it is able in itself, it endures unwillingly this empty life, which is transitory and filled with hardships, **but because of him,** namely, he endures it, **who has subjected it in hope,** namely, of that future revelation; that is, he humiliates it by afflicting it in this life, so that he may exalt it in that life for which he hopes.

[8.21] What that hope of the creature truly is, that is, what the afflicted faithful hope for here, he adds, saying, **Because the [creature] itself [shall also be freed from slavery to corruption];** that is, they hope for this: that they will be freed then

---

137. *b. conjugali* 21.16. There is a pun here between "effect," *effectus,* and "inner disposition," *affectus,* which here cannot be accurately rendered as "affect" or "affection."

138. Ps 125.6.   139. Cf. Gn 1.26–27.

140. Phil 1.23.

from the yoke of passible and corruptible flesh, by which they are oppressed here unwillingly. He calls **the freedom [of the glory of the sons of God]** the glory of that life in which there will be no oppression, when no one will incur anything against his own will.

[8.22–23] **For we know...** He shows through the parts that the creature was afflicted here for that which he hopes for there, to pant after *the freedom of the glory* with complete desire, because both those who are lesser among the faithful and those who are greater [do so]. But he distinguishes the lesser ones through what he says, **every creature**, and the greater ones through what he adds: **[we also] who have the firstfruits of the Spirit.** Therefore, when he says *every creature,* it is as the same thing as saying, these who are entirely creatures, or who are all creatures, not creators, not being able to create or generate anything for God through preaching. Indeed the apostles and (221) their vicars are in a certain manner creators of others, so to speak, as we said, according to what this very Apostle says elsewhere, "For I gave you birth through the Gospel in Christ Jesus";[141] and again, "My little children, with whom I am in labor again, until Christ is formed in you."[142] **...groans and is in labor;** that is, by groaning it is in labor. But the groans of the faithful arise here from the earthly affliction according to those words, "Going, they went and wept, sowing their seed,"[143] or from the desire for the heavenly dwelling-place, just as it says, "Woe is me that my dwelling is prolonged,"[144] and again, "Upon the waters of Babylon, there we sat and wept while we remembered you, Zion."[145] But they are in labor; that is, with the greatest labor they eagerly try to bring forward the fruit of good works, **up to now,** that is, not for a time, but as long as they live. For "I am in labor" is a term expressing desire to act, not past action,[146] and therefore is well adapted for the lesser and imperfect ones who are, as it were, in the beginning of thought, not in the perfection of working. But

141. 1 Cor 4.15.   142. Gal 4.19.
143. Ps 125.6.   144. Ps 119.5.
145. Ps 136.1.

146. Peter uses the present active indicative form, first person singular, *parturio*, indicating continuing action in the present, as opposed to the perfect form, *parturivi,*, indicating past completed action.

these words of the Apostle, when he says, *groans and is in labor,* are in harmony with those words of the Lord, "When a mother is in labor, she has sorrow," etc.[147]

Having the firstfruits of the Spirit, that is, the greater gifts of the Holy Spirit, such as the holy preachers [have] who gain themselves and others for God. In his first epistle to the Corinthians the Apostle himself exhorts us to this duty of preaching, as if to the greatest gift of the Holy Spirit, saying, "But be zealous for the better gifts. And I show to you a more excellent way."[148] And a little later he says, "Pursue charity, be zealous for spiritual gifts; but even more that you may prophesy";[149] that is, that you may receive the office of prophets by preaching.

And we groan, burdened with the passibility and corruption of the flesh as the others are, but having comfort from hope, which hope is like the anchor of our ship amidst the waves of this world. (222) He immediately adds this comfort, saying, **longing,** that is, hoping with assurance, **for the adoption of the sons of God** from the Gentiles themselves; that is, that they will be adopted by God and established as heirs in the heavenly kingdom. I call this *adoption* **the redemption of our body,** that is, of the Church whose members we are. For our adoption by God is nothing else than our redemption from the power of the devil or from the yoke of sin through his Only-begotten, so that this entire adoption may be attributed to divine grace, not to our merits.

[8.24] **For in hope [we were saved].** He said above that we wait for *the revelation of the sons of God* by hoping and that we are subjected to the vanity of the present life in this hope, lest we despair on account of our labors. And lest someone object that that hope is not certitude and therefore we should not put our trust in it, he therefore says that all of us, however many we are, are saved through hope. And he immediately adds that hope is rightly said only of those things which do not appear, saying, **But hope which [is seen],** that is, the knowledge which is of the things appearing, should by no means be called hope, **for that which someone sees,** that is, **why does he hope for** something

147. Jn 16.21.   148. 1 Cor 12.31.
149. 1 Cor 14.1.

which he sees? As if he should say, what he hopes for by seeing is nothing, so that if someone sees that he became rich, and perhaps he had hoped for this before, he now does not have hope or an opinion concerning this, but certitude.

[8.25] **But if . . .** He shows how we may become saved by hope, because that hope, which is spoken of the future life, makes us patient, lest we fail in the tribulation of the present life. And this is what he says: for *if,* namely, because, **we hope for what we do not see, we hope** for it patiently, not failing in the anguish of the present struggle.

[8.26] **But likewise . . .** Just as hope helps us by furnishing patience, so the Holy **Spirit also helps our weakness** in this anguish, by supplying necessary prayers to us. And this is what he says: **For we do not know what we should pray for, as is proper** and necessary for us, since we are frequently placed in tribulations, doubting in many of them that it is useful for us, as was the case with the Apostle himself when (223) he prayed three times to the Lord that Satan's torment be removed from him.[150] **But the Spirit himself prays for us;** that is, he causes us to pray for what we do not know, namely, by teaching and inspiring his greatest desire.

[8.27] **But he . . .** I said that he causes us to pray **with indescribable groans,** that is, with such great desires that they can be felt rather than described. But although they are indescribable, nevertheless they are known to him **who searches the hearts** and is "the inspector of the heart,"[151] who considers the things which dwell in the heart rather than those which are brought forth from the mouth. **[Knows] what [the Spirit] desires,** that is, causes us to desire, **because he prays for the saints,** that is, he causes the saints to pray, **according to God's [will],** that is, according to what the Spirit of God has received from God, because he has his being from God, namely, by proceeding from him, and according to what he knows is ordered in the very disposition of God. Therefore, it is certain that God cannot be concealed when he disposes what the Spirit does.

[8.28] **But we know [that for those who love God all things**

150. 2 Cor 12.8.
151. Prv 24.12.

work together]... As if an opponent should say, How does the
Spirit help the saints, so many of whom we see laboring with
afflictions? He says that he even converts those afflictions and
whatever things happen to the saints, favorable as well as ad-
verse, **for good** and leads them to their advantage. Who they
are **who love God** he adds, saying, f**or those who were called
to be saints;** that is, they were sanctified by the inspiration of
an internal calling, **according to God's purpose** rather than according to their preceding merits, that is, according to what
would be acceptable to divine grace rather than according to
what they might merit.

[8.29] **For those he foreknew**...He diligently describes how
they are sanctified *according to God's purpose,* that is, what is acceptable to divine grace, saying that *those he foreknew,* he later
made them **conformed** to Christ by predestining them. God is
said "to know" those things which he approves and which are
worthy of his knowledge, according to that passage, "The Lord
knows the way of the righteous,"[152] just as on the contrary he
is said "to ignore" or "not to know" evil, according to what the
Son says to the wicked, "I do not know you."[153] Therefore, he is
said to have foreknown those (224) whose future election he
approved before they existed. Therefore, whomever he thus
foreknew, he later **predestined** them; that is, he prepared them
with the gifts of his grace. For divine predestination is called
"the preparation of grace,"[154] which is only in the elect.

He predestined them, I say, **to be conformed,** that is, for this purpose: that they may become like **to the image of his Son,** that is,
of Christ, who is "the image of God,"[155] that is, the express likeness of the Father, equal to him in all good things according to
divinity, according to that passage which says, "Philip, he who
sees me also sees the Father,"[156] as if he should say that of what
nature or how good the Father is can be known wholly through
me. But at that time we are conformed to Christ if, laying aside
"the old man with his deeds,"[157] we put on Christ himself, just

---

152. Ps 1.6.   153. Lk 13.25, 27.
154. Augustine, *praed. sanct.* 10.19; Abelard, above, 1.4.
155. Col 1.15.   156. Jn 14.9.
157. Col 3.9.

as it is written, "He who says he abides in Christ, ought to walk just as Christ walked";[158] so, I say, we are conformed **so that he,** namely, Christ, **may be firstborn among many brothers;** that is, among many who are sons of the same Father through adoption, he who by nature is the Son excels in dignity in the manner of the firstborn; he is not equal to them in the same way as he is equal to the Father, whose image he is called.

[8.30] **But those whom [he predestined, he also called; and those whom he called, he also justified; but those whom he justified, he also glorified].** The elect are predestined; that is, illuminated through faith, they are prepared for eternal life, which faith they first receive as if it were "the foundation of all good things";[159] later they are called, having been enticed through hope; when they have known the mercy of God and the power of the sacraments, they are attracted to acting well, on account of the reward of eternal things; finally they are justified by the inner disposition of genuine charity, adhering to God not so much on account of his [good things] as on account of himself; and finally they are magnified, raised into the heavenly homeland.

Question

(225) A question imposes itself in this passage, namely, concerning divine providence or predestination. These things seem to remove free choice from us, since it is necessary that all things happen just as they were foreseen by God, and since it is not possible that anyone who was predestined should perish. For it is certain that all things, before they happen, have been foreseen by God in the way in which they will be, whether they are good or bad, and his providence cannot be mistaken in anything. Since, therefore, he foresaw that this man will commit adultery who perhaps will commit adultery, it is necessary that he commit adultery. Because if it is necessary that he commit adultery, it is inevitable; it is not now in his free choice or power to avoid this sin. Therefore, he should not be judged guilty on account of this sin, which he could in no way avoid. And so all evil things seem to be led back to God's providence, as if their

158. 1 Jn 2.6.
159. Ps.-Augustine, *symb.*, Exordium; see below on 15.13 and 16.25.

necessary cause, and thus all things seem to arise unavoidably in that way in which they happen, since they were thus foreseen by God not to be able to turn out otherwise in any way.

We concede, however, that he who will commit adultery will inevitably commit adultery, since God foresaw it; but it is not therefore appropriate to be said simply that he will inevitably commit adultery. For this wording, with its qualification, does not imply that simple thing. We reserve a more diligent explanation of this and the difference between providence and predestination or fate for our *Theology*.[160]

[8.31] **What therefore...** Since God is so solicitous for our salvation that he foreknows, he predestines, he calls the predestined, he justifies the called, he makes great the justified; **What shall we say to these things;** that is, what hindrance could we find against this? Nothing at all, because although by ourselves we are weak, **who** could prevail **against us, if God is for us,** that is, when we have God as our advocate?

[8.32] Concerning his advocacy or protection by which we are able to be untroubled, he adds, recalling his singular love,[161] which he showed to us, **He who did not even spare** (226) **his own Son,** that is, [his] consubstantial, not adopted, [Son,] **but handed him over,** namely, to death, **for us all,** namely, those he foreknew, or, as was said, predestined, so that he might cleanse the stains of our sins in his blood. The words *even his own Son* mean that God did not spare his other adoptive sons before for us, such as Isaiah or Jeremiah or some of the other prophets, who, having been sent to God's people, were killed as martyrs for man's salvation.[162] **How did he not even [grant all things to us with him];** that is, by what reason can it be said that in so great a gift as the handing over of his Son he did not give **all things to us,** namely, things necessary for our salvation?

[8.33] **Who will make accusation [against God's elect]?** Since God, as was said, is solicitous for our salvation, whose accusation could assert anything against us? The accusation of God himself, who not only does not accuse, but also, as is said, **justifies?** As if he should say, No.

160. *TSch* 3.96–111.   161. *Dilectio.*
162. Cf. Lk 11.47–51.

[8.34] **[Who is it who condemns?]** Or if the accuser should
stop, who would persist in our condemnation? **Christ** himself,
who showed us such great love[163]—as he himself says, "No one
has greater love than this"[164]—that he died for our salvation? As
if he should say, No.

Indeed, he who… As if correcting what he had said, **Who
died,** that is, of weakness, he adds the glory of the resurrection
shown and promised to us in himself, which especially encourages us in all tribulation; and since there was a resurrection
of some who had died twice, such as Lazarus,[165] or will be [a
resurrection] of the wicked to be placed at the left hand, he
adds, **Who is at the right hand of God;** that is, he who continues
in eternal blessedness in terms of his revived humanity, there
also is not unmindful of our salvation, where, as if an advocate,
he intercedes for us with the Father, by always showing to the
eyes of the Father that humanity in which he suffered so many
things for us, and by reconciling us in this way to him as a mediator, so to speak.[166]

Therefore, *he intercedes;* as was said, as an intermediary he
intercedes between us and God through that substance of our
nature, as was said. We say that even the saints themselves in-
tercede and pray for (227) us, by the affection of charity or the
intercessions of their merits rather than the utterance of the
voice. Therefore, when we also say, "Saint Peter, pray for us,"[167]
it is the same thing as if we should say, "Have mercy on us, O
Lord, on account of the merits of blessed Peter."

[8.35] **Who therefore [shall separate us from the charity of
Christ?]** Since God showed to us and confirmed in himself such
great grace with such great benefits, what thing could separate
us further from his love?[168] As if he should say, None. And he
immediately proves that through those things which especially
seem to be able to turn men away from God. And first he mentions those things that are hostile: **Tribulation?** As if he should
say, No. Any affliction of the body, such as a flogging, is called

---

163. *Dilectio,* also in the quotation of Jn 15.13.
164. Jn 15.13.   165. Jn 11.43–44; 12.1.
166. Cf. 1 Tm 2.5.   167. From the litany of All Saints.
168. *Dilectio.*

a *tribulation,* any anxiety of mind, such as fear, is called **distress,** any driving off from place to place is called **persecution,** any armament of death is called **danger,** and death itself is called a **sword.**

[8.36] **Just as it is written,** namely, in Psalm 43, as if he should say that it is especially true that none of these things could separate, **Because,** just as the prophet says, **on account of you [we are put to death],** that is, we cling to you inseparably; afflicted by the dangers of [this] life, we depend on you **the whole day,** that is, for the whole time of our life, which in comparison to the life of unbelievers, who walk in darkness, should be called day, illuminated by faith. **We are considered as...** It is written concerning the wicked, to those speaking of the righteous, "We considered their life madness";[169] **sheep for the slaughter,** that is, worthy of slaughter and having nothing of any further use, not yielding any food for eating, even from their own death, not resisting in any respect the slayers, sometimes because of the feebleness of their nature, sometimes because of their tameness.

[8.37] **But in all these things [we overcome]...** I said that all those oppressions could not overcome our constancy to the point of separating [us] from God, but on the contrary we conquer all these things by persevering through the grace of God rather than by our own power. And this is what he says: **on account of him who loved**[170] **us,** that is, on account of his helping grace.

[8.38] **I am certain...** Therefore, I speak so confidently concerning the divine grace which helps the faithful, that for no reason could they be separated from God, because now I have not only attained faith with these things, (228) but even a certitude with great proofs, because **neither** threatened **death, nor** promised **life,** namely, in this world, **nor angels,** that is, the angelic dignity, promised to us by the one who tempts us, just as the devil promised Eve that they would be as gods, **nor sovereignties, nor virtues,** that is, the superiority of those orders which is greater than the dignity of the angelic order.

169. Cf. Wis 5.4.
170. *Diligere.*

Blessed Gregory diligently distinguishes these orders when he says, "In Greek 'angels' means 'messengers,' and 'archangels' means 'most high messengers.' Angels announce the small events, but archangels announce the greatest. Hence it is that not just any angel was sent to Mary, but Gabriel the archangel."[171] Again he says, "Virtues are those [spirits] through whom signs and miracles happen more frequently. Powers are those [spirits] who received this more powerfully than others in their own order, so that the contrary virtues might be subordinate to their authority, by whose power they are restrained, lest they prevail in tempting the hearts of men as much as they wish. Sovereignties are those who also have charge over those good spirits of angels; they rule over others who are subjected [to them] for the purpose of perfecting their service, while they arrange for those things which are to be done."[172]

[8.38–39] **Neither things present,** that is, the present goods and evils, **[nor things to come,] nor might,** that is, the fury of some power, **neither height nor depth,** that is, the exaltation of some human glory, or the debasement and humiliation into some degree of lowness, as if he should say, neither some human prosperity nor adversity, **nor any created thing,** other than those mentioned above, that is, angelic powers and all the rest, **[can separate us] from the charity of God,** by which we love[173] him purely for himself, **which is in Christ Jesus,** that is, through Christ our Savior, inspired in us or built and rooted and founded in him.

[9.1] **I speak the truth...** He wishes to prove by his own experience his statement that he and the faithful like him could not be removed from the charity of God, (229) saying, namely, that he, when he was the greatest persecutor of the Church, worked for this purpose: that he might from that time turn away his own people converted to faith in Christ;[174] and this is what

171. Gregory the Great, *homil.* II, hom. 34.8.

172. Ibid., 34.10. See also the translation of David Hurst, *Forty Gospel Homilies* (Kalamazoo: Cistercian Publications, 1990), 288, which influenced my translation.

173. *Diligere.*

174. 1 Tm 1.13; Acts 8.3; 9.1–2.

he says: **in Christ Jesus,** that is, swearing through Christ Jesus, *I speak* truly, as far as the occurrence of that thing is concerned, that it is so, that I speak and **I do not lie, my conscience bearing witness to me;** that is, I am not guilty of a lie since I thus believe as I speak. For someone can, as far as the occurrence of the thing is concerned, have the truth in words through ignorance, and nevertheless speak against conscience and through this incur the guilt of a lie. For he does not lie in God's presence; that is, he is not reckoned by him as guilty of lying, unless he speaks in duplicity. To the one who speaks, his conscience bears witness when the disposition does not differ from the words, that is, when it is believed by him just as it is spoken. *To me,* he says, I who know it, although not "to us,"[175] *my conscience,* I say, existing **in the Holy Spirit,** that is, founded and rooted in the charity of God,[176] from which charity a lie cannot come forth. Therefore, he is rightly called "the Spirit of truth."[177]

[9.2] I speak this truth **because I have great sadness** in quantity of remorse, and continually in duration of time, **in my heart,** that is, not simulated in the exterior manner of life, but truly in the very inner disposition of the rational soul.

[9.3] And where the *sadness* comes from, he adds: because indeed **I wished** at one time, not now, **I myself,** who now seem to be something great and to oppose Judaism before others and contrary to the former life, *I wished,* I say, **to be anathema from Christ for my brothers,** that is, I strove in every way to become the separation of my countrymen, that is, of the Jews, *from Christ,* so that not only might I be separated from Christ but I myself might be the separation of the others, and with both words and deeds turn away from him those also who had adhered to him through faith, just as it is written, "Saul, still breathing threats," etc.;[178] or, in this way, in order to turn my brothers away from Christ, I desired to turn away everyone in general, just as it is written, "So that if he found men of this way,"[179] not (230) only Jews, etc. But he indicates that he generally calls "brothers" whoever are of his own race, that is, any Jews, saying, **who are**

175. Peppermüller: "to you." 176. Cf. Eph 3.17.
177. Jn 14.17; 15.26; 16.13. 178. Acts 9.1.
179. Acts 9.2.

my kindred according to the flesh, that is, from my fleshly kindred, and therefore at that time my mind was more ardently preoccupied with them, so that I might do the most for them.

[9.4] And lest we only understand those who belong to the tribe of Benjamin, from which the Apostle came, but indeed [that we should understand] generally the whole race of Jews, he adds, **who are Israelites,** that is, from the race of Jacob the patriarch, who was first called Jacob by his parents and later Israel by the Lord, that is, "a man who sees God."[180] Therefore, also especially the entire posterity that was marked with his name boasted as if it were granted to them alone to see, that is, to know, God, as if they did not require further the doctrine either of Christ or of anyone else; so that Paul himself on this account might also explain that he despised the discipline of Christ with some reason and on account of the things which follow, namely, from the commendation of those who were at one time the special people of God,[181] when he says, **To them belongs the adoption of sons,** that is, who first were adopted by God through grace as sons and are especially shown to be loved[182] by him by the exhibition of countless benefits; **and glory,** that is, boasting in the present time proceeding from that adoption, by which those now in the Church wished to set themselves before the Gentile converts.

But from what place this *adoption* or boasting of theirs proceeded he diligently pursues, saying that **the covenant** is theirs and was offered to them first, not to the Gentiles, as it is written, "He did not do so for every nation, and he did not manifest his judgments to them."[183] To this matter pertains what he had said above, *Therefore, what advantage is there for the Jew? Or what is the advantage of circumcision? Much in every way. First, the utterances of God were committed to them.*[184] **[And the law,] and the worship,** that is, the public duty of divine worship in the tabernacle and the temple, **and the promises,** countless promises, concerning both the land of Canaan that was to be occupied and earthly comforts, (231) and spiritual goods given through Christ, who was to be born from them.

---

180. Cf. Gn 32.30.
182. *Diligere.*
184. Rom 3.1–2.

181. Cf. Dt 7.6; 14.2; 26.18.
183. Ps 147.20.

[9.5] In the same way, he presently adds these words: **To them belong the fathers,** according to the flesh rather than according to the imitation of faith, they **from whom is Christ** himself **according to the flesh,** namely, the patriarchs Abraham, Isaac, and Jacob, to whom the promises concerning Christ were made, that in their seed all the nations are blessed. Because he had said they were the *fathers* of Christ, lest, through this, Christ seem to have been born from those fathers, he adds, **who is blessed over all,** that is, to be praised and glorified **forever,** that is, through all the successions of times, set in order in the best way by him as if by divine wisdom. **Amen,** that is, it is true. The doubling of the declaration indicates a profession of the mouth as much as of the heart, just as it says, "Amen, amen, I say to you," and "Let your word be, 'yes, yes,' 'no, no.'"[185]

Here ends the third book; the fourth begins.

185. Mt 6.2; 5.37.

BOOK FOUR

(232)
[9.6] **UT IT IS NOT** that [the word of God] failed. Perhaps someone might say: And how were the divine promises made to the Israelites, which that people, always rebellious towards God and now thoroughly convicted by him, cannot obtain because of their wickedness? To this the Apostle says: The promises were *not* made to them in such a way *that the* very *word* of promise *failed,* that is, that the promise is void and in no way fulfilled. For the promise which is fulfilled is said to stand or endure, but the one which is not is said to fail. Consider what was said above. For when it was asked, *What is the advantage of circumcision?* and answered, *Much in every way; first,* etc., it was added, *For what if some of them did not believe, does not their unbelief nullify faith in God?*[1] Therefore, it is also said in this passage that the promise made to the Israelites, as was said, was not emptied, if it was never fulfilled in some who are of the nation of Israel according to the flesh. **For not all [who are of Israel are Israelites].** For only they should be counted among the sons of Israel who remain in the worship of the one God and imitate the faith of their father Israel, that is, Jacob.

[9.7] He demonstrates this at once in a comparison regarding Abraham, saying, **Not all who are of the seed of Abraham,** namely, according to the flesh, are counted among the **sons** of Abraham. He confirms this immediately with the testimony taken from Genesis, where, after Sara had ordered her maidservant Hagar to be driven out with her son, the Lord said to Abraham, "All the things which Sara said to you, hear her voice, **because in Isaac shall your seed be named.**"[2]

1. Rom 3.1–3.
2. Gn 21.12.

[9.8] **That is, [these are the sons of God,] not those who [are the sons of the flesh].** The Apostle explains what was said before: *In Isaac shall your seed be named.* He calls sons of the flesh those who derive only their fleshly origin from Father Abraham, and who do not take him as the example of faith. But when it seems that he should say, "these are the sons of Abraham," the Apostle says rather, *these are the sons of God,* showing that no others should be called the sons of Abraham except those who are the sons of God, that is, those who are faithful. For Abraham signifies faith; therefore, they alone are rightly called the sons of Abraham (233) whom the Lord adopts to himself for faith, both from the Jews and from the Gentiles, just as the Apostle himself mentions above when he says of Abraham, *that he may be father of all who believe, not only of these who are circumcised, but also of these who follow the footsteps of the faith of our father Abraham, which is in uncircumcision.*[3]

But those who are sons of the promise... He calls sons of the promise those who belong to faithful Isaac, namely, by imitating him through faith, whom Abraham begot from an old and barren mother by the promise of God alone, not through fleshly nature.... **are deemed as his seed,** namely, Abraham's; that is, they must be reckoned among the sons of Abraham.

[9.9] But with what words was the promise made to Abraham concerning his future son, Isaac? He adds this, saying, **For [this is the word] of promise,** etc. These are the words of the angel who spoke to Abraham: **At this time,** that is, at such a time, as it is now, namely, when a year has passed, **I shall come and [Sara] shall have [a son];** that is, through my coming and working rather than through nature, then Sara shall conceive. But this meaning is expressed with these words in Genesis: "I shall come back to you at this time, and Sara your wife shall have your son."[4] Likewise later: "The Lord visited Sara, just as he had promised, and fulfilled what he said, and she conceived and gave birth to a son in her old age, at the time which God had foretold to her."[5] By these words it is not sufficiently clear, when it is said, *Sara shall have a son,* whether this should be understood con-

3. Rom 4.11–12.   4. Gn 18.10.
5. Gn 21.1–2.

cerning his conception or his birth. But when it is said "in her old age," it is clearly intimated that he said that this son is not so much of the flesh as of promise, that is, not of nature but of grace.

[9.10] And although it was said, *In Isaac shall your seed be named,* nevertheless this was not the case with all who were to be born from Isaac according to the flesh, since Esau himself was immediately rejected and Jacob alone was chosen by God. He now follows this up, saying, **but not only did she,** that is, Sara (understand:...have the promise of offspring from the Lord), **but also Rebecca** already had children in her womb, before she received that promise; she had, I say, children in her womb **from one husband, Isaac our father,** not so much through flesh as through faith.

[9.11] And truly she also received that promise (234) concerning the choice of the younger son, namely, that the older would serve the younger. And this is what he says: **For when they were not yet born,** namely, those whom she bore from Isaac, **or [had done] anything [good or evil],** that is, they did not yet have any merit from their good or bad works. For it could happen that, illuminated in the womb in the manner of Jeremiah and John the Baptist, they knew God, and by loving[6] or not loving him they might merit something, so that through this, that they had not yet deserved anything, **the purpose of God according to election might endure** in one of them, that is, in Jacob, and not in Esau; this is according to what God had declared in himself and ordained in his providence from eternity, that the choice of Jacob should endure, that is, his predestination should remain unmoved.

[9.12] **Not by works,** that is, on account of some merit of the works of the one who was chosen, **but** only **by** God **who calls** him, that is, by the grace alone of him who later drew him to himself through internal inspiration, **it was said to her,** that is, to Rebecca, **that the older,** that is, Esau, who was to be the firstborn, **will serve** the later brother, that is, Jacob. This servitude should be understood not so much in the persons of the

6. *Diligere.*

two brothers as in their posterity, that is, in the peoples who
were promised to be born from them, when the Lord said to
Rebecca, "Two nations are in your womb, and two peoples will
be divided from it, and a people will subdue a people, and the
older will serve the younger."⁷ For if you consider the persons
of the brothers, you will find that Esau never was obligated to
or became subject to Jacob in anything, but on the contrary Jacob always especially feared Esau and humbled himself extensively before him.⁸ But it is clear that this should be understood
concerning the peoples, since even according to the commandment of the law it was forbidden to the Israelites to have slaves
from their own people, but only from the Gentiles. Therefore,
it is written in Leviticus, Chapter 84: "If your brother is forced
into poverty and sells himself to you, you shall not oppress him
with the servitude of slaves, but he shall be just as a hired servant or sojourner. He shall work for you up to the year of Jubi-
lees, and afterwards he shall go out with his children and return
to his kindred and (235) the possession of his fathers. For they
are my servants. Let them not be sold in the status of slaves; you
must not afflict him with might. Let your slaves and maid-ser-
vants come from the nations; you shall have them for servants,
and you shall pass them on by hereditary right to your descendants and possess them forever."⁹

[9.13] [*The God*] *who calls* him, I say, **just as it is written,**
namely, in the prophet Malachi, with these words: "Was not
Esau Jacob's brother? says the Lord," and, **I have loved**¹⁰ **Jacob,
but I have hated Esau;**¹¹ that is, I have called one by choice, but
I have rejected the other. Concerning such a choice the same
Apostle said above, *And those he called he also justified.*¹²

[9.14] **What therefore [shall we say?]** The Apostle next states
an appropriate objection from the remarks, as if to accuse and
assault God, who, before Esau could have merited anything,
judged him worthy of his hatred by not predestining him; and

---

7. Gn 25.23.   8. For example, Gn 32.20–21.
9. Cf. Lv 25.39–46. "Chapter 84" refers to an older numbering of the text,
prior to the current one.
10. *Diligere.*   11. Mal 1.2–3.
12. Rom 8.30.

to the extent that he gave grace to the other brother, who likewise had merited nothing before, he withdrew it from him, with
the result that when it was withdrawn from him he could not act
well, and thus it seems that the blame falls not so much to Esau,
wherein he was unjust, as it does to God himself, who did not
give to him the grace by which he could have done well. But the
Apostle himself later adds the solution to this objection when
he says, *O man, who are you,* etc.[13] Up to that point, all that was
interposed concerned the objection.

To continue, seeing that Jacob no more obtained his election
and calling by his own merits than did Esau, but only by the
choice of the one who calls, and that Esau did not previously
give it up by his own merits, *what shall we say?* That is, what will
we be able to say and answer to an objection of this sort? That
which immediately follows: **Is there iniquity with God?** That is,
by what reasoning will we be able to defend God from blame
and demonstrate that he is not guilty of iniquity, who, by withdrawing his grace from him who did not yet have merit, made
him reprobate? For thus it is said, *When they were not yet born or
had done anything good or evil.*[14] The Apostle immediately says on
his own part, **In no way** should iniquity ever be believed to exist
in God. But before this he shows why God should not (236) be
said to be unjust on the basis of the charges; he corroborates
the objection up to this point in the manner of a good argu-
mentator, such that the stronger the objection was, the
more difficult or admirable the solution would appear later.

[9.15] **For [he said] to Moses,** as if he should say, It was
rightly asked with respect to the question at hand, so that we
may be capable of defending God from blame, because God appears to be thoroughly culpable and inexcusable in such things
from the very testimonies of scripture, since he has the power to
grant mercy to whomever he wills, by which they are saved; and
without his mercy no one can be saved. That he has this power
he premises, saying, **I will have mercy [on whom I have mercy],**
etc. He immediately adds that someone can be saved only by his
prevenient mercy when he says, *therefore, not to the one who wills.*[15]

13. Rom 9.20.   14. Rom 9.11.
15. Rom 9.16.

[*I will have mercy*] *on whom I have mercy*, by predestining, namely, before a man has any merit, *I will have mercy* by calling him later through internal inspiration; and finally *on whom I have mercy* by calling, **I will grant mercy**, in the very prize of a celestial calling.

[9.16] **Therefore**, the Apostle says, speaking as the person in opposition, this (bestowing of divine mercy, understood) belongs **not** to the man **who wills** however so much, **nor to him who runs**, that is, to the one who makes haste and strives however so much to obtain it, **but** only **to God, who has mercy.** That is, it is not in our power to receive it, but in his hand to give it, so that through this it may seem to be demonstrated that no one is to blame, if there is anyone estranged from that mercy, except him who had it to bestow but did not wish to.

[9.17] **For [scripture] says [to Pharaoh]**...He shows by contraries that it belongs *to God who has mercy* that men are saved, and to him who hardens that they are condemned, just as is clear in Pharaoh from the very testimony of God. He does not only say "hardens" but, as it were, compels to evil, when it says, **I raised [you] up.** And in order to enlarge the blame of God, he adds, **that I may show in you [my virtue],** as it were to condemn others that he may glorify himself and seek his glory in the death of others, which does seem most unjust. **For this very purpose,** that is, for afflicting the people (237) or pursuing them or not hearing me, just as it is written, "I will harden Pharaoh's heart."[16] *I raised you up;* that is, by opposing you I caused your malice to flare up against me even more, so that, just as it is written, "He who is righteous, let him be even more righteous," cleansed like gold in the forge of tribulation, "and he who is filthy, let him be even filthier."[17] *My virtue*, that is, power, as much in the plagues of Egypt as in the drowning of the Egyptians.

So that through this **my name may be made known [in all the earth],** that is, that the fame of my power may be spread everywhere in the world. The words *so that* through this seem to show more effect than cause, just as it is customarily said concerning someone that "he went out in order to die"; that is, he

16. Ex 4.21; 7.3; 14.4, 17.
17. Rv 22.11.

went out, and from that cause death resulted. So it is also said here that *I raised you up,* and through this I later showed *in you my virtue,* that is, in these things which I did concerning you and your people.

[9.18] **Therefore, [he has mercy] on whom he wills;** that is, it seems so. The Apostle still speaks as the person in opposition, and says that *he has mercy on whom he wills,* **and he hardens whom he wills;** that is, because of his willing and his choice rather than because of their own merits, men are either saved through his mercy or condemned in their sins through his hardening. He causes this hardening by not having mercy, so that the whole thing may appear to be ascribed to the divine choice of men for salvation or condemnation.

[9.19] **Therefore, you say to me,** says the Apostle in his own person, or of each of the faithful, who praise God in all things; that is, You, whoever you may be, on the basis of the testimonies and reasons spoken above, seemed to speak and oppose rationally that which follows, **Why does he still complain?** That is, does God complain; that is, how can he justly move any complaint against us concerning our offenses, which all seem to happen by his fault alone, or especially so, since, as was said, he hardens whom he wills, and, as is now said, no one **can resist his will?** *Still,* that is, (238) after such clear testimonies or reasons accusing him. *His will,* that is, his decree, concerning which it is written, "Whatever he willed, he did."[18] God is even said in another way to will, namely, not by disposing, but by taking counsel with us, that we may do those things through which we may be saved, according to those words, "How often have I wished to gather [you]," etc.,[19] and "Who wishes all to be saved,"[20] that is, he takes counsel that they may act.

[9.20] **O man, you...** In this passage the Apostle for his own part answers the objections cited above which seem to draw God thoroughly into blame, and sufficiently refutes them, with a suitable example drawn from the potter. He therefore says, answering and satisfying the question with a question, *O man,* that is, carnal and animal rather than spiritual, who until now

18. Ps 113.11; 134.6.   19. Mt 23.37.
20. 1 Tm 2.4.

have attacked God, as it were, by accusing him of iniquity, just as was begun in that passage, *Is there iniquity with God?* [21] And later it was amplified with examples and reasons.... **Who are you,** I say, **who respond to God,** that is, you who justify yourself? You who accuse God in the ways mentioned above, answer him,[22] that you may defend yourself from what is unsuitable, if he himself should question you in this way, saying, **Does the thing created say [to the one who made it, "Why did you make me like this?"],** that is, can it justly complain about the potter that he made such a *thing*, that is, a vessel made, that is, composed of clay? Here "make" means "compose."

[9.21] **Or does not [the potter] have the power;** that is, is not the potter allowed, without any injustice which he might bring upon his vessels, **to make one vessel for honor,** that is, for some honorable service, **and another for disgrace,** that is, for some vile and abject use? And this **from the same lump** of earth, that is, if there is no reason for this disgrace on account of the quality of the material, which is the same. **The potter of clay,** that is, the shaper of moist and flexible earth, not the creator of that material. From this it appears that he has less right in his work than God (239) has in his, who is not only the shaper but also the Creator of the material.

Whatever that man might respond to the premises, he is, as it were, wounded with a horned syllogism.[23] For if he answers that the potter does not have this power, he thoroughly condemns the work of potters and impudently disparages the public welfare and the common convenience and necessary use. But if he should choose what is evident, namely, that he should do such things without inflicting any injustice on the vessels of disgrace, it is likewise clear, indeed much more so, that God, who is held guilty of no crime, is allowed to treat and dispose his creature in

21. Rom 9.14.

22. So Buytaert. Peppermüller reads: "that is, you who accuse God in the ways mentioned above, who are adequate to answer him." The manuscripts feature several different readings. Peppermüller's reading is taken from manuscript *A,* while Buytaert prefers *m.*

23. Peppermüller (III, 634, n. 5) cites three sources as the background for this term: Boethius, *diff. top.*1.7.9; Jerome, *Ep.* 69.2; and Seneca, *ep. mor.* 49. It might also be translated as "the horns of a dilemma."

whatever way he wishes, before that creature deserved anything. Otherwise, all the animals created for labor could rightly murmur and complain against him, why he made them for labor only, and the service of men, since they never merited an affliction of this kind, which lasts until death. Because if they are rightly conceded to have been created for labor, for his own glorification or some usefulness to men, it should certainly be conceded by the same reasoning that God justly withdrew his grace from some and did not free them from iniquity, since there is no iniquity which God does not use for the best and he allows nothing to happen without cause, even in the judgment of worldly wisdom. Therefore, Plato also says in his *Timaeus*: "For nothing comes into being that is not preceded by a legitimate cause and reason."[24]

For who among the faithful does not know how [God] used for the best that great impiety of Judas, by whose accursed betrayal he accomplished the redemption of the entire human race? Certainly he accomplished this more expediently in the wickedness of Judas than in the righteousness of Peter, and he used the evil work of the former much better than the good work of the latter; not, I say, as far as it pertains to Judas, but to the common welfare of all, which should always be put before a friend. (240) Some were converted and saved by Peter's preaching and the example of his life, but that treason of Judas was turned into the salvation of all, which was accomplished equally by the Father and the Son, but with a different intention.[25] Thus, whatsoever malice may happen, it is best arranged by the divine disposition, and in all the things which he does or allows to do, he himself knows the reasons, although they are hidden from us and incomprehensible, why it is appropriate to do or permit it. Otherwise, he would do or permit some things irrationally.

Question

But I think that it should be rightly asked, even if God cannot be accused of injustice because he did not give his grace to some, how it should be imputed to wicked men, to whom

24. *Tim.* 28a. See above, in 3.8, and in *TSch* 3.7, *TChr* 5.7.
25. That is, different from Judas's intention.

God did not give his grace that they might be saved, that they are condemned, so that they may be said to be condemned by their own fault? Or if it is not their fault, by what merit of theirs are they said to be condemned by God, *who renders to each one according to his works?*[26] But again, what fault is it of a man if he is not saved, to whom God never wanted to give the grace through which he may be saved, and without which he could not be saved?

But perhaps someone may say that it is his fault, insofar as God did not wish to give that grace to him which he equally offered to him just as he did to the righteous, but he did not wish to receive it when it was offered. To this I respond that it cannot be that he received [it] without the grace of God. Since God did not wish to give this grace of receiving the offered gift, and he could not receive it without this grace, the fault is falsely ascribed to him insofar as he did not receive the offered grace. For example, a physician comes to a sick person and offers a potion by which he can be cured, but the sick person in no way was able to raise himself up to receive the medication unless the physician himself also held him up; what fault is it of the sick person if he did not receive the offered remedy? Or what commendation is it of the physician in offering the medicine if he withdraws the efficaciousness of the medicine by not holding him up?

We therefore say that it is not necessary that a new grace be imparted to us by God in individual good works, (241) so that we may in no way be able to do or to will new things without a new, preceding gift of divine grace; but often, when God distributes an equal gift of his grace to some, it does not happen that they work equally. On the contrary, he often works less who has received more grace for working. For as it happens with love[27] or desire for temporal things, so it happens with true and eternal goods. Some powerful person comes and shows and offers his riches in reward equally to the needy, if they will fulfill what he orders them. One of these people, inflamed with desire for the reward shown and promised to him, applies himself and

26. Rom 2.6; cf. Mt 16.27; 2 Tm 4.8.
27. *Amor.*

completes the labor of the task. But another, since he is lazy and unwilling to endure hard work, is inflamed less with that desire the more he is discouraged by the magnitude of the toil; and often it turns out that he who is stronger in body is lazier in mind, and he who is poorer is more sluggish. Why is it, therefore, that, when wealth is shown and offered in reward to each one, one person, inflamed with desire for them, endures labor that he might become rich, while another neglects to work and chooses lasting poverty instead of sustaining work to the end? What is this, I pray, except the honesty of the former and the sloth of the latter? What did the rich man, who equally showed and promised an equal reward to each one, do more for one than for the other? In the one, you will say, so much desire burned that it made him patient in his work and caused him to complete it. But this, I say, followed from that action of the rich man; it did not at all follow from the action itself; that is, it is not some part of it. What impediment was there in the other, that he did not similarly accomplish it? You will certainly not be able to show anything, except the sloth of him who refused work.

So also, when God offers the Kingdom of Heaven to us every day, one person burns with desire for that kingdom and perseveres in good works, while another grows sluggish in his sloth. Nevertheless, God offers it equally to each and brings about what is his own, and works to such a degree in relation to each, by offering and promising the blessedness of his kingdom, which should be enough for inflaming the desire of each one apart from another new grace added on. For the greater the reward is known to be, the more it attracts each one naturally with desire for it, especially since the will alone is enough to obtain it, (242) and it can be reached by all with much less expense or labor or danger than in the acquisition of earthly kingdoms.

Therefore, for the purpose of inflaming our desire in God and desiring the celestial kingdom, how necessary is it that grace precede, unless so that that blessedness to which it invites us, and the way by which we can arrive at it, is set forth and believed? But he equally imparts this grace both to the reprobate and to the elect, by instructing each one equally about this, so that by the same grace of faith which they obtained, one is aroused to good works, and the other is rendered inexcusable through the negligence of his sluggishness. Therefore, this faith, which works in the first through love,[28] and is of no effect, inactive, unfruitful, and inoperative in the other one, is the grace of God, which goes before each of the elect, so that he may begin to desire well; and again it follows the beginning of a good will, so that that will may persevere. It is not necessary that apart from that faith God give another grace through new individual good works which daily follow, by which faith we believe that through these things which we do we will obtain such a great reward. For the worldly merchants, since they undergo so many great labors, endure all things with the one hope of earthly reward which they conceived from the beginning; and although they do different things, they are not pushed onward to them by a different hope, but they are drawn by one and the same hope.

[9.22] **What if [God,] wishing...** The Apostle shows by a fitting likeness drawn from the potter that God in no way can be accused of injustice if he did not wish to give grace to some people, by which grace they are saved, such as to Pharaoh or Esau, concerning whom the objection arose. Now then, he turns this same thing which was done concerning them to the commendation of God, by showing that God endured the malice of Pharaoh with much patience, that he might come to his senses; and when he showed that he was completely incorrigible, he made excellent use of the rod of his malice (243) for the common welfare of the others, so that that freed people, seeing this, or the whole world hearing this, might be restrained from evil at least by the fear of punishment and aroused to good.

To continue: Just as it was shown, God should not be accused of injustice, if he should will not to bestow his grace on some people, by which grace they may be saved. And you, man, who at first accused God, you do not have anything to answer to him, having been driven from the present likeness, but much more should you praise him concerning this, since even in these

---

28. *Dilectio.*

things, in which he especially seems to you cruel, his mercy should be proclaimed. And this is what he says: *What if,* namely, what should you answer or be able to say, since, in what he did to Pharaoh, in order to deter other wicked people, **he wished to show his wrath,** that is, his vengeance, which he exercises on the wicked, and his power which he executed in miracles, both in the plagues of Egypt and in the drowning of the Egyptians? **He endured with great patience,** that is, through his great patience, **vessels of wrath;** that is, he endured those wicked people for a long time, although they thoroughly deserved to be obliterated by him. He calls those who are filled with all vices *vessels of wrath,* with whom he should immediately be angry. And this is what he adds, determining that they are **fit for destruction,** that is, thoroughly worthy of being obliterated. *He endured,* I say, not without cause, but for this purpose: so that in accordance with the fact that the malice of oppression abounds, the power of divine compassion may also abound to the oppressed, by which power he may save them to the praise of himself.

[9.23] **[That he might show] the riches of his glory,** that is, the excellence of his power by which he is glorified **in the vessels of mercy,** towards his chosen, whom he mercifully preserves, lest they be crushed with adversities. Rightly does he say *vessels of wrath* and *vessels of mercy* according to the example at hand concerning the vessels of the potter, **which,** namely, *the vessels of mercy,* **he prepared for glory;** that is, he predestined them to the blessedness of eternal life or to his glory, so that they may glorify him, praising him for the mercy they have obtained.

[9.24] **These he also called...** According to the meaning of the thing, not (244) the property of the term used before, he uses the relative pronoun *quos,* in the masculine gender, not *quae* in the neuter, even though the term used before, *vasa,* "vessels," to which the relative refers, is neuter. Vergil also uses this change of gender according to meaning when he says, "Praeneste, at its foot."[29] *These,* namely, the elect, *he also called;*

29. Vergil, *Aeneid.* 8.561. *Praeneste* is neuter; *ipsa,* "its," is feminine. Abelard is showing that the relative pronoun *quos,* though masculine, in fact refers back to the neuter *vasa,* vessels; grammatically he argues that it refers to the "elect," *electos,* in the masculine, not mentioned in the Vulgate text.

that is, he drew them to himself with an internal inspiration; they did not come to him by themselves, especially in those miracles which he showed to all concerning Pharaoh, just as was said above, *So that my name may be made known in all the earth.* **Not only from the Jews,** I say, did he call them, **but also from the Gentiles,** since the Gentiles had heard what a great hand he exercised against Pharaoh, just as Rahab confessed to the spies she received.[30]

[9.25] **Just as he,** namely, the Lord himself, **says in Hosea,** that is, Hosea the prophet. Paul first introduces the testimony concerning the calling of the Gentiles, and then of the Jews: *But Isaiah,* etc.[31] **I shall call [a people not my own, My people];** that is, I shall subjugate to myself the Gentiles, who in no way became subject to me first, with a fear of terrible things, "because the fear of the Lord is the beginning of wisdom,"[32] but its completion is charity, since from servants they become friends, just as he quickly adds, saying, **and her who is not loved, Beloved;** that is, later I shall transform them from servants into friends, just as it is written: "Now I will not call you servants," etc.[33] *I shall call;* that is, I will truly cause to be called. **And she who has not obtained mercy, One who has obtained mercy.** It is much more to become a son than to obtain mercy. For the latter is a beginning, the former a perfection. We obtain mercy when we, by the call and warning of God, "unless we are converted,"[34] are converted to him lest we be punished by him. We are made sons when "perfect charity casts out" this "fear."[35]

[9.26] Therefore, these two things are related individually to the two things said before, as it were, a confirmation and exposition of the things said before. **In the place,** that is, in the land of the Gentiles, **where** they were first **not my people;** (245) that is, they were not subject to me through fear; **[there they shall be called] sons,** that is, they serve with filial reverence. He says **of the living God** in distinction to the gods which the Gentiles, deluded by a fickle error, had established for themselves before, either from insensate things or from dead men.

30. Jos 2.10.
32. Ps 110.9.
34. Cf. Mt 18.3.
31. Rom 9.27.
33. Jn 15.15.
35. 1 Jn 4.18.

[9.27] **But Isaiah [cries out on behalf of Israel]…** Hosea prophesied the aforesaid calling of the Gentiles, but Isaiah openly prophesied in this way concerning the future conversion of the Jews: **If [the number of the sons of Israel] were…,** that is, although the Jews were innumerable in their barrenness, that is, persevering in unbelief, **just as the sand of the sea,** which is innumerable and sterile, nevertheless a **remnant** of them **will be saved,** which the Lord left for himself, driving away the others from his grace and casting them away from himself. Or "remnant" means the simple and ignorant among the people who were cast away among them, just as the apostles and many adhering to Christ from the masses were, just as those wicked profess, saying, "Did any of the most eminent believe in him? But this crowd, which does not know the law, they are cursed."[36]

[9.28] As if someone might ask by whose preaching that calling of both peoples occurred, he answers, By the very preaching of the incarnate Lord himself. And this is what he says: **Because the Lord will confer** through himself **his shortened word over the earth,** that is, an abridged preaching, according to which it is said, a wise man is known for few words.[37] *Over the earth,* that is, which rises above every teaching of earthly and human wisdom, just as that great John professed of the Lord, saying, "He who is of earth, speaks of earth. He who comes from heaven is over all."[38]

But he mentions before how this teaching rises above all the others, saying that **he completes the word and shortens it in equity;**[39] namely, he will cause. "To complete" is "to perfect," namely, when that which is begun is brought to perfection. Therefore, the preaching of the Gospel, which the Lord gave through himself, (246) completed, that is, perfected, the necessary edification begun in the old law, namely, by adding the things that were lacking for the fullness of righteousness, just as he himself professes, saying, "Unless your righteousness abounds," etc.[40] *Completes in equity;* that is, he supplies what had been less in the equity, that is, what had been lacking from the

36. Jn 7.48–49.
37. Sextus, *sent.* 145, per Peppermüller, 3.650.
38. Jn 3.31.
39. Equity, *aequitas,* here means much the same as righteousness, *iustitia.*
40. Mt 5.20.

perfection of righteousness and virtues; and when the count-less carnal observances have been disregarded, *he shortens* that equity, namely, in the two commandments of charity, where he answers that rich man who took counsel with him concerning the salvation of his soul: "Do this and you shall live, for on these two commandments hang all the law and the prophets."[41]

We can even say how much this applies to the multitude of words in the New Testament, which teaches a shortened Old Testament, because they are few which the Lord, when he hand-ed on the New Testament, taught to the apostles on the moun-tain, in comparison to those which he taught through Moses, and the volumes of the four Gospels are small in comparison to the five books of Moses. Therefore, great is this commendation of the Gospel, that it may be both more perfect in meaning and shorter in words.

[9.29] **And just as** the same **Isaiah foretold: Unless the Lord Sabaoth,** that is, of Hosts, who daily sends his warriors against the kingdom of the devil, just as it is written, "as an army of the camps, set in order."[42] **...had left us seed,** that is, when he blinded our people, that is, the Jewish people, because of their fault, and removed them from his grace, and, as it were, cast out the spoiled grain from the threshing floor and preserved some for himself as if seed, such as the apostles and the other faithful of the primitive church; **we would have been like Sodom and like Gomorrah,** where parents were destroyed at the same time with their children, so that they might not leave seed. In the seed the usefulness of the previous crop is preserved, and the ancient seeds are revived and renewed, and from a few seeds many are produced. Thus in the apostles and the other mem-bers of the primitive church, the usefulness of the preceding fathers was made good, and religion came to life again, (247) and the great abundance of the divine harvest spread through the whole world from that time.

[9.30] **What therefore...** Since he made *her who was not loved, Beloved,* and since now we see conversely that the one be-loved has become not loved, that is, when the Gentile people

---

41. Conflation of Lk 10.28 and Mt 22.40.
42. Song 6.3.

were chosen and almost all Israel was rejected, for what reason shall we say that it happened, namely, in the matter of the rejection of his people? And this is what he says: **What shall we say**—namely, regarding this, that the Gentiles, who at first did not know **righteousness,** that is, the faith which leads to righteousness, now **have taken hold of righteousness,** namely, that true **righteousness** of the soul **which comes from faith,** not that which consists in exterior works?

[9.31] **But Israel,** that is, the people of the Jews, **by pursuing the law of righteousness,** that is, by practicing the austerity of bodily discipline, **did not arrive at the law of righteousness;** that is, it did not receive the perfect teaching of the Gospel which alone justifies.

[9.32] **Why** this? I say: **Because** it did **not** take hold (understand: of the righteousness which is) **by faith, but as it were** the righteousness, not in fact the righteousness which is **by works,** that is, following the letter of the law that kills in exterior and carnal observances, he is not justified and vivified by the spiritual and mystical understanding which edifies faith in Christ, just as is written, "The righteous lives by faith."[43] And this, therefore, because **they stumbled on the stone of stumbling;** that is, they were scandalized by Christ, whom by no means did they believe to be God on account of the weakness of his human nature. Their feet are accustomed to stumble upon and be hit against small stones which can scarcely be blamed for their smallness. In the same way Christ, who was despised by the Jews, became a stone of stumbling to them because of the smallness of the humility which he showed to the world, so that the Jews who did not believe in him might be offended at the things which he said.

[9.33] **Just as it is written,** namely, in Isaiah, **Behold, I place [in Zion]**...They are the words of the Father and the promise concerning the sending of his Son. *Behold, I place;* that is, now before me, I ponder the foundation that is to be placed in the Church, (248) humble but strong, that is, the incarnate Word. Because it is a stone, it is strong; because it is a stone

43. Hab 2.4; Rom 1.17; Gal 3.11; Heb 10.38.

of stumbling, it is humble and to be trod upon by those stumbling on it. **Everyone,** either Jew or Gentile, **[who believes] on him,** not only trusting in him or believing that he exists, **will not be ashamed;** that is, he will not be embarrassed, disappointed in his hope. He likewise says, **a stone of stumbling** and **a rock of scandal.** And it happens frequently in the prophets that the words in the same sentence are varied. The Church is called **Zion,** that is, a watchtower, which, raising itself on high through desire, carefully considers each one of its actions which it has here, lest it hinder its celestial desire.

[10.1] **Brothers...**Lest the Apostle, who had withdrawn from the Jews, appear to have disparaged them from some hatred rather than from a desire to correct them, he shows in the effect how much affection of charity and compassion he has for them, saying that he prays to God intently for their salvation. For when he says, **The will of [my] heart and prayer,** he shows that the prayer issues from the devotion of the heart, and that it consists more in devotion than in words. As if he should say, Although I disparage you in this way, nevertheless, O *brothers,* I do not cease to pray **for them** that they may be saved. Therefore, the Church has a special prayer for the Jews every year: "That God may take away the veil from their hearts and that, when the truth which is Christ has been acknowledged, they may be converted to him."[44] The Apostle calls those to whom he writes *brothers,* according to what the Truth says, "You have one Father, who is in heaven,"[45] that they might receive his correction more willingly, as if from a brother and an equal, and not from a superior. Therefore, this custom took root in the Church, so that at the beginning of the readings which are taken from the apostolic epistles, the word "Brothers" is announced beforehand.

[10.2] But why he should pray for the Jews or especially feel pity for their error he adds, saying, **For [I bear them] witness,** from myself, who once acted similarly. **[They have] an enthusiasm** (249) **[for God, but] not according to knowledge,** that is, a zeal for God, neither rational nor good, because it is erroneous,

44. *Liturgia Romana,* prayer for Holy Saturday.
45. Mt 23.9.

thinking that, namely, which is not according to those words of the Truth: "But the hour is coming when everyone who kills you will think that he is offering a service to God. And they will do these things because they know neither the Father nor me."[46] Any zeal, either good or bad, is called a fervor and agitation of the soul inflamed to doing something.

[10.3] But how this enthusiasm is *not according to knowledge* he immediately adds, saying, **They do not know the righteousness** which God approves, which comes, of course, from faith in Christ, wishing **to establish,** that is, to be preserved immovable, **their own [righteousness],** that is, what they regard and approve in place of righteousness, namely, in carnal observances. **They were not subject,** that is, obedient, **to the righteousness of God,** that is, to those commandments of God which justify those obeying them (as, for example, "You believe in God; believe also in me").[47]

[10.4] **For [Christ is] the end…** They are truly ignorant of God's righteousness, because they do not have the faith in Christ by which each one who believes is justified. Because each person is truly justified through faith in Christ and not through his own righteousness, namely, of the works of the law, he thus says that **to everyone who believes,** that is, to each faithful person, **Christ,** that is, faith in Christ, **for righteousness,** that is, for this purpose, that through it he may be justified, is *the end* of **the law,** that is, of legal works, because as long as they place the hope of salvation in those works, Christ will not profit them. Therefore, he also says to the Galatians, "If you are circumcised, Christ will profit you nothing,"[48] and Christ says through himself, "The law and the prophets were until John."[49]

[10.5] **For Moses [wrote that]…** He shows in the testimonies of Moses the law-giver that no one attains eternal life, nor was it promised, through fulfilling the righteousness of the law, namely, in those carnal works; rather, one attains it through faith in Christ. **The man who shall perform the righteousness which is from the law,** that is, who has fulfilled the legal works, **shall live** upon the earth, namely, **on it;** that is, on account of the observance of the law he will enjoy the good things of this life, not of eternal life.

[10.6] **But the righteousness which is from faith...** Since faith (250) is not from the things which are visible,[50] it promises that eternal life which is hidden in Christ rather than the present life, and invisible goods rather than visible ones. And this is that *righteousness which is from faith,* namely, in Christ, that is, that faith held in Christ, which justifies us. So he says in the same place, namely, Deuteronomy,[51] through the same Moses, who truly was righteous through that faith, encouraging us that we may be lacking in nothing or despair in no adversities. And this is what Moses himself **says** about that righteousness which he then had: **Do not say in your heart,** that is, do not even think it, O man, whoever you are, or you, the people of Israel, **Who shall ascend into heaven?** That is, do not despair of that heavenly life in which faith in Christ consists, and of its promise by which Christ especially draws us to himself, as if human nature could by no means ascend to that life, because this would be, the Apostle says on his part, **to bring Christ down** from that life, that is, to believe that he did not ascend to that place in the human nature which he assumed.

[10.7] **Or, who will descend into the abyss?** That is, even as far as hell itself, so that he might lead those whom he freed from that place to heaven with himself, because this would be **to call Christ back from the dead,** that is, by believing to bring Christ back or to call him back from that descent by which he freed his faithful dead from hell and brought them to heaven with himself.

[10.8] **But what does scripture say?** the Apostle says; that is, pay attention to what is added in the same place by Moses himself, namely, this: **The word is near, [in your mouth];** that is, it is easy for you to confess or believe that this was complete in Christ, namely, concerning the ascent of man to heaven and the descent of man to hell; therefore, it is easy because it is not in opposition to reason but especially compatible with divine mercy. **This is,** says the Apostle, **the word of faith [which we preach],**

50. Heb 11.1.
51. Dt 30.12–13.

that is, the word concerning that which faith possesses and concerning (251) that which, when believed, makes [people] faithful; we apostles were sent to preach this word. And justly, because our salvation consists in the confession of this word and in faith.

[10.9] And this is what he says: **Because if you,** whoever you are, **[confess with your mouth that Jesus is Lord and believe with your heart that God raised him from the dead, you will be saved].** He confesses with his *mouth* who understands what he asserts; he believes with his *heart* who applies his heart and will to what he believes, so that faith itself draws him to works, just as when someone, by believing that Christ was raised *from the dead* into eternal life, tries as he is able in order that he may arrive at the blessedness of the same life by following his footsteps.

We should note that it frequently happens that, when some testimonies from the Old Testament are brought into the New, it is easy for the testimonies brought in to be applied to confirming that for which they were brought in, if through them they may be examined closely. But if we pay attention to the contexts of that passage from which the testimonies were taken and to how things preceding or following that passage in the scripture are compatible with what was taken from there, our understanding has an especially sharp focus. It touches on this same testimony which is now expounded.

That we may consider this more diligently, let us open more broadly the words of scripture itself. Therefore, it is written in Deuteronomy, Chapter 57,[52] when, after the law was given, Moses exhorted the people to the observance of the law with these words: "This commandment which I teach to you today is not above you, neither is it placed far away nor located in heaven, so that you could say, 'Who of us can ascend to heaven to bring it down to us, that we may hear it and fulfill it with a work?' It is not placed across the sea, that you may plead and say, 'Who of us could cross the sea and bring it back to us, that we may be able to hear and do what is commanded?'"[53] Likewise, in Chap-

---

52. As at 9.12, these chapter numbers refer to an older numbering system.
53. Dt 30.11–13.

ter 58: "But the word is very near, in your mouth and in your heart, that you may do it."[54]

Behold, from these words, if we follow them according to the letter, he seems to admonish the Jews alone, so that they may not complain about the difficult understanding of the law, as though something were spoken obscurely, through an enigma; (252) but all things are commanded openly, so that they may be self-evident, and if someone differs in obeying the commandments because he cannot understand them, he does not have any excuse. But since it especially invites us to follow the Apostle, who was most skilled in the law, it is proper for us to adapt the things which are said according to its meaning for faith in Christ.

Therefore, Moses, knowing that the law which he had given was full of mystical and obscure meanings, which were only to be explained through the coming and ascension of Christ—just as it is written: "And beginning from Moses and all the prophets, he interpreted the scriptures to them,"[55] and just as Christ himself says, "Unless I go away, [the Paraclete will not come],"[56] and again, "But the Paraclete, [the Holy Spirit,...will teach you all things and make known to you everything I say to you]"[57]—warns the people lest they despair concerning the spiritual understanding of the law, as if it were never to be explained, as though the world were not to have him who came from heaven to explain the meaning of God which was in the law; in fact the Son of God was about to come from heaven and to ascend again, to supply this understanding to the world both through himself and through the Holy Spirit, who was to be sent for this purpose after the ascension.

We should note that the Apostle added this: *Or who will descend to the abyss,* which is not at all contained in the words of Moses cited above, but spoken there in place of these words: "It is not placed across the sea," etc. The Apostle, having followed the meaning, added these words, or perhaps, according to another translation which we now use, he only gathered

---

54. Dt 30.14.
56. Jn 16.7.
55. Lk 24.27.
57. Jn 14.26.

those words which he saw coincided with the meaning set forth.
<What is said, "It is not placed across the sea," can be under-
stood in this way: that it is not located in the abyss, that is, in
hell; that, on account of it, it is necessary that someone descend
there and enter the sea of this world in order to arrive at that
depth of hell, so that it may be "beyond the sea," as if "down-
ward," "after the sea" should be said, that is, in that remote bitterness of hell after the misery of the present life.>[58]

(253) [10.10] **For with the heart...** I rightly said, *confess* and
believe, because each is necessary, because *with the heart* **it is believed to** this end, that he may be justified who believes, because
"without faith it is impossible to please God";[59] and later **confession is made** concerning what he believes, so that the faithful
one may be added to the Church and share in its sacraments.

[10.11–12] **For [scripture] says,** as was expressed above in
Isaiah. **For [there is] no [distinction]...** I said, **Everyone [who
believes],** namely, either Jew or Gentile, and justly, because the
diversity of peoples is of no importance for obtaining this salvation, while there is one faith by which we believe **on him,** rather than trusting in him or believing in him, as we mentioned
above.[60] **He is rich toward all,** that is, sufficient to enrich *all* with
true riches, **who invoke him,** not who call. For the calling is the
sound of exterior words, concerning which it is said, "Not everyone who says to me, 'Lord, Lord,' will enter into the Kingdom
of Heaven."[61] The invocation is an interior cry, that is, the devotion of the soul sighing to God, concerning which it is said to
Moses, "Why do you cry to me?"[62]

[10.13] **For everyone [who calls upon the name of the Lord
will be saved],** by the authority of Isaiah.[63] *The name of the Lord;*
that is, he desires with devotion the knowledge of him and his
revelation, concerning which it is said, "And I will reveal myself
to him,"[64] and the psalmist says, "I will be satisfied when your
glory appears."[65]

---

58. This last sentence is a *Lectio Abaelardi,* found only in *mOR.*

59. Heb 11.6.   60. E.g., 3.22; 4.5; 4.23–24; 9.33.
61. Mt 7.21.   62. Ex 14.15.
63. Actually Jl 3.5; Acts 2.21.   64. Jn 14.21.
65. Ps 16.15.

[10.14] **How, therefore,...** He commends his service and that of the other apostles, namely, by showing how necessary their preaching is that men may believe and be saved.

To continue: Since he who **will invoke** [the Lord] will be saved, therefore he should be invoked by men that they may be saved. But **how will they invoke him on whom they have not believed?** As if he should plainly say, In no way. **[Or how shall they trust] him;** that is, not only did they not believe on him, but they did not trust him, that is, his commandments or admonitions, **whom they have not heard,** neither through [Paul] preaching him or through another who preached him. **[But how will they hear] without a preacher,** either himself or another?

[10.15] **[How] shall** anyone **preach, unless they are sent?** In the same way the Son was sent by the Father, and the apostles by the same Son when he said to them, "Just as the Father sent me, I also send you."[66] Here he refers to the false apostles who, not having been sent by God, come by themselves to preach. (254) Concerning these the Truth says, "All who came before were thieves and robbers."[67] **Just as it is written, ["How beautiful are the feet of those proclaiming the good news of peace and good things."]**[68] Origen says, "This example seems to have been taken from Isaiah."[69] Ambrose says, "The prophet Nahum says this."[70] The feet of the apostles were beautiful because their affections were clean from the contagion of earthly desire and pure in God. They sought not the things which are their own from their preaching, but the things which are Jesus Christ's, and served not the stomach but God. Therefore, their feet were washed well by the Lord;[71] he prohibited these feet from being hidden in shoes on account of this mystical beauty of theirs,[72] because what is hidden is deformed, and where light is misused it is hidden. *Of those proclaiming the good news of peace,* that is, of those preaching and teaching reconciliation with God. In this mystery, they were instructed to say to every house which they entered, "Peace to this house."[73] **Good things,** namely, those

66. Jn 20.21.
67. Jn 10.8.
68. Cf. Is 52.7 and Na 1.15.
69. *Rom.,* 8.5.
70. Ambrosiaster, *Rom.,* 10.15.
71. Jn 13.5–14.
72. Mt 10.10; Lk 10.4.
73. Lk 10.5.

true things which "the eye has not seen."[74] In this life we gain this peace and reconciliation with God through penance, just as it is written, "Turn back to me and I will turn back to you."[75] Those good things come later on, in the future life. Therefore, he rightly said *peace* before, and *good things* after.

[10.16] **[But not all obey] the Gospel,** that is, the divine proclamation. **[For Isaiah says, Lord,] who has believed [our preaching];** that is, who has had faith through this [Gospel] which he heard from us? As if he should say, None or few.

[10.17] **Therefore,** that is, from that testimony it appears that **faith** is **from hearing, [and hearing is] through the word of Christ** rather than through ours, because we do not speak from ourselves but from that which he taught us, so that whatever happens through our preaching might especially be directed to his glory or displeasure.

[10.18] **[But I say,] did they not [hear?]** That is, can some part of the world claim ignorance as an excuse for its unbelief, as if the preaching of the Gospel did not come or was not about to come to everyone? As if he should say, Not at all. He refutes this immediately with the testimony of the Psalmist, saying, **And indeed,** although not everyone may obey, **their sound,** that is, the fame of the apostles or of the preachers of the Gospel, **[has gone out into every land,] and their words,** through which they preached, as far, even, **as the ends of the earth.**[76]

(255) [10.19] I said *to the ends,* that is, to the farthest parts of the world which, it is certain, are inhabited by the Gentiles. But **did not** the Jews know that the preaching went out as far as the nations? That is, can they therefore be excused as though the preaching were not offered to them, and ascribe this to the fault of the preachers? He does not say only that [*Israel*] *did not hear,* but even **it did not know;** that is, it does not consider the truth of that preaching, as if he should say, it in fact did this, although it might resist with the zeal of malice and of envy or of earthly desire. Therefore, its sin against the Holy Spirit remains unpardonable. And he demonstrates this with the testimony of Moses himself, who wrote as the **first** of the prophets and

74. 1 Cor 2.9; Is 64.3.   75. Zec 1.4.
76. Ps 18.5.

first prophesied this malice of theirs in writing. **I** (the words are God's) **will incite you** to envy and hatred both of myself and of my people, **to hostility,** that is, through me, by preaching, says the Son of God. But because envy is hatred of another's good, he truly shows that they knowingly transgressed against Christ. **I will send you to those who are not a nation by a foolish nation;** that is, through your dispersion, to be brought about by the unbelieving Romans, I will cause you to be not a people. For a people or a nation is not rightly called such unless there is a community of men. *I will send you,* even when dispersed, **in anger** toward other men, so that they may always oppress and afflict you with dread exactions.[77]

[10.20] **But Isaiah...** Not only Moses but also Isaiah openly **dares** to speak openly of their condemnation and the election of the Gentiles, even if he foresaw that he was to be killed by them. **[I was found] by those who were not seeking me,** that is, by the Gentiles, says the Lord. **[I appeared] openly,** because the Church is much more learned about God than the synagogue is. **[...to those who] did not ask [about me];** that is, they have learned to seek nothing from me, whom they thoroughly disregarded.[78]

[10.21] **But to Israel,** that is, the Jews, **all day long,** that is, the whole time of my preaching, which should truly be called "day" and "the illumination of the world," **I spread out my hands [to a people that does not believe];** that is, I offered myself voluntarily to gather them, by my own hands; that is, my works were shown to them daily, and I turned away thoroughly from the way of the Gentiles (256) so that I might be entirely available to them. **But [Israel] contradicts,** which is worse, and slanders me in every way.

[11.1] **I say, therefore.** Because he had refuted the Jews with so many authorities and had taught most recently that the election of the Gentiles and condemnation of the Jews were clearly prophesied, lest on this account the Gentiles, understanding, as it were, that that people was thoroughly condemned, should especially undertake the opportunity of boasting against the Jews in their debate, he begins to remove this boasting from the Gentiles, and despair from the Jews.

77. Dt 32.21.   78. Is 65.1.

He returns to the invective against the Gentiles.

And now he returns to the invective against the Gentiles so
that he may also destroy their pride.

To continue: Since the condemnation of the Jews was confirmed with such clear testimonies, therefore *I say,* that is, I consider that what follows should be examined and resolved. **He
has rejected his people,** that is, the Jews, entirely, so that he may
receive not one more from there.[79] **[For I am an] Israelite,** that
is, a Jew, not a proselyte, and from the lineage of **Abraham,** not
descending through Ishmael or Esau but through **Benjamin,**
and from the lineage of cursed Saul, whose posterity was rejected from the throne.

[11.2] **[God has not rejected] his people, whom he foreknew,** that is, those whom he once predestined from that peculiar people of his. **[Or do you not know what scripture says]
about Elijah,** that is, what it says about Elijah in the Book of
Kings, **how he,** namely, Elijah, **intercedes with God against Israel,** that is, by praying or complaining, he stirs God to vengeance
against the wickedness of the Jews persecuting him?

[11.3] **[Lord,] they have killed [your prophets],** under Jezebel; **they have dug under [your altars];** that is, they have completely overturned them from the foundation, so that they may
worship only idols.[80]

[11.4] **But what does [the divine answer] say [to him]?** That
is, did he think that he alone remained? But he was shown to be
in error by the testimony of God himself. **I have left to myself
[seven thousand men who have not bowed the knee...];** that is,
I have not cast away from my grace. **[...before] Baal,** that is, the
idol of Ahab and Jezebel.

(257) [11.5] **So therefore [in this time].** Since we have introduced the example of Elijah, let us testify to what was introduced. And this is what he says: that even now **there is a remnant,** that is, those whom the Lord did not cast away, **[saved]**

79. If we take Peter's citation literally, as has been done here, without adding the important, missing words of the biblical text, then we must read Peter
as virtually contradicting Paul. On the other hand, if we add the missing words,
we could render this passage as follows: Has God rejected his people, that is,
the Jews, entirely, so that he may receive not one more from there? [In no way.]

80. Missing biblical text: "And I alone am left, and they seek my life."

according to the election of the grace of God, not their merits.

[11.6] **But if by grace,** that is, (*they were saved*, understood) through grace, **it is no longer on account of works,** that is, on account of their merits. He does not say "through merits," but *on account of* merits, because the grace of God does not exclude the merits of Paul and of others. But it was on account of merits, not on account of grace, if the beginning proceeded from our merits and the grace of God did not go before, which [grace] at the least inspired faith or guided the preachers. **Otherwise,** that is, if what is now **grace,** that is, something given gratis, with our merits not preceding the grace of God, had turned out differently, in a manner contrary to what I say, it **would not be grace** but merit alone. The Apostle introduced a suitable comparison from Elijah for our time and began to refute the rash judgment of the Gentiles with a suitable example, since they saw that such a great man was reproved by the Lord because of an entirely similar disobedience. We know that John the Baptist, another Elijah[81] as it were, preceded the first coming of the Lord, and he harshly accused the people of the Jews, as if he despaired of their salvation, with these words: "Race of vipers," etc.,[82] so that those things which are now said of Elijah may appear to resound in this time of grace, concerning which it is written, "The law and the prophets [were] until John."[83]

[11.7] **What then?** Since only the *remnant* of Israel *was saved* —on account of the election of the grace of God rather than on account of their own merits—therefore, *what* (understand: should we say)? It is clear, namely, that which follows: that **what Israel sought,** that is, he asked from God, as it were, for his own, and, as it were, what was owed to him through works, **he did not obtain,** namely, eternal life or an earthly[84] inheritance. **But the election,** that is, the few who were chosen from that people through the grace of God, *which* [*Israel*] *sought,* that is, eternal

81. Buytaert reads "Isaiah," which makes much less sense than Peppermül-ler's "Elijah," which Peppermüller elsewhere points out is read by all four manuscripts ("Ausgabe," 94).

82. Lk 3.7; cf. Mt 3.7.   83. Mt 11.13; Lk 16.16.

84. Buytaert, following two of the manuscripts, reads "eternal inheritance." Peppermüller, following the other two manuscripts, offers this reading, which makes more sense.

life, **obtained** what they sought; **but the others were blinded;** not (258) only did they not attain what they sought, but lest they believe further, they were thoroughly condemned.

[11.8] **Just as it is written, [God] gave to them a spirit of confusion.** Origen says,

Thus far I have not been able to find where it is written, "God gave to them a spirit of confusion, so that their eyes may not see and their ears not hear up to this day."[85] But I think that the Apostle spoke in this way: "The others were blinded, and, just as it is written concerning them, he gave to them a spirit of confusion." But these are the words which were spoken through Isaiah concerning the blindness of the eyes and the hearing of the ears: "You will hear with the hearing and not understand, and seeing you will see and not see. For the heart of this people has been hardened," etc.[86] Now, therefore, the Apostle seems to have revealed the meaning of Isaiah with his words. He likewise asserts concerning these things which scripture proclaims from [the person of] David, "Let their table become [a snare]," etc.[87]

A spirit of confusion, that is, of envy and hatred, with which their minds were afflicted, that is, incited against Christ and his people. Eyes, that is, reason that is not able to see by itself, *and ears,* that is, not understanding when another teaches.

[11.9] **Let their table become…** Origen says, "This seems to be taken from Isaiah or David, with one meaning somehow expounded in both." Likewise, "The word 'trap' is not found written in the Psalm, neither in the Septuagint nor in the Hebrew. Also, in the Psalm there are the words 'before them,' though the Apostle did not cite them."[88]

Let their table **before them,** that is, the scriptures of the Old Testament handed on to them and frequented by them, from where intelligent souls receive their food. **Be a snare and a trap,** that is, *a snare* in which they do not capture others, but are captured and detained, lest they walk in the way of Truth, which says, "I am the way, the truth, and the life,"[89] while they understand nothing there mystically but expound everything according to

85. St. Paul seems to have conflated Dt 29.3 and Is 29.10.

86. Cf. Is 6.9–10.   87. Origen, *Rom.,*8.8, edited.

88. Ibid. Paul is quoting Ps 68.23, imperfectly, as Origen points out, though he takes nothing from Isaiah. "Trap" likely comes from Ps 34.8, which uses very similar language.

89. Jn 14.6.

the letter which kills; *and a trap,* (259) while they are captured and bound often by the Lord or the holy doctors who often conflict with them, by these testimonies which are put before them from scripture, so that they cannot extricate themselves from the objections; such is that which the Lord set against them, when he says, "Therefore, how does David, in the Spirit, call him Lord when he says," etc.[90] **And a stumbling stone and a recompense,** that is, in recompense for the stumbling of their soul, that is, for damnation, not for salvation, according to the word of the Lord, who says, "It is Moses who accuses you,"[91] and according to what the Apostle says, *And whoever has sinned in the law shall be judged by the law.*[92] The law became a stumbling stone to them, that is, the cause of offense and indignation, since they saw Christ and his disciples say and do many things which they believed to be contrary to the law. Therefore, they said, "We have heard from the law that the Christ remains forever."[93]

[11.10] **Let [their eyes] be darkened [that they may not see].** From where the stumbling stone or the trap proceeds he adds, namely, from their blindness and the desire for earthly things, which always especially reigns among the Jews. **Bow...** This is an imperative, as if he should say, You, God, *bow* **their backs** so that by their eagerness to strive for earthly things they may not be raised up to heavenly things.

We should note that words of this kind, which seem to be words of condemnation, since they are spoken by the saints, belong more to prophetic proposition than to the desire for vengeance, so that when somebody says *fiat,* "let it be done," it is the same as if *fiet,* "it shall be done," was said before. For just as, at one time or another, scripture uses the future of an indicative verb in an imperative way—for example, *diliges,* "you shall love," in place of *dilige,* "love," or *non occides,* "you shall not kill," in place of *non occide,* "do not kill"—it does the reverse a few times.[94] What harm does it do if some holy man, illuminated by the Spirit, approving the divine judgment, prays that the pun-

---

90. Mt 22.43–44; Ps 109.1.   91. Jn 5.45.
92. Rom 2.12.   93. Jn 12.34.
    94. That is, scripture uses both a future indicative in place of an imperative, and vice versa, as well as a jussive subjunctive in place of a future indicative, as in 11.10, and vice versa.

ishment of the wicked may occur, which he rightly understands must occur, and sees that it was fixed beforehand in the divine will? What is the injustice in wishing what is just to happen? Otherwise, some judgment would displease us, and we would also detest that known judgment of the Lord. But (260) we will treat this more diligently in our *Theology*.[95]

[11.11] **I say therefore...** Since their condemnation was prophesied, **did they offend,** namely, God, **so that** not only did they waver in faith but thoroughly **fell;** that is, were they condemned without recompense of some reward from God, who uses all evil well? **[May it not be so.] But by their transgression [the Gentiles have salvation];** when [the Jews] drove away the preaching of Christ from themselves, and the apostles went over to the Gentiles, the more easily they were received by the Gentiles, the more they saw them driven out and afflicted by the Jews, their greatest enemies; or in this, even, because [the Jews] are dispersed through the world, in perpetual captivity on account of the sin committed against Christ, they especially confirm our faith and supply the great praises of the power of Christ. **So that they might emulate them;** that is, turning the order around, the Gentiles do to the Jews what the Jews engaged in proselytization once did to the Gentiles, that is, with zeal for God, convert or rouse them to imitation of them. To emulate someone is a zeal, that is, to have a strong desire toward him that the one may imitate the other or vice versa, according to what he is about to say: *if somehow I may provoke my own flesh to emulation.*[96]

[11.12] **Now if...** They emulate them, and justly, because if God uses their transgression so well, that is, if so much benefit followed from it that the whole world advanced in the Gentiles, how much benefit will there be from their conversion in like manner with the Gentiles? And this is what he says: *Now if* **their transgression means riches for the world,** that is, if by their transgression and the condemnation of one people, the rest of the world is enriched spiritually; **and their diminution [means riches for the Gentiles],** that is, because the world now has less in them of spiritual goods, it is compensated in the Gentiles.

95. Cf. *TSch* 3.117–18.
96. Rom 11.14.

How much more will their fullness (be, understand) *riches for the world;* that is, if they also, equally with the Gentiles, fill the world with good works, how much more will it be enriched? And the term "now," *quod,* is like an adversative "but," *sed,* for this reason: namely, that he had said this first concerning their sin and now speaks concerning their conversion, so that according to the letter it may be connected to what was said before: in this way, by their transgression the world is enriched in the Gentiles, but *if their transgression,* etc.

(261) [11.13] **For [I speak] to you [Gentiles].** As if someone might despair concerning this future fullness, believing that the Jews are further thoroughly condemned by God, he shows by his own example that we should not despair because he also labors daily for this, since he is **the Apostle to the Gentiles,** that he may convert some of the Jews. Indeed, this is his duty, namely, of preaching, to **honor,** that is, to commend especially [his **ministry**], since he wins them through the bountiful God. He was not established as their Apostle, that is, their missionary; he is *the Apostle to the Gentiles,* although least of all to the Jews.

[11.14] **If somehow [I may provoke]**...both with words and with examples, both with authority and with reason, both with plain truth and with useful simulation or dissimulation, concerning which he says elsewhere, "I became a Jew to the Jews, and all things to all people, so that I may win over all."[97] **My own flesh,** that is, the Jews who are of my race; **to emulation,** that is, to imitating me in conversion; **[and save] some [of them]** at least, if not many.

[11.15] **For if...** I justly persist in this that I may convert them also, because although their **loss** is **the reconciliation of the world** in the Gentiles and is beneficial on account of this, much more miraculous and beneficial will be their **acceptance,** which will be, as it were, the resurrection of the dead. For it is more miraculous to raise the dead than to animate something that has not lived, that is, to restore life than to give it. For we know that flesh is animated naturally, daily, in the wombs of mothers, and we do not wonder; but to revive the dead [flesh] was a miraculous act rather than an act of nature. Therefore, we

97. 1 Cor 9.20, 22.

can say that when the Gentiles, who before did not live through faith, were converted to God they were animated, that is, vivified rather than resurrected. This is also true of the Jews, if they return to God and "the hearts of the fathers are converted to the sons,"[98] as if the dead are raised, since that people did live before through faith. And certainly it is more difficult to raise a righteous person when he has fallen than to draw him who remained a sinner to righteousness. We prove this daily in the convents of religious, when we see those monks who are converted from the malice of the world to the monastic life persevering willingly in a good intention, monks who scarcely or never become worldly again.

(262) *The loss* of the Jews is rightly called, since God let them go through their unbelief,[99] those whom he had previously held subject through faith. He designates the Gentiles with the term *world,* those who, lacking sense and reason, were to be counted more among the insensible parts of the world, at the time when they worshiped idols, than among human beings, that is, rational creatures. **What,** that is, of what kind, will the *acceptance* of the lost Jews be, **except life from the dead,** that is, except the resurrection of those dead in sins?

[11.16] **For if the sample…** A *sample* is a taste of some part taken from a whole, through which it can be examined of what nature the whole is, that is, its taste. But there was always a **mass** of faithful among the Jewish people, of those expecting the incarnation of God and his passion for their redemption, such as Zachariah and Elizabeth,[100] Simeon and Anna,[101] Nathanael,[102] Nicodemus,[103] and others who were found in the time of Christ; that person was revealed and conclusively shown to them from heaven, concerning whom they believed that the promise they had expected was to be completed. And perhaps such were all the holy apostles before. Therefore, they so willingly followed Christ when he called, either inspired by God beforehand or taught by the testimony of John.[104] Of these, Andrew alone, a

98. Lk 1.17.
99. Peter contrasts "loss," *amissio,* with "let them go," *amiserit.*
100. Lk 1.5–6.   101. Lk 2.25–32, 36–38.
102. Jn 1.47.   103. Jn 3.1–21.
104. Cf. Jn 1.40.

disciple of John, said to Simon his brother, "We have found the Messiah,"[105] and Philip said to Nathanael, "We have found the one about whom Moses wrote in the law and the prophets, Jesus."[106] From these words it is shown that they, instructed in the law and the prophets, had expected the Christ, but they did not yet recognize the predetermined time or the person ordained. The divine grace received them so that they could recognize this or manifest it to others. And when they were received from the *mass* of preceding believers, and so willingly followed Christ at the utterance of the one command, having left behind everything they had, it was as if a *sample* was made in which it could be shown from what faith that *mass* arose. Therefore, they were received as a *remnant* to show visibly or with the thing itself that which they held by faith.

To continue, the Apostle[107] says, how could some of them be received from such a worthless people, always so rebellious? Rightly, (263) says the Apostle, and more easily according to the nature of their origin than from the Gentiles, because it was necessary that the mass from which the *sample* **was** made **holy** be holy at that time, because as the *sample* is, so is the *mass,* and vice versa, just as he presently adds, **and if the root is holy, so also are the branches.** For he calls that mass of faithful predecessors a root; he calls those who were received from it branches rising from it.

[11.17] **For if some of the branches,** that is, some of that mass of faithful which beforehand had believed correctly, waiting for what was still to be, **were broken,** that is, they lost the pristine state of faith that they once had, **but you,** namely, the Gentiles, **since you are a wild olive tree,** that is, naturally barren and uncultivated, **you have been inserted into them,** that is, substituted in their place by an outside action, **[and you were made] a sharer of the root of the** fruitful **olive** through faith, **and of its richness** through charity. For richness is of a warm nature and therefore signifies the fire of charity, and faith is the root and foundation of charity.

105. Jn 1.41.   106. Jn 1.45.
107. Buytaert reads "someone," following the interlinear correction in A, though all four mss. read "Apostle" in their text. Though Buytaert's reading makes more sense, we here follow the majority reading.

[11.18] **Do not boast against the branches,** that is, abuse them because of the loss of their breaking, or be proud because of your status, ascribing this, namely, to your own merits or virtue. **But if you boast,** know that **you do not support the root [but the root supports you];** that is, what you have came to you from their root, not to the root from you, because the people of the Jews are a faithful she-ass, the mother of a foal, that is, a woman giving birth to the Gentile people in faith.

[11.19] **Therefore, you say...** Because you cannot boast against the root, you wish at least to place yourself before those branches in this: that **they were broken** so that you **may be planted in;** that is, *they were broken* and not planted in again, but you were planted in, in their place.

[11.20] **Indeed,** says the Apostle; that is, what you say is true, but therefore you cannot boast, because they were not broken on account of your good which you had before, by which God chose you to be planted in: but **on account of** their evil, that is, their **unbelief. [But you stand by faith.] Do not be high-minded,** namely, by being proud against (264) them, **but fear,** namely, to do such a thing by which you also may be broken off. In truth, it is necessary for you to fear also.

[11.21] But what he should fear, he adds: **For if [God] did not spare,** namely, from breaking, **the natural branches,** that root of theirs from which they came, (understand here "fear") **lest perhaps [he not spare you].**

[11.22] And in order that you may fear this, either reproached by the example of the others or kindled by the love[108] of the grace received, pay full attention to **the goodness** of the grace **[of God]** and the **severity** of his righteousness, **[severity toward those who have fallen, but the goodness of God toward you,] if you remain in** that **goodness** which you have received, that is, if you have not lost by your own fault the grace you have received. **Otherwise,** that is, if what I warn happens in another way, **you will be cut away** from the holy root in which you were implanted as if through a fall, and were not born from it.

[11.23] **But they also, [if they do not remain in unbelief,]** even after they have been broken off, **may be grafted in** where

108. *Amor.*

you were cut off, just as you were first grafted in, in the place of those broken off. And, as if it might be asked who could do this, since God broke them off on account of their fault, he says that he who broke them off on account of their own fault can do this through his own mercy. And this is what he says: **God is able,** that is, after your implanting and his own breaking off. I said that *God is able* **to graft them in again,** and it is not marvelous that it appears easier and more expedient for nature, according to the parable of the olive tree cited above, that the proper branches could be planted in than the foreign ones.

[11.24] And this is what he shows, going from the lesser [to the greater], saying, **For if you,** a Gentile, **were cut off from a wild olive tree, natural** to yourself, that is, taken from the unfruitful tree of the Gentile people **against nature,** that is, against the custom of grafting. For unfruitful trees are not usually grafted onto fruitful ones, nor wild onto domesticated, nor does the shoot usually bear the fruit of the root, but bears the fruit of its own kind. **How much more,** that is, how much more easily, **will they be grafted onto their own olive tree,** from which, of course, they were born, **according to the nature** of their origin.

[11.25] **For I do not want you,** as if he should say, therefore I recall so often, O Gentiles, the grace of your election and the righteousness of their condemnation and, later on, their future conversion, because *I do not want you* **to be ignorant of this mystery,** that is, this hidden judgment of the divine dispensation, (265) **because partial blindness has seized Israel;** that is, some of the Jews who have been blinded did not recognize the coming of Christ, through whom they might have been illuminated in their faith, **until the fullness of the Gentiles went in,** that is, until many were converted from the entirety of all the nations and built the spiritual city of God, that is, the Church.

[11.26] **And so,** finally, that is, after their entrance, **all Israel [will be saved],** namely, according to their individual tribes. Therefore, many will be converted in the end, by the preaching of Enoch and Elijah. Nevertheless, not all will be converted, since the Truth says to them concerning the Antichrist, "Another will come in his own name, and you will receive him,"[109] so

109. Jn 5.43.

that not all the Jews will be converted at the end of the world, just as they were not at the coming of Christ, but only the Lord's remnant. Therefore, Jerome writes this in his letter *To Hebidia* on the ninth question: "Isaiah cries out concerning Israel, 'If the number of the sons of Israel was as the sand of the sea, a remnant will be saved';[110] that is, although the multitude did not believe, nevertheless a few will."[111]

But concerning the end of the world, so says Isidore in Book 2, Chapter 5, of *Against the Jews,* "Malachi also says that before the end of the world Elijah must be sent to convert the Jews: 'Behold, I will send to you Elijah the prophet, before that great and terrible day of the Lord comes, and he will convert the hearts of the fathers to the sons, and the hearts of the sons to their fathers.'"[112] Again he says, "This people is to be converted at the last, who, under the figure of Benjamin, the patriarch Jacob prophesies is a devouring wolf in the morning and at night divides the spoils,[113] because in the beginning he received the law, but in the evening of the world he will believe and will divide it between the New and Old Testaments."[114] He says again, in Chapter 12, "Amos the prophet says, 'The house of Israel (266) has fallen, and it will not rise again. The virgin Israel is cast down on her land, and there is no one who will lift her up.'[115] There follows in the same prophet, 'The end has come upon my people Israel.'[116] All these passages pertain to the carnal kingdom of that people or to its worship, because they will be beyond repair. For those promises of repair which the word of their [prophets] expresses are promised to that portion of the Jews which will believe on God. For not all the Jews are to be redeemed, and not all will be saved. But all those who are to be chosen by faith will be saved."[117]

The Apostle himself, where he says *and so all Israel will be saved,* also seems to agree with some of the saints who say that at the end they will be converted through the preaching of Elijah

---

110. Is 10.22.   111. *Ep.* 120.10.

112. Mal 4.5; Isidore of Seville, *fid. Cath.* 2.5.3.

113. Gn 49.27.   114. Isidore, *fid. Cath.* 2.5.8.

115. Am 5.1–2.   116. Am 8.2.

117. Isidore, *fid. Cath.* 2.13.3–5.

and Enoch, either according to all the tribes (we should not understand it individually, as we said), or perhaps those who at first acknowledged the Antichrist when he restored the Judaic rites, and who were corrected later through the preaching of Enoch and Elijah, and when the destruction has been seen of him concerning whom the Truth says, "Unless those days were shortened, not all flesh would be saved,"[118] those converted to Christ will be saved. Gregory says in Book 35 of his *Moralia* that at the end all Israel will run together to faith when the preaching of Elijah is recognized, and then that extraordinary banquet is celebrated with a manifold gathering of the peoples.[119]

Remigius says about Psalm 13, "'When the Lord turns away the captivity,' etc. Since the Jewish treachery was unrepentant in its harshness, it entangled itself in the harsher snare of captivity. Nevertheless this captivity will be ended with the preaching of Elijah and Enoch, since all the Jews will believe in Christ at their preaching."[120]

Haymo says, "He will turn ungodliness from Jacob fully, just as it is written, 'And he will redeem Israel from all his sins,' and when *the fullness of the Gentiles* has gone in, then *all Israel will be saved.*"[121]

(267) [11.25] **So that you may not be wise in yourselves;** that is, therefore, *I do not want you to be ignorant* concerning that hidden mystery, lest when you see their blindness, on account of the illumination of wisdom which you have, you scoff proudly at them, boasting about the gift of God, as if it were your own property; this was what he meant about being wise to themselves rather than to God, that is, to apply one's wisdom to one's own glory, and not to that of the one who gives it. Haymo says, "A *mystery* is a hidden thing containing something secret in itself … and for that reason he cast down the Jews, at one time his own people, and joined the sinful nations to himself through faith."[122]

[11.26] **Just as it is written, [There will come from Zion one**

---

118. Mt 24.22.   119. *moral.* 35.14.34.
120. Remigius of Auxerre on Ps 13.7.
121. Haymo of Auxerre, *Rom.* 11.26, edited.
122. Ibid., edited.

who will deliver and turn away iniquity from Jacob]... Origen
says, "In Isaiah, from whom Paul took this testimony, it is written, 'He will come for Zion's sake,'[123] and what he says here,
'When I shall take away their sins,' is not at all written there.[124]
It is taken for granted by the authority of the Apostle."[125] He
refers to *Zion,* that is, Jerusalem, in place of Judea, namely, the
part which is the capital of the kingdom in place of the whole. It
is the same as saying, *there will come* from Judea, he who will save
the Jews, by being born in that place; or, according to the words
of Origen, "There will come for Zion's sake," namely, in order
to save it, just as he indicates, saying, *he who will deliver* it and
free it from captivity to the devil or from the yoke of sin, which
captures the soul from God. And explaining this, immediately
he says, *and turn away iniquity from Jacob,* that is, from the people
of the Jews. We can thus also distinguish: *He will deliver* from the
original sin with which we are born, and from those sins which
he finds in them, *and turn away* from the rest those which they
will commit unless he turns them away. Observe that when he
says that he will be born in Judea or will come "for Zion's sake,"
he ascribes a certain glory to the Jews by which he restrains the
proud insults of the Gentiles.

[11.27] **And this is my [covenant] with them,** says the Lord.
Our word *covenant* means "pact" in Hebrew, that is, a firm promise, for the things which are confirmed with a covenant are
especially enduring; the promise, I say, will be fulfilled at that
time, **when I shall take away,** that is, forgive, **their sins.**

(268) [11.28, Ms. *A*][126] **According to the Gospel they are indeed enemies for your sake, but according to election they are
most beloved for the sake of their fathers.** I said that *all Israel
will be saved,* that is, the Jews. But still they are *enemies* to us, and
they intensely hate us on account of the preaching of the Gospel converting you Romans and others to faith in Christ; but
nevertheless they are *most beloved* to us *for the sake of their fathers,*
namely, the patriarchs and the prophets, most acceptable to

123. Is 59.20, LXX.   124. Cf. Is 27.9.
125. Origen, *Rom.,* 8.12, edited.
126. The manuscripts diverge significantly in their comment on 11.28; *A*
gives the following, shorter reading; *mOR* give the second, longer reading.

God and chosen by him. Therefore, we also especially desire to convert them to the faith, whose conversion may offer the greatest testimony to the Christian faith.

[11.28, Mss. *mOR*] **According to the Gospel.** It is not sufficiently apparent on what those two nominative plurals, **enemies** and **most beloved,** depend with regard to the order of arrangement, unless they refer to those things said long before, namely, where it says, *How much more will they, according to nature, be grafted onto their own olive tree;* **indeed,** I say (understood: although) they are *enemies* now *according to the Gospel* **for your sake,** etc. Perhaps according to the usage of the Hebrew language the Apostle used a nominative form without an absolute verb, just as it says: "The Lord, in converting [the captivity of Zion]," and "The Lord, his throne in heaven."[127] In the epistle to the Galatians, Paul himself accuses Peter of destructive hypocrisy, saying, "If you, although you are a Jew, live like the Gentiles and not like a Jew, how can you compel the Gentiles to live like Jews?"[128] And again, "But if I preach circumcision, brothers, why do I still suffer persecution?"[129] From these things it appears that Paul especially and other preachers of Gospel freedom endured the greatest hostility from the Jewish converts on account of the burdens of the law, burdens which they did not impose on the Gentiles, knowing that those legal observances were now entirely useless and that the Gentiles could scarcely or never be led into them. And this is what Paul now (269) is mindful of when he says, I say that they are *enemies,* resisting me and those like me, *as regards the Gospel,* that is, as is clear from our preaching, when their boasting is especially troublesome, when it thoroughly forbids the burdens of the law, and this on account of you, O Gentiles, on whom we do not wish to impose these burdens. But nevertheless they are *beloved* to us; that is, before the others we cling to our desire that, having been converted, they may be saved, **for the sake of their fathers,** who were most righteous and of great authority, namely, the patriarchs and proph-

127. Pss 125.1 and 10.5. These translations are here given literally to make Peter's grammatical point clearer.
128. Gal 2.14.
129. Gal 3.11.

ets. Nevertheless, more than according to their own merits, it is **according to the election** of God, who chose them through his grace and wonderfully exalted them, having rejected the Gentiles. For it is not unknown that God himself showed his grace toward the sons on account of the fathers, and we know that he did not spare the idolatry of Solomon on account of his righteous father,[130] and that Moses begged for and obtained favor for his delinquent people on account of the merits of their fathers.

[11.29] **For [the gifts and calling of God] are without repentance.** As if someone should say, What concern is there for that election of the ancient fathers, for either the promises or benefits made to them once by God, since in fact it now appears in the malice of their sons that those things which the Lord did among the fathers now displease him? The Apostle answers, Indeed, (270) *the gifts and calling of God are without repentance;* that is, it never displeases him that he gave something to someone or called someone to faith, because his will is entirely unchangeable; not ever does he condemn having done that which he once judges must be done, which at any rate would be to repent of his deed. Nevertheless, in another way God is sometimes said to repent, namely, by changing or abolishing what he did, not by condemning his deed, that is, not by judging that it was evil, because repentance is properly spoken of by the philosopher: "Repentance follows an evil deed."[131] Among the elect of God his gifts precede their calling, while he prepares their will so that they may assent to the one calling them to himself and that they may obey the one commanding them.

[11.30] **For as [at one time you also did not trust God, but now have obtained mercy...]** I said that after the full number of Gentiles has been converted, the Jews also will be converted to faith.[132] Do not wonder if it should happen in this way concerning them, O you Gentiles, just as it also happened concerning you. And this is what he says: *For as [at one time you also did not trust God, but now you have obtained mercy]* **on account of their unbelief.** At the time when they were rejecting preaching from

130. 1 Kgs 11.4–8, 31–39.   131. Boethius, *diff. top.* 2.7.29.
132. Rom 11.25.

themselves, the apostles were compelled to pass over speedily to the Gentiles.

[11.31] **So they also,** that is, the Jews, **now have not believed on your mercy, [so that they also may obtain mercy]**; that is, they have not received the preaching by which you obtained mercy from God, so that after you, they also may come to faith later and be made more humble by this: that they follow you to faith, taught as it were from this source, the instruction of your example.

[11.32] **But [God] has shut up [everyone in unbelief, that he may have mercy on everyone]**; that is, he has given everyone up to be bound with the blindness of unbelief, both Jews and Gentiles, so that in the conversion of everyone later on, he may show his great clemency. It stands that they have no merit before faith, "because without faith it is impossible to please God."[133]

(271) [11.33] **O the depth...** It is the exclamation of one who regards with wonder that large abyss of the divine judgment concerning the first election of the Jewish people and the condemnation of the Gentiles, and now the new election of the Gentiles in the conversion of many and the condemnation of the Jews, with so few converts from that time but a fuller number of them to be converted later, so that they who once preceded the Gentiles in faith later follow them, and the last become the first.[134] *Depth,* that is, a profundity hidden to us, **of the** rich and plentiful **wisdom of God** as far as his foreknowledge is concerned, **and of his knowledge** as far as the accomplishment of his work is concerned, from which those foreseen things can be known. **How incomprehensible;** that is, how powerless we are to understand those causes of dispensation or of his providence, for what reason he decreed something was to be done before his works were done, and even after the accomplishment of his works, **his ways are unsearchable.** For the *ways* of God, by which one comes to knowledge of him, are his works, just as the same Apostle mentions above, saying, *For his invisible things were understood from the creation of the world.*[135] Therefore, the works of God, which we experience daily by sense, are unsearchable to us be-

133. Heb 11.6.   134. Cf. Mt 19.30.
135. Rom 1.20.

cause we are not yet sufficient to discuss their hidden natures with reason.

[11.34] No wonder: **For who has known the mind of the Lord,** that is, could understand by himself the reason which God had in his foreknowledge concerning these things which he was about to do? Or whom did he consult concerning these things which he was about to do, that he might be instructed by that person's counsel as to what he should do and how he should act?

[11.35] **Or who [has given to him first, and it was repaid to him?]** After the supreme and incomprehensible wisdom of God, he shows his supreme goodness by which he bestows all things on us sooner than he receives anything from us.

[11.36] Finally, the Apostle ends his wondering in thanksgiving by saying, **Because all things are from him,** that is, the nature of each substance was, so to speak, created by him, so that it might exist; preserved **through him,** so that it might remain; **in him** as (272) if perfected in the best end, while the greatest workman and disposer [of all things] is glorified and praised in them, on account of which he established and preserves them, just as it is written in Proverbs, "God created all things for himself, the wicked also for the evil day."[136] As blessed Augustine mentions in his commentary on Genesis, any creature, to the extent that it is in itself, is the evening; to the extent that it has returned to the praise of its Creator, it is called the morning, because, when it is considered with respect to itself, it is deficient, so to speak, but has made progress in the praise of the Creator.[137]

Perhaps someone may ask how the nature of each substance is preserved so that it may remain, since the spirits of irrational animals are thoroughly believed to be covered with flesh and to die with the flesh? Indeed, if those spirits, just as also ours, are of certain substances, a certain rarity of elements as it appears to some, when the spirits cease to exist, that is, when they cease to make their bodies alive, nevertheless the substances do not cease to exist; just as the flesh also, with which they are said to

136. Cf. Prv 16.4.
137. Cf. Augustine, *Gn. litt. imp.* 12; *Gn litt.* 4.31.

perish when the flesh ceases to exist, does not lose the nature of the bodily substance.

It can even be asked, since God should be praised on account of himself rather than on account of his works, how the Apostle says that he should be praised on account of his works, that is, that he is worthy of greatest praise? For he is good or worthy of praise by himself rather than on account of his works, and his works should be praised or good on account of himself, rather than he on account of his works. But although he is good or worthy of praise by himself rather than by his achievements, nevertheless that thanksgiving or the execution of our praise, which we render to him, follows from the works through which we know him; just as the praise of any artisan is known in his works, and although he is now made worthy of praise on account of the knowledge which he has, his praise follows from the knowledge of his works.

The Apostle does not say in this passage that God is worthy of praise on account of the works which he does, but he exhorts us to his praise (273) on account of his works which we know: **To him be glory,** he says, that is, the best and highest renown extending widely, **forever,** that is, through all successions of time. **Amen,** that is, let it be so, which is an adverb of choosing, sometimes even of confirming, when it is used in place of "it is so" and "it is true."

[12.1] **Therefore, I urge [you, brothers].** Because he "from whom are all things,"[138] and *through whom*, etc., is so distinguished and so great, *I urge you* to prepare yourselves as a sacrifice for him rather than slaughtering your cattle for him. As if by swearing an oath he compels them when he says, **through the mercy of God,** as if he should say, just as you confide in his mercy, so, in order to obtain it, to the extent that you are able, you should prepare yourselves. The bodies of cattle, when they were offered in sacrifice, were killed; but our **bodies,** when they are offered to God, die to vices in such a way that they are not deprived of life. And this is what he says: **a living sacrifice.** And indeed, at the time of our offering, it is a **reasonable service, [holy and pleasing to God,]** if we offer ourselves in this way

138. 1 Cor 8.6.

rather than slaughter our cattle to him, or kill ourselves for his sake.

[12.2] **[Do not] be conformed to this world,** that is, [do not] imitate worldly people who love the present life; **but be transformed,** that is, strive to restore and renew the understanding of human reason, which was darkened with sins a long time ago. **That you may prove,** that is, be able to know or show in others, and be able to prove rationally **what is the will of God,** that is, what God wills that we do that we may be **good** in ourselves and from that time on to others also; or being **well-pleasing** to God and, finally completed, **perfect** in virtues, by always growing into better things and in the heavenly life of perfect happiness.

[12.3] **For I say…** I said, *Do not be conformed to this world, but be transformed,* and I justly warn you about this, because *I say* this **through (274) the grace which has been given to me;** that is, through the authority enjoined on me over you, I am compelled to say **to all who are among you,** that is, to the converts among the Gentiles, whose specially appointed Apostle I am, **Do not be wiser than is fitting, but be wise to the point of sobriety.** He is wiser than is fitting who not only discerns evil things from good with the knowledge of reason, according to what the philosopher says, "For the knowledge of evil cannot be lacking in the righteous man,"[139] but also learns them from experience, regarding which it is called "the tree of the knowledge of good and evil."[140] And this is the understanding of the world, that is, of worldly and carnal men, such that they know those evil things by the experience of pleasures, as if they were seduced by the sweetness of a certain taste.[141] In this experience they exceed the bounds of a sober and honorable life while they disgracefully serve their own pleasures. **And to each one,** namely, of us, do I say this, that is, *do not be wiser,* etc., **just as God has apportioned a measure of faith,** that is, just as he believes it should be done, so he fulfills this.

[12.4] **For just as [we have many members in one body, but**

139. Boethius, *diff. top.* 2.2.15; see Peppermüller, 3.722, n. 67.
140. Gn 2.9, 17.
141. Abelard here plays on the similarity between the words *sapor* ("taste") and *sapere* ("to be wise").

not all the members have the same function], as if someone
should ask, Is there a diverse opinion among the faithful about
the discernment of good and evil? The Apostle answers that
there is, but the gifts of divine grace among them are also diverse. And this is what he demonstrates with a suitable comparison, saying, *For just as,* etc., **they do not have the same function,**
that is, the same duty.

[12.5] **So [we, though] many, [are one body in Christ].** According to the diversity of persons in the one head, Christ, and
united in the same sacraments, we are **members one of another,**
that is, completing their duty on behalf of the other and manag-
ing for him what he is not able to complete. For then the eye is
made, as it were, a member of the hand when it furnishes vision,
so that the hand may be able to work; and likewise, each of the
faithful ought to supply the gift of grace which he has to another, so that the faithful may especially be gathered to one another
in charity, (275) when they come to help each other and each
one recognizes that the other is necessary to him in something.

[12.6] I said that *each is a member one of another,* but justly, because **they have** different gifts of the **grace** of God conferred on
them. He immediately subdivides these gifts, saying, **whether
they have prophecy,** that is, the grace of interpreting, that is, of
expounding the divine words. Therefore, he also says to the Corinthians, "For he who prophesies speaks to men for their edification."[142] **According to the reasoning of faith.** He uses prophecy
who moderates his words in his preaching according to what he
believes is necessary for his hearers, and discerns what is fitting
to be preached to these persons or to those according to their
capacity, so that sometimes he gives milk to the children, sometimes solid food to the adults, just as Paul himself teaches by his
own example, writing to the same Corinthians.[143] The Psalmist
foresaw this discretion of the apostles when he said, "Day ut-
ters the word to day, and night declares knowledge to night."[144]
Therefore, such it is *according to the reasoning of* his *faith,* as if it
should be said, according to the discretion which he believes he
has; when, if perhaps he errs, charity excuses his ignorance.

142. 1 Cor 14.3.   143. 1 Cor 3.2.
144. Ps 18.3.

[12.7] **Whether ministry in ministering.** In this whole passage
we should understand the words *according to the reasoning of faith,*
in such a way that we may do all things with discernment, according to which we believe they should be done. He calls *ministry* the duty of bodily work, such as sewing or building. He has
ministry in ministering to others who seeks the benefit of others
more than his own, just as the same Apostle says elsewhere, "Let
no one seek his own good, but that of his neighbor."[145] **Or he
who teaches,** let it be **in teaching;** that is, let him teach what he
believes should be taught.

[12.8] Likewise, **the one who exhorts,** that is, who speaks in
order to persuade, *according to the reasoning of faith.* He now distinguishes prophecy, which he understood above, by means of
teaching and exhortation. For whoever speaks for the purpose
of edification, speaks either by teaching something (276) or by
exhorting to something. Expound it in this way: *Or he who teaches
according to the reasoning of faith,* let him discern **in exhorting,** as
much as he is able, what will persuade and in the same way teach
these men, according to those words of the Truth: "Do not give
what is holy to dogs, nor cast your pearls before swine."[146]

He who gives, that is, he bestows what is his on those in
need (understand: let him do it) **in simplicity,** that is, let him
not have a twofold intention there, both for temporal reward
and eternal. The Lord also forbids this elsewhere when he says,
"When you offer alms, let not your left hand know what your
right hand is doing."[147] *In simplicity* can also mean, Let not the
end be twofold in intention, that he may establish the end of
his alms both in himself and in God, but only in God; or thus,
let him not act deceitfully as the hypocrites do, who feign something other than what they intend, since they feign to do for
the sake of God that which they do more for the sake of human
glory; or just as they do who, when they bestow something on
someone, hoping that they will receive more from them, feign
that they do by charity what they do by desire instead.

He who rules over others, that is, who carries on the duty of
the prelate (understand: "let him rule") **in care,** namely, by seek-

145. 1 Cor 10.24.
146. Mt 7.6.
147. Mt 6.2.

ing their advantage rather than his own. Solomon gives advice concerning this care by prelates toward their subjects when he says, "My son, if you pledge for your friend, you have fastened your hand to a stranger; you have been entrapped with the words of your mouth and seized by your own words. Therefore, do what I say, my son, and free yourself, because you have fallen into your neighbor's hand. Run, hurry, awaken your friend. Do not give sleep to your eyes, do not let your eyelids fall asleep."[148]

He who has mercy, [in joyfulness]; that is, joyful, he forgives those transgressing against him, and does this without any bitterness of soul; he does not bring shame against the penitent, nor does he shamefully impute his own sin to him, (277) as if to show that he is more sorrowful concerning his own wrong than joyful concerning the conversion of the sinner.

[12.9] **Love** (understand: "should be") unchangeable, genuine, **not feigned,** just as it is written elsewhere, "Little children, let us not love with word or tongue, but in deed and truth."[149] **Hating** vices, **clinging** to virtues, or withdrawing from the conduct and habits of the perverse man and imitating **good,** giving heed to what is written, "With the holy you shall be holy."[150]

[12.10] **[Loving] the charity of the brotherhood,** that is, exercising the effects of fraternal charity **mutually,** so that each one may help the other as if he were his brother, and obey God as if he were his father. He urges that not only should they provide for the benefit of their neighbors, but also for their honor, saying **preceding each other in honor,** namely, one to the other, providing this among yourselves so that when someone else wishes to honor you, you should honor him first and let his benefit precede yours, so that it may be returned to you as if it were a debt, rather than given. But there are those who do not need our benefits and who are drawn to love more by honor than by usefulness; therefore, the Apostle also diligently looks after honor, after the usefulness of the benefit.

[12.11] **Not lazy in care,** that is, not delaying to fulfill the accomplishment of our care towards those who are subject, just

148. Prv 6.1–4.
149. 1 Jn 3.18. "Love" is here, and in 12.10, *dilectio* or *diligere.*
150. 2 Sm 22.26; Ps 17.26.

as it is written, "Whatever your hand is able to do, do it immediately."[151] **Fervent in spirit,** as if he should say, although you will not be able to fulfill the aforesaid things thoroughly, you may at least be fervent with the zeal of charity for fullfilling these things, and the will for a good desire suffices with God. **Serving the Lord.** After fraternal charity towards one's neighbor, he ascends to the charity of God by which he is devoted to him. But the Apostle rightly placed *fervent in spirit* before when he was about to say *serving the Lord,* so that this may be understood as a filial service of reverence, (278) a subjection out of love,[152] rather than as a slavish service out of fear, Christian more than Jewish. We serve the Lord alone, to whom we devote our service, if we establish the total end of our subjection in God, if the total reverence that we show to prelates, we show to them for the sake of God, whose vicars they are and from whom they received the office of ecclesiastical dignity. For he who devotes service to the legate or vicar of some prelate on account of that prelate only, by whom they are appointed, is said to be devoted to that prelate alone in this, and to devote service and honor to him only, on account of whom only it is done.

[12.12] **Rejoicing in hope,** namely, that you may be **patient in tribulation.** Therefore, the Apostle James also says, "Consider it all joy, my brothers, when you meet with various trials, knowing that this testing [of your faith works patience]."[153] He rightly placed *rejoicing in hope* before *patient in tribulation,* so that the surpassing hope of reward may counteract powerful sufferings, while they give heed to that which is written, "Vexed in few things, they are well disposed in many," etc.[154] *Rejoicing in hope,* that is, in the expectation of future happiness, since hope concerns only the good and what is yet to be. And because we cannot have this constancy against suffering from our own virtue, in order that we may resort to prayer in regard to this, he urges the following when he says, **pressing in prayer,** that is, standing in prayer in regard to this rather than lying prostrate.[155] For

---

151. Cf. Eccl 9.10.   152. *Amor.*
153. Jas 1.2–3.   154. Wis 3.5.
155. Peter here plays on *instantes,* the word of the biblical text, and *stantes,* standing, and contrasts them with *iacentes,* lying.

they pray lying prostrate, as it were, who do not raise themselves up to God through devotion, so that their prayer may attain its result, and they prepare their words only, and not their hearts. Concerning these, the Lord laments through Isaiah, "This people honors me with their lips, but their heart is far from me."[156]

[12.13] **Sharing in the needs of the saints,** that is, having compassion on the faithful who suffer need or adversity, so that we may be made sharers in their need or tribulation, while what we withdraw from ourselves, we devote to them, or we incur danger and harm for them either by rescuing or defending them. <Therefore, he also says elsewhere, "Bear one another's burdens.">[157] (279) **Pursuing hospitality,** not only devoting, since we follow after those withdrawing from ourselves so that we may draw to hospitality even those who are resisting, just as Lot did in the taking-in of the angels.[158]

[12.14] **Bless those persecuting you;** that is, pray also that it may be well for them, that you may establish charity for them, just as it is written, *For then you will heap coals of fire on his head;*[159] or, therefore, that your prayer may accomplish its result the more easily, the more acceptable it will be to God, who says, "For if you love[160] those who love you, what reward do you have?"[161] The Lord himself as well as his proto-martyr Stephen showed us this perfection of love in their passions by praying for their enemies.[162] **Bless and do not curse.** He says *bless* twice, so that we may have a blessing both in our mouth and in our heart. He did not say, "lest you curse," but *do not curse.* For when we excommunicate someone for the obstinacy of his sin, we actually throw the sentence of cursing at him. We read in the Acts of the Apostles that Paul himself cursed the one to whom he said, "The Lord destroy you, you whitewashed wall."[163] But because the saints do such things constrained by the zeal of righteousness, they have the power to curse, but not the will. Indeed, in

156. Is 29.13; Mt 15.8.
157. Gal 6.2. This is a *Lectio Abaelardi,* found in *mOR.*
158. Gn 19.1–3. 159. Rom 12.20.
160. *Diligere* and *dilectio,* in the next sentence.
161. Mt 5.46. 162. Lk 23.34; Acts 7.60.
163. Acts 23.3.

this passage it is not said that they should not curse at all but that they should not wish to curse, so that namely, the will to curse is prohibited and not the action,[164] just as the Lord also says, "Do not swear";[165] he forbids the will to swear rather than the action. So also the judge, when compelled by the law to kill someone, not voluntarily, is excused of murder because it is not performed willingly by him to whom it is entirely displeasing, because he who is punished is guilty of that for which the law orders him to be killed, so that the law kills him more than the man does, indeed God himself who provided the law, who said, "I will kill and make alive,"[166] and, "Vengeance is mine, I will repay,"[167] rather than the minister of God.

(280) It does not seem unjust to ask why we should pray to him with words, since God looks at hearts rather than at words. But I judge that it is done for two reasons: the first is for the honor of God; the second is adapted for our benefit. For when we ask for something from God by praying, we show by those words of ours that we can only have from him what we pray for. Those words that we bring forth arouse and stir our affection and devotion toward God by their understanding, so that the prayer is more efficacious, the greater the devotion is in the one who prays.

[12.15] **To rejoice with those who rejoice.** He uses the infinitive in place of the imperative, namely, by saying *gaudere*, "to rejoice," and *flere*, "to weep," in place of *gaudete*, "rejoice," and *flete*, "weep"; that is, exult with the faithful in their progress and show sorrow by having compassion in their failure. For the joy of the wicked is a false joy, with which one should not rejoice, and their sorrow is a false sorrow, which one should by no means share. Therefore, the Lord says, "The world will rejoice, but you will be sad,"[168] and Solomon says in Proverbs about the perverse, "They who rejoice when they do evil and exult in the most evil things."[169]

But since the same Solomon says elsewhere, "Whatever hap-

---

164. *Actio,* which can also mean the power delegated to someone, as in the previous sentence. Peter uses both senses of the word.

165. Mt 5.34.   166. Dt 32.39.
167. Cf. Dt 32.35; Heb 10.30.   168. Jn 16.20.
169. Prv 2.24.

pens to the righteous, it will not sadden him,"[170] and the Apostle says above, *We know that all things work together for good for those who love God,*[171] what can happen to the elect that would cause one to weep? Or how rational are those tears of Rachel concerning the murder of her children, who passed over from misery to beatitude?[172] Therefore, it is written concerning that weeping of the faithful at the death of blessed Martin, "Since they perceived that they should rather rejoice, if the power of sorrow would allow a reason."[173] And in his letter *To Tyrasius* concerning the death of his daughter, Jerome says,

She has escaped such great and extreme tempests of life, so many assaults of the devil, (281) so many wars of the body, so many worldly disasters, and do we shed tears as if we do not know what we suffer daily? On account of this the Lord also advises his disciples, "If you love me, you will certainly rejoice because I go to the Father."[174] He clearly wept for dead Lazarus, he lamented that he was not sleeping but rather rising, and he wept for him whom he was compelled to recall to the world to save others. The Lord groaned giving this life which you lament is destroyed. Your tears fight against his. He did not wish to restore to labors the one whom he loved, and you believe that you love the one to whom you wished the torments of labors to remain. She has departed from her hostile homeland to heaven. The Apostle says, "As long as we are in this world, we are exiled from God."[175]

Therefore, why these tears of Rachel? Why the compassion of the faithful concerning the murder of the righteous ones, which ends their misery and bestows glory on them? Or, since all the things which happen to the elect work together for good for them, as was said, and they are not saddened, whatever happens to them, why is it appropriate for us to grieve over them, or for them to repent of something, when it is nevertheless certain that, although they remember their sins, they are in no way oppressed with the sorrow of penance in the other life, because they consider that those sins worked together for good for them? Finally, since we should not doubt that all things are best disposed by

170. Prv 12.21.   171. Rom 8.28.
172. Jer 31.15; Mt 2.17–18.
173. Cf. Sulpicius Severus, *Ep.* 2; Abelard, *TSch* 3.117.
174. Jn 14.28.
175. Cf. 2 Cor 5.6; Ps.-Jerome, *Tyras.* 40.2–4.

God to such a degree that it is good that there also exist those evils, and according to that word of Truth "it is necessary that stumbling-stones come,"[176] what can happen whereby one may reasonably grieve? For if, as blessed Augustine mentions, it is good that evil exists,[177] whoever grieves about evil actually grieves about something whose existence is good, and whoever wishes that it not exist, certainly wishes that there not exist what it is good exists; and so he seems to be contrary both to the divine disposition and to reason, and it is uselessly said to God, "Your will be done,"[178] (282) whose will or disposition he opposes as much as he can. But because this discussion belongs to higher philosophy, we reserve its completion for our *Theology.*[179]

[12.16] **Being of one mind towards one another,** reckoning others as oneself through the affection of charity, according to those words of the Truth, "What you wish men to do to you, do also the same to them,"[180] and, "What you do not wish to be done to you, do not do to another."[181] *Being of one mind* with others, let us consider their goods and their losses, as it were, to be ours. Or, *being of one mind,* that there may be no schisms from the Catholic faith. It seems especially to pertain to this, because he adds, **not minding high things,** that is, not proudly presuming something through heresy while we seek to boast on account of some novelty; **but consenting,** joining ourselves in the unity of faith **to the humble,** to whom God, resisting the proud, gives grace.[182] He teaches us how to do this when he adds, **Do not be wise among yourselves,** that is, do not convert your knowledge, if you have it, to boasting, nor boast about it among yourselves; I even say to you, *returning evil for evil to no one,* that is, avenging no one because he injured you, but rather because it is just. We can understand what is said, *Do not be wise among yourselves,* in this way, that it may be added to that passage more fittingly. For he is called wise in himself who strives entirely by his own judgment, so that he may wish to carry out whatever he declared to

---

176. Mt 18.7.

177. See the discussions of 3.6, 8, where Abelard quotes Augustine to similar effect, from *ench.* and *civ. Dei.*

178. Mt 6.10.   179. *TSch* 3.117.

180. Mt 7.12.   181. Tb 4.16.

182. Jas 4.6; 1 Pt 5.5.

be righteous, so that since his wrath may seem unjust to no one who is angry, he thinks he is to be avenged against whomever it is by whom he is offended.

[12.17] He resists this danger, saying, **Returning evil for evil to no one.** He had said above, *Do not curse those persecuting you;*[183] here he prohibits evil deeds just as he did evil words there. **Providing good things,** that is, striving as much as we are able, that our good works may be seen not only **by God but** also **by men,** so that they may wish to imitate them and glorify God thereafter, just as the Truth also says, "Let your light shine before men," etc.[184]

[12.18] **If it is possible, have peace with all men,** as we said, *returning evil for evil to no one* (283) and by *providing good things before men.* **This,** namely, to have *peace with all,* **is in you;** that is, you have this by your own nature, that you may especially be united to those whom you see to be closer by nature. Therefore, another Apostle also says, "How can he love God whom he does not see, who does not love his neighbor whom he sees?"[185] For the closer we are by nature, the more it summons us to love.

[12.19] To such a degree, I say, *have peace with all men* so that if you went to excess and offended someone, you should **not defend yourselves,** that is, excuse your own sins, **but give place to wrath,** that is, yield submissively to the angry and offended brother, enduring his anger, not rousing him up again through your excuse. For were we to resist his wrath at that time, so that it might burn all the more or remain in him, we would not yield so that it might pass from him. **For it is written,** namely, in Proverbs,[186] **Vengeance is mine,** as if he should say, therefore, when you offend others, you ought to endure patiently those offended and appease their anger as much as you are able, because even if you are offended by them, the Lord exhorts you not to avenge yourselves after that, but to reserve vengeance to him who says, (understand "reserve") *Vengeance to me,* **and I will repay** it, so that I may avenge you.

And we should note that, if this is understood as an exhorta-

183. Rom 12.14. 184. Cf. Mt 5.16.
185. 1 Jn 4.20; *diligere,* and, in the next sentence, *dilectio.*
186. Actually, Dt 32.35.

tion to perfection rather than as a command, just as the Truth also says, "And you should not demand back what is yours,"[187] that which was said above, *Do not defend yourselves,* can be understood as an exhortation to perfection, so that, although we may be able to defend ourselves from persecutors, he nevertheless may say that it is more perfect not to defend at all; but enduring that force brought against you rather than wounding your soul by defending your body, you perhaps cannot defend yourselves from him otherwise than by killing him through anger.

(284) But just as above we explained the former as a command, the latter can perhaps also be understood as a command: *Vengeance is mine,* etc. For just as when the judge, bound by the law and the love[188] of God, who established the law, kills the guilty man, he is not said to do this so much as the law or God is, who commanded him to do this and uses the judge for doing this just as he would use a tool; so also, when [the judge] avenges with the zeal of justice and love, this vengeance should be imputed to God rather than to him. Therefore, because God commands vengeance to be reserved for himself so that he may carry it out, it means that no one may presume to take revenge unless, as was said, God does this through him, [God] who says, "I will kill, and I will make alive."[189] Therefore, Augustine says in Chapter 71 of his *Questions on Leviticus,* "When a man is justly killed, the law kills him, not you."[190] He also says in Book 1 of *The City of God,* "*You shall not kill,* with the exception of those whom God orders to be killed."[191]

But he does not kill who owes his office to the one who commands, just as the sword owes service to the one using it. Therefore, a man kills when he does so on his own account, and not God's. But when he does this by the divine institution or command, God does it as if through an instrument, rather than the man himself. For we thus say that someone powerful builds or does something when it is carried out according to his direction. Therefore, it is prohibited for a man to kill, not for God.

187. Lk 6.30.
188. *Amor,* here and later in the sentence.
189. Dt 32.39.   190. *Qu. Lev.* 68.
191. 1.21.

Perhaps we are thus also forbidden to demand back what is our own, because it is our own, just as we are forbidden to love those who love us, that is, because they love us. For we ought not to have these things for our own sake, that we may establish the end of this possession in ourselves, and much less should we demand back the things that were taken away for our own sake, because God perhaps wishes to dispose them better through others than through us, or he foresaw that they would be injurious to us. Therefore, we are allowed to demand back the things which are God's rather than the things which are ours, that is, that we may dispose them according to his will, for God's sake, rather than for our sake; and then God (285) demands back what is his own in us rather than we demanding our own, when we do this that we may cause them to be God's rather than our own.

[12.20] **But if [your enemy is hungry, feed him; if he is thirsty, give him something to drink.]** I said that you should not avenge yourselves, but rather let God do so, as was said, but on the contrary, do good to those doing evil. And this is what he says: *But if [your enemy is hungry, feed him; if he is thirsty, give him something to drink.]* **For [by doing] this.** He gives the reason why we should do this for our enemies: because by this we can easily bring them to salvation. **[You will heap on his] head,** which is the principal part in the body, supplied as it were with all the senses of the body, and it signifies our mind or soul. **Coals of fire** are fires of charity or laments of penitence, with which the penitent soul is tormented and kindled against itself as if with some flames of indignation. Therefore, we should heap these coals on the mind of our enemy by doing good to him, while through this we kindle him to love[192] toward us or to penance for the evil deeds which he inflicted on us.

[12.21] **Do not be overcome [by evil, but overcome evil with good];** that is, be subdued by your vice, if anger dominates you to such an extent that you return evil for evil, but **overcome** and restrain that anger of yours, through good recompensed for evil. For it is not evil to serve man, but to serve vice. Therefore, he immediately adds,

[13.1] **Let every soul,** that is, every rational creature, **be sub-**

192. *Amor.*

ject, that is, obey willingly. He says this in answer to the opinion of certain of the faithful to whom it seemed entirely unjust and unsuitable that whoever has now been converted to faith in Christ may devotedly serve and obey earthly power even more, as if such powers had not been at all established by God. Therefore, the Lord himself exhorted us to this by his own example when he thought it worthy to pay the census to Caesar for himself and Peter.[193] **To higher powers,** that is, to those set in authority over them, namely, by God, just as he immediately adds, saying, **For there is no power,** either good or bad, it may seem, **except from God,** that is, established through his (286) decree. For when princes are good, it is a divine favor. But when they are evil, either for vengeance against perverse men or for the cleansing and testing of the good, they are directed by God, who also disposes each impiety well. Therefore, the power of the devil or of whatever wicked person is asserted to be good, although their will is the worst and their working is perverse. For they receive power from God, but they have an evil will from themselves. Therefore, the Truth says to unjust Pilate, "You would have no power over me except that which was given to you from above."[194] And the devil could attack Job in nothing until license for this power was granted to him by God.[195] **And those that exist,** namely, they are established **by God,** not only permitted. For God himself permits sins; he does not establish them. **Are ordained,** that is, reasonably established.

[13.2] **Therefore, they who [resist the power, resist the ordinance of God],** namely, since all power is established by God. **[But they who resist,] acquire damnation [for themselves],** that is, deserve to be condemned for doing this, because they resist God rather than man. It is one thing to resist the tyranny of an evil ruler, and another thing to resist his just power, which he received from God. For when he does something through violence that does not pertain to his power and rule, truly when we resist him in this, we oppose his tyranny more than his power, the man, namely, rather than God, because he claims this wrongly through himself; he does not do this through God. But

193. Mt 17.24–27.   194. Jn 19.11.
195. Jb 2.6.

when we resist him in these things for which he was legitimately established, then we infringe on his power.

[13.3] **For princes [are not a terror to good work, but to evil];** that is, their power should not be feared by those who do good, but by those who do evil. He immediately shows this, saying, **Do you,** anyone, **wish not to fear power** rather than man? Do good, and by sparing you he will approve your works, and he will bear witness that you act well.

[13.4] **[For he is the minister of God to you for good. But if you do evil, fear, for he does not] bear the sword [without reason];** that is, not without reason is he instructed to kill, because (287) he serves God in this, who established him for this purpose: that he may punish evil. And this is what he says: **For [he is the minister] of God, an avenger for wrath [to him who does evil],** that is, an avenger who rages against the one who does evil rather than against the man, that is, against his malice rather than against his substance.

[13.5] **Therefore,** because *he is the minister of God,* **you must be [subject,]** obedient to him, as if to God, and this **by necessity,** that is, for the plain benefit which you get from the office of the princes, **not only on account of** their **wrath, but also for the sake of** your **conscience,** that is, not only on account of the terror of the wrath of those who immediately punish you who are disobedient to them, but also because you are conscious in yourselves that they are necessary to you for restraining malice.

[13.6] **For that reason [you also pay taxes to them];** because, indeed, they are necessary to you; namely, for punishing those who act evilly, as was said, you pay taxes to them. **[For they are the ministers of God], serving** God **for this purpose,** that they punish evil, and for this reason, because they receive taxes, they are able to fulfill their duty, which they by no means could exercise without these payments, and *therefore,* because you are conscious of this or because in this way they serve God as soldiers.

[13.7] **Pay everyone** what you owe because of this; **to the one** to whom you owe **taxes,** pay **taxes.** Origen says, "Taxes from the land, tolls from business."[196] Haymo says,

---

196. Origen, *Rom.,* 9.30, paraphrased.

To the one to whom you ought to pay taxes, pay them, just as the Creator himself paid the didrachma for himself and Peter.[197] The word "tax," *tributum,* comes from "tribunes," *tribunis,* and this comes from "three," *tribus.* Further, Romulus divided the people subjected to him into three parts, namely, into senators, who were also called consuls, into soldiers and farmers; and for each part he established a single prince who was called a tribune, because he was set over one of the parts. The payment that was collected from his subjects was called a "tax," *tributum.* **To the one** you owe **revenue.** "Toll," *vectigal,* is a fiscal tax, and comes from "carrying," *vehendo,* because it is received from "the things carried," *vectitiis,* that is, from the revenues brought in.[198]

(288) **To whom fear [is owed, fear].** Fear should especially be shown to angry people in power, lest the anger of the one aroused punish more than is fitting. The gentle should be more greatly honored to the extent that patience makes them more worthy and beneficent.[199]

[13.8] **Owe no one anything;** that is, free yourselves from all debts, so that you may acknowledge that you owe nothing except charity. This should always be paid, that it may always be owed, and should always be so expended that it may be retained especially at the time when it is expended. But when money is paid out, it belongs to him to whom it is given, and departs from the one giving. To love[200] another person is to wish well to him for his own sake. **[Except to love] each other,** that is, between yourselves, that there may be mutual love. **[For he who loves his] neighbor [has fulfilled the law.]** By neighbor, understand every man who is united to us by human nature and draws a common origin with us from the same father Adam. For if the Apostle understands the *neighbor* as the Jew only, according to what is said in the law, "You shall not charge interest to your neighbor, but to a foreigner,"[201] what he says can in no way stand, that *he who loves his neighbor* does not commit adultery, etc., since these things could be committed among the un-

---

197. Mt 17.24–27.

198. Haymo, *Rom.,* 13.7, slightly edited.

199. Manuscript *m* here ends Book Four and begins Book Five. Of the other three manuscripts, only *O,* in a later marginal note, so divides the text.

200. *Diligere,* here and in the rest of the paragraph.

201. Cf. Dt 23.19–20.

believers. He speaks of the law of Moses, where the commandments he adds are contained.

[13.9] **For you shall not commit adultery.** The law seems to
describe adultery as every unlawful intercourse. Otherwise, it
would nowhere exclude that fornication which is committed by
those who are not married. Therefore, when he says, *You shall
not commit adultery,* he substitutes the species for the genus, just
as he conversely substitutes the genus for the species when he
adds, **You shall not kill.** For he does not forbid an animal to
be killed by a man, but a man [to be killed]. But a man kills a
man, and it is not God who kills through him, as we also suggest
above, at the time when he does this by his own will, not bound
by the sanction of the divine law. Indeed, the Lord teaches Peter about this unjust murder when he says, "He who takes the
sword will die by the sword."[202] He who takes it by himself, he
says, not the one to whom it is delivered by [divine] power for
administering justice, (289) deserves to die by the sword. At
that time when he does that by himself only, apart from God,
a murder occurs since he acts to fulfill his own will and not to
administer justice. Therefore, Augustine says in Chapter 27 of
his *Questions on Exodus,* "When the minister of the judge kills
him whom the judge ordered to be killed, if he actually does it
willingly, it is murder, even if he kills him who he knows ought
to be killed by the judge."[203]

You shall not steal; that is, you shall not deceitfully take away
what belongs to another person. For the Hebrews did not commit theft when by the divine command they plundered the
Egyptians of those things that belonged to God more than to
them.[204]

[You shall not give] false testimony, namely, by speaking
against conscience.

You shall not covet what belongs to another person; it is not
merely that you shall not take it away.

---

202. Mt 26.52.   203. Augustine, *Qu. Exod.* 39.
204. Ex 12.35–36.

On charity

And if [there is any other] commandment (understand: "of love"),[205] it is fulfilled **in this** commandment: **You shall love [your neighbor as yourself].** It is one thing to say *as yourself,* and another to say "as much as yourself." For in the first a similarity is shown; in the second, an equality. Therefore, when the Truth says, "Be merciful just as your heavenly Father is,"[206] he expresses a similarity rather than an equality of mercy. But if I ought to love each person as much as myself, everyone should be loved equally by me. But since it appears that no one should be loved except for God's sake, each one is worthy to be loved more, the more dearly he is held by God and the better he is. For if God, because he is better, is to be loved above all, whoever are better after him should be loved more than others. For charity is not otherwise ordered.

But we love him more whom we wish to be happier, although we may minister less to his bodily goods or to his health less than to our own, and give care to those who cling to us spiritually.[207] But then we love each one as ourselves when we wish him to reach happiness just as we do, namely, with the same intention held towards him (290) as for us, because we consider this good to be for him just as it is for us. For perhaps when one person hates another, he wishes that the other were now in paradise, where he can wish nothing better for him; nevertheless he does not therefore love him, since he does that not so much for the sake of the other as for his own sake, in order to be freed from him.

[13.10] **Love of neighbor...** Truly, he who loves his neighbor will not commit adultery, will not kill, etc., because he **works** absolutely **no evil.** Therefore, it appears that David, at the time when he committed fornication with Bathsheba, and Uriah went forth to death,[208] in no way loved his neighbor; but since another Apostle says, "For how can he love God whom he does not see, who does not love his neighbor, whom he does see?"[209]

---

205. *Dilectio* and *diligere* throughout this discussion in 13.9–10.
206. Lk 6.36.
207. Buytaert; Peppermüller reads "especially," following manuscript *m*.
208. 2 Sm 11.4–5, 14–15.
209. 1 Jn 4.21.

certainly he does not seem to have loved God at that time. How can he be said to love the other as himself when he truly does not love himself, who by sinning does not spare himself from the death of the soul? For it is written, "He who loves iniquity hates his own soul."[210]

Therefore, the fullness [of the law]... Since love of neighbor also fulfills the law, as was said, therefore it is established that this is inferred much more from its genus, which **is love.** Since, however, the entire essence of our merits consists in the love of God and neighbor, we should diligently describe each one, if we are able; and moreover we should demonstrate how, since the love of God, which is greater, was passed over, the Apostle dared to say that love of neighbor fulfills the law.

Love of God from the whole heart is in us that best will toward God, by which, the more we strive to please him, the more we know we must please him. But we do that from the whole heart or rather the whole soul, when we direct to him the entire intention of our love, that we may consider not so much what is useful for us as what is pleasing to him. Otherwise we might make ourselves rather than him the object of our love, that is, the final and supreme cause. The love of God toward us is that disposition of divine grace for our salvation. Truly he loves his neighbor (291) as himself who, for God's sake, has so good a will toward him, that he may thus strive to conduct himself for [the neighbor's] sake, lest the other be able justly to complain about him, just as the first does not wish anything to be done to himself by the latter concerning which he might justly be able to complain.

But to this love of neighbor there belong those two commandments of the natural law: "What you do not wish to be done to you, do not do to another,"[211] and, "Do to others what you wish men may do to you."[212] The understanding that one should have of these commandments is perhaps not clear to all. For we often give honor or favor to others out of charity which we refuse to receive from others, or we often punish or even kill others in the service of justice, although we in no way wish to suffer this from them. Who does not know that sometimes

210. Ps 10.6.   211. Tb 4.16.
212. Mt 7.12.

we wish those things to be done to us that are not proper? Nevertheless, we should not do those things to others. So that if I may wish that someone assent to me in evil, should I likewise assent to others in order to sin? Often even those in power require such services from their subjects which are by no means fitting for them to render to their subjects; and the poor wish many things to be done for them by the rich which they can by no means do for others, so that they may be able to fulfill this commandment, "[Do to others] what you wish men may do to you," unless perhaps it is said that this is not a general commandment but is enjoined only on those who can make recompense for the benefits, just as, when it is also said, "Give alms,"[213] and "Break your bread with the hungry,"[214] it is imposed only on those who can do this.

But so that we may respond briefly to the objections, since it is said, "What you do not wish [to be done] to you, [do not do to another],"[215] and "[Do to others] what you wish men may do [to you],"[216] they should be understood in such a way that you may understand the former concerning injuries to be avoided, and the latter concerning benefits to be granted, as if it should be said, Just as you do not wish yourself to be wronged, so refrain from wronging others; and just as you wish to be helped mercifully in your needs, so also help others, if you can, in theirs. But no one good declares that he is able to do that which he believes is not of his law or is by no means fitting for himself. But since God should be loved only for his own sake, (292) but one's neighbor for God's sake, it is established that love of God is included in the love of neighbor, since it cannot exist without the love of God. Therefore, when we described it, we prudently added "for God's sake." Indeed, the love of God, since it is naturally superior to the love of neighbor, just as God is naturally superior to the neighbor, thus does not conversely or inevitably include the love of neighbor, since God can be loved without the neighbor, just as he can exist without him. Thus the Apostle seems rightly to have said that the love of neighbor fulfills the law, rather than the love of God.

213. Lk 11.41.   214. Is 58.7.
215. Tb 4.16.   216. Mt 7.12.

Question

It can be asked, not unjustly, whether we should also love
those who are in hell or who are not predestined to life, or
whether the saints love every neighbor as themselves even in
the other life, both those whom they now see damned or those
they foresee, by the revelation of God, to be damned, as well
as the elect. But since, as we said, we should understand every
man in the neighbor,[217] how will they preserve the love of neighbor, if they do not love some? Or how are they considered to
be more perfect there [in the other life] than here if the love
of neighbor in them is diminished or shattered? For it is not
the case that, since we love the holy angels, we must love the
wicked ones. Therefore, how is either their love or ours rational
if we also are included in the devil's members? Because we do
not know who are predestined in this life and who are not, do
we therefore act rationally by loving everyone or by praying for
everyone? Or if it is not rational that this be done, how are we
commanded to do that for them and not rather for ourselves,
since it helps us more than them? How upright, even, is the intention that is erroneous? For because we believe that will benefit them, we do it. Or if ignorance still excuses us, why do we
respond, concerning this, that—since we know that not all will
be saved, but very few, according to those words of the Truth:
"Many (293) are called, but few are chosen,"[218] and "Narrow is
the way which leads to life," etc.[219]—nevertheless we want everyone to be saved and we pray for everyone, knowing that neither
our will nor our prayer should be accomplished?

But you mention those words of Augustine, "Have charity
and do as you will,"[220] and call to mind those words of Jerome,
"Charity has no measure."[221]

---

217. Rom 7.6.   218. Mt 20.16.

219. Mt 7.14.

220. The literal Latin citation is not found in Augustine, though it may be
found in Ivo, *decret.*, Prol., where it is attributed to Augustine. A similar statement, "Love and do as you please," is found at *ep. Io.* 7.4.8.

221. Rather, of Paula and Eustochium, *To Marcella*, among the epistles of
Jerome, *ep.* 46.1.

Question

Therefore, charity often compels us to exceed measure in such a way that we wish to happen what is in no way good or righteous to happen, and on the contrary not to happen what is good to happen, just as the saints are killed or afflicted. These things *work together for good* for them. But we reserve this discussion for our *Ethics.*[222]

[13.11] **And knowing this...** Construct it in this way: *and knowing* **this time, that now is the hour for us to rise from sleep.** *Therefore, let us cast off the works of darkness,* etc.[223] *From sleep,* that is, from negligence of or sluggishness in a good work. When he says *hour,* which is a small amount of time, not a day or a week or a month or a year, he exhorts us to do it without delay. For where the time is shorter for something to be done, it must be done more quickly. **For now [is our salvation nearer...]** Therefore, we must rise swiftly from sleep because *now,* with the good works of our faith added besides, we are nearer to obtaining the prize of eternal life **than when we** first **believed,** namely, at the very beginning of our conversion.

[13.12] He follows up with suitable words the metaphor by which he said that now we must rise from sleep, saying that now night, which is the time for sleep, **has passed,** and day has arrived. (294) **Night** is the ignorance of salvation, and **day** is its knowledge and illumination. Do not wonder if we were sluggish in our actions while we were oppressed by this night. The blindness of our unbelief is driven out from our hearts with the arrival of the teaching of Christ, who says, "I am the light of the world."[224] We did not withdraw from this night so much as it did from us, and we did not approach [the day] so much as it did us, because, since we are in no way seeking it, the divine grace worked in this way, just as it is written concerning the Lord himself, "I was found by those not seeking me."[225]

---

222. Buytaert cites Chapter 3, PL 178.636–37, as the place where this is discussed, although David Luscombe, in his critical edition and translation of *Ethics,* says that this discussion was only projected, and never included; this seems to be more accurate (*Peter Abelard's* Ethics [Oxford: Clarendon Press, 1971], 130–31, n. 2).

223. Rom 13.12.   224. Jn 8.12.
225. Is 65.1; Rom 10.20.

Therefore, let us cast off... Since that *night has* now *passed* and the *day* **has drawn near,** he does not now say that "they should be cast off," but *let us cast off,* because now, illuminated by faith, we are able to act. He calls evil works **the works of darkness,** according to those words of the Truth, "Everyone who does evil hates the light";[226] this also applies to the works of the unbelievers and those in the dark over whom "the sun of righteousness"[227] has not yet risen, that it may illumine their hearts. **The armor of light** is the virtues of the faithful, with which they fight against vices and diabolical temptations.

[13.13] So, I say, *let us put on the armor of light,* so that, dressed in this way, **we may walk decently,** as if **in the day,** when each one is dressed with more precious clothes. **Not in...** He teaches first what the works to be cast away are. *Not in* **revelries.** Understand: "Let us walk"; that is, let us not place our feet, which are understood as the inner dispositions of the soul, in them. Revelry is called a feast gathered from various households, where each one offers something of his own, and therefore eats more securely as if eating from his own, and more eagerly, lest he seem to be injured as if consuming less and using equally, and the more unrestrainedly he indulges the appetite the more he is aroused by the examples of many. Therefore, a revelry, *comessatio,* as it were, a common eating, comes from *comedendo,* that is, from eating at the same time.

Jerome says, "A *comessatio* is a *mensae collatio,* a contribution to the table."[228] Solomon forbids such revelries when he says, "Do not be in the feasts of the drinkers, nor in the revelries of those who bring meat for eating, because in giving themselves to drinking and giving contributions for the feast they are eaten up."[229] Haymo says, "*Comessatio* comes from (295) *mensae alternatio,* a changing of the table. For there are feasts that are celebrated alternately and prepared by partners on alternate days. There are others which are in common, when one brings bread,

226. Jn 3.20. 227. Mal 4.2.
228. Pelagius, *Rom.,* 13.13. Here, based on Abelard's other comments, I follow Peppermüller's translation of "mensae collatio" (*Beisteuern zum Mahl,* 3:787) as opposed to De Bruyn's translation of "luxurious banquet" (139).
229. Prv 23.20–21.

another meat, another wine," etc. "We call a goblet, *briam,* in the masculine gender, a chalice ready for drink, from which comes drunkenness, *ebrietas,* which is excessive drinking."[230]

But what the Apostle says in this passage, *Not in revelries* **and drunkenness,** looks back to what the Lord says in the Gospel, "Watch, lest your hearts be burdened in gluttony and drunkenness,"[231] that is, in excessive food and drink. **Not in debaucheries.** He consequently adds the things which follow revelries and drunkenness, so that the more they are corrupted, the worse are the things that arise from them. Debaucheries belong to wild and irrational animals, with which the beds of drunks are compared, in which, when the image of God, that is, reason, has been killed by drunkenness, they were made "like horse and mule which have no understanding."[232] **Lewdness** also follows drunkenness. Therefore, also the same Apostle elsewhere exhorts, "Do not get drunk with wine, in which there is dissipation."[233] The drunkenness of blessed Lot shows this to us with the worst example.[234] Therefore, such are his words, *in debaucheries and lewdness,* as if he should say, in lewd debaucheries, where apart from all reverence, the drunken indulge in dissipation like cattle. The preacher of lewdness, Ovid, exhorts fornicators to come especially to these revelries and [engage in] drunkenness, so that they may thereafter easily receive the opportunity for their fornications.[235]

Not in contention [and envy]. Drunkenness is disorderly, it quarrels, and breaks forth easily into contention. He calls evil zeal *envy,* that is, agitation of hatred against another, which especially follows from the reproaches and insults of contentions. For nearly all men, and especially those who are free, are kindled into hatred more by the foulness of words than by loss of damaged goods.

[13.14] After *the works of darkness* which he says are to be cast away, he adds *the armor of light,* that is, the virtues of Christ which we should put on; he says, **But put on…**Whoever assumes the

230. Haymo, *Rom.* 13.13.
231. Lk 21.34.
232. Ps 31.9.
233. Eph 5.18.
234. Gn 19.30–38.
235. *Amores.* 1,4, per Peppermüller, 3.788, n. 14.

habit of the mild or harsh is said to "put on" the lamb or the lion; but he is also said to "put on" **[the Lord Jesus] Christ,** (296) who is the fullness of all virtues, and, by following his footsteps, he strives to adorn himself with all virtues to the extent that he can. The same Apostle says elsewhere concerning Christ, "Who was made wisdom for us by God and righteousness and sanctification and redemption,"[236] as if he should say openly that he becomes for us all the virtues, so that, when we are adorned with the virtues, we may rightly be said to put on Christ.

And so that you may be able to put on Christ spiritually, lest you live carnally, since the flesh lusts against the spirit,[237] that is, Christ, **make no provision [for the flesh] in its desires.** *In its desires,* he says, that is, not in the excess of pleasures, but in the necessity of food. For it is also fitting that necessary things be applied to our body just as excessive things are subtracted, so that the substance of nature may be preserved and the stimuli of vices be denied. He does not, therefore, simply say that you should have *no provision for the flesh,* but *in its desires,* that is, in pleasures rather than in necessities. For we should be enemies not of nature but of vices.

[14.1] **But [receive] the weak [in faith, not with disputes about opinions.]** Since he had said above, *not in contention,* he is here especially eager to impose an end to the perverse contention that arose immediately in the primitive church. For some Jews, recently converted to the faith and not yet sufficiently instructed concerning the freedom of the Christian faith, thought that the carnal observances of the law should still be retained, and especially that now also they should abstain from pork and other foods which the law forbade, perhaps to such an extent especially that whatever seems to belong to abstinence is reckoned to virtue. Therefore, just as earlier he forbade excessive revelries, so here he considers excessive abstinences, lest, through the discord of this contention, he scandalize those of the Jewish converts still having weak, that is, imperfect, faith, to such a degree that they return to Judaism, if they were for-

236. 1 Cor 1.30.
237. Gal 5.17.

bidden from these abstinences which the law, indeed, the Lord himself through the law, had established.

(297) Therefore, the Apostle takes counsel with those among the Romans who were of perfect faith and doctrine in such things, so that if someone among the newly converted Jews was still weak, that is, imperfect, in faith, not yet believing that Christ and evangelical doctrine were sufficient for salvation without the carnal observances of the law, they therefore should not cast him off, but *receive* him who comes to conversion, not disputing about his opinions, that is, not contending about that which he believes about such things. For it could easily happen that he who is still of imperfect faith, in the beginning of his conversion, having been instructed gradually, after a while may come to perfection.

[14.2] **For one...** Therefore, he explains that disputes, that is, contentions, are of this sort, saying that *one,* the one mentioned previously, who is imperfect of faith, **believes that he may eat everything,** that is, that he is allowed to eat food of any kind, so that he may thereafter incur no guilt on account of the law. **But he who...,** as if he should say, but he who does not believe this abstains from these foods which he fears, lest in acting against his own conscience he sin. And this is what he says: *He who* **is weak,** namely, in this belief about foods, fearing that he will be contaminated by certain foods, **let him eat vegetables;** that is, I advise him to use those foods which he can easily have and thereby cause less scandal to others, and receive some commendation of his religion. For if he should eat some meats and not others, he would be easily shown to Judaize. But since he openly abstains from them all and is content with viler foods, it is reckoned to religion rather than to an error of faith.

[14.3] **He who...** He said a while later that we should not contend about such things, and he even says that one person should not be haughty against another in his heart, so that *he who* **eats** everything **may despise** him in his heart as if by boasting about the perfection of his faith, and, as it were, he believes that he will be condemned who does not eat everything, that is, who abstains from some things. **And he who does not eat,** namely, everything, in a similar manner, therefore **should not judge,**

that is, (298) believe to be condemned, **the one who eats** as if
he is a transgressor of the law. **For God [receives] him,** the one
who eats as much as the one who abstains; he does not cast him
off. For many were converted to the faith, still erring in many
things, and later were gradually corrected and taught. Note that
he says "received" by God rather than "coming through him,"
according to that word of the Truth, "No one comes to me unless my Father, who sent me, draws him."[238]

[14.4] **Who are you...?** As if he should say, Who do you think
you are **to judge** another's **servant,** that is, to dispose according
to your choice concerning those things which are to be done by
him? Which is to say, abandon **to the Lord** this ordering of the
life of the servant who instructs him concerning these things
when he wishes, either by himself or through his deputies. You
who are a fellow slave did not come to command but to obey; in
the same way, he should be left *to his Lord,* that is, to the choice
of his Lord, both his good standing in faith and his falling into
error, and to him only does each servant look, from whom he
will receive what he deserves.

But he will stand, as if he should say, I said that **he stands
or falls;** but because we should interpret or explain in a better
sense the things which are uncertain, I say rather that *he will
stand,* that is, he will not be condemned on account of this, because he abstains, if you will, out of zeal for the law, lest he sin
against conscience. **For [God] is able,** as if he should say, Therefore, I judge and claim charitably what is better, because there
seems to be no reason why this should not be hoped. And this
is what he says: *God is able.* For God is said to be able to do that
which seems to be impeded by no reason and contradicted by
no authority that might prevent its successful accomplishment
by him. Therefore, it is such, *God is able,* as if it should be said,
No reason appears to infringe on his ability to do this.

[14.5] **For one [judges]...** Therefore, the Apostle adds,
some may judge or blame others in this way, by their own con-
sciences, since *one* believes that in abstinence of the things said
above there should be an observance **between day and day,**

238. Jn 6.44.

that is, one day interposed with another day, just as it is now the custom that on Wednesdays and Fridays one should abstain especially from all meat, for the sake of (299) conquering the flesh, not on account of some commandment of the law; but **another [judges] that every day** should be observed apart from these meats which the law forbids. **Let each one** in such things, namely, in these things to be judged or deliberated, concerning which no inquiry was yet made, either with reason or authority, **abound in his own understanding;** that is, let him follow his own opinion more than another's. For a clear reason had not yet been passed on to those Romans by the Apostle or by the other doctors as to why this abstinence should not be preserved on account of the commandment of the law.

[14.6] **He who discerns the day, [discerns it in honor of the Lord,]** as if he should say, Therefore let everyone of you still be henceforth given up to judgment in such things, because he otherwise sins by acting against his conscience, just as it is later said, *Everything which is not of faith is sin.*[239] And this is what he says: *He who discerns the day;* that is, he believes that some day ought to be observed; he does this to the honor of the Lord, whom he believes he pleases through this moderate abstinence. **And he who eats;** that is, he believes he should not ever abstain from any foods, since he perceives no rebellion of the flesh, which must be subdued, nor suffers any weakness which is contrary to abstinence. For we believe that in the time of the apostles, the abstinence of Lent and Fridays was not yet established or confirmed. . . . **eats to the Lord;** that is, he does so likewise in honor of him, on account of this which he immediately adds: that **he gives thanks** to him, that is, he renders praise, namely, for the meal provided to him by the Lord. From this we should consider how great a sin it is not to give these thanks to the Lord after food. **And he who does not eat,** that is, who on account of the law abstains thoroughly from these foods which it prohibits, **does not eat** for the honor of the Lord; that is, he abstains. For he does not show this reverence of obedience to the law, except on account of the God who gave it; and when he

239. Rom 14.23.

abstains from the taking of other food granted and provided by God, *he gives thanks.*

(300) [14.7] **For no one [of us lives to himself, and no one dies to himself.]** Therefore, both he who eats and he who abstains do this to the honor of the Lord, because the elect always honor and glorify the Lord by living as much as by dying. They glorify by living according to that word of the Truth, "Let your good works shine and glorify your Father who is in heaven."[240] Death also glorifies the God of the righteous, just as it is said of Peter, "signifying by what death he would glorify God,"[241] since the righteous person also does not cease from good works and prayer or from the praise of his Creator at his death. For the more carefully anyone prepares himself, the more closely he approaches the taking of his crown. He is said to live to himself or to die to himself who intends to dispose these things for his own gain or glory rather than to the honor of God. For indeed many, displaying the greatness of their soul by their death, desired to obtain glory for themselves; or bringing hands against themselves, they believed that their tortures would be ended with death.

[14.8] **For whether...** Since **we** who are the elect do not **live** or **die** to ourselves, as was said, therefore we do so **to the Lord;** and in view of this, *whether we live,...* [*or whether we die*]; that is, our life as much as our death should be ascribed to God, in whose honor it happens, rather than to ourselves; that is, because of this it should be called his rather than ours.

[14.9] **For to this end,** as if he should say, *to this end,* because **he died,** namely, for us and on account of our sins, **and rose again,** likewise for us and *on account of our justification,*[242] just as the same Apostle said above; he merited to rule over our death as much as our life, so that, just as he did each for us, so by dying as much as by living we may seek only to obey him and to fulfill his will. For otherwise he is not **Lord of the dead,** but, as it were, an enemy because of his punishments, unless we persist until death (301) in his obedience, having prepared our soul not only for its confession, but also to lay it down for the brothers.

---

240. Mt 5.16.   241. Jn 21.19.
242. Rom 4.25.

[14.10] **But you, why [do you judge...].** After he said, *Who are you to judge another's servant?* he now adds **your brother,** so that if he does not give this up as an injury which he does to his Lord, he thus ceases, at least for fraternal love, to judge his brother lest he scandalize him. **Or,** if you do not judge, **why do you despise [your brother]** in such things, in which the intention should be explained more than the action, since no definite judgment on it has yet been issued? For with reference to establishing these and similar things concerning which the Romans were disputing, the Apostle said in the beginning of his epistle that he wishes to come to them *that* he *might have some fruit* among them *just as among the other Gentiles.*[243]

For we all..., as if he should say, you should not presume to judge difficult things, you who will be judged by God on certain things with all other men; but reserve this judgment rather for him who must judge rightly about them all. And this is what he says: *For we all...* Concerning this the Truth also says, "Do not judge and you will not be judged";[244] that is, you should not desire to judge lest you be judged and condemned on this account; and the Apostle himself says elsewhere, "Do not judge before the time, until [the Lord comes]."[245] But if we consider more diligently, just as it belongs to God to kill rather than to us, so it is with judging; and at last, just as we ought to do all things to his glory, so he ought to work all these things through us, rather than we ourselves. At that time God makes the judgment rather than man, when he instructs us what should be said, either through some law or an internal inspiration, so that his judgment should later be read out by us, and not carried out.

Therefore, it seems that one first judges in three ways concerning some question: namely, through God himself, just as we have explained, through some manifestation of the matter, and through a man relying vainly on his own opinion. But when what had been uncertain is manifested in some outcome of the matter, (302) the thing itself is said to judge, not the man. Therefore, in uncertain things only man is said to judge. This is prohibited completely, when, following his own opinion

243. Rom 1.13.
245. 1 Cor 4.5.

244. Lk 6.37; Mt 7.1–2.

alone, he presumes to decide, since neither yet through God
nor through the very experience of the thing does it happen
that he is certain.

We will stand, he says, as if upright, so that we can be recognized by all, **before the tribunal,** that is, the judiciary seat
of the **God** who cannot err and who is righteous, rather than
of man. Understand that this seat of God is the humanity assumed by the Word. For the Father "has given all judgment to
the Son, ... because he is the Son of Man."[246] For the Son of God
died as much as he was raised in this assumed humanity, just as
he now has said; and the judgment of condemnation especially
threatens us from that time, if our death as much as our life is
not prepared for obedience and does not adhere inseparably to
him who died for us, as was said, and was raised for us.

[14.11] **For it is written ...** He shows by the testimony of Isaiah that all are to be judged by God. **"As I live,"** [says the Lord,]
as if he should say, I swear by my unfailingly living self. The
knee is bent to the judge when his judgment is humbly awaited,
which cannot be resisted.[247]

[Mss. *AmR*:] **Every tongue** shall make a confession of praise
to God in that judgment, because no one's conscience will be
able to mutter against the uprightness of that judgment. Therefore, the evil who also repent and sigh among themselves will
confirm, in this very thing that they will do, that they receive a
just sentence of damnation.

[Ms. *O*:] **Every tongue** will confess to the Lord in that judgment, because by the conscience of each one, concerning which
it is said, "They spoke in the heart and with the heart,"[248] it will
be proved that he is the true Lord of all, since the rewards and
punishments of all are ordained in accordance with his choice,
and no strong man will be able to resist his judgment.

[All Mss.:] Therefore, in that judgment those who judge
as much as those who will be judged, or even those who were

---

246. Jn 5.22, 27.

247. So Peppermüller, who follows the minority reading of ms. *A*, against
the majority reading of Buytaert ("The knee is bent to the judge when his sentence is completed ...").

248. Ps 11.3.

judged, will bend the knee since they will all humble themselves
either by fear of punishments or by the benefit of grace obtained under such a judge.

(303) [14.12] **Therefore,** because we all will thus appear *before the tribunal* of such a judge, **[each one of us] will render account [for himself to God];** that is, to the extent that reason demands, he will receive from the Lord concerning punishment
or reward.

[14.13] **Therefore, [let us] not [judge...],** because he must
thus judge concerning all things, and especially concerning
those things of which there is an uncertain intention, **each
other,** namely, one judging another by reckoning that the other
should be condemned for such things, **any more,** that is, after
this exhortation or command of ours; **but rather judge this:**
that is, resolve to take care, **lest you set up a stone of offense
for your brother,** that is, lest you do something and he fall, corrupted by that example, or, scandalized and exasperated by our
guilt, he withdraw from faith.

[14.14] And since all this contention was born from foods
forbidden by the law, he says that no one is defiled by the quality
of the food but only by consciousness of transgression, if he eats
them against his conscience. And this is what he says: **I know
and [am confident in the Lord Jesus, that nothing is common
by itself];** I say this not of myself but boldly, from the teaching
of the Lord, who says that a man is contaminated only by those
things which go forth from the heart, not by those things which
enter into the mouth;[249] and, sending his disciples to preach,
he said, "Eat and drink what is set before you,"[250] because no
food is common, that is, unclean, by itself, that is, of its own
self, but rather by the conscience of the one who eats. And this
is what he says: **except to him,** as if he should say, but **to him
who considers anything [to be common, it is common],** that is,
any food to be unclean, that is, from which his soul is defiled,
to him it is unclean because he sins by eating it against his conscience. The more unclean the things which are made common
or public are, the less they are defended, and therefore "com-

249. Mt 15.11.
250. Lk 10.7.

mon" is substituted for "unclean." "Therefore, also in the Acts of the Apostles," Origen says, "the Lord says to Peter, 'What God has cleansed, you should not call common.'"[251] Even Mark (304) the Evangelist substitutes "make common" for "contaminate" when he says, "You should not understand that everything which enters into a man from the outside can make him common, because it does not enter into his heart but proceeds into his stomach. The things which go out from a man make him common."[252]

[14.15] **For if...** I said that you should not set up a stone of offense for your brother, because whoever you are, **if [your brother is grieved] because of** your **food, [you are not walking according to charity,]** that is, if you persist in offending him in this way. **Do not [destroy him with your food].** After a stone of offense, he also forbids a stone of stumbling, because, having taken offense, he might easily withdraw from faith; **for whom,** namely, the one to be saved, **Christ died;** as if he should say, lest you hold in contempt the salvation of him for whom so great a price was given.

[14.16] **Therefore, do not [let our good...].** He generally warns us to avoid all blasphemy, through which we drive away others from our faith; as if he should say, because men should be won by the example of Christ rather than lost by us, we should avoid, as much as possible, doing that through which our good faith might **be blasphemed.**

[14.17] **[For the Kingdom of God] is not [food and drink];** that is, we earn no kind of food or drink, that God may rule or dwell among us. For whatever things seem to happen well outside, and which especially pertain to abstinence, are equally common to the reprobate as to the elect, and to the hypocrites as to the truly faithful. **But righteousness,** that is, that equity through which "what you do not wish done to you, do not do to another";[253] **and peace,** arising from it, that is, harmony with the brothers, **and,** finally, spiritual **joy [in the Holy Spirit],** arisen from this source.

[14.18] **For he who [does] this,** namely, what I mentioned,

251. Acts 10.15; Origen, *Rom.*, 9.42.
252. Mk 7.18–20.   253. Tb 4.16.

that he may avoid the stumbling stone of a brother and pursue righteousness and peace, as was said, **serves Christ;** that is, he obeys him who teaches this, **[pleases God] and is approved by men;** that is, he is approved, that is, praised and commended, by the judgment of men also.

[14.19] **Therefore,** that is, in this way also, as I said, by avoiding stumbling stones, **let us pursue** first **the things** which belong to **peace,** as I said; that is, (305) let us especially strive to maintain harmony with the weak brothers also, as was said; **and** henceforward **let us keep the things that are edifying towards one another;** that is, one who is more complete in faith instructs the still incomplete faith of another, and aims to bring it to completion.

[14.20] **Do not...,** you who have a more complete faith and eat everything, by scandalizing a brother newly converted and still weak, **destroy** in him **the work of God,** that is, the portion of faith which he now has, **[on account of food]. Indeed, all things [are clean, but it is evil to the man who eats with offense],** as if he should say, In fact we agree with you that no kinds of food eaten by him defile the soul, but it is destructive nevertheless to eat this knowingly when a brother is offended.

[14.21] **It is good** for man **[not to eat meat and not to drink wine],** as if he should say, Thus, as I said, it is evil to eat, but on the contrary it is beneficial to abstain entirely in order to avoid the stone of offense of the brother. By the example of Daniel, who also abstained from the wine of the unbelieving king, the converted Jews resolved to abstain from all the wine of the unbelievers. **[Or to do anything in which your brother] is offended,** by withdrawing entirely from faith; or at least **is scandalized,** that is, he is disturbed with himself as if judging that such a faith, to which he was converted, is contrary to the law and perverse; **or is weakened** in the faith of his profession, by doubting it, if not condemning it completely.

[14.22] **You have faith;** as if he should say, you who believe that all things are to be eaten, you have faith within yourself; that is, it is approved by your judgment; but have it also **before God,** that is, that it may please him and be approved by his judgment. For we can see and perceive those things that are before us, and God is said to know those things that he approves, and not to know the things he condemns. **Blessed is he who does not judge himself,** that is, who does not obtain damnation for himself from those things which he, rather than God, **commends,** that is, he approves, or does not reject, their implementation; as if he should say, (306) He who has such discretion that he thus takes precautions concerning those things which he believes may be done, lest he incur the damnation and wrath of God by acting indiscreetly. For, as Solomon says, "There are ways of a man which seem right, but his last way leads to death."[254] And the Lord said to Cain, "If you offer properly, but you do not properly divide, have you not sinned?"[255]

[14.23] **But he who [discerns, if he eats, is condemned],** as if he should say, Just as he is blessed who abstains from lawful things, lest by using them indiscreetly he incur damnation for the stumbling of a brother; so on the contrary, he sins who uses lawful things even against his own conscience. And this is what he says: *But he who discerns;* that is, he distinguishes certain foods, namely, by believing that they should not be eaten on account of the prohibition of the law, and nevertheless eats them against his conscience. As long as he believes that he should not eat them, he is determined to be guilty through this **because** what he does **is not from faith;** indeed, he acts against his own faith; that is, he acts against what he believes. For he believes that they should not be eaten and nevertheless he eats them, and through this he sins. **But everything [which is not of faith];** as if he should say, Because whatever is done against what is believed, whether in eating or in other things, **is sin.** For God, "who is the inspector of the heart,"[256] observes not so much the things that are done as with what disposition they are done.

Question

It can be asked, not unjustly, concerning those who killed the faithful whom they thought to be seducers (according to that word of the Truth, "The hour is coming when everyone who kills you thinks that he is fulfilling a duty to God"),[257] wheth-

254. Prv 14.12.
255. Cf. Gn 4.7.
256. Prv 24.12.
257. Jn 16.2.

er they sinned in this. For if they believed they were seducers
of souls and therefore worthy of death, how should they have
shown mercy to them against their conscience? For if they
had shown mercy, they would have acted against their conscience and so would have sinned. But again, since they kill the
innocent, indeed, the chosen of God, which is unjust, shall we
say that they do not sin or that they have a good intention in
this which goes very wrong, and therefore it is held to be good
but in fact is not? How does ignorance (307) excuse them from
sin, since it is established that some sins are said to be of ignorance? Otherwise, how could the Psalmist say to God, "Pour out
your wrath on the nations which do not know you,"[258] and how
could the Truth say concerning his persecutors, "Father, forgive
them, because they do not know what they are doing"?[259] For
where sin has not preceded, why is the work to be forgiven? For
if ignorance or even an error of faith should excuse thoroughly
from sin, therefore are the Jews and Gentiles or any unbelievers to be condemned for their unbelief, since each one thinks
his faith to be right? For who willingly persists in a faith that he
believes to be heretical, or chooses the worse part for himself?
Concerning such people the Truth nevertheless says, "He who
does not believe is already judged."[260] But we reserve the discussion of this matter for our *Ethics*.[261]

Question

I also think we should ask why the Apostle in this passage
considers abstaining from lawful foods on account of the stumbling stone to weak brothers, since in the epistle to the Galatians he says that he resisted Peter in this "because it was reprehensible"?[262] But we reserve this to be defined in that place.[263]

Question

We must now ask if, according to the Apostle himself, "All
things are clean to the clean" and nothing should be rejected

---

258. Ps 78.6.   259. Lk 23.34.
260. Jn 3.18.
261. *Ethics* 13, ed. Luscombe, 54–57.   262. Gal 2.11.
263. In Abelard's comentary on Galatians, which did not survive.

among the foods because it should be received with thanksgiving, why the apostles and holy fathers forbade some foods to us just as the law did. Concerning this, there is contained in the Acts of the Apostles, "There arose certain of the sect of the Pharisees who had believed, saying that it is necessary for them to be circumcised, and to instruct them also to keep the law of Moses...Standing up, Peter said to them,...'Why do you test God, to place a yoke upon the neck of the disciples which neither our fathers nor we could bear? But we believe we are saved, just as they are, through the grace of the Lord Jesus.'"[264] Likewise, "James answered, saying, (308) 'His work is known to the Lord from of old. On account of this I judge that we should not disturb those who turn to God from the Gentiles, but write to them to abstain from the contaminations of idols, from fornication, from meat that has been strangled, and from blood. For from ancient times, in every city, Moses has those who proclaim him in the synagogues, where he is read every sabbath.'"[265]

Origen, in his commentary on Romans, says about the words, *If, therefore, the uncircumcised [keeps the righteousness of] the law,* "But do you wish to see," up to "is its blood," which you will find above in the second quire.[266]

Ambrose, in his commentary on Galatians, says about the apostles,

In addition, when they gave the law that those who believed among the Gentiles should not be bothered, but that they should observe that prohibiting them from these things only: that is, from blood, fornication, and idolatry...at any rate, they were not prohibited from murder, since they were commanded to observe the prohibition from blood. But they understood what Noah had learned from God, that they should observe the prohibition from eating blood with meat...The sophistical ones among the Greeks do not understand these things; nevertheless, knowing they should abstain from blood, they have adulterated the

264. Acts 15.5, 7, 10–11.   265. Acts 15.13, 18–21.

266. Peter here refers the reader to Origen's comments on Rom 2.26–27, *Rom.* 2.13, which he himself uses in his comment on 2.16, pp. 137–38. "The second quire" refers to a gathering of manuscript pages, usually four to six leaves, each of which could hold four pages, folded over and written front and back. A quire thus normally contained between sixteen and twenty-four pages. Manuscript *A* reads, "on the fourth page of the second quire."

Scripture, adding a fourth commandment to be observed, "and from meat that has been strangled," which, I think, they will now understand by the will of God, because what they added was said above."[267]

Jerome, in his commentary on Ezekiel, says,

"The priests shall not eat any body, of bird or animal, torn by a beast."[268] And according to the letter, this refers specifically to Christians who were anointed with spiritual oil, concerning which it is written, "God, your God, has anointed you with the oil of exultation before your comrades";[269] these precepts are applicable to the entire chosen race, royal and priestly,[270] that it should not eat a body, (309) of birds as much as of animals, whose blood was in no way shed, which is called "strangled" in the Acts of the Apostles, and the epistle of the apostles of Jerusalem advises that it is necessary that these things should be observed; and a body "torn by a beast" because it was likewise strangled.[271]

From the *Penitential Book* of Theodore:

Animals that are mangled by wolves or dogs are not to be eaten, neither a deer nor a goat if they were found dead, unless perhaps they were first killed by a man while alive, but they may be given to swine and dogs. Birds and other animals, if they are strangled in snares, are not to be eaten, not if a bird of prey seized them and if they are thus found dead, because in the Acts of the Apostles it is commanded to abstain from fornication, from strangled blood, and from idolatry.[272]

Again,

If swine or chickens eat the blood of a man, they should be killed directly and the entrails cast away, and the remaining flesh may be eaten. But if the killing is delayed, they should not be eaten. But if they mutilated the bodies of the dead, they should be weakened and eaten after the course of a year. But if swine should kill a man, they should be killed immediately and buried.[273]

Again, "He who eats meat that is unclean or naturally dead or torn by beasts must do penance for forty days. But if it happens

267. Ambrosiaster, *Gal.*, 2.1, edited.
268. Ezek 44.31.
269. Ps 44.8; Heb 1.9.
270. Cf. 1 Pt 2.9.
271. Jerome, *Comm. in Ezech.* 13 (44.31).
272. Theodore, Archbishop of Canterbury, *Capitula* 15; Burchardus of Worms, *Decretorum libri XX*, 19.85.
273. Theodore, 17; Burchard, 19.87.

because of hunger, it is much lighter."[274] Again, "If he who eats is defiled by blood or anything unclean and does not know, it is light."[275] Again, "He who drinks blood or semen in place of some other thing must do penance for four years."[276] Again, "A fish found dead in the river must not be eaten. If it was touched by fishing and found on the same day, he who does not hesitate may eat it; but he who hesitates may not eat it."[277]

(310) From the Council of Gangra, after the Council of Nicaea, Chapter 2: "If someone believes that a person who eats meat by faith with devotion, apart from blood and meat sacrificed to idols and meat that has been strangled, should be condemned just as a person who does not have hope who eats those things, let him be anathema."[278]

In his work *To Peter on Faith*, Augustine says, "Hold firmly and in no way doubt that every creature of God is good and nothing should be rejected which is taken with thanksgiving, and that the servants of God who abstain from meat or wine do not reject the things made by God as if they were unclean; but abstain from stronger food and drink for the correction of the body alone."[279]

But if we inquire diligently in the apostles and apostolic fathers about the basic intention regarding these things, which seem contradictory, we will find that these things and others are now prohibited, now conceded, according to time and place; and sometimes prohibitions were provided in connection with integrity of life more than with devoutness of faith. For thus does blessed Ambrose in his commentary on the Hexaemeron prohibit garlic to be eaten for food, which he allows to be eaten for medicine, because respectable men are easily offended by its odor.[280] We believe that this is done with some other base foods on account of the integrity to be preserved.

274. Theodore, 19; Burchard, 19.88.

275. Theodore, 19; Burchard, 19.90.

276. Not found in Theodore, but found in Burchard under Theodore's name, 19.91.

277. Not found in Theodore, but in Burchard, 19.92.

278. Ch. 2, ed. P. P. Joannou, Fonti IX, *Discipline générale antique* (Grottaferrata, 1962), 90; Mansi II, 1101–1102; Ivo of Chartres, *Decretum* 4.30.

279. Fulgentius of Ruspe, *De fide ad Petrum* 85.

280. Ambrose, *In Hex..*, 4.4.28.

Do not wonder if the Apostle says here with discretion that we should abstain from some foods on account of the stumbling stone to the weak brothers; James also, in the early church, which was still weak in faith, prohibited those foods to be eaten by which he considered the believers were at that time especially offended. For the Apostle himself, although he completely forbids circumcision, nevertheless yielded once by permitting Timothy to be circumcised, and by consecrating him himself in the Jewish rite with some Jewish converts.[281] That which, therefore, some of the holy fathers in certain (311) times and places reasonably prohibited on account of the stumbling stone to those with whom they lived, later others, now strengthened in our faith as much as they could be, laudably allowed. Otherwise, the Apostle would be found contrary to Moses, if what is prohibited or permitted at one time is always to be maintained.

There can be a question concerning the Jews and proselytes, concerning those making their profession and vow through the observances of the law before the coming of Christ: whether those converted to faith later can transgress a vow either in food or in other things. For at that time, when the law still retained its position, it seems that a vow of this kind was lawfully made. Therefore, in no way does it seem that it should be violated. And he who made that vow at that time, who later became a Christian, seems not to have been absolved from that abstinence from foods, especially since he lives more negligently by abstaining from no foods than by abstaining from some. He may not legitimately neglect a vow well made, unless he ascends to better things which may hinder keeping it.

I think we should respond to this that, if he now observes this not so much on account of the strictness of the law as for the disposition of his vow, he should in no way be blamed and he should not be absolved from this vow, unless perhaps on account of the stumbling stone to some other believers, [namely,] that he still observes Jewish practices in this matter, as if he now also believes that the law retains its position and he now abstains because of this. He does not seem to have made such

281. Acts 16.1–3.

a vow legitimately and rationally at that time, but he seems to have professed a promise through an error, since he believed that the law would persevere in its pristine vigor.

[15.1] **But we [who are stronger] should [bear the weaknesses of the weak].** I said above that *nothing is common*, indeed, *all things are clean* to the faithful; but nevertheless we should endure the weakness of those who believe otherwise and who are weaker in the faith, (312) **and not please ourselves,** that is, not fulfill our will concerning them by rejecting them, but seek their well-being by enduring them.

[15.2] **[Let each one of you] please [his neighbor in good];** that is, he should strive to please in what is not blameworthy, for the sake of [his neighbor's] **edification.** For he could not otherwise be edified by us unless he received our teaching; and we should do this by the example of Christ.

[15.3] And this is what he says: **For [Christ did not please himself];** that is, that human nature assumed by the Word, who is especially called Christ according to his special anointing, strove to fulfill the resolution not so much of the human will as of the divine. Therefore, he himself also says, "I have not come to do my own will but that of him who sent me."[282] For that is properly called the will of man which, introduced by the weakness and passibility of the flesh, naturally desires that rest which is afflicted by no troubles but is thoroughly immune from every punishment, just as was granted to our first parents before the sin and will be fully granted to us in the life to come. For just as it is established that the compensation of misery is rest, and just as everyone desires what belongs to blessedness and rest, so everyone flees from what belongs to misery and hardship. Therefore, such a desire in us is called human will; and every one follows this will by obeying it.

But, you will say, how is it that *Christ did not please himself,* if he pleased God the Father? Can what pleases one displease the other? Do all the righteous please Christ as they do the Father? Or is the will of the Father different from the will of Christ? What then? *Did Christ not please himself,* and did he come not to

282. Jn 6.38.

do his own will, save that the assumed human nature never desired to do anything because he hoped that this would be pleasant to himself, but because he believed this would be pleasing
to God? All the others, however holy they may be, because they
are not completely free of sin, desire some things by (313) the
weakness and passibility of the flesh, not for any other reason
except that they may satisfy the weakness and avoid the present
suffering and affliction. This is to please himself and do his own
will, that is, to do it only and especially because it is believed
to be pleasant to himself, establishing the end of this action of
his in himself, which was very far from Christ. Therefore, this
is what he says: *Christ did not please himself,* but God the Father,
since the human nature desired nothing because it was pleasant
to him, but because he knew that God approves this and because he kept his command in this. He himself says this to him:
"Because of the words of your lips I have kept hard ways."[283]

The Apostle immediately adds this laborious suffering on account of the obedience he received, so that he may show through
this that [Christ] pleased the Father more than himself: **But just
as it is written** in Psalm 68, **The reproaches [of those reproaching you have fallen upon me].**[284] Whoever upbraids someone's
messenger or strikes and insults him in something, this should
be ascribed not so much to him who is sent as to him who sends.
Therefore, it is said to Saul, "Saul, Saul, why do you persecute
me?" "Me," I say, rather than "mine," because you do this on account of me rather than them. But what is it to reproach God the
Father except to mock the birth which is in divinity, which their
carnal understanding could not accept? Therefore, this mocking
fell upon Christ, because while he proclaimed this birth and said
that he was the Son of God, by seeking the glory of the Father
in this, not his own, not only was he held in mockery from that
time, but he was also handed over to death, just as it is written,
"He boasts that he has God as his father; let us see if his words are
true,"[285] and in the Gospel, "He trusted in God; let him deliver
him now if he wants, for he said, 'I am the Son of God.'"[286]

[15.4] **For whatever things were written,** as if someone should

283. Ps 16.4.
285. Wis 2.16–17.

284. Ps 68.10.
286. Mt 27.43.

say, What concern is the testimony of the Old Testament to us, who teach the New Law, especially since we reject its works? (314) He answers that *whatever things were written,* in the Old Testament as in the New Testament, **[were written] for our [instruction],** that is, of Christians. For they who follow the letter that kills are not taught in the Old Testament but are blinded; but they especially who break the outer crust are stuffed with inner bread. But God permitted secular literature to be written only for some teaching, either of morals or of learning, and so that the Holy Scriptures might bring aid in some way, although the writers of that literature did not know this.

So that... We are instructed and taught by them for this reason, I say: *so that* **through patience** in misfortunes **and the consolation** provided in the scriptures, namely, of the prize of eternal blessedness, we may be strengthened by **hope** in God through all things, knowing that "if we suffer with him, we will reign with him,"[287] and "in your patience you will possess your souls."[288] But this hope is that concerning which it was said above, *But hope does not confound.*[289] But since he had previously spoken well of adversities when he said, *The reproaches of those reproaching,*[290] he added *patience* against those reproaches, a necessary thing, *and the consolation* **of the scriptures.**

But since in the beginning of this epistle I had said that every scripture aims at either teaching or exhorting, how is it now said that *whatever things were written were written for our instruction,* unless, indeed, because those things which admonish *were written for instruction,* not so that they may teach what should be done but so that the teaching may be effectual, that is, that we may wish to fulfill what we were taught?

[15.5] **But may the God [of patience and of comfort];** that is, just as *Christ did not please himself* but God, and sought not his own glory but the Father's, so *may God* himself, whose it is to give both patience and comfort, **grant that you** (315) **may be of one mind towards one another,** that is, to seek this among yourselves, that one may please the other in good **in the same way as Jesus Christ,** that is, by his example, as was said.

---

287. Cf. 2 Tm 2.12.   288. Lk 21.19.
289. Rom 5.5.   290. Rom 15.3.

[15.6] **So that with one mind,** that is, both the weak in faith and the strong together, you may praise **God** with a harmonious **mouth,** for the mercy of our redemption shown to us through his Son. Therefore, when he had also said *God,* he furthermore adds a synonym: **and Father of our Lord Jesus Christ,** who is praised not only for his own glory but for having such a Son for our salvation, so that through him who came down to seek brothers he may be our Father.

[15.7] **Therefore,** so that God may thus be honored by all together, **receive one another;** that is, let not one cast off or provoke the other, but he who is stronger and more complete in faith should support him who is weak. And act by this example of **Christ,** who did not reject you but **received you,** even you stiff-necked Jews, not only the weak in faith but those dead in unbelief; indeed, he even drew you, **[to the honor of God,]** to glorify and praise God, as much for our conversion as for that of others through you.

[15.8] **[For I say that Jesus Christ] was the minister to the circumcision,** that is, to the Jews, to whom alone he ministered by himself, by preaching the word of life, just as he himself says, "I was not sent except to the lost sheep of the house of Israel."[291] **For the sake of the truth of God,** that is, that the promise of God might endure, who especially and frequently had promised to send to them a savior. And this is what he adds: **for confirming,** that is, that those **promises** made to the ancient **fathers** concerning the sending of Christ to them might remain firm and unchanged. For he wished to continue as a debtor through his promises, that he might become the deliverer by his pardoning.

[15.9] **But the Gentiles,** as if he should say, *I say that Christ was the minister* [*to the circumcision*], but also the *Gentiles, I say* (understood), **are to honor God for** the **mercy** now especially granted to them by God. (316) The farther they had been from God at one time through idolatry, the more they have now drawn near to the worship of God with a greater number, so that where sin abounded, grace also superabounded.[292] And

291. Mt 15.24.
292. Rom 5.20.

note that above, on account of the promise made to the Jews, he did not so much pronounce mercy as he understood a debt. The more suitably he invoked mercy among the Gentiles, the less it was due to them, according to the manifold fault of their error.

Just as it is written in the Psalm that speaks in the person of Christ, who says to the Father, **Therefore, I will confess to you among the Gentiles, [O Lord];**[293] that is, I will cause you to be praised, even by the Gentiles converted and won to you by me. Of these, the first fruits were the Magi and those Samaritans to whom he became known through that Samaritan woman,[294] and perhaps those Gentiles who, around the Passion, desiring to see him, approached him through Philip and Andrew. Concerning these he said, "Now is the Son of Man glorified."[295] **And [I will sing] to your name;** I will cause them to be free for spiritual songs to your honor and for spreading your fame. The word *therefore* is a continuation of what he said earlier in the Psalm, "You will lift me up by those rising up against me."[296] For he is lifted up by those who believed they could wipe out his name by crucifying him. Concerning this lifting-up, he himself also had foretold: "And I, if I am lifted up from the earth, I will draw all things to myself,"[297] not only by converting the Jews but also the Gentiles.

[15.10] **And again, [Rejoice, O Gentiles, with his people].** Foreseeing through Isaiah[298] a church to be gathered as much from the Jews as from the Gentiles, he exhorts both commonly to exult and praise God for their conversion. He calls the Jews the people of God and, at one time, his special people.[299]

[15.11] **And again,** through David himself: **[Praise the Lord, all you Gentiles,] magnify him,** that is, praise his good works, **all**

---

293. Ps 17.50.

294. The Magi: Mt 2.12; the Samaritans: Jn 4.7–42.

295. Jn 12.20–22.

296. Ps 17.49. The meaning is actually "You will lift me up *from* those rising up against me," but Peter chooses to read the preposition *ab* as meaning "by" instead of "from," as suggested by the next sentence, in which he uses *per,* "by those . . ." He thus sees these verses as a prophecy of Christ's crucifixion.

297. Jn 12.32.   298. Actually, Dt 32.43.

299. Dt 7.6; 14.2; 26.18.

the peoples, that is, each multitude of the faithful, not only that gathered from the Gentiles.

(317) [15.12] **[And again Isaiah says,] There shall be a root** ... Another testimony concerning the conversion of the Gentiles,[300] after the Incarnation of the Lord, of those to be ruled by him and of those who will hope in him. Just as the root is the remainder of the cut tree, and just as, if it is concealed in the earth, it issues many shoots of little branches, so **Jesse,** the father of David, when he had died and was cut off from the present life as from a tree, had Christ as if a root and remainder of his own, to be born long afterward from his seed. This root was concealed in the earth, buried while in that flesh of his which is of earthly substance, according to which he says concerning himself, "Just as Jonah was in the belly of the whale," etc.[301] By rising again he sprouted in a large shoot of the faithful according to that parable of his, "Unless a grain of wheat," etc.[302] But we know both that each root sprouts especially at that time and that it is, as it were, enriched so that it may multiply, if manure and dung are applied to it, according to the Lord's parable: "Let it go this year also, that I may put manure on it."[303] But what are the manure and dung applied to this root, except the filth of our sins, which he took up through his suffering and bore in his own body, so that fruits of an uncountable offspring might spring forth in the Church from himself, as if from the root and origin of all things? For, "It profited nothing to be born, unless it profited to be redeemed."[304]

Therefore, the Spirit says, foretelling this through Isaiah, *There shall be a root of Jesse;* that is, when it has died, posterity will be left to it from its seed, through which what perished in the tree may be restored more fruitfully in the offshoot, because more faithful [people] will arise than existed before Jesse. **And who,** as if he should say, and he will be that root who **will rise [to rule the Gentiles]** by growing furiously, until his body, which is the Church, is extended everywhere; he will always be set over their government as their head, just as he promises, saying,

---

300. Is 11.10. 301. Mt 12.40.
302. Jn 12.24. 303. Lk 13.8.
304. Easter praeconium "Exultet" of the Latin liturgy.

"Behold I am with you always, until the end of the world."[305] Concerning this ruler the same prophet says elsewhere, "And a little boy (318) will lead them."[306] **In him [will the Gentiles hope];** that is, they will trust because of his grace, not because of the law or their own strength; this is the *root* concerning which the same prophet speaks in a certain passage: "The root of Jesse who stands for a sign of the peoples, the Gentiles will pray to him, and his sepulcher will be renowned."[307] Concerning this sepulcher, that rising *root* grew into a great tree of branches.

[15.13] **But may the God...** I said, *Rejoice, O Gentiles,* and, *In him will the Gentiles hope,* and may he **fulfill** this in you Romans. And this is what he says: May *the God* **of hope,** that is, whose grace should be hoped for by all. Only the elect can have **all joy,** both in this life in hope and in the next life in reality; **and peace,** by removing from you that proud contention, for the checking of which this epistle was written. **In believing, so that [you may abound in hope],** as if he should say, *so that* by faith, through which one believes, and which is "the foundation of all good things,"[308] you may progress in hope and charity, which naturally follow from that. For he calls the love of God in us **the power of the Holy Spirit,** which is strong against everything, just as it is written, "Love is strong as death,"[309] and again, "It suffers all things, it endures all things."[310]

[15.14] **But I myself am certain [of you, my brothers]...** Those whom he had long frightened by finding fault, he soothes in the end by praising, lest they despair, by saying that among them there are those who **are full of love and...knowledge,** that they may wish and be able to instruct others. And this is what he says: *I am certain,* as if he should say, As if I should correct or warn you, **since you also;** that is, just as among some persons you are full of proud contention and ignorance, so also among some *you are full [of love and] all knowledge,* **so that,** that is, you have knowledge sufficient for this, *that* **you may be able** to encourage one another to doing good.

305. Mt 28.20.   306. Is 11.6.
307. Is 11.10.
308. Ps.-Augustine, *symb.,* Exordium; see above on 8.30 and below on 16.25.
309. Song 8.6.   310. 1 Cor 13.7.

(319) [15.15] **But more boldly in part,** that is, with somewhat greater trust **have I written to you** who are in a place committed to me, who am especially "the teacher of the Gentiles,"[311] rather than of the Jews. And this is what he explains, saying that, inasmuch as he is anxious for you **on account of the grace [which was given to me by God],** that is, the apostolic duty of preaching to the Gentiles enjoined on me. Concerning this grace he himself says, "Freely you have received, freely give."[312]

[15.16] **[T]he minister of Christ** is a preacher as long as he seeks not his own profit but Christ's. And because some preach well and live badly, he adds, **sanctifying [the Gospel of God];** that is, my life also commends the preaching which I perform concerning God, that **the offering [of the Gentiles],** that is, my prayer which I make for them, **may be accepted** by God **and sanctified in the Holy Spirit,** that is, through the Holy Spirit, who, as was said above, teaches us what should be prayed for, and *prays for us with indescribable groans,*[313] that is, he accomplishes a holy effect, that he may make us all holy.

[15.17] **Therefore, I have . . .** Because I act in this way, namely, by seeking the things which are Christ's, *I have* **glory** on this account before Christ, whom I serve in the presence of **God;** that is, I acquire on this account the price by divine, if not by human, judgment. By saying this, he rouses them by his example to concern for brotherly love.

[15.18] **For I do not [dare to speak of any of those things which Christ does not accomplish through me].** He shows how he sanctifies and commends his preaching, saying that he does not presume *to speak of anything,* that is, to attribute to himself through boasting of those things which he has not accomplished, just as the pseudo-apostles did. **For the obedience of the Gentiles;** that is, on account of this, that I may draw the Gentiles to myself for obedience, *Christ accomplishes* these things, **in word,** that is, through my preaching, **and deeds,** that is, through miracles.

[15.19] He immediately subdivides these deeds, saying, **in the virtue,** that is, through the power conferred on me, **of signs**

311. 1 Tm 2.7.   312. Mt 10.8.
313. Rom 8.26.

and wonders, (320) that is, of miraculous signs. For there are certain natural signs concerning which we do not wonder, just as it is written concerning the planets, "That they may be for signs and seasons."[314] These wonders, *prodigia*, which happen against nature, that is, the customary course of nature, such as cleansing lepers and raising the dead, are said to be worthy of admiration. Therefore, "wonder," *prodigium*, is said to come from "to be revealed with a finger," *prodendum digito*. **In the virtue of the Holy Spirit,** that is, by the power conferred on me through the grace of God, to be distinguished, namely, from the miracles of the Antichrist and sorcerers.

Origen says, "Those things are called signs in which, when there is something miraculous, something yet to be is made known; those things are called 'wonders' in which only something miraculous is shown. Scripture sometimes improperly uses 'wonders' in place of 'signs,' and 'signs' in place of 'wonders.'"[315] Haymo says, "*Signs and wonders* are understood in this passage as one thing."[316]

So that... *I have glory before God,* I say, so much on account of my labor, that **I have filled** the whole land **from Jerusalem as far as Illyricum** with the preaching of the Gospel, that he may show himself worthy to be heard by the Romans, he who was heard by so many and so great. Haymo says, "Illyricum is a province, the end of Asia and the beginning of Europe."[317]

[15.20] **But [I have] so [preached this Gospel, not where Christ has been named],** namely, with *word and deeds* and *the virtue of signs* in these places where absolutely nothing had ever been heard about Christ before, that it may not be miraculous if my preaching has an opportunity among you, who are already converted to Christ. **Lest [I build] on [another's foundation],** as if he should say, When this happens to me, that I should not erect the edifice of faith upon the preaching of others who went before, which would be, as it were, the foundation of my preaching. In this he shows that what he did there was more difficult than what he desired to do among the Romans.

[15.21] **[But just as] it is written** in Isaiah, that is, in order

314. Gn 1.14.
316. Haymo, *Rom.,* 15.19.
315. Origen, *Rom.,* 10.11, edited.
317. Ibid., 15.19.

that there may happen through me (321) what was prophesied about him, that is, Christ, **[they to whom] he [was not spoken of] will see,** namely, by understanding. He explains this immediately when he says, **and they who [have not heard will understand].**[318]

[15.22–23] **On account of this,** namely, that I turned entirely to converting so many of the ignorant, **I was hindered;** [he says this] that he may exclude the fabrications of the pseudoapostles, of those who say that he does not dare to come near to such important persons, and especially into their presence, or that he may excuse himself with a good reason. He says **greatly,** that is, especially, because there could have been some other reasons for this hindrance.

[15.23] **[But now, having no more] opportunity,** namely, a reason for preaching or delaying, when all [the churches] have been well established.

[15.24] Origen says, "He seems to say these things while located in Achaea, near Corinth."[319] **[When I begin to set out] for Spain.** He promises to see them in passing, as if hinting to those who had now been converted that he must not dwell with them for long, just as at the beginning of the epistle he also said that they must be confirmed in some things, rather than converted. It is fitting that every good man should promise less than he does, and the stay of the good teacher becomes more welcome and is desired more, the more briefly he is awaited. He therefore anticipates them, that they may prepare themselves for his coming and foresee those things about which they wished to be instructed. **I hope [that when I pass by I may see you],** taking nothing for granted in myself about myself, but committing everything to God. **And [that I may be led there] by you.** For he wishes them to be companions on his journey, first that the other nations subjected by the authority of the Romans may be converted more easily, and then that they may be able to prove his preaching, which they heard, against the pseudo-apostles and all those disparaging him, and he thus at least compensates those traveling about with him for a long time as he preaches,

318. Is 52.15.
319. Origen, *Rom.,* 10.13.

to the extent that he will see them in passing. He rightly says
that he is accompanied by them, as if showing that he is secure
through the protection of those who rule others. In this he also
encourages them for his stay among them, as if placing this in
their power.

(322) **If [first I have enjoyed] your company.** Haymo says,
"To enjoy is to possess and embrace and see something with delight."[320] And pay attention because, since enjoyment especially
pertains to God, as blessed Augustine mentions,[321] he does not
simply say here "to enjoy," but to enjoy **in part,** just as in his epistle to Philemon, when he said "that I may enjoy you," he immediately added, "in the Lord."[322] For we enjoy God wholly at the
time when we desire to obtain him only for his own sake, and
we enjoy our neighbor *in part,* at the time when we embrace
him in this way through love for the sake of his benefit, so that
we may place the end of this enjoyment, that is, the final and
supreme cause, in God. For the neighbor is partly the cause, but
God is the supreme cause. Therefore, we enjoy our neighbor *in
part,* but we enjoy God wholly, because he is the entire cause of
his own enjoyment, but the neighbor is not the entire cause of
his own enjoyment, since God is superior, although we should
think about our neighbor also for God's sake.

Note that he says, *I begin to set out,* because, when he comes
to the Romans for their sake, he does not ascribe setting out for
Spain to himself, except when he withdraws from them to do
everything for the Spaniards. And pay attention because, when
he says, *If first [I have enjoyed] your company,* he lays hold of their
good will in such a way, as if he should judge it necessary for
himself that he not be able to act otherwise for the Spaniards
unless he should first visit them.

[15.25] **But now [I will set out for Jerusalem],** because I
do not have any further opportunity here; *now,* that is, before
I come to you, although he had received the apostolate especially for the Gentiles, concerning which he alone is called the
"teacher of the Gentiles."[323] He shows how much care he has
for the Jewish converts in what he says elsewhere, "Concern for

320. Haymo, *Rom.,* 15.24, edited.   321. *doc. Chr.* 1.5.5.
322. Phlm 20.   323. 1 Tm 2.7.

all the churches."[324] Perhaps he offers this as a kind of excuse for himself, if he should postpone coming to them. **To minister to the saints,** that is, to those faithful converts who are there in Judea, to bring to them the food gathered by me for their need. For, as is often shown, the Apostle had customarily (323) the greatest concern for the bodily needs of that church in Jerusalem, once converted by Christ himself and by Peter and James and the other apostles, so that he might administer bodily food, at least, to those to whom the preaching of the others administered spiritual food.

He especially considered that they should be helped for many reasons. For that converted people gave much authority to our faith; they alone received the law from God, and were called his special people; and since they had been the first to believe, as if placed in the foundation of our faith and as an example to others, they were especially to be supported, lest they disappear. Finally, just as one reads in the Acts of the Apostles, they were converted with such devotion that, entirely abandoning their own property, they placed everything they had at the feet of the apostles;[325] and just as he himself mentions in the epistle to the Hebrews, they endured the greater violence of the Jews in the loss of their property.[326]

But on this account especially the Apostle sets forth a pattern and example to bishops, that when they see poor churches and monasteries, their preaching should collect food for them.

[15.26] **For [Macedonia and Achaia] have seen fit...** See how carefully he challenges the Romans by the example of others likewise to make this act of mercy to the Jerusalemites, saying that they who give these things by themselves have seen fit to do it; that is, they approved doing it, rather than by some compulsion or exhortation of the Apostle. Therefore, he also says that *they have seen fit,* that is, approving it as if it was by their own decision, [as if] they compelled me to this.

Haymo says, "They who did not have the knowledge of preaching, that they might be able to go to preach to the nations, were in Jerusalem, free for continuous prayer and fasting.

324. 2 Cor 11.28.   325. Acts 2.45; 4.32–35.
326. Heb 10.32–34.

From whatever provinces and places in which they preached, the apostles tried to send to them whatever money, silver, gold, grain, and clothing they received, especially Paul, who (324) preached to many nations. Therefore, the teachers say that at some time he sent to them more than three or five measures of silver."[327] Again, "*Macedonia and Achaia,* which is called Achaea, by which its people are called Achaeans, are most excellent provinces of the Greeks lying near to each other, which the Apostle filled with churches."[328]

When he says *Macedonia and Achaia,* he substitutes that which contains for that which is contained, that is, the names of the lands for the names of the inhabitants, just as we call a drink a cup. **[To make] a contribution,** which we call a "symbol" in Greek,[329] where different things are gathered together and given by different people, just as is customarily done at common meals. They, however, did not gather their own meals, but meals for the poor, from their own substance.

[15.27] **For it pleased [them],** as if he should say, I rightly said that *they have seen fit* to do this voluntarily, rather than to be coerced, because they do this on account of their own will more than on account of our agitation; and it justly *pleased them,* because **they are debtors.** He immediately demonstrates this from the lesser thing, saying, **For if [the Gentiles were made sharers],** that is, **of the spiritual goods** which they had, just as they were [sharers] of the law and the prophets, and even of the prayers and of the divine services which they celebrate daily for the salvation of the Gentiles, [the Gentiles ought to minister to them as well in physical things].[330]

[15.28] **Therefore,** because *it pleased them,* as is righteous, **when I have accomplished this,** that is, when I have completed this mission, and, arriving there, **have conveyed to them this yield,** namely, these alms, that is, I specified who sends these to them so that they may pray for them as for benefactors, **I will set**

327. Haymo, *Rom.,* 15.25, edited.
328. Ibid., 15.26.
329. Peter may be referring to one of the classical meanings of σύμβολον, that of a pledge on which money was advanced.
330. This last clause is found only in mss. *A* and *m.*

out [for Spain]. Although the Apostle may say that he *will set out for Spain,* it is uncertain whether he accomplished this, according to the opinions of different people.

(325) Jerome says in Book 4 of his commentary on Isaiah, "'They will fly in the ships of foreigners, and they will plunder the sea at the same time.'[331] We should interpret this only in reference to the example of the Apostle Paul, who was borne 'in the ships of foreigners' to Pamphylia, Asia, Macedonia, Achaia, and different islands and provinces, to Italy also, and, as he himself writes, to Spain."[332] Cassiodorus says in his commentary on this epistle of Paul, "*I will set out for Spain through you.* He often says this, but we never read that this was completed. Therefore, it is spoken of as something desired, but it is not completed in the manner of a prophetic truth. No one accuses the Apostle of a lie if he did not fulfill what he believed. For he did not speak through duplicity, that he might say something other than what he intended, that is, that he had in his mouth something other than what he had in his heart."[333]

[15.29] **But I know [that when I come to you],** that is, I learned by the Spirit's revelation, although I said that I must come to you while in transit elsewhere. In this we should note that, while he says that he knows this was revealed to him, he hints that he said this before about Spain as an opinion, rather than making this known as a declaration. **[I will come] in the abundance of the blessing [of the Gospel of Christ],** so that, just as it is read about Joseph, the Lord may pour out upon you a large blessing of heavenly grace "at my coming",[334] that is, may he give you increase in spiritual goods.

[15.30] **I implore you, therefore, [brothers],** that I may accomplish what I wish **through the Lord [Jesus Christ, and through the charity of the Holy Spirit],** if you wish to accom-

331. Is 11.14, according to the Septuagint.

332. Jerome, *Commentarii in Isaiam* 4, on 11.14.

333. This is not found in the commentary of Pelagius revised by Cassiodorus and published in the Patrologia Latina under the name of Primasius (cf. PL 68.504A), nor in his *Complexiones* (PL 70); it is likely from a now-lost commentary.

334. Cf. Gn 30.30, where Jacob, not Joseph, says something like this.

plish more in him and if you have the love[335] of God. **[That you help me in your] prayers [to God for me],** for he believes that the prayers of many faithful, although imperfect, people obtain much with God.

[15.31] **[That I may be delivered] from the unbelievers [who are in Judea],** while I thus labor for the faithful (326) who are there. **[And that the offering] of my service,** that is, the service enjoined on me by those who send this through me, and by the Lord, who made me a minister and steward of the Church. *Offering,* a sacrifice, so to speak, brought through me to the altar of God for them; **acceptable [to the saints in Jerusalem],** that is, pleasing and joyous. For if something serious should happen to me there on account of this, they will be greatly saddened.

[15.32] **[That I may come to you in joy by the will of God and] be refreshed [with you],** first by resting from prolonged labor, and then by fulfilling my desire.

[15.33] **May the God...** Either I will come or I will not. **Of peace [be with you all. Amen],** that is, pacify you from mutual proud contention. Reserving this for the end of the epistle, toward which the epistle itself especially moves, he teaches also what the final cause and intention of it is.

[16.1] **I commend [to you],** namely, with my prayers, **Phoebe,** through whom Paul is believed to have sent this epistle to the Romans from Corinth; she is said to have been a wealthy and noble woman, who from her own means and those of others supplied the needs for the faithful who were **at Cenchreae,** by the example of the holy women who are said to have done this for the Lord and the apostles. But she had specific business for which she needed to come to Rome. Therefore, the Apostle exhorts the Romans on her behalf and asks them to receive her with respect and to help her in her business as much as they are able. **Our sister,** in faith, not in the flesh. **[Who is] in the ministry [of the church],** that is, in the service of those faithful who are *at Cenchreae,* that is, in that place which is so called, and said to be, the port of Corinth. Therefore, Haymo says, "Cenchreae is the port of Corinth."[336]

---

335. *Dilectio.*

336. Haymo, *Rom.,* 16.1.

[16.2] **That you may receive [her]** with hospitality **in the Lord,** that is, in the love of God, and (327) so *receive* her with respect and kindness, just as it is proper and appropriate for **the saints** to receive a saint. **And assist her [in whatever business she may have need of you];** that is, help her. **For [she has assisted many, including me].** This is owed from her many preceding merits, so that this may not be given to her so much as returned.

Origen says, "He teaches with apostolic authority that women are appointed in the ministry of the Church. He honors Phoebe, placed in this office with the church *which is at Cenchreae,* with great praise and commendation, because she assisted in the apostolic needs and labors. This passage teaches two things: both that women are ministers in the Church and that such persons who assisted many should be received into ministry, and who through good service deserve to attain apostolic praise."[337]

Jerome says, "*In the ministry of the Church,* just as now in eastern churches women deaconesses are seen to minister among their own sex in baptism and the ministry of the Word, because we find that women taught privately, such as Priscilla, whose husband was called Aquila."[338] He also says in his commentary on Timothy, "But refuse to appoint the younger widows in the ministry of the diaconate."[339]

Saint Epiphanius says in his letter to John of Jerusalem, "I have never ordained deaconesses, and I sent them to other provinces, and I did not do anything whereby I might split the Church."[340] Known in former times as deaconesses, that is, ministers, we now call these women abbesses, that is, mothers.

Cassiodorus says on this same passage, "It shows that Phoebe was a deaconess of the mother church; therefore, in regions of the Greeks today it is done for the sake of service; to them the practice of baptizing in the Church is not denied."[341]

Claudius also, in his exposition of this epistle: "This passage teaches that women are appointed in the ministry of the

337. Origen, *Rom.,* 10.17, edited.
338. Pelagius, *Rom.,* 16.1.
339. Pelagius, *1 Tim.,* 5.11, edited.
340. Among the epistles of Jerome, 51.2.
341. Also from Cassiodorus's lost commentary.

church; (328) the Apostle honors Phoebe, placed in this office with the church *which is at Cenchreae,* with great praise and commendation."[342]

[16.3] **Greet...** At the end of the epistle he especially commends some, greeting them by name, so that the others may especially acquiesce in the counsel and authority of those who were more perfect. The Apostle here addresses **Prisca,** who is called Priscilla in the Acts of the Apostles,[343] perhaps with some beautiful allusion to her name, so that he might teach that she was an old woman in her understanding and mature in her conduct. But Priscilla was the wife of **Aquila,** and both were converts to Christ from Judaism.[344] **[My helpers] in Christ [Jesus];** that is, for Christ they were the Apostle's helpers in many things, whom the Apostle found at Corinth when he came there, when they were expelled from Rome by Claudius with the other Jews, and, because he was skilled in the same craft, that is, in tent-making, he joined himself to them that they might work together.[345]

Therefore, Bede also says in his commentary on Acts,

"For they were tentmakers by trade." As if exiles and wanderers, they build tents for themselves, which they use on their journey. For tents, *tabernacula,* are called *scenae* in Greek,[346] and the term draws its etymology from "shading," *obumbrando,* and with the Greeks *umbra,* "shelter," is *scena.* For *scenae* or *scenomata,* "dwelling-places," means "shelters," *umbracula,* which the ancients built with linen or woolen or woven blankets, or from the branches of trees or bushes. Mystically, however, just as Peter draws us from the waves of the world by fishing, so Paul defends us, in word and deed, from the rain of sins, from the heat of temptations, and from the winds of traps, by raising up shelters of protection.[347]

Chrysostom says in his first sermon on the Epistle to the Hebrews,

342. Claude of Turin, *Rom.,* unedited; cf. Paris BN Lat. Ms. 2392, f. 64ra; Paris BN Lat. Ms. 12,289, f. 78va. This is obviously taken from the passage of Origen cited above.

343. Acts 18.2, 18, 26.   344. Acts 18.2.

345. Acts 18.1–3.

346. The Vulgate text of Acts 18.3 describes Paul, Priscilla, and Aquila as *scenofactoriae artis,* from σκηνοποιοὶ τῇ τέχνῃ; hence Bede's explanation.

347. Bede, *Super Acta Apostolorum expositio* 18.

"Who is the splendor of his glory and stamp of his substance." O the apostolic wisdom, but more, the wonderful grace of the Holy Spirit. For he did not say this from his own understanding. (329) For whence did this come to him? From knives or skins or in the workshop? This is the working of majesty. For he did not bring forth these understandings with his own mind, which then was so feeble and extreme that he had nothing more, apart from [what] the common people [had]. For how could he understand something divine who spent his whole life and all his energy on the business of selling and the tanning of hides?[348]

Ambrose says concerning Prisca and Aquila, "These believers were made sharers in the Apostle's work, so that they might exhort others to faith. Finally, although he was well versed in the scriptures, Apollos was more diligently taught the way of the Lord by them. Therefore, [Paul] calls them sharers of his work, although *in Christ Jesus*. For they were his fellow-workers in the Gospel."[349] Therefore, he especially teaches the extent to which the Romans should obey them.

Origen says, "But it can happen that at that time, when the Jews were driven from the city by the command of Caesar, they came to Corinth; when the severity ceased, and they were allowed by edict to return again to Rome, they were greeted by Paul. Nevertheless, when Paul was in danger from the plots of the Jews, it appears that they offered themselves, that he might depart a free man."[350]

[16.4] **[Who risked their necks]** for my life; that is, to save my life, they exposed themselves to death. **[To them not only I, but] all the churches [of the Gentiles give thanks],** of whom the Apostle is especially called preacher and teacher.

[16.5] **[And the church that meets in their] home,** that is, their entire family, likewise converted to the faith. **[Greet my beloved Epaenetus,] the first fruits of Asia [in Christ].** Haymo says, "Either because (330) he was the first of all to believe or because he was of great eminence and nobility, such that he might show the nobles how to come to the faith and through this attract the foremost Romans to the faith."[351]

348. John Chrysostom, *Heb., Serm.* 1; see especially *Mutiani* 1; Heb 1.3.
349. Ambrosiaster, *Rom.* 16.3, edited.
350. Origen, *Rom.*, 10.18; Acts 18.1–3.
351. Haymo, *Rom.*, 16.5, edited.

[16.6] **[Greet Mary,] who [has labored] much [among you].** Origen says, "Here he teaches that even women ought to labor for the churches. They labor when they teach young women all the things written which refer to the duties of women."[352] [*Who*] *has labored.* Ambrose says, "For their exhortation."[353] Haymo says, "[*Who*] *has labored,* namely, by devoting herself to the duty of preaching to the women of her sex in their homes, for women did not teach in the churches."[354]

[16.7] **[Greet Andronicus and Junias, my] kin.** Ambrose says, "Both according to the flesh and the Spirit."[355] **[And] fellow prisoners.** Haymo says, "They were made exiles from their own home on account of the grace of God, just as Paul was."[356] **[Who are of note] among the apostles,** that is, among the preachers. He seems to mention a woman apostle in this passage, unless perhaps, we do violence [to this passage] by referring that *who* only to Andronicus and the men mentioned above.[357] **[Who were also before me] in Christ,** that is, in faith in Christ.

[16.9][358] **[Greet Urbanus,] our [helper in Christ],** namely, of myself and the others. **[And Stachys, my] beloved,** though not a helper.

[16.10] **[Greet] Apelles, [approved in Christ].** Origen says, "I think this Apelles, after many tribulations, passed away wisely, and therefore was proclaimed *approved,* according to what Paul said elsewhere: that *patience works approval.*[359] We should consid-

352. Origen, *Rom.,* 10.20, edited.

353. Ambrosiaster, *Rom.* 16.6, edited.

354. Haymo, *Rom.,* 16.6, edited.

355. Ambrosiaster, *Rom.* 16.7, edited.

356. Haymo, *Rom.,* 16.7, edited.

357. Peter here seems to believe "Junias" to be a woman's name, and that Paul here mentions a woman doing apostolic work. Atto of Vercelli also believes she is a woman, the wife of Andronicus, though he does not refer to her doing apostolic work (PL 134.282A); and Herveus of Bourg-Dieu speculates that they were among Christ's seventy-two disciples, and were therefore entitled to be listed among the apostles, though he does not say that Junias was a woman (PL 181.807D). I know of no other commentators who raise the issue of a woman apostle.

358. Peter omits any discussion of 16.8, "Greet Ampliatus, my beloved in the Lord."

359. Rom 5.4.

er whether he is not the one who is named 'Apollos the Alexandrian, learned in the scriptures' in the Acts of the Apostles."[360] Ambrose says, "He greets this Apelles not as a friend (331) or sharer in his work, but because he was approved in temptations and found faithful in Christ."[361] Haymo says, "Although some say that these are two proper names, 'Greet Apelles and Probus,' it is not so; it is one proper name with an adjective: *Greet Apelles, approved...*, that is, approved in faith and worthy of praise."[362] **[Greet those who are of] Aristobulus's [household].** Perhaps he was now dead whom he praises adequately by greeting his family and by commending his faith among them. Ambrose says, "That man is understood to have been a convenor of the brothers in Christ."[363] Origen says, "He mentions neither those beloved nor those approved nor his helpers; but perhaps they had nothing useful in their merits, and so he honored them only with a notice of greeting."[364]

[16.11] **[Greet Herodion my] kinsman.** Ambrose says, "The one he only calls *kinsman*, he shows to be devoted in charity; nevertheless he does not describe his watchfulness."[365] **[Greet those who are of] Narcissus's household [who are in the Lord].** Origen says, "There seem to have been many in Narcissus's house or family, but not all were *in the Lord*."[366] Ambrose says, "Narcissus is said to have been an elder at that time, just as is read in other manuscripts. But because he was not present, he salutes the saints who were of his house. But this elder Narcissus performed the duty of a pilgrim, strengthening the believers with exhortations."[367]

[16.12] **[Greet Tryphaena and Tryphosa, who] labor in the Lord.** Origen says, "Many labor, but not in the Lord."[368] Ambrose

---

360. Origen, *Rom.*, 10.23, edited; Rom 5.4; Acts 18.24. Origen speaks of Apelles as having sustained ordeals, not as having passed away, but Abelard edits out key words and phrases. See Scheck, v. 2, 294–95.

361. Ambrosiaster, *Rom.* 16.10.   362. Haymo, *Rom.*, 16.10.
363. Ambrosiaster, *Rom.* 16.10.   364. Origen, *Rom.*, 10.25, edited.
365. Ambrosiaster, *Rom.* 16.11, edited.
366. Origen, *Rom.*, 10.27.
367. Ambrosiaster, *Rom.* 16.12, edited.
368. Origen, *Rom.*, 10.28, edited.

says, "He declares them worthy in Christ with one word."[369] *Labor,* namely, by ministering (332) to the saints. **[Greet most beloved Persis,] who [has labored] much [in the Lord].** Origen says, "This woman seems to be praised more."[370] Ambrose says, "This labor is in exhortation and the ministry of the saints and in difficulties and in need on account of Christ, because they abandoned their homes to those who had been put to flight and were a rebuke to the treacherous."[371]

[16.13] **[Greet Rufus,] chosen in the Lord.** Haymo says, "That is, promoted to the priesthood."[372] **[And] his [mother] and mine.** It can be read in this way: *his mother* and *my mother,* that there are two of them; or that it is the same mother: the mother according to the flesh of the one, [and] of the Apostle according to the kindness with which she perhaps supported him at one time in another place from her own substance, as if she were his mother; and out of reverence for her holiness he calls her his mother, to whom honor should be given, as if to a mother.

[16.14] **[Greet] Asyncritus, [Phlegon, Hermas, Patrobas, and Hermes, and those who are brothers with them].** Ambrose says, "He greets these together, because he knew they were harmonious in Christ, that is, united in Christian friendship,"[373] and not idle in friendships. *Hermas.* Origen says, "I think that Hermas is the writer of that small book which is called *The Shepherd,* which seems to me a very useful writing and, as I think, divinely inspired. The reason why Paul added no praise was, I think, that he seems to have been converted to penitence after many sins, as the writing shows. It is understood that they lived together, whose greeting is combined."[374]

The Ecclesiastical History says in Book 3, Chapter 3, "And the small book of Hermas, which is called *The Shepherd,* whom Paul

---

369. Ambrosiaster, *Rom.* 16.12, edited; Ambrosiaster reads, "of one honor," which makes more sense.

370. Origen, *Rom.,* 10.29, edited.

371. Ambrosiaster, *Rom.* 16.12. Peter originally attached this passage to that of Origen preceding; the attribution to Ambrose and the words "This labor" have been added.

372. Haymo, *Rom.,* 16.13.   373. Ambrosiaster, *Rom.* 16.14.

374. Origen, *Rom.,* 10.31, edited.

PETER ABELARD

mentions in his epistles, was not received by most, (333) but it was judged necessary by others for the sake of those who are first instructed in order to establish faith. Therefore, it is also read in some churches, and many of the ancient writers used its testimony."[375]

Jerome says in Chapter 10 of his *Distinguished Men,* "Hermas, whom the Apostle Paul mentions when he writes to the Romans: *Greet Phlegon, Hermas,* etc., they claim to be the author of the book which is called *The Shepherd,* and it is even read publicly in some churches in Greece. In fact, it is a useful book, and many ancient writers made use of testimonies from it. But among the Latins, it is almost unknown."[376]

[16.15] **[Greet] Philologus and Julia, [Nereus and his sister, and Olympias, and all the saints who are with them].** Origen says, "It could be that they were married, and the others were members of their family."[377] Jerome says, "He teaches us by his example what kind of person we ought to greet in our letters, not the wealthy, adorned with the riches of the world, but those enriched with the grace of God and faith."[378] The same, a little before, "We understand by their names that the first-fruits of the Asian church, all those whom he greets, were wanderers, by whose example and teaching we think, not irrationally, that the Romans believed."[379]

[16.16] **[Greet] each other,** namely, yourselves. Because he could not greet them all individually, he instructs them for his part and from his position that they should greet each other mutually, just as he would do if he were present, and so, reconciled to *each other* **with a kiss,** they may put an end to their proud contention. **With a holy kiss,** not lustful or deceitful (as was the kiss of Judas the betrayer),[380] but which unites us in brotherly love. **All the churches [of Christ greet you],** that is, the congregations of Christians, in contradistinction to the church of "malicious people" that the Psalmist indicates,[381] pray and plead

375. Eusebius, *hist. eccl.*, 3.3.6.

376. Jerome, *vir. ill.* 10.

377. Origen, *Rom.*, 10.31.

378. Pelagius, *Rom.*, 16.15.

379. Ibid, 16.5.

380. Mt 26.49; Mk 14.45; Lk 22.47–48.

381. Ps 25.5.

for your welfare with the same affection of love[382] with which I greet you. For he who, in greeting another, says to him, "Health (*Salve*)," actually prays that he may be healthy (*salvus*).

(334) [16.17] **Now I ask [you, brothers].** He speaks of the false apostles, that they may beware of them, lest their faith be corrupted through them. **That you watch [those]...,** that is, set [them apart]. **[Who cause] dissensions,** that is, disputes over words, **and offenses,** that is, dangerous errors in faith. They exist, I say, **apart from** sound **teaching [which you have learned]; turn [from them];** that is, withdraw.

[16.18] **[For such persons do not serve Christ our Lord,] but their own belly;** that is, they are turned to fleshly weakness. **[And through] pleasing words,** that is, flattery. Jerome says in Book 2 of his commentary on Amos, "A flatterer is excellently defined among the philosophers as a charming enemy. The truth is bitter. Therefore, the Apostle says, 'I have become an enemy to you by speaking the truth,'[383] and the comic poet, 'Allegiance produces friends, truth produces hatred.'"[384] On this account we eat the paschal lamb with bitter herbs, and the Vessel of election[385] teaches that the Pasch should be celebrated "in truth and purity."[386] **[And] blessings,** as if they confer the gifts of the Holy Spirit through the imposition of hands and confirmation, **[they lead astray the hearts] of the innocent,** that is, of the simple and ignorant, who are not able to detect them.

[16.19] **For your...** Therefore, *I ask you* this, because the more dangerous the deceit that endangered you, the more the **obedience** of your faith **is made known [in every place],** as if it were established in the capital of the world. **Therefore, I rejoice [in you],** because it *is made known* in this way, namely, by discerning **in good. [But I want you to be...] simple in evil,** as if not knowing how to plot against anyone, according to that word of the Truth: "Be clever as serpents and simple as doves."[387]

(335) [16.20] **May the God...,** as if he should say, *I ask* in

382. *Dilectio.*
383. Gal 4.16.
384. Terence, *Andria* I.1.41; Jerome, cf. rather *Exod.*
385. Acts 9.15.   386. 1 Cor 5.8.
387. Mt 10.16.

this way that it may happen, but may **the God of peace** rather than of dissension accomplish this as I ask. **Crush Satan,** that is, every enemy of your soul, **under your feet;** that is, may he subject him powerless to you, that you may be able to prevail over him in all things and trample all his tricks, such as those things which are pressed under your feet; **swiftly,** namely, at my coming. Meanwhile, you should note this, just as I ask. **May the grace,** that is, the free gifts **of Christ** through which you can accomplish this, **be with you.**

[16.21] **Timothy [greets you].** Although he had said *All the churches greet you,* nevertheless he decided to greet them especially and by name on the part of those whom he held as distinguished, so that the written epistle might be strengthened by the testimony of such men. **[My] helper,** namely, in preaching, "as if a co-bishop," as Ambrose says.[388] This is that disciple of Paul, "a son of" a certain "believing Jewish woman and of a Gentile father," whom Paul himself was compelled to circumcise, just as is contained in the Acts of the Apostles.[389] Origen says,

Some say that **Lucius** is Luke, who wrote the Gospel, in view of the fact that occasionally names are customarily cited according to the native Greek and Roman declension. **Jason** is the one concerning whom it is written in the Acts of the Apostles that during the Thessalonian insurrection he gave himself to the turbulent crowds in place of Paul and Silas, that he might obtain for the apostles the freedom to leave.[390] **Sosipater.** I surmise that this may be he who in the Acts of the Apostles is named Sopater of Beroea, son of Pyrrhus.[391]

(336) [Origen] will ponder how Paul, a Hebrew, is called the blood relation of Timothy and Jason and Sosipater: "Now indeed, although he should in no way confer this title on others, it is certain that he uses some designation; this kindred or blood relationship he undoubtedly knows . . ."[392] Ambrose says,

---

388. Ambrosiaster, *Rom.* 16.21.   389. Acts 16.1–3.

390. Acts 17.5–9.

391. Acts 20.4; Origen, *Rom.,* 10.39, edited.

392. Origen, *Rom.,* 10.39. Abelard's citation of Origen is here so highly edited and paraphrased that it makes little sense as it is. Origen is speaking of terms which Paul applies to his friends, reserving the title of kinsman to some, and using other terms for others; the term of kinsman comes from the paternity which is named in heaven by Christ (Eph 3.14–15).

"He calls them kindred partly by reason of birth, partly by reason of faith."[393]

[16.22] **[I,] Tertius, [who wrote this epistle, greet you in the Lord.]** This is the proper name of him who, by Paul's dictation, wrote this epistle as if he were the Apostle's secretary, just as the apostolic chancellor now is. Perhaps this was done by a certain divine presentiment, in order that he might be called *Tertius* who was third in operation.[394] For the Holy Spirit inspired what the Apostle dictated, and made known what he who is called *Tertius*, as was said, wrote with his own hand. Ambrose says, "This is the scribe of the epistle, whom the Apostle allowed to greet the Roman people with his own name."[395] This was not done unjustly, so that he might use his own words, which were made known only with human consciousness.[396]

[16.23] **[Gaius] my host [greets you].** Origen says, "He seems to indicate that he was a hospitable man, who not only received Paul but also offered a place of assembly to the whole church in his own home. It is asserted by the tradition of the elders that this Gaius was the first bishop of the Thessalonian church."[397] Ambrose says, "This is the Gaius to whom, I think, John the Apostle wrote, rejoicing in the charity which he showed to the brothers, furnishing the necessary expenses for them."[398] Haymo says, "He is the fellow-prisoner Gaius who was baptized by the Apostle, just as he says in the epistle to the Corinthians, 'I baptized none of you except Crispus and Gaius.'"[399]

(337) **And of the whole church.** Ambrose understands here a nominative plural, as if it should be said, "All the churches greet you."[400] But it is better as a genitive singular, as Origen has it, so that it may be understood in this way: "My host and the host of the whole church."[401] For since the Apostle had said above that

393. Ambrosiaster, *Rom.* 16.21.
394. *Tertius* means "third" in Latin.
395. Ambrosiaster, *Rom.* 16.22.
396. I.e., without divine inspiration.
397. Origen, *Rom.,* 10.41, edited.
398. Ambrosiaster, *Rom.* 16.23; 3 Jn 1–8.
399. Haymo, *Rom.,* 16.23; 1 Cor 1.14.
400. Ambrosiaster, *Rom.* 16.23.
401. See previous passage of Origen cited. The Latin text reads, "Salutat vos Gaius hospes meus et universae ecclesiae." The last two words can legitimately

All the churches of Christ greet you,[402] what need was there to repeat here, "All the churches greet you"?

Erastus, treasurer of the city, [greets you, and Quartus, a brother]. Origen says, "I think that Erastus is the one whom he says remained at Corinth; he calls him a treasurer, that is, a steward of that city whose founder is God."[403] According to Jerome, he is called *treasurer of the city* according to that which he once was, now is not.[404] Haymo says, "A *treasurer*, that is, a leading man and steward, because he had charge of the public treasury, where the money of the king's taxes and tolls was placed. *And Quartus,* a proper name, just as Tertius is."[405]

[16.24] **The grace of our Lord [Jesus Christ be with you all. Amen].** Jerome says, "This is what his hand writes in all his epistles, so that he may remind them of the benefits of Christ."[406] Haymo says, "*Grace* is said to be that which is given gratis, and we ought to understand by the term 'grace' whatever good the elect freely receive from God, namely, faith, hope, charity, and the remission of sins."[407]

[16.25–27] **Now to him…** Origen says, "Marcion, by whom the evangelical and apostolic writings were falsified, completely removed this paragraph from this epistle. But he also cut off everything from that passage where it is written, *But everything which is not of faith is sin,*[408] up to the end. (338) Indeed, in other examples, which were not desecrated by Marcion, this paragraph is found to be placed in different ways. For in some manuscripts, after that passage, *But everything which is not of faith is sin,* there is found immediately, **Now to him who is able to strengthen you.** Other manuscripts have it at the end, as it now is placed."[409]

When their greeting is finished, he ends his epistle in thanksgiving, as if returning thanks for his completed work to him

---

be interpreted in either of the ways Peter describes, as well as a singular dative, meaning to or for the whole church.

402. Rom 16.16.

403. Origen, *Rom.*, 10.42, edited; 2 Tm 4.20; Heb 11.10.

404. Pelagius, *Rom.*, 16.23.   405. Haymo, *Rom.*, 16.23, edited.

406. Pelagius, *Rom.*, 16.24.   407. Haymo, *Rom.*, 16.24.

408. Rom 14.23.   409. Origen, *Rom.*, 10.43.

who inspired this in him. *Now to him,* as if he should carry on in this way: *Grace to you,* I say, but *to him who is able,* let there be uninterrupted **glory.** And we should note that although it is said *To him who is able,* what he adds at the end seems to be superfluous with regard to the meaning and construction: **to whom,** since at first he had said *to him,* unless perhaps it is said to be done on account of the long insertion. For many things are inserted between *To him,* which was mentioned before, and **honor and glory,** which is joined at the end. Therefore, let not the unskilled reader forget to what *honor and glory* is connected: *to whom* is added. In order that the construction of the letter may be composed in whatever way, join the beginning of this verse to the end: *Now to him who is able,* etc., *honor and glory* ("may there be" understood), and again, when *to whom* is said, "belongs" is understood, as if it should be said, "May there be *honor and glory to him* to whom it belongs"; as if it should be said, just as it in fact is, May it be, I say, **through Jesus Christ,** through whom the Father should be glorified.

In conformity with this end of the epistle, I think that the teachers of the Church conclude their expositions and sermons with very similar endings, namely, in thanksgiving to God.

[16.25] **To strengthen [you],** namely, in faith, which is "the foundation of all good things";[410] **according to my Gospel,** that is, the doctrine of my **preaching,** which is **about Jesus Christ,** (339) not another preaching, because I preach the same thing that he does. I say *my Gospel* and *the preaching of Christ,* done **according to the revelation of the mystery;** and *to strengthen according to* my *revelation.* It is called a "secret" and "hidden" mystery. Therefore, a mystical discourse is called figurative, which is not plain.

[16.25–26] The mystery **which is now laid open** is the very means of our redemption, which means once was concealed in the prophetic scriptures that were not yet explained, but *now* is revealed both by those things expounded by Christ and those expounded by us. For it is written concerning Christ that "beginning from Moses and all the prophets, he interpreted to them

---

410. Pseudo-Augustine, *symb.,* Exordium; see above on 8.30 and 15.13.

in all the scriptures."[411] **Kept secret from eternity,** that is, always
hidden until *now*, and not ever revealed further through explanation, although those translators of the Septuagint are indeed
believed to have kept silence and to have hidden things in their
translations which are said concerning the Son of God. He says,
[through the writings] of the prophets, rather than of the law,
because this mystery is especially contained in the prophets,
in which it was prophesied more openly and fully concerning
Christ. *It is now laid open,* I say, **among all the nations according
to the precept of the eternal God,** that is, of the Christ who says,
"Go [into all the world]," etc.;[412] *of the eternal God,* I say, although
it had its beginning according to man. *It is laid open,* he says, for
this reason: not only that all the nations may believe, but even
more, that they may obey him, that is, that they may act according to faith.

[16.27] *To him,* I say, [who is] now known **through Jesus
Christ. To the only wise God,** that is, to him who now appears
exceedingly wise by that which he did through Christ in this
mystery of our redemption. Concerning him Job says, "By his
prudence he struck the proud."[413] He alone is called wise, in
comparison with whom no one should be called wise, just as no
one should be called good, according to that word of the Truth,
"No one is good except God."[414] Also, only (340) he is called
wise, because he has that unique and singular wisdom which
nothing can hide. **Honor and glory,** that is, a glorious and singular honor. **Amen.**

411. Lk 24.27.   412. Mk 16.15.
413. Jb 26.12.   414. Mk 10.18.

INDICES

GENERAL INDEX

Aaron, 137

Abel, 183

abbots, 272

Abraham, 35, 101, 139, 164, 172, 173, 193–94, 288–89; bosom of, 164; circumcision of, 136–37, 178–87, 194; example of, 194–95, 196–99, 289; exultation of, 203–4; faith of, 169, 194, 196–203; father of Jews and Gentiles, 178–87, 196–98; hope of, 198; justified by faith, 173, 177, 204; lineage of, 101, 314; promises made to, 101, 202, 287; signifies faith, 289

abstinence, 235, 355, 357–59, 363, 370

Achaia, 382

Adam, 30–32, 47, 51–52, 54, 147, 210–11, 222–23, 225–26, 230; author for death and punishment, 209; father of fleshly people, 210, 346; humanity incurs damnation through, 212; likeness with Christ, 210, 212; sin of, 167, 208–15

adoption: Christ not adopted, 66, 103, 281; of believers, 35–36, 103, 272–74, 277, 280, 286, 289

adultery, 36, 57n229, 59–60, 75, 141, 149, 247, 255, 261, 280–81, 346–47

Ahab, king of Israel, 314

Andrew, apostle, 320–21, 375

angels, 26, 127, 130, 151, 153, 164, 179, 182, 198, 246–47, 283, 289, 337, 351; fall of, 113, 208; orders of, 283–84; pictures of, 123

anger, 113, 128–29, 139, 166–67, 225, 300, 313, 341–43, 346

Anna, prophetess, 153, 320

Antichrist, 323–25, 379

Apelles, 389–90

Apollos, 388, 390

Aquila, 386–88

Aristobulus, 390

atonement, 38, 43–51, 163, 167. *See also* reconciliation, redemption

Baal, 119, 314

Balaam, 100, 184

baptism, 13, 26, 31, 40, 52, 55, 78–79, 142, 169–71, 215, 218–19, 225, 395; administered by deaconesses, 386; and circumcision, 180–81, 183, 187; and original sin, 225; as death of sin, 229; as rebirth, 103; baptized have sins blotted out, 230; forgiveness of sins in, 269; likeness of death of Christ, 229; sanctifies small children, 176; unbaptized children, 210

Bathsheba, 348

benevolence: attribute of God, 115

Benjamin, 92–93, 95–97, 286, 214, 324

blasphemy, 142, 151, 189, 363

blessing, of enemies, 337

blindness, spiritual, 120–23, 153, 316–17, 323, 329, 352

body, 112, 115, 120, 130, 143–44, 171, 190–92, 238, 343, 355; affliction of, 282–83; and sin, 233–34,

INDEX OF HOLY SCRIPTURE

New Testament

INDEX OF CLASSICAL AND
PATRISTIC CITATIONS

spir. et litt.
29.50: 172
Trin.
15.17.30:
160

Bede
Acta
18: 368

Boethius
c. Eut.
8: 147
diff. top.
2.2.15: 332
2.7.29: 328
in Per.
3.9: 217
syll. hyp.
I: 109

Burchardus of Worms
Decretorum libri XX
19.85: 368
19.87: 368
19.88: 369
19.90: 369
19.91: 369
19.92: 369

Cicero
inv.
1.34: 116
2.56: 86

Claudius of Turin
Rom.
16.1: 386–87

Cyprian
eccl cath.
14: 274
ep.
31.4: 274

Eusebius of Caesarea
Hist. eccl.

2.14, 15: 89
3.3.6: 391–92

Fulgentius of Ruspe
fid.
41: 216
70: 220
85: 369

Gangra, Council of
Ch. 2: 369

Gratian
Decret.
cap. 63, causa XI:
165

Gregory of Tours
Franc.
1.24: 89

Gregory the Great
homil. 2,
hom. 32.6: 219
moral.
4.3: 142, 169, 180
33.4: 134
35.14.34: 325

Haymo of Auxerre
Rom.
Argumentum: 89
Prol.: 90
1.23: 119
2.17: 140
3.28: 171
4.11: 178
6.23: 239
8.15: 273
11.26: 325
13.7: 346
13.13: 354
15.19: 379
15.24: 381
15.25: 383
15.26: 383
16.1: 385

16.5: 388
16.6: 389
16.7: 389
16.10: 390
16.13: 391
16.23: 395
16.24: 396

Hilary of Poitiers
Trin.
13.3: 103–4

Horace
Ep.
Bk 1, ep. 1.32: 253
Odes
3.16.18: 242

Isidore of Seville
etym.
7.1.5: 115
fid. Cath.
2.5.3: 324
2.5.8: 324
2.13.3–5: 324
sent.
1.15.9: 184
1.22.3: 269

Ivo
decret.
Prol.: 351
4.30: 369

Jerome
Ep.
21.37: 153
22.20: 94
46.1: 351
49.13: 94
51.2 (Epipha-
nius): 386
58.1: 94
68.1: 128
120.10: 324
Ezech.
4 (16.8): 218